BEGINNING ANDROID® PROGRAMMING WITH ANDROID STUDIO

BEGINNING

Android® Programming with Android Studio

J. F. DiMarzio

Beginning Android® Programming with Android Studio

Published by
John Wiley & Sons, Inc.
10475 Crosspoint Boulevard
Indianapolis, IN 46256
www.wiley.com

Published simultaneously in Canada

ISBN: 978-1-118-70559-9
ISBN: 978-1-118- 70742-5 (ebk)
ISBN: 978-1-119-19609-9 (ebk)

Manufactured in the United States of America

10 9 8 7 6 5 4 3 2 1

Library of Congress Control Number: 2016952673

To my children Christian, Sophia, and Giovanni;
Katie, Sarah, and Joe; and my love Jennifer.

CREDITS

Project Editor
Charlotte Kughen

Technical Editor
Chád (Shod) Darby

Production Editor
Athiyappan Lalith Kumar

Development Editor
Rick Kughen

Manager of Content Development and Assembly
Mary Beth Wakefield

Production Manager
Kathleen Wisor

Marketing Manager
Carrie Sherrill

Professional Technology and Strategy Director
Barry Pruett

Business Manager
Amy Knies

Executive Editor
Jim Minatel

Project Coordinator, Cover
Brent Savage

Proofreader
Nancy Bell

Indexer
Nancy Guenther

Cover Designer
Wiley

Cover Image
© iStockphoto.com/Leo Blanchette

ABOUT THE AUTHOR

J. F. DIMARZIO began developing computer programs—specifically games—in 1984 as a wide-eyed, curious child of the Atari age. Starting on the TRS-80 Color Computer II, in BASIC, he wrote several small text-based games and simple inventory applications. After leaving the Music program at the University of Massachusetts, J. F. moved into professional computer development; working for the United States Department of Defense, Walt Disney Imagineering, TechData, and The Walt Disney Company. In 2008, he started developing apps on the newly introduced Android platform (then on version 0.8). He has had 14 books published to date, 7 of which are on Android and Android game development.

ABOUT THE TECHNICAL EDITOR

CHÁD (SHOD) DARBY is an author, instructor, and speaker in the Java development world. As a recognized authority on Java applications and architectures, he has presented technical sessions at software development conferences worldwide (in the U.S., U.K., India, Italy, Russia, Netherlands, Singapore, Japan, and Australia). In his 20 years as a professional software architect, he's had the opportunity to work for Blue Cross/Blue Shield, Merck, Boeing, Red Hat, and a handful of startup companies.

Chád is a contributing author to several Java books, including *Professional Java E-Commerce* (Wrox Press), *Beginning Java Networking* (Wrox Press), and *XML and Web Services Unleashed* (Sams Publishing). Chád has Java certifications from Oracle and IBM. He holds a B.S. in Computer Science from Carnegie Mellon University.

ACKNOWLEDGMENTS

J. F. DIMARZIO would like to thank Charlotte Kughen, Jim Minatel, Rick Kughen, and the team at John Wiley & Sons publishing; and Stacey Czarnowski, Katrina Bevan, and the team at Studio B.

CONTENTS

INTRODUCTION

I first started playing with the Android Software Development Kit (SDK) before it was officially released as version 0.8. Back then, the tools were unpolished, the application programming interfaces (APIs) in the SDK were unstable, and the documentation was sparse. Android is now one of the most popular mobile operating systems in the world.

Every day, more developers are trying Android development using Android Studio, either as a hobby or professionally. The current challenge for many beginning developers who want to move into the exciting world of android development is trying to determine where to start.

It was with this challenge in mind that I was motivated to write this book, one that could benefit beginning Android programmers and enable them to write progressively more sophisticated applications.

This book is written to help jump-start beginning Android developers, covering the necessary topics in a linear manner so that you can build on your knowledge without being overwhelmed by the details. I adopt the philosophy that the best way to learn is by doing. The numerous Try It Out sections in each chapter first show you how to build something. Then the follow-up How It Works sections explain how everything works. I have also taken this opportunity to further improve the previous edition of this book by addressing feedback from readers and adding additional topics that are important to beginning Android developers.

Although Android programming is a huge topic, my aim for this book is threefold: to get you started with the fundamentals, to help you understand the underlying architecture of the SDK, and to appreciate why things are done in certain ways. It is beyond the scope of any book to cover everything under the sun related to Android programming. However, I am confident that after reading this book (and doing the exercises), you will be well equipped to tackle your next Android programming challenge.

WHO THIS BOOK IS FOR

This book is targeted for the beginning Android developer who wants to start developing applications using Google's Android SDK. To truly benefit from this book, you should have some background in programming and at least be familiar with object-oriented programming (OOP) concepts. If you are totally new to Java—the language used for Android development—you might want to take a programming course in Java programming or grab one of many good books on Java programming. In my experience, if you already know C# or VB.NET, learning Java doesn't require too much effort. If you're already comfortable with C# or VB.NET, you should be comfortable just following along with the Try It Outs.

For those totally new to programming, I know the lure of developing mobile apps and making some money is tempting. However, before attempting to try out the examples in this book, I think a better starting point would be to first learn the basics of programming.

> ***NOTE*** *All the examples discussed in this book were written and tested using version N (Nougat) of the Android SDK on Android Studio 2 previews (1 through 6). Although every effort is made to ensure that all the tools used in this book are the latest, it is always possible that by the time you read this book a newer version of the tools will be available. If so, some of the instructions and/or screenshots may differ slightly. However, any variations should be manageable.*

WHAT THIS BOOK COVERS

This book covers the fundamentals of Android programming using the Android SDK. It is divided into 12 chapters and one appendix.

- **Chapter 1: Getting Started with Android Programming** covers the basics of the Android OS and its current state. You are introduced to the features of Android devices, as well as some of the popular devices on the market. You also find out how to download and install Android Studio to develop Android applications, and then you see how to test them on the Android emulator.
- **Chapter 2: Using Android Studio for Android Development** walks you through many of the different elements within Android Studio. You are introduced to the IDE (Integrated Development Environment) and its pieces. Finally, you discover how to publish a finished application
- **Chapter 3: Activities, Fragments, and Intents** gets you acquainted with these three fundamental concepts in Android programming. Activities and fragments are the building blocks of an Android application. You find out how to link activities to form a complete Android application using intents, one of the unique characteristics of the Android OS.
- **Chapter 4: Getting to Know the Android User Interface** covers the various components that make up the user interface (UI) of an Android application. You are introduced to the various layouts you can use to build the UI of your application. You also learn about the numerous events that are associated with the UI when users interact with the application.
- **Chapter 5: Designing Your User Interface with Views** walks you through the various basic views you can use to build your Android UI. You learn three main groups of views: basic views, picker views, and list views. You also find out about the specialized fragments available in Android 3.0 and 4.0.

- **Chapter 6: Displaying Pictures and Menus with Views** continues the exploration of views. Here, you see how to display images using the various image views, as well as display options and context menus in your application. This chapter ends with some additional cool views that you can use to spice up your application.
- **Chapter 7: Data Persistence** shows you how to save, or store, data in your Android application. In addition to being introduced to the various techniques to store user data, you also find out about file manipulation and how to save files onto internal and external storage (SD card). In addition, you learn how to create and use a SQLite database in your Android application.
- **Chapter 8: Content Providers** discusses how data can be shared among different applications on an Android device. You see how to use a content provider and then build one yourself.
- **Chapter 9: Messaging** explores two of the most interesting topics in mobile programming—sending SMS messages and email. You learn how to programmatically send and receive SMS and email messages, as well as how to intercept incoming SMS messages so that the built-in Messaging application is not able to receive any messages.
- **Chapter 10: Location-Based Services** demonstrates how to build a location-based service application using Google Maps. You also find out how to obtain geographical location data and then display the location on the map.
- **Chapter 11: Networking** explores how to connect to web servers to download data. You see how XML and JSON web services can be consumed in an Android application. This chapter also explains sockets programming, and you see how to build a chat client in Android.
- **Chapter 12: Developing Android Services** demonstrates how you can write applications using services. Services are background applications that run without a UI. You learn how to run your services asynchronously on a separate thread, and how your activities can communicate with them.
- **Appendix: Answers to Exercises** contains the solutions to the end-of-chapter exercises found in every chapter.

HOW THIS BOOK IS STRUCTURED

This book breaks down the task of learning Android programming into several smaller chunks, enabling you to digest each topic before delving into a more advanced one.

If you are a total beginner to Android programming, start with Chapter 1. After you have familiarized yourself with the basics, head to Chapter 2 and get to know the Android Studio IDE. When you are ready, continue with Chapter 3 and gradually move into more advanced topics.

A feature of this book is that all the code samples in each chapter are independent of those discussed in previous chapters. This gives you the flexibility to dive into the topics that interest you and start working on the Try It Out projects.

WHAT YOU NEED TO USE THIS BOOK

All the examples in this book run on the Android emulator (which is included as part of the Android SDK and Android Studio). However, to get the most out of this book, it would be useful to have a real Android device (though it's not absolutely necessary).

CONVENTIONS

To help you get the most from the text and keep track of what's happening, a number of conventions are used throughout the book.

TRY IT OUT These Are Exercises or Examples for You to Follow

The Try It Out sections appear once or more per chapter. These are exercises to work through as you follow the related discussion in the text.

1. They consist of a set of numbered steps.
2. Follow the steps with your copy of the project files.

How It Works

After each Try It Out, the code you've typed is explained in detail.

As for other conventions in the text:

- New terms and important words are *highlighted* in italic when first introduced.
- Keyboard combinations are treated like this: Ctrl+R.
- Filenames, URLs, and code within the text are treated like so: `persistence.properties`.
- Code is presented in two different ways:

```
We use a monofont type with no highlighting for most code examples.
```

```
We use bolding to emphasize code that is of particular importance in the
present context.
```

> ***NOTE*** *Notes, tips, hints, tricks, and asides to the current discussion look like this.*

SOURCE CODE

As you work through the examples in this book, you may choose either to type in all the code manually or to use the source code files that accompany the book. All the source code used in this book is available for download at `www.wrox.com`. When at the site, simply locate the book's title (use the Search box or one of the title lists) and click the Download Code link on the book's detail page to obtain all the source code for the book.

You'll find the filename of the project you need at the end of the title of the Try it Out features:

TRY IT OUT Understanding the Life Cycle of an Activity (Activity101.zip)

After you download the code, decompress it with your favorite compression tool. Alternatively, go to the main Wrox code download page at `www.wrox.com/dynamic/books/download.aspx` to see the code available for this book as well as for all other Wrox books.

> ***NOTE*** *Because many books have similar titles, you might find it easiest to search by ISBN; this book's ISBN is 978-1-118-70559-9.*

ERRATA

We make every effort to ensure that there are no errors in the text or in the code. However, no one is perfect, and mistakes do occur. If you find an error in one of our books, such as a spelling mistake or faulty piece of code, we would be very grateful for your feedback. By sending in errata, you might save another reader hours of frustration and at the same time help us provide even higher-quality information.

To find the errata page for this book, go to `www.wrox.com` and locate the title using the Search box or one of the title lists. Then, on the book details page, click the Book Errata link. On this page, you can view all errata that has been submitted for this book and posted by Wrox editors.

> ***NOTE*** *A complete book list, including links to each book's errata, is also available at* `www.wrox.com/misc-pages/booklist.shtml`.

If you don't spot "your" error on the Book Errata page, go to `www.wrox.com/contact/techsupport.shtml` and complete the form there to send us the error you have found. We'll check the information and, if appropriate, post a message to the book's errata page and fix the problem in subsequent editions of the book.

P2P.WROX.COM

For author and peer discussion, join the P2P forums at `p2p.wrox.com`. The forums are a web-based system for you to post messages relating to Wrox books and related technologies. There, you also can interact with other readers and technology users. The forums offer a subscription feature that enables you to receive emails about topics of interest (of your choosing) when new posts are made to the forums. Wrox authors, editors, other industry experts, and your fellow readers are present on these forums.

At `p2p.wrox.com`, you will find a number of different forums that will help you not only as you read this book but also as you develop your own applications. To join the forums, follow these steps:

1. Go to `p2p.wrox.com` and click the Register link.
2. Read the terms of use and click Agree.
3. Complete the required information to join as well as any optional information you want to provide and click Submit.
4. You will receive an email with information describing how to verify your account and complete the joining process.

> ***NOTE*** *You can read messages in the forums without joining P2P, but in order to post your own messages, you must join.*

After you join, you can post new messages and respond to messages posted by other users. You can read messages at any time on the web. If you want to have new messages from a particular forum emailed to you, click the Subscribe to This Forum icon next to the forum name in the forum listing.

For more information about how to use the Wrox P2P, be sure to read the P2P FAQs for answers to questions about how the forum software works, as well as many common questions specific to P2P and Wrox books. To read the FAQs, click the FAQ link on any P2P page.

1

Getting Started with Android Programming

WHAT YOU WILL LEARN IN THIS CHAPTER

- What is Android?
- Android versions and its feature set
- The Android architecture
- The various Android devices on the market
- The Android Market application store
- How to obtain the tools and SDK for developing Android applications
- How to develop your first Android application

> ***CODE DOWNLOAD*** *There are no code downloads for this chapter.*

Welcome to the world of Android! This chapter explains what Android is and what makes it so compelling to both developers and device manufacturers. It also shows you how to obtain and set up all the necessary tools so that you can test your application on an Android emulator in Android Studio 2 and how to get started with developing your first Android application. By the end of this chapter, you will be equipped with the basic knowledge you need to explore more sophisticated techniques and tricks for developing your next killer Android application.

WHAT IS ANDROID?

Android is a mobile operating system that is based on a modified version of Linux. It was originally developed by a startup of the same name, Android, Inc. In 2005, as part of its strategy to enter the mobile space, Google purchased Android, Inc. and took over its development work (as well as its development team).

Google wanted the Android OS to be open and free, so most of the Android code was released under the open source Apache License. That means anyone who wants to use Android can do so by downloading the full Android source code. Moreover, vendors (typically hardware manufacturers) can add their own proprietary extensions to Android and customize Android to differentiate their products from others. This development model makes Android very attractive to vendors, especially those companies affected by the phenomenon of Apple's iPhone, which was a hugely successful product that revolutionized the smartphone industry. When the iPhone was launched, many smartphone manufacturers had to scramble to find new ways of revitalizing their products. These manufacturers saw Android as a solution, meaning they will continue to design their own hardware and use Android as the operating system that powers it. Some companies that have taken advantage of Android's open source policy include Motorola and Sony Ericsson, which have been developing their own mobile operating systems for many years.

The main advantage to adopting Android is that it offers a unified approach to application development. Developers need only develop for Android in general, and their applications should be able to run on numerous different devices, as long as the devices are powered using Android. In the world of smartphones, applications are the most important part of the success chain.

Android Versions

Android has gone through quite a number of updates since its first release. Table 1-1 shows the various versions of Android and their codenames.

TABLE 1-1: A Brief History of Android Versions

ANDROID VERSION	RELEASE DATE	CODENAME
1.1	February 9, 2009	
1.5	April 30, 2009	Cupcake
1.6	September 15, 2009	Donut
2.0/2.1	October 26, 2009	Éclair
2.2	May 20, 2010	Froyo
2.3	December 6, 2010	Gingerbread
3.0/3.1/3.2	February 22, 2011	Honeycomb
4.0	October 18, 2011	Ice Cream Sandwich

ANDROID VERSION	RELEASE DATE	CODENAME
4.1	July 9, 2012	Jelly Bean
4.4	October 31, 2013	KitKat
5.0	November 12, 2014	Lollipop
6.0	October 5, 2015	Marshmallow
7.0	TBD	Nougat

In 2016, Google released Android 7.0; the following are the key changes in Android 7.0:

- Split-screen multi-window mode
- Redesigned notification shade
- Refined "Doze" feature
- Switch from JRE (Java Runtime Environment) to OpenJDK

One important thing to keep in mind as you are looking at Android versions is that each version has its own features and APIs (application programming interfaces). Therefore, if your application is written for the newest version of Android, and it uses an API that was not present in an older version of Android, then only devices running that newer version of Android will be able to use your application.

Features of Android

Because Android is open source and freely available to manufacturers for customization, there are no fixed hardware or software configurations. However, the base Android OS supports many features, including

- **Storage**—SQLite, a lightweight relational database, for data storage. Chapter 7 discusses data storage in more detail.
- **Connectivity**—GSM/EDGE, IDEN, CDMA, EV-DO, UMTS, Bluetooth (includes A2DP and AVRCP), Wi-Fi, LTE, and WiMAX. Chapter 11 discusses networking in more detail.
- **Messaging**—Both SMS and MMS. Chapter 9 discusses messaging in more detail.
- **Media support** H.263, H.264 (in 3GP or MP4 container), MPEG-4 SP, AMR, AMR-WB (in 3GP container), AAC, HE-AAC (in MP4 or 3GP container), MP3, MIDI, Ogg Vorbis, WAV, JPEG, PNG, GIF, and BMP.
- **Hardware support**—Accelerometer sensor, camera, digital compass, proximity sensor, and GPS.
- **Multi-touch**—Multi-touch screens.
- **Multi-tasking**—Multi-tasking applications.
- **Tethering**—Sharing of Internet connections as a wired/wireless hotspot.

Android's web browser is based on the open source WebKit and Chrome's V8 JavaScript engine.

Architecture of Android

To understand how Android works, take a look at Figure 1-1, which shows the various layers that make up the Android operating system (OS).

The Android OS is roughly divided into five sections in four main layers:

- **Linux kernel**—This is the kernel on which Android is based. This layer contains all the low-level device drivers for the various hardware components of an Android device.
- **Libraries**—These contain the code that provides the main features of an Android OS. For example, the SQLite library provides database support so that an application can use it for data storage. The WebKit library provides functionalities for web browsing.
- **Android runtime**—The Android runtime is located in the same layer with the libraries and provides a set of core libraries that enable developers to write Android apps using the Java programming language. The Android runtime also includes the Dalvik virtual machine, which enables every Android application to run in its own process, with its own instance of the Dalvik virtual machine. (Android applications are compiled into Dalvik executables). Dalvik is a specialized virtual machine designed specifically for Android and optimized for battery-powered mobile devices with limited memory and CPU power.
- **Application framework**—The application framework exposes the various capabilities of the Android OS to application developers so that they can make use of them in their applications.
- **Applications**—At this top layer are the applications that ship with the Android device (such as Phone, Contacts, Browser, and so on), as well as applications that you download and install from the Android Market. Any applications that you write are located at this layer.

Android Devices in the Market

Android devices come in all shapes and sizes including, but not limited to, the following types of devices:

- Smartphones
- Tablets
- E-reader devices
- Internet TVs
- Automobiles
- Smartwatches

Chances are good that you own at least one of the preceding devices. Figure 1-2 shows the Samsung Galaxy Edge 7.

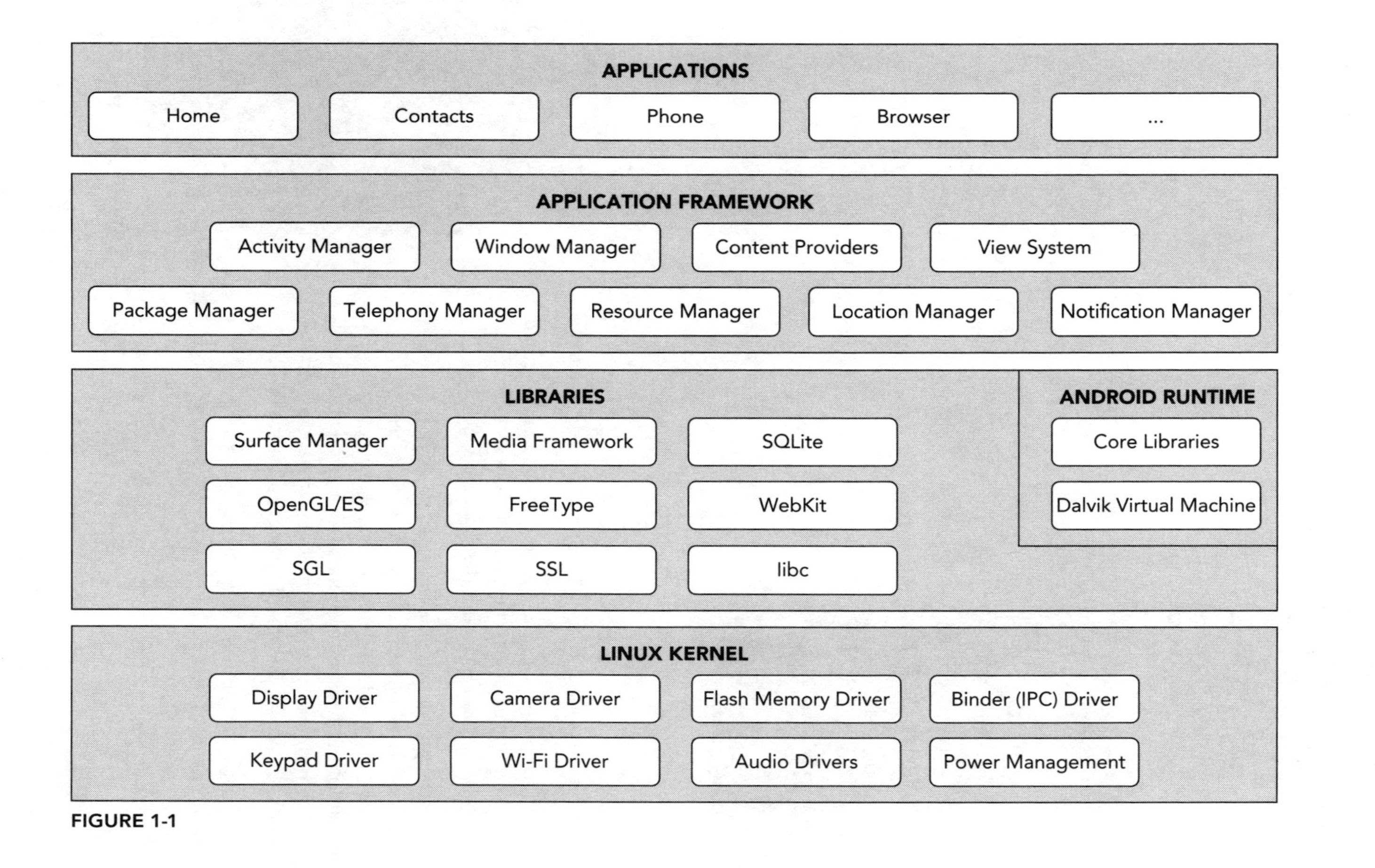
APPLICATIONS
Home
Contacts
Phone
Browser
...
APPLICATION FRAMEWORK
Activity Manager
Window Manager
Content Providers
View System
Package Manager
Telephony Manager
Resource Manager
Location Manager
Notification Manager
LIBRARIES
Surface Manager
Media Framework
SQLite
OpenGL/ES
FreeType
WebKit
SGL
SSL
libc
ANDROID RUNTIME
Core Libraries
Dalvik Virtual Machine
LINUX KERNEL
Display Driver
Camera Driver
Flash Memory Driver
Binder (IPC) Driver
Keypad Driver
Wi-Fi Driver
Audio Drivers
Power Management

FIGURE 1-1

FIGURE 1-2

Another popular category of devices is the tablet. Tablets typically come in two sizes: 7″ and 10″, measured diagonally.

Besides smartphones and tablets, Android is used in dedicated devices, such as e-book readers. Figure 1-4 shows the Barnes and Noble's NOOK Color running the Android OS.

In addition to the popular mobile devices I've already mentioned, Android is finding its way onto your wrist. Smartwatches, and "wearables" in general, have become a major segment of the Android population. Figure 1-3 shows the Motorola Moto 360 Smartwatch, which runs Android Wear (a version of Android OS specifically designed for wearables).

FIGURE 1-3

At the time of writing, the Samsung Galaxy Nexus (see Figure 1-4) is the only device running a pure version of Android. Many manufacturers add their own modifications to the Android OS for use on their specific devices. Motorola devices have Motoblur, HTC devices have HTC Sense, and so on. However, the Nexus devices always run a clean version of Android with no modifications.

FIGURE 1-4

The Android Market

As mentioned earlier, one of the main factors determining the success of a smartphone platform is the applications that support it. It is clear from the success of the iPhone that applications play a very vital role in determining whether a new platform swims or sinks. Also, making these applications accessible to the general user is extremely important.

Users can simply use the Google Play application that is preinstalled on their Android devices to directly download third-party applications to their devices. Both paid and free applications are available in the Google Play Store, although paid applications are available only to users in certain countries because of legal issues.

> ***NOTE*** *Chapter 13 discusses more about Google Play Store and how you can sell your own applications in it.*

OBTAINING THE REQUIRED TOOLS

Now that you know what Android is and what its feature set contains, you are probably anxious to get your hands dirty and start writing some applications! Before you write your first app, however, you need to download the required tools.

For Android development, you can use a Mac, a Windows PC, or a Linux machine. You can freely download all the necessary tools. Most of the examples provided in this book are written to work on Android Studio. For this book, I am using a Windows 10 computer to demonstrate all the code samples. If you are using a Mac or Linux computer, the screenshots should look similar. Some minor differences might be present, but you should be able to follow along without problems.

Let the fun begin!

JAVA JDK 8

The Android Studio 2 makes use of the Java SE Development Kit 8 (JDK). If your computer does not have the JDK 8 installed, you should start by downloading it from `www.oracle.com/technetwork/java/javase/downloads/jdk8-downloads-2133151.html` and installing it prior to moving to the next section.

Android Studio

The first and most important piece of software you need to download is Android Studio 2. After you have downloaded and installed Android Studio 2, you can use the SDK Manager to download and install multiple versions of the Android SDK. Having multiple versions of the SDK available enables you to write programs that target different devices. For example, you can write one version of an application that specifically targets Android Nougat, but because that flavor of Android is on less than 1% of devices, with multiple versions of the SDK you can also write a version of your app that uses older features and targets Marshmallow or Lollipop users. You can use the Android Device Manager to set up device emulators.

You can download Android Studio 2 from `http://developer.android.com/sdk/index.html` (see Figure 1-5).

Android Studio 2 is packaged in an executable. Run the install process to set up Android Studio 2. After you've downloaded and run the setup executable, use the following steps to go through the installation process:

1. Accept the terms and conditions shown in Figure 1-6.
2. If you have an older version of Android Studio already installed on your computer, the Android Studio Setup prompts you to automatically uninstall it. Even though the old version of Android Studio will be uninstalled, the settings and configurations are retained. You have an opportunity to reapply those settings and configurations to Android Studio 2 after the setup has completed. Figure 1-7 shows the screen where you are prompted to uninstall an old version of Android Studio.

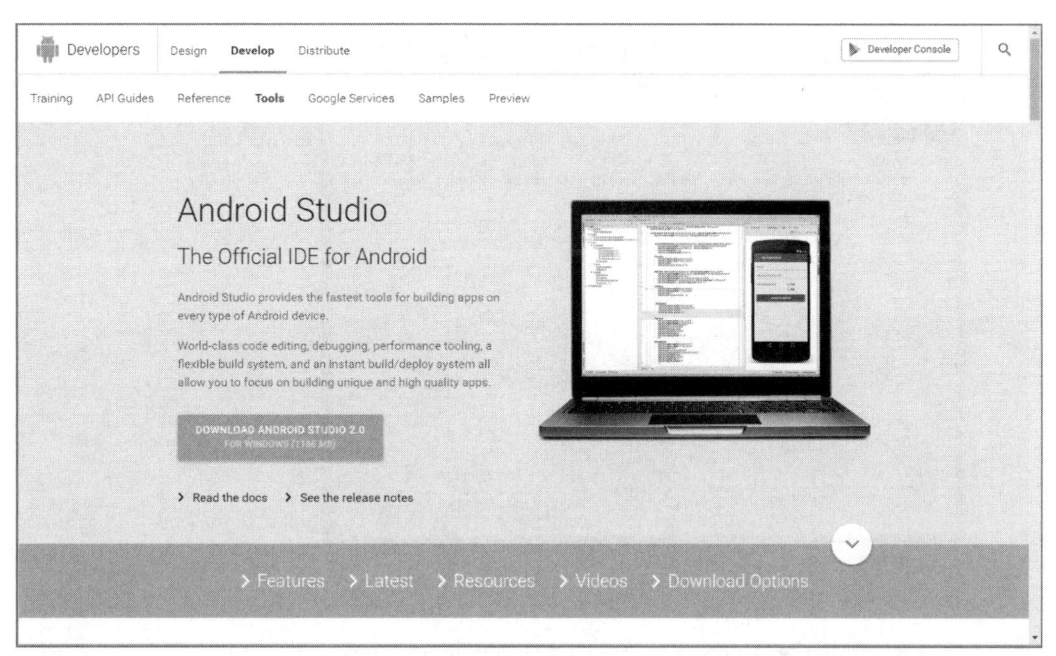

FIGURE 1-5

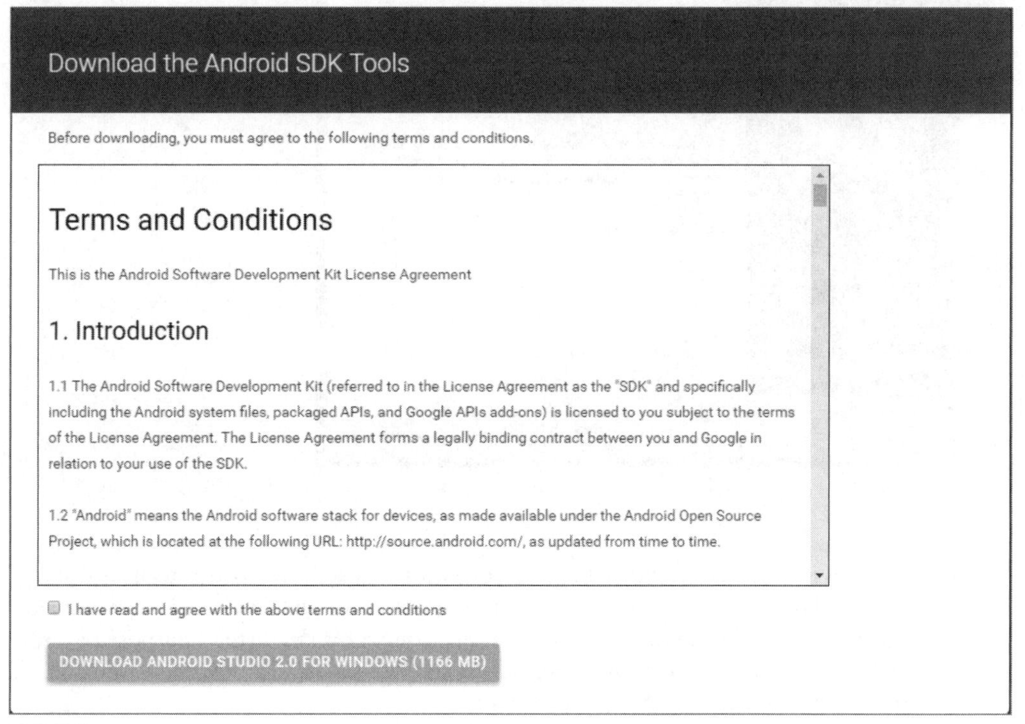

FIGURE 1-6

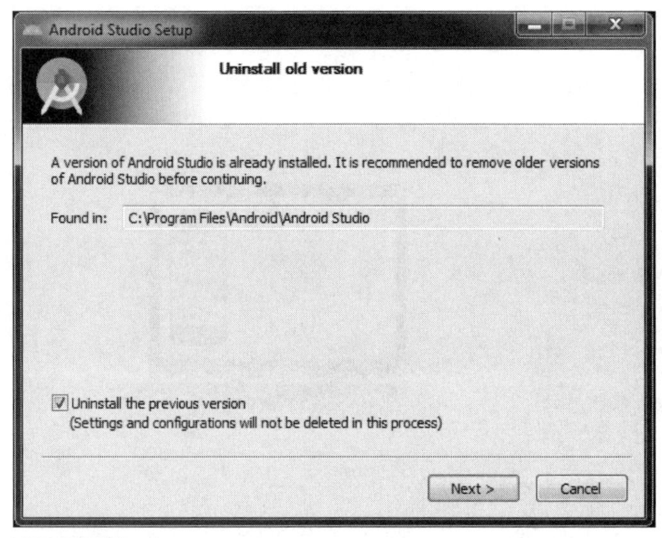

FIGURE 1-7

3. Click Next on the Welcome to Android Studio Setup screen (see Figure 1-8).

FIGURE 1-8

4. Pick which components of Android Studio you want to install from the screen shown in Figure 1-9. Android Studio is selected by default (and cannot be deselected), which makes sense given that you are going through all of this trouble for the distinct purpose of installing Android Studio. Android SDK and Android Virtual Device are also selected by default. Click Next to accept the default choices and continue.

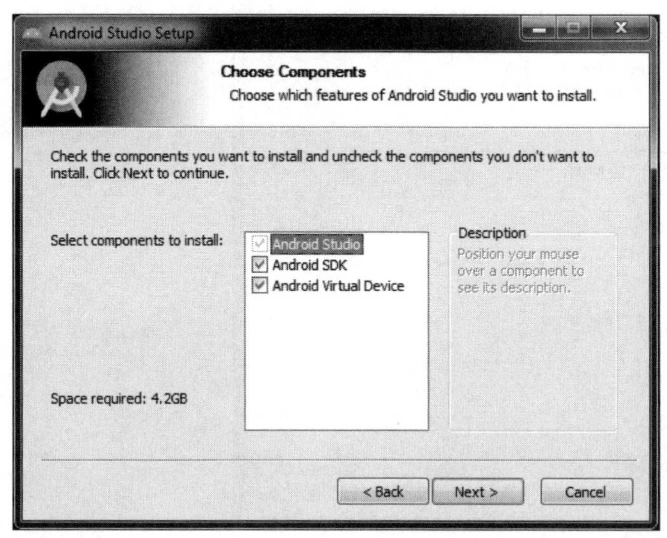

FIGURE 1-9

5. You are presented with the License Agreement, as shown in Figure 1-10. Click I Agree to continue.

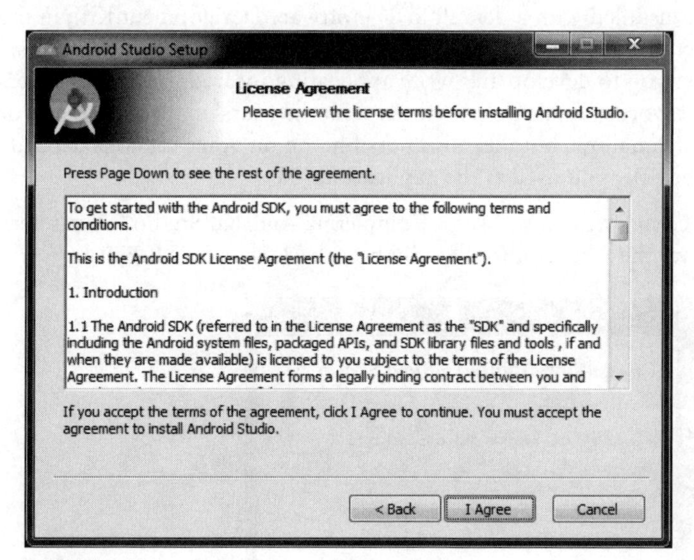

FIGURE 1-10

6. On the configuration settings screen, it is best to accept the default locations specified by the setup process and click Next to continue. You see the Choose Start Menu Folder screen (shown in Figure 1-11). Click Install to kick off the Android Studio 2 installation.

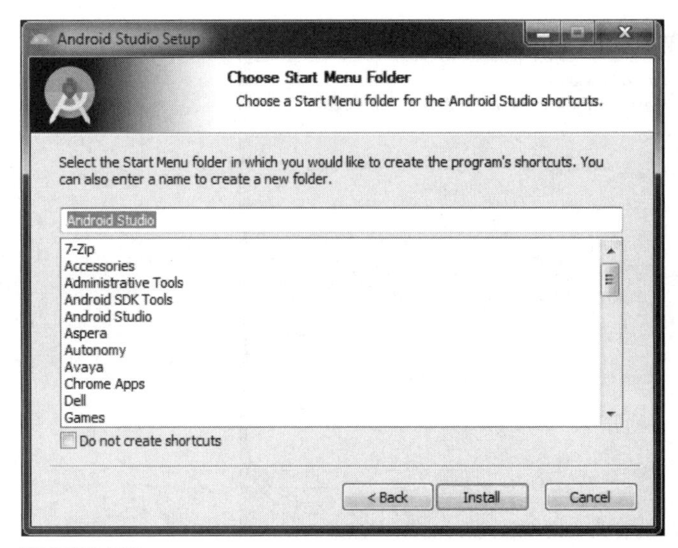

FIGURE 1-11

7. Installing Android Studio 2 could take a few minutes, depending on the speed of your computer. You are presented with a progress bar to help you track the state of the installation. Android Studio 2 is installed with a default SDK (Software Development Kit), in this case Marshmallow. Later in the process you have the opportunity to install other SDKs. The Android SDK allows you to develop and write applications geared for a specific version of Android. In other words, applications written with the Marshmallow SDK run on Android devices running Marshmallow, but they also possibly run on other versions depending on which features of the SDK you used in the application.

8. When the install is complete, you will see a Completing Android Studio Setup screen (shown in Figure 1-12). Leave the Start Android Studio box checked and click Finish.

FIGURE 1-12

9. Android Studio 2 prompts you to either import settings from a previous version of Android Studio or continue with new settings. If you uninstalled a previous version in the first step of the installation process, Android Studio offers you a chance to recover the settings used in that previous version and apply them to Android Studio 2 (see Figure 1-13).

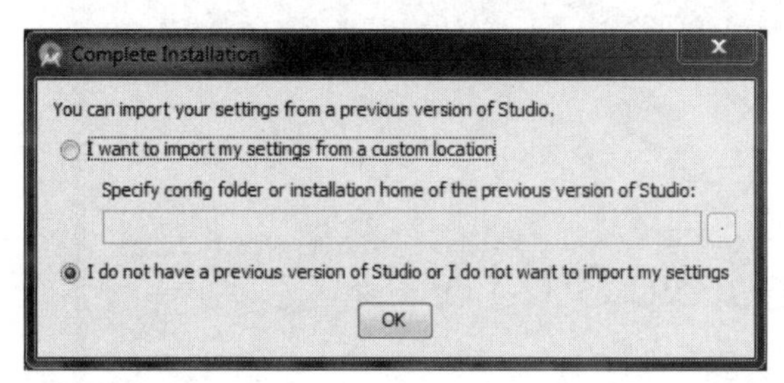

FIGURE 1-13

Now that Android Studio 2 is installed, you need to adjust the settings and options using the following steps:

1. Click Continue at the Welcome screen and choose Standard from the Install Type selection screen shown in Figure 1-14. Click Next to continue.

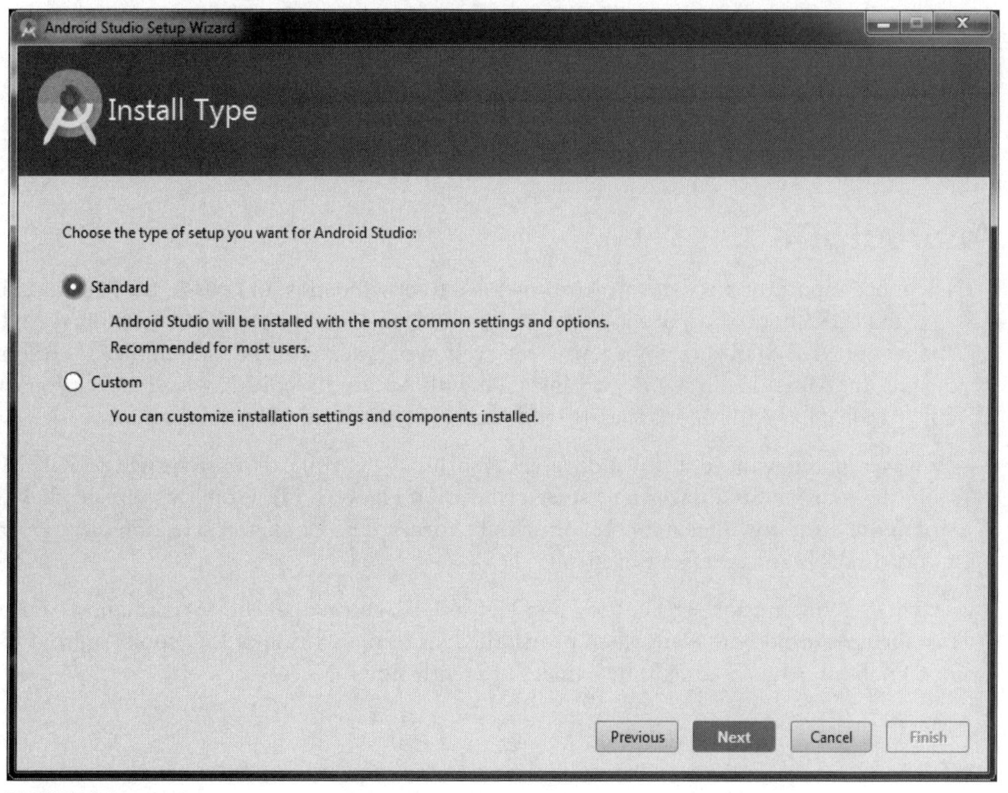

FIGURE 1-14

2. Click Finish on the Verify Settings screen, and Android Studio 2 finalizes the setup process. You know the process is complete when you are greeted with the Welcome to Android Studio screen (see Figure 1-15).

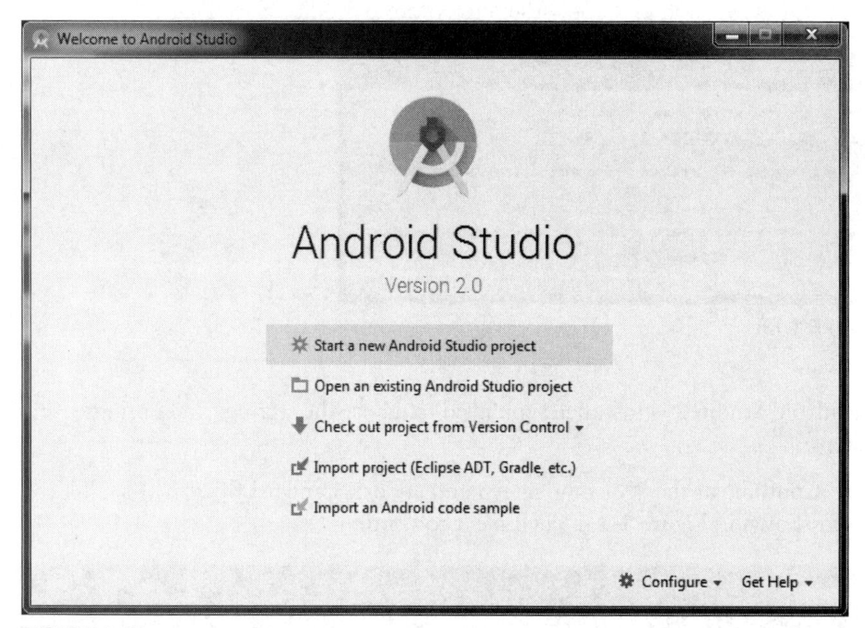

FIGURE 1-15

Now that Android Studio is set up, it's time to install the latest and greatest Android SDK.

Android SDK

The most important piece of software you need to download is, of course, the Android SDK. The Android SDK contains all of the packages and tools required to develop a functional Android application. The SDKs are named after the version of Android OS to which they correspond. By default, the Marshmallow SDK was installed with Android Studio 2, which means you can develop applications that will run seamlessly on devices with Android Marshmallow.

However, if you want to install a different Android SDK, you can do so using the SDK Manager from the Android Studio welcome screen (shown in Figure 1-15). From this screen, click the Configure drop-down menu in the lower-right corner. The Configure selection menu opens. Choose SDK Manager from this menu.

The SDK configuration screen, shown in Figure 1-16, shows that the Marshmallow SDK is already installed. Android N is available to be installed (as of the writing of this book Android Nougat was in a finalized beta, so it might be named differently now).

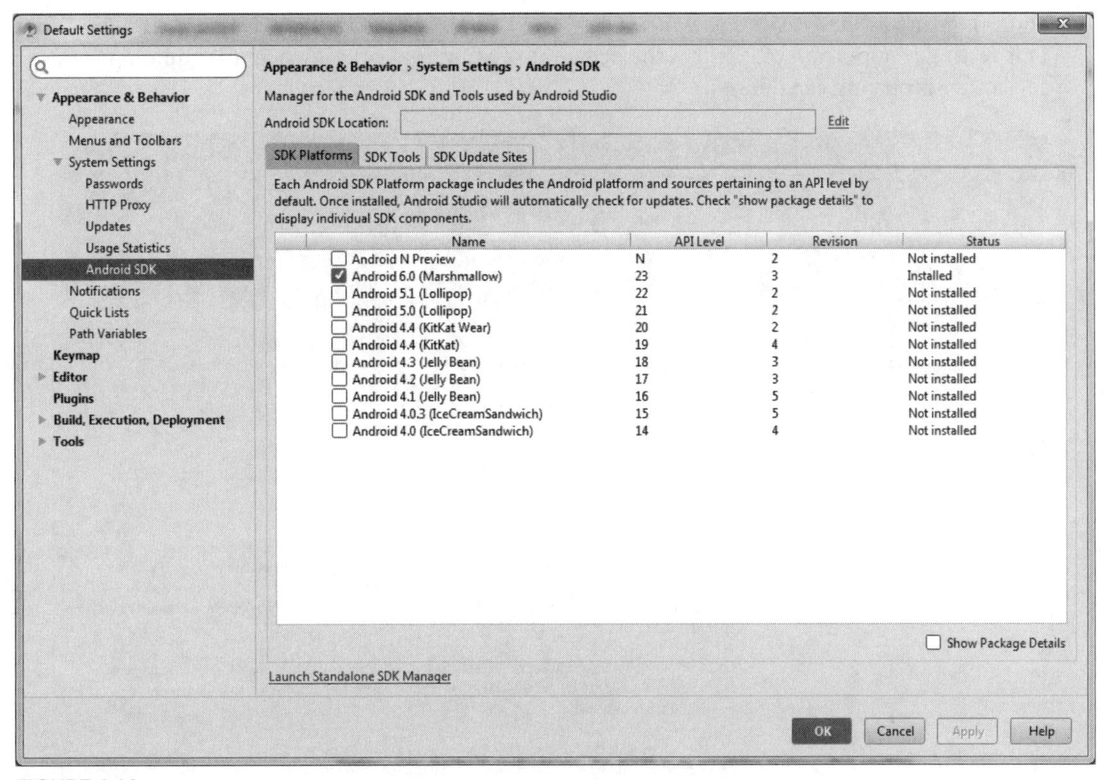

FIGURE 1-16

Select Android Nougat, click Apply, and then click OK. However, before the SDK is installed you must accept the licensing agreement as shown in Figure 1-17.

The setup process for Android Studio is now complete. The next section explains how to set up an Android Virtual Device that you can use to test your applications.

Creating Android Virtual Devices (AVDs)

The next step is to create an Android Virtual Device (AVD) you can use for testing your Android applications. An AVD is an emulator instance that enables you to model an actual device. Each AVD consists of a hardware profile; a mapping to a system image; and emulated storage, such as a secure digital (SD) card. One important thing to remember about emulators is that they are not perfect. There are some applications, such as games (which are GPU heavy) or applications that use sensors such as the GPS or accelerometer. These types of applications cannot be simulated with the same speed or consistency within an emulator as they can when running on an actual device. However, the emulator is good for doing some generalized testing of your applications.

You can create as many AVDs as you want to test your applications with different configurations. This testing is important to confirm the behavior of your application when it is run on different devices with varying capabilities.

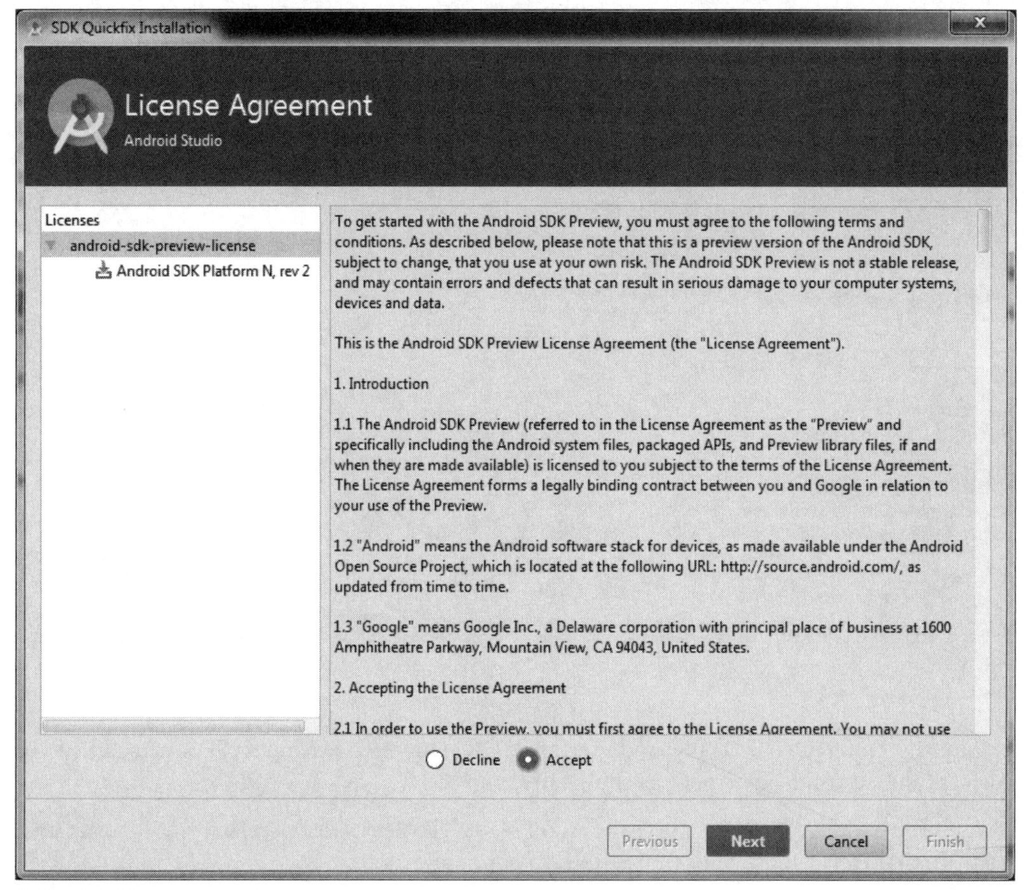

FIGURE 1-17

Use the following steps to create an AVD. This example demonstrates creating an AVD (put simply, an Android emulator) that emulates an Android device running Android N on the Nexus 5x hardware specs.

1. Start Android Studio so that the Welcome screen is visible (refer to Figure 1-15). Click Start a New Android Studio Project. You see the Create New Project Wizard shown in Figure 1-18.
2. Set up a HelloWorld project (that you will use in the final section of this chapter). Type **Chapter1Helloworld** in the Application Name field.

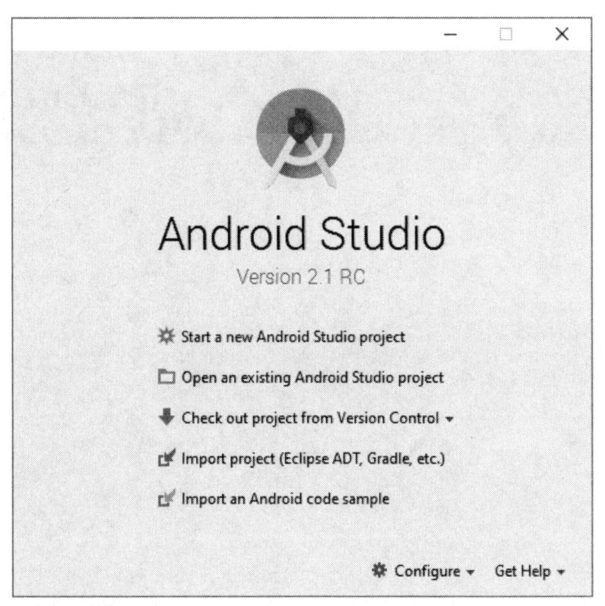

FIGURE 1-18

3. You can keep the default values for the other fields on the New Project screen (they will be explained in more detail in later chapters). Click Next.

> ***NOTE*** *For the purposes of setting up a quick Hello World project and creating an AVD, you will be accepting many of the default values, without explanation, during the project setup process. This is fine for now, as all of the settings are explained in much greater detail in subsequent chapters.*

4. You should see the Targeted Android Devices screen. By default, the Create New Project Wizard selects for you the Android SDK level that has the greatest activity based on statistics gathered from Google Play. At the time this book was written 74.3 percent of the active devices on Google Play were written using Android Jelly Bean. For now, accept the default, as shown in Figure 1-19, and click Next.
5. On the Add an Activity to Mobile screen, accept the default choice—Empty Activity (see Figure 1-20)—and click Next.

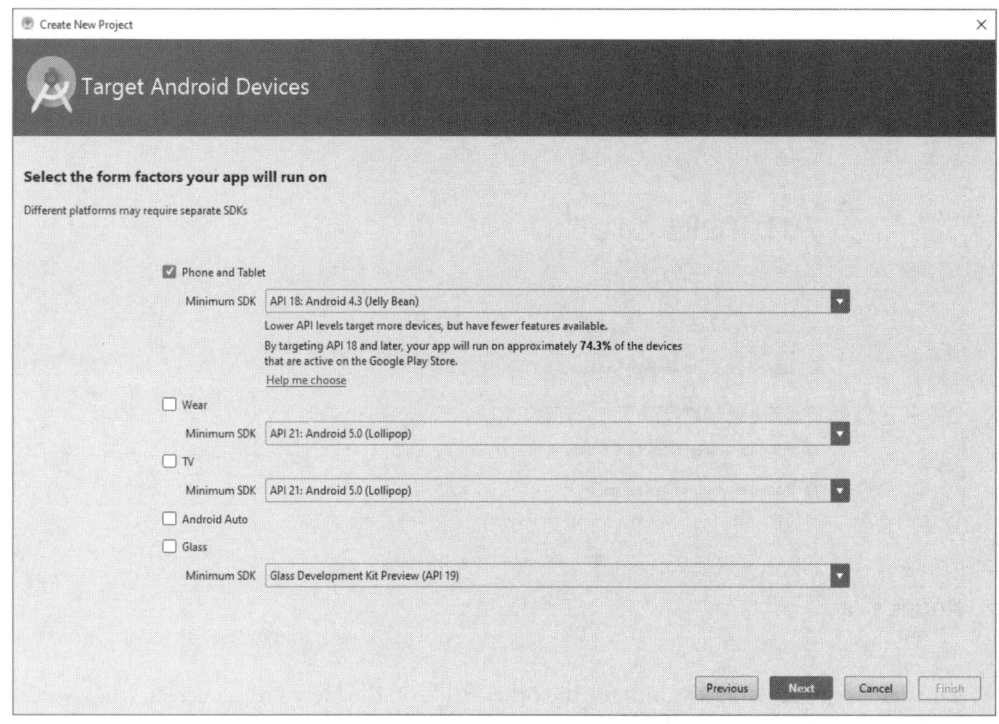

FIGURE 1-19

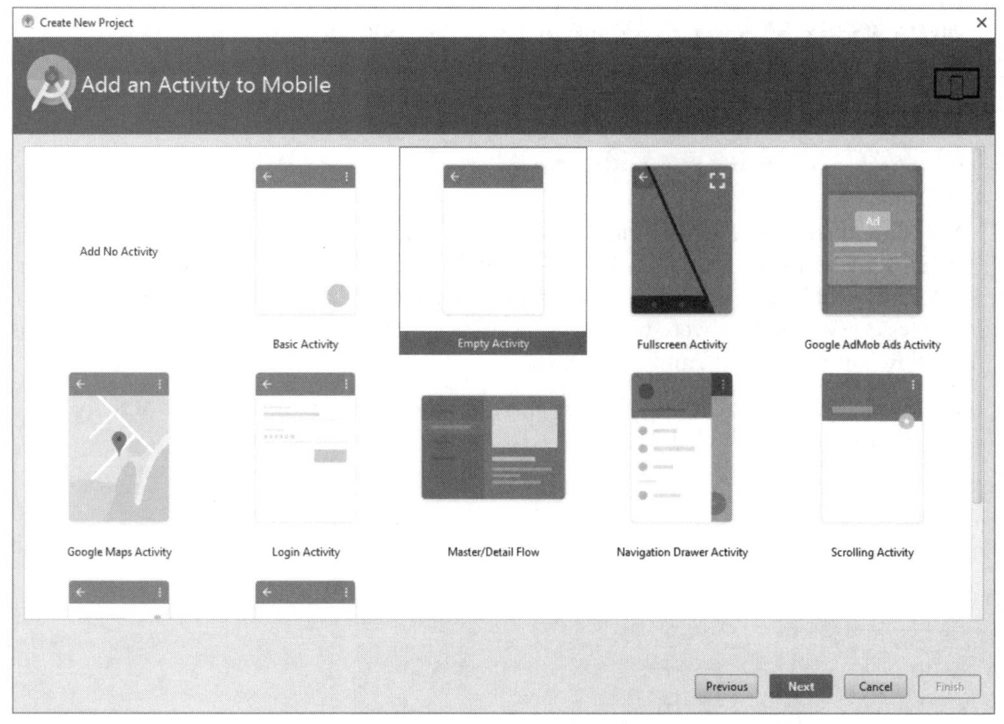

FIGURE 1-20

6. Accept all of the defaults on the Customize the Activity screen, as shown in Figure 1-21, and click Finish. Figure 1-22 shows the open Android Studio IDE.

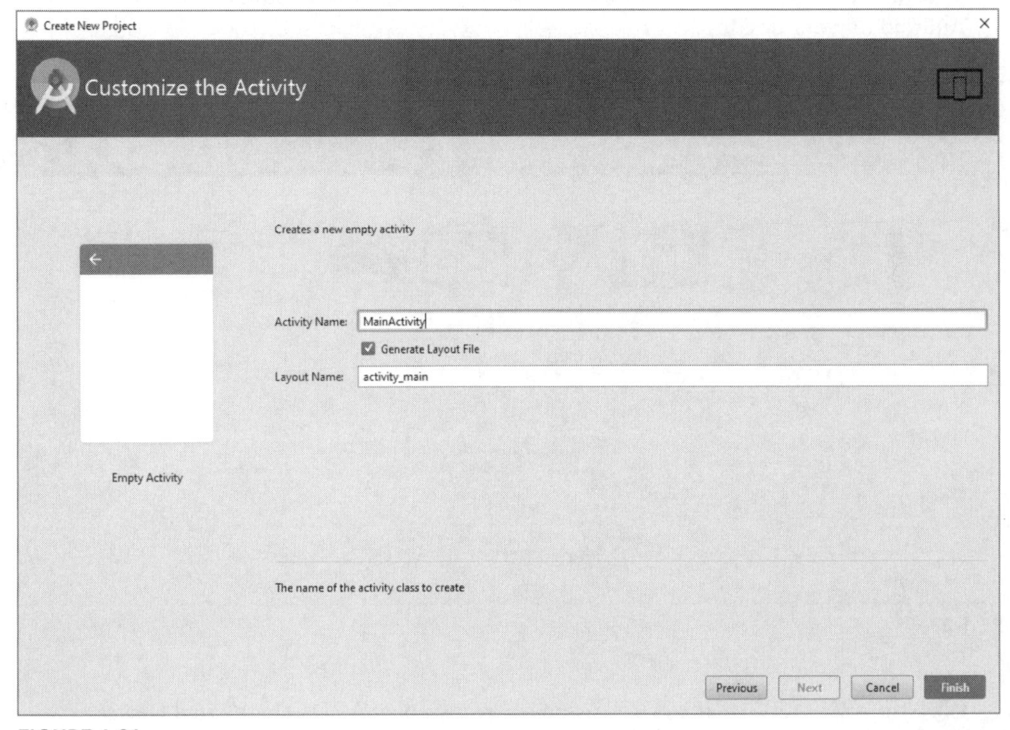

FIGURE 1-21

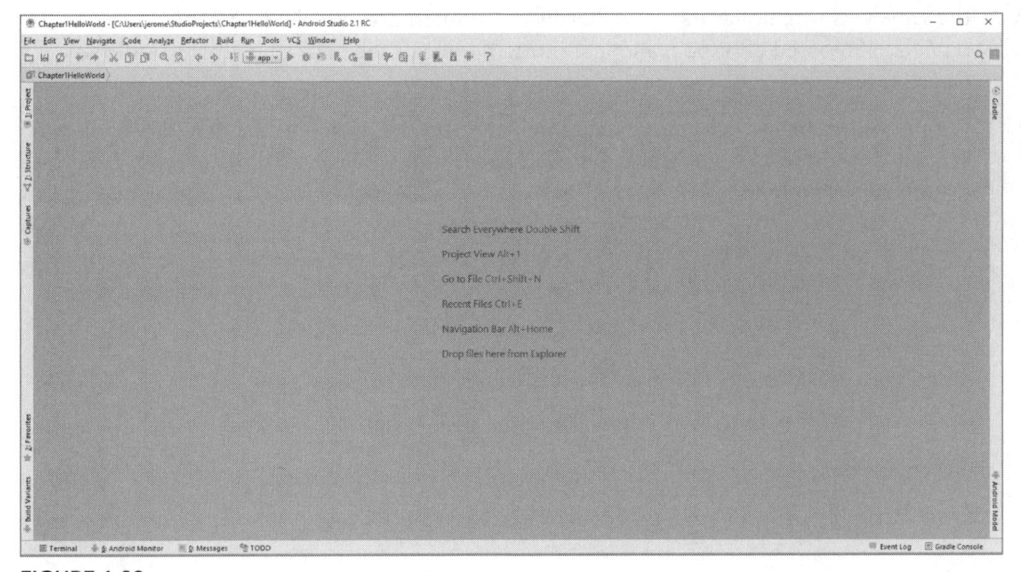

FIGURE 1-22

7. Launch the AVD Manager by selecting Tools ➪ Android ➪ AVD Manager or using the AVD Manager button from the toolbar. Figure 1-23 shows the Android Virtual Device Manager Wizard, which is where you set up AVDs to be used when you emulate your application in Android on your desktop.

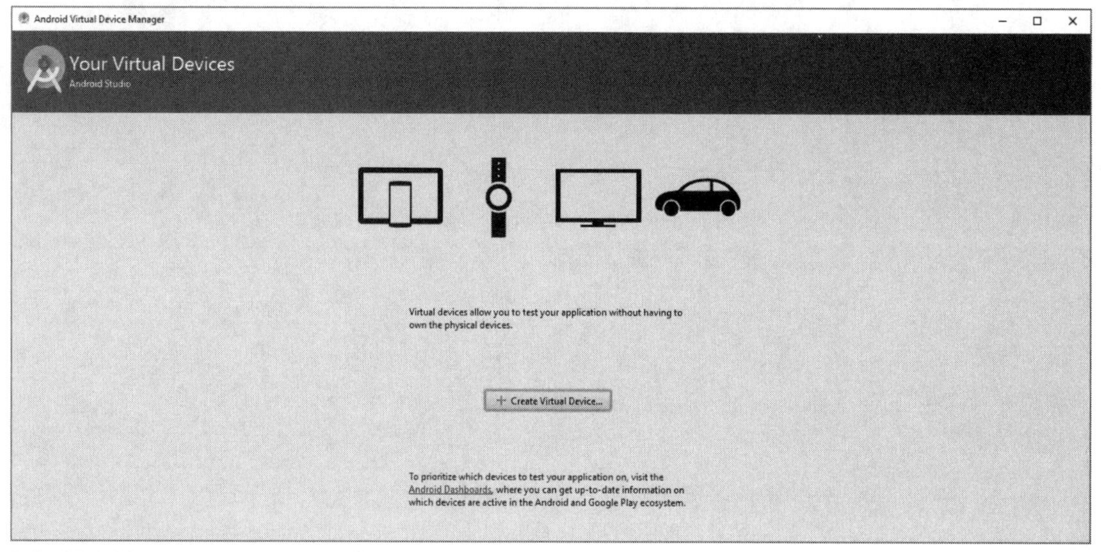

FIGURE 1-23

8. Click the + Create Virtual Device button to create a new AVD. The Virtual Device Configuration screen opens as shown in Figure 1-24.
9. Select the Nexus 5x hardware profile and click Next. Although none of the emulators offers the same performance as its actual hardware counterpart, the Nexus 5x should run well on most x86-based desktops, and it still offers some of the mid- to high-end Android device specs.
10. For the system image, select and install the latest option, which at the time this book was written is Android Nougat. Click the x86 Images tab (see Figure 1-25), select N from the list of images, and then click Next.

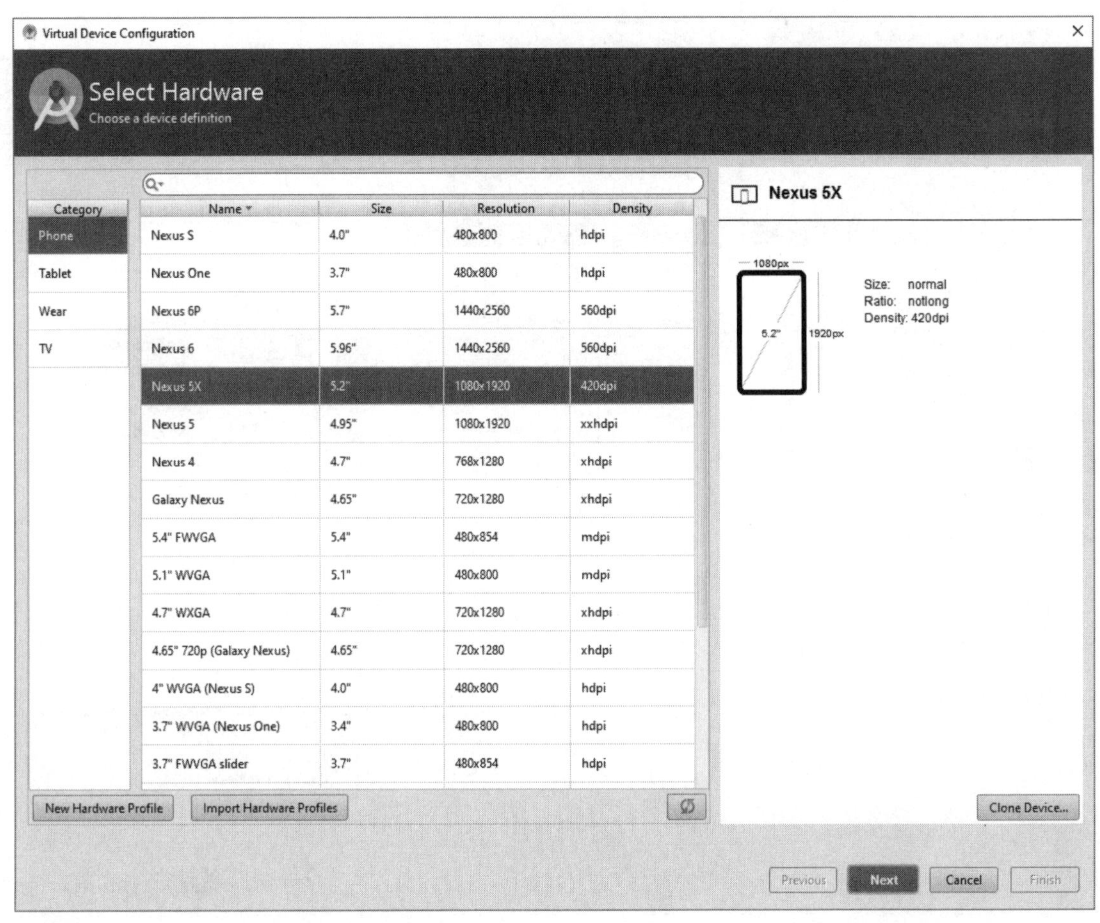

FIGURE 1-24

11. In the Android Virtual Device (AVD) dialog, accept the defaults as shown in Figure 1-26. Click the Finish button to begin building the AVD.

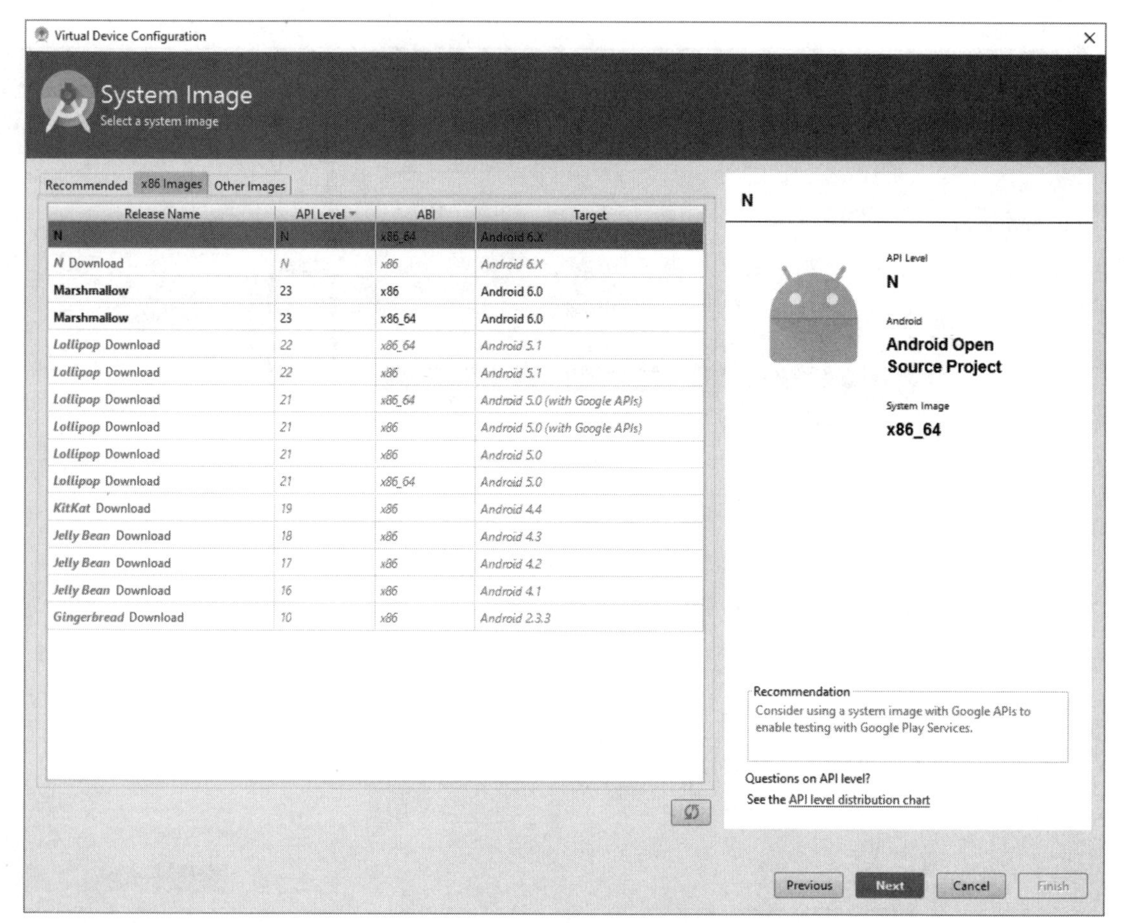

FIGURE 1-25

> ***TIP*** *It is preferable to create a few AVDs with different API levels and hardware configurations so that your application can be tested on different versions of the Android OS.*

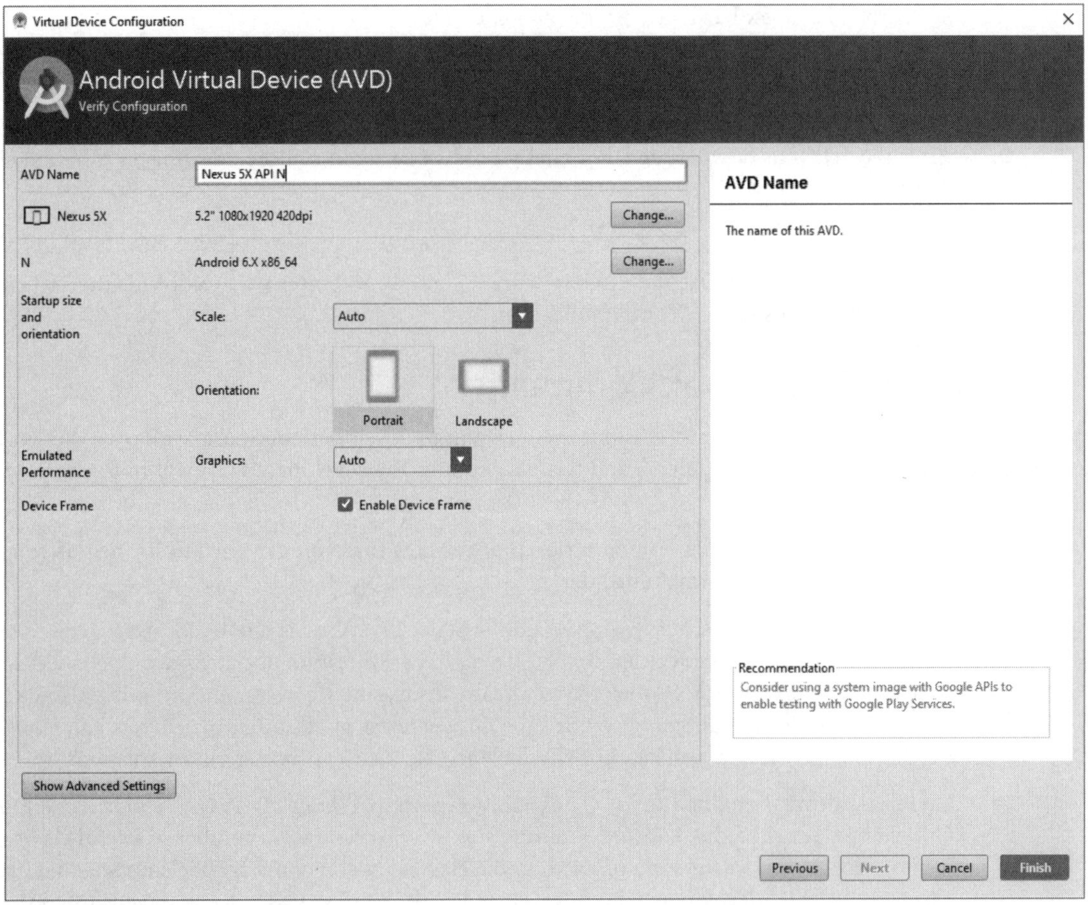

FIGURE 1-26

TRY IT OUT Creating a Jellybean Emulator

When you created your first Android project earlier in this section, the setup process determined that Jelly Bean was the most active version of Android on Google Play. In this Try It Out, you create an AVD for Android Jelly Bean.

1. Launch the AVD Manager by selecting Tools ➪ Android ➪ AVD Manager or using the AVD Manager button from the toolbar.
2. In the Android Virtual Device Manager Wizard, click the + Create Virtual Device button.

3. Select the Nexus 5x hardware profile and click Next.
4. Click the x86 Images tab, select Jelly Bean from the list of images, and then click Download.
5. Accept the agreement and download the Jelly Bean SDK.
6. After the SDK has downloaded, click Jelly Bean once again (on the x86 Images tab) and click Next.
7. In the Android Virtual Device (AVD) dialog, accept the defaults and click the Finish button.

After you have created your ADV, it is time to test it. There is no better way to do this than to create and launch the ubiquitous Hello World application.

The Android Developer Community

Now that Android is in its seventh version, there is a large developer community all over the world. It is easy to find solutions to problems and to find like-minded developers with whom to share app ideas and experiences.

The following are some developer communities and websites that you can turn to for help if you run into problems while working with Android:

- **Stack Overflow** (`www.stackoverflow.com`)—Stack Overflow is a collaboratively edited question-and-answer site for developers. If you have a question about Android, chances are someone at Stack Overflow is probably already discussing the same question. It's also likely that someone else has already provided the answer. Best of all, other developers can vote for the best answer so that you can know which are the answers that are most trustworthy.
- **Google Android Training** (`http://developer.android.com/training/index.html`)—Google has launched the Android Training site, which contains a number of useful classes grouped by topics. At the time of writing, the classes mostly contain code snippets that are useful to Android developers who have started with the basics. After you have learned the basics in this book, I strongly suggest you take a look at the classes.
- **Android Discuss** (`http://groups.google.com/group/android-discuss`)—Android Discuss is a discussion group hosted by Google using the Google Groups service. Here, you will be able to discuss the various aspects of Android programming. This group is monitored closely by the Android team at Google, so this is good place to clarify your doubts and to learn new tips and tricks.

LAUNCHING YOUR FIRST ANDROID APPLICATION

With all the tools and the SDK downloaded and installed, it is now time to start your engine. As in most programming books, the first example uses the ubiquitous Hello World application. This will give you a detailed look at the various components that make up an Android project. This is also the easiest Android project you will ever make.

Believe it or not, the Hello World application is already finished. By default, when you create a new application in Android Studio, it creates a Hello World application. Let's launch this application and, in the process, also launch the Android emulator to see how everything works.

1. Select Run ➪ Run *app* from the Android Studio menu bar. You should see the Select Deployment Target dialog as shown in Figure 1-27.

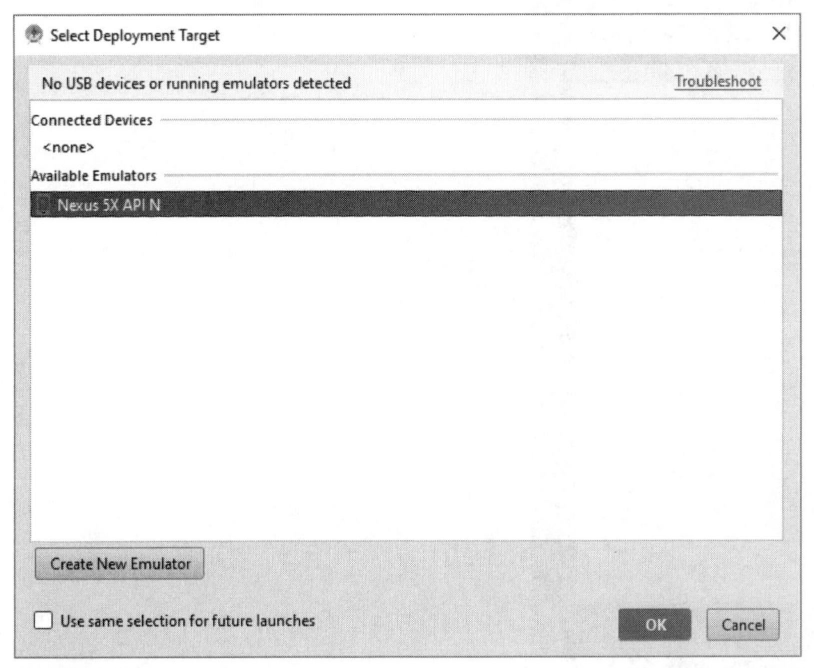

FIGURE 1-27

2. Select the Nexus 5X API N (feel free to select the Nexus 5x API 18, which is the Jelly Bean emulator that you created in the Try It Out for the last section), and click Next.

> ***NOTE*** *Note that If there's ever a time when you have not already created the emulator, you can create an emulator at this point.*

3. It can take up to five minutes, and sometimes longer (depending on the hardware specs of your desktop) for the emulator to start and fully load. During this time (the first time you launch the emulator) the application might time out. If a message pops up in Android Studio telling you that the application timed out waiting for the ADB (Android Debugging Bridge) to start, or another similar message, just wait for the emulator to fully load, and then once again select Run ➪ Run *app* from the Android Studio menu bar.

With the emulator fully loaded and started, Android Studio can install your Hello World application. The application will display as shown in Figure 1-28.

FIGURE 1-28

This was a very quick example of how to create and launch your first Android applications. However, what this example has really done for you is introduce you, on a general scale, to most of the major skills you will fine tune throughout this book.

SUMMARY

This chapter provided a brief overview of Android and highlighted some of its capabilities. If you have followed the sections on downloading the tools and the Android SDK, you should now have a working system—one that is capable of developing Android applications that are more interesting than the Hello World application. In the next chapter, you find out about the inner workings of Android Studio before moving on to more complex Android application development concepts.

EXERCISES

1. What is an AVD?
2. Why was Jelly Bean selected for you by default in the Targeted Android Devices dialog?
3. What does SDK stand for?
4. What tool is used to download new Android SDKs?

You can find answers to the exercises in the appendix.

▸ WHAT YOU LEARNED IN THIS CHAPTER

TOPIC	KEY CONCEPTS
Android OS	Android is an open source mobile operating system based on the Linux operating system. It is available to anyone who wants to adapt it to run on their own devices.
Languages used for Android application development	You use the Java programming language to develop Android applications. Written applications are compiled into Dalvik executables, which are then run on top of the Dalvik virtual machine.
Google Play	Google Play hosts all the various Android applications written by third-party developers.
Tools for Android application development	Android Studio, Android SDK, and virtual devices.

2

Using Android Studio for Android Development

WHAT YOU WILL LEARN IN THIS CHAPTER

- How to move around in the Integrated Development Environment (IDE)
- How to use code completion to make writing applications easier
- How to use breakpoints to debug your applications

> ***CODE DOWNLOAD*** *There are no code downloads for this chapter.*

Chapter 1 covers how to install and initially configure Android Studio for the purposes of developing Android applications. This chapter explains how to navigate the intricacies of Android Studio in a way that helps you develop applications more easily and with great efficiency.

Android Studio contains myriad features to help everyone from the greenest novices to the most senior superstar developers. By the time you finish this chapter, you will be able to navigate through the features of Android Studio with confidence, produce code that is easy to read and easy to reuse with the help of refactoring, save and share your code to GitHub, and use breakpoints to quickly find problems in your applications.

Let's begin by examining the features of Android Studio.

EXPLORING THE IDE

In this section you explore the Android Studio Integrated Development Environment, which is also known as the IDE. Basically, the IDE is the interface between you and Android Studio. The more you know about the tools, windows, and options that are available to you in Android Studio, the faster you will be able to produce code and the more confident you will be at creating applications.

1. If you haven't already, open Android Studio. If you worked through Chapter 1, you created a very quick Hello World project. You are going to create another quick project for this chapter; this time, however, you explore the different options available as you start up and work with your project.

2. Now that you have opened Android Studio, you see should a screen that looks like Figure 2-1.

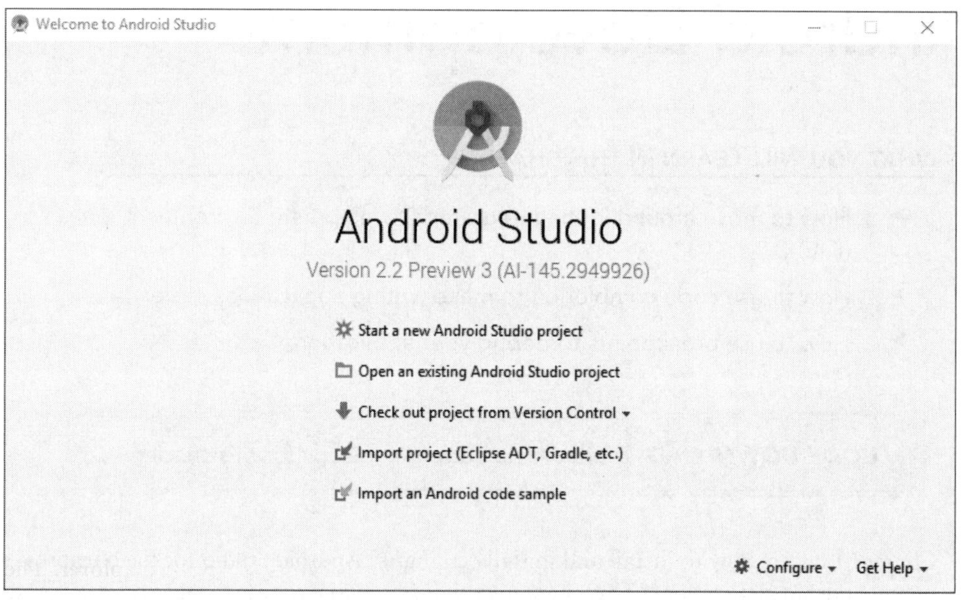

FIGURE 2-1

> ***NOTE*** *If you do not see the screen in Figure 2-1 and instead see the last* `Hello World` *project from Chapter 1, simply locate the File option on the menu bar. Click File ⇨ Close Project to return to the screen shown in Figure 2-1.*

3. The Android Studio welcome screen contains an option for you to open existing projects that you might have already created in Android Studio. It also presents options for opening a project from VCS, and importing projects from other IDEs, such as Eclipse.

4. Click the Start a New Android Studio Project option from the Android Studio welcome screen. You should now see the Create New Project screen (shown in Figure 2-2), which enables you to configure some of the basic options for your project.

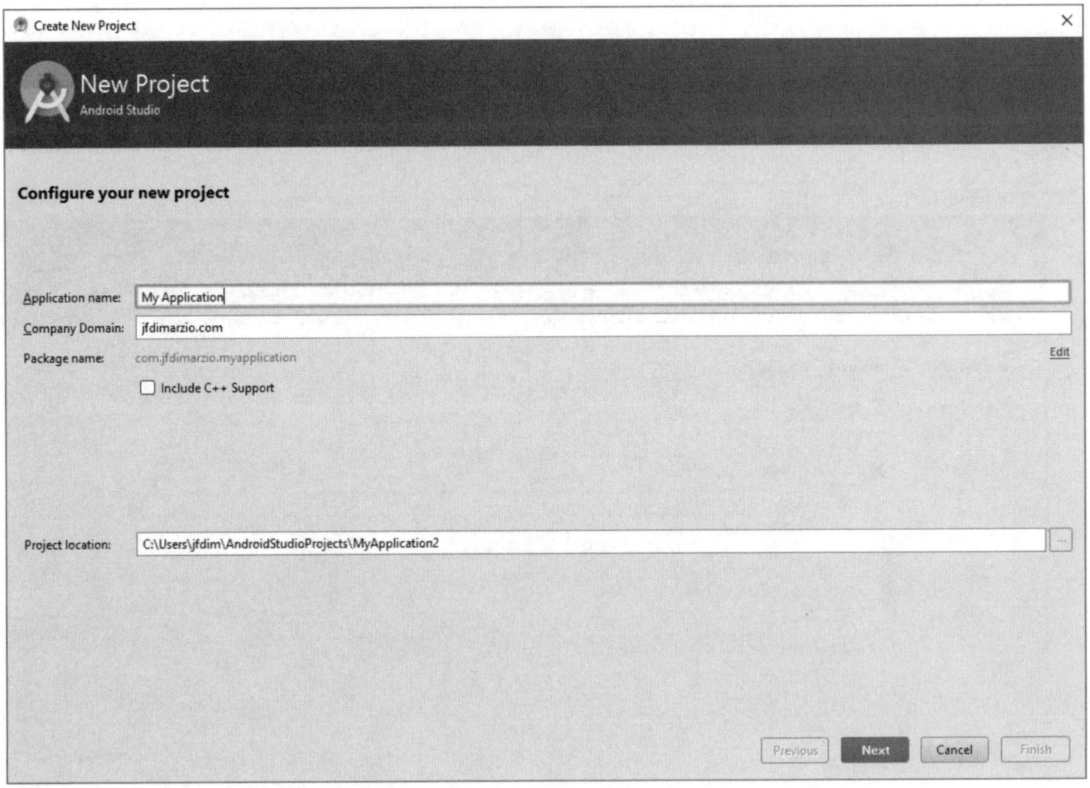

FIGURE 2-2

The first option you have is to name your project. Let's call this one **IDEExplorer**. The second option—the Company Domain—is very important because it is used to name the Java package to which your code will belong. You can type any name that you want into this field. There is no validation to check that you actually own the domain that you specify, but you should try to use a valid domain. I have used `jfdimarzio.com`. As you can see from the Package Name line, Android Studio automatically reverses your company domain to create the package name.

> ***NOTE** The package name is used in almost every code file in your project. It helps Android Studio identify which files belong to your project (and which, for example, belong to the core Java libraries). Throughout this book, when you look at the provided code samples, I remind you to replace all instances of my package name (`com.jfdimarzio`) with whatever package name you select here. If you do not, Android Studio doesn't know that the example code should belong to your project rather than mine.*

The final option on the Create New Project screen is the path to which Android Studio will save your new project. I typically accept the default here because it makes it easier for me to find projects in the future. However, feel free to specify any valid location that you want to use—it will not affect this tutorial. Click Next to continue.

The next screen allows you to select the form factor on which your application will run (see Figure 2-3). For the purposes of this book, you exclusively use Phone and Tablet. The version of Android is Android N (or Nougat, depending on the version of the SDK you downloaded. As of the writing of this book, the name was officially announced as Nougat, but the SDK was still labeled N).

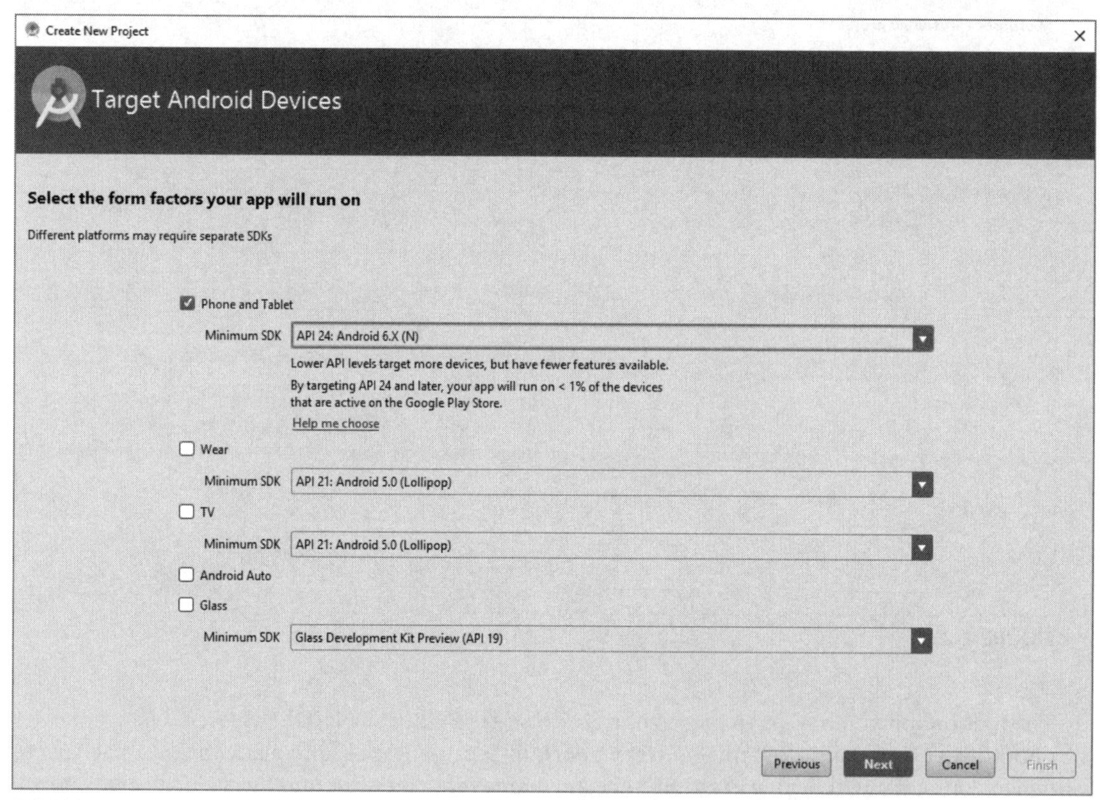

FIGURE 2-3

The other options on this screen allow you to create applications that run on Android Wear, Android Auto, and the elusive Google Glass. If you are feeling adventurous after reading this book, feel free to try some of these other application form factor options. For now, make sure to select Phone and Tablet and Android N and click Next to continue.

The next screen is the Add an Activity to Mobile screen, as shown in Figure 2-4. This screen is a helper that adds commonly used features to your project at the time the project is created.

The options on this screen range from Add No Activity to Tabbed Activity. For example, if you were to select the Google Maps Activity option, Android Studio would create for you a project with a basic activity that contains a Google Map in it already. This can drastically cut down on the amount of time needed to create some types of applications.

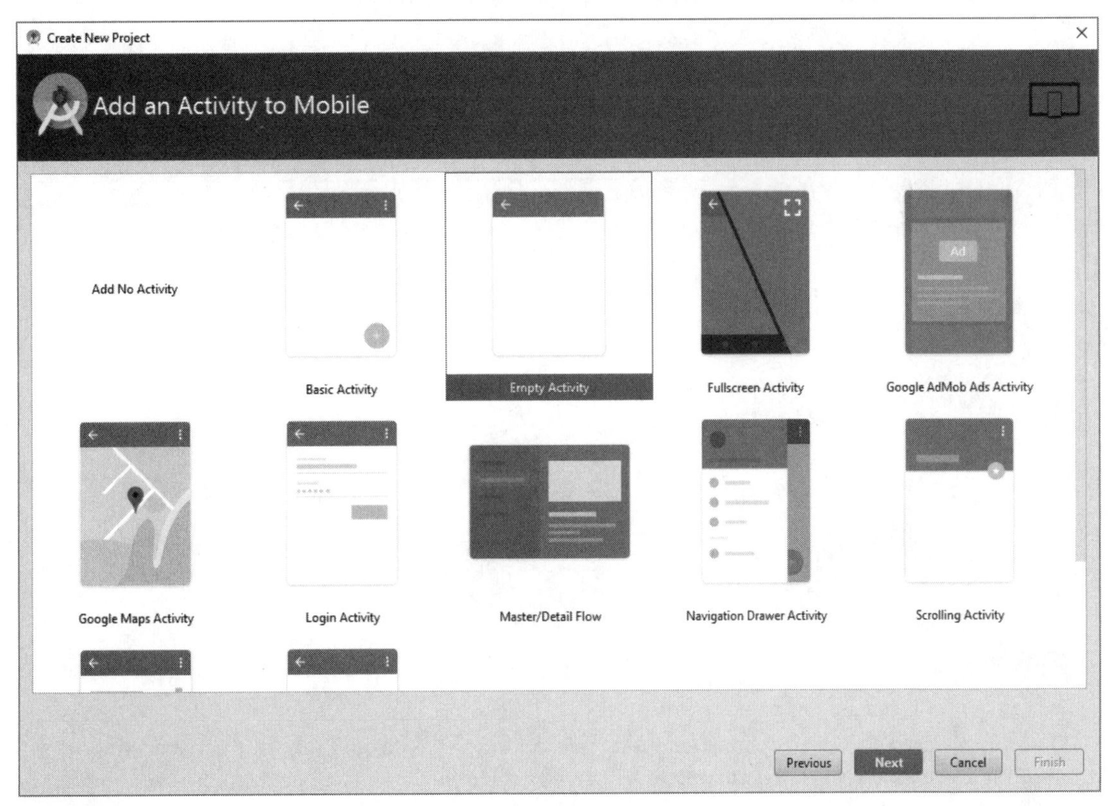

FIGURE 2-4

The default option is Empty Activity. This is the most useful for our examples because it creates a basic activity for you, with no code in it—thus allowing you to easily follow the examples in this book.

> ***NOTE*** *Unless otherwise specified in this book, all of the examples in the chapters assume you select the Empty Activity option.*

Click Next to go to the Customize the Activity screen, as shown in Figure 2-5.

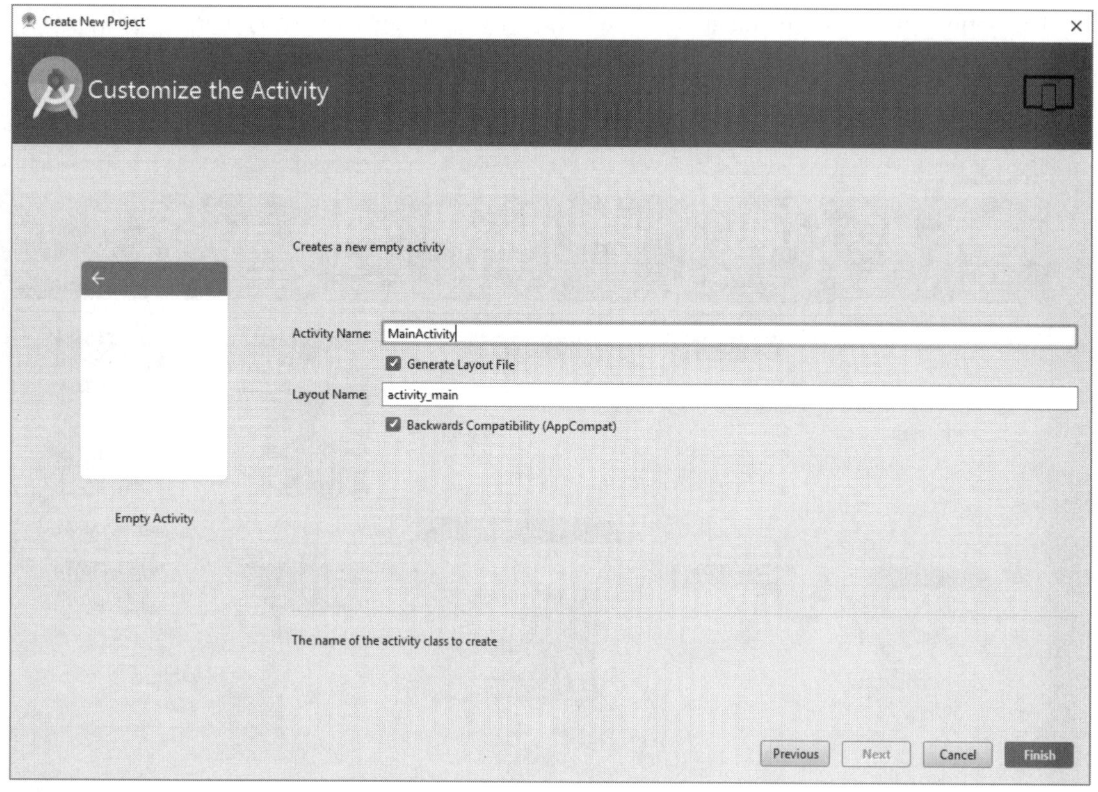

FIGURE 2-5

The Customize the Activity screen contains two options, one for naming your activity, and one for naming the main layout (presumably to be used by the main activity). Let's explore these two options.

- It is accepted practice in Android development to name your main activity—that is, the activity that is loaded on startup by your application—as `MainActivity`. The reason for this is to make it easier to locate the startup code for your application. If anyone else needs to look at or work with your application, they should know that the `MainActivity` is the starting point. All other activities can be named by their function, for example `InputFormActivity` or `DeleteRecordActivity`.
- The layout file follows the "name" naming convention. The startup layout, that is the layout for the screen elements that will be displayed when your application is started by the user, is the `activity_main` layout. All other layouts should be named according to the activity that they support (`activity_input`, `activity_delete`).

> **NOTE** *Unless otherwise specified, all of the examples in this book assume that you accept the defaults on the Customize the Activity screen of* `MainActivity` *and* `activity_main`.

Click the Finish button to finish creating the project and jump into exploring the IDE.

The Android Studio IDE should now be visible to you as shown in Figure 2-6.

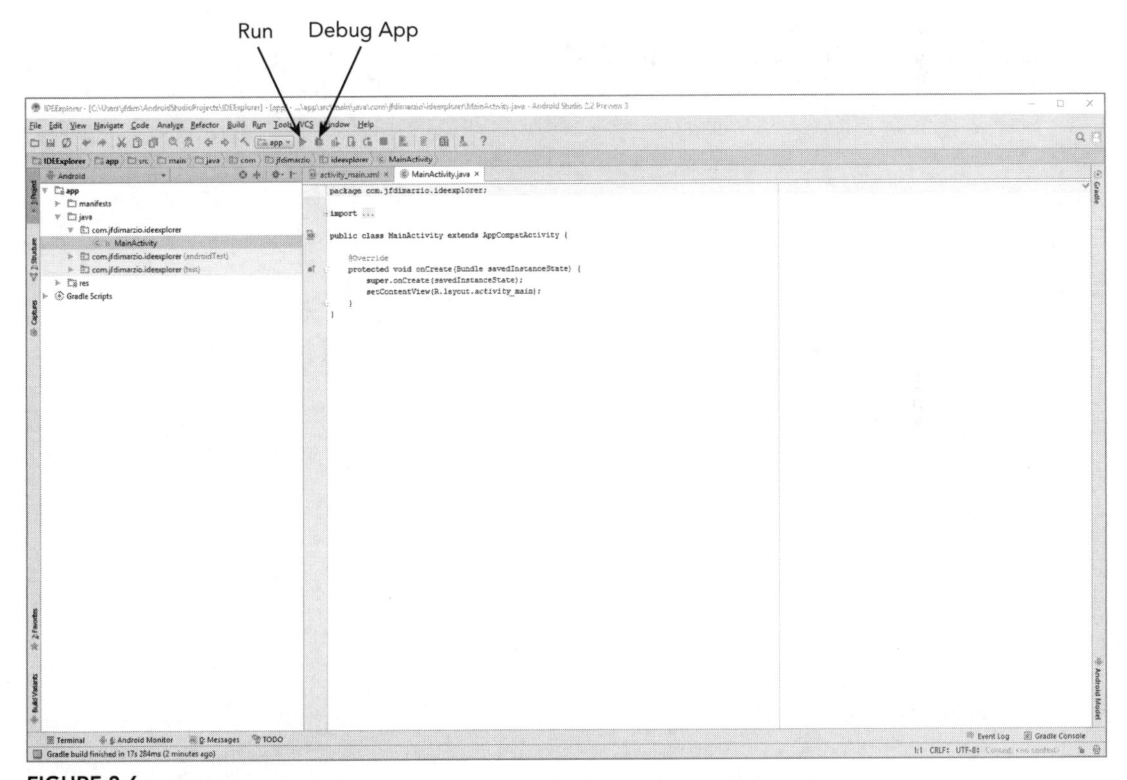

FIGURE 2-6

The upper portion of the IDE represents the menu bars or ribbons. Here, as with most applications that you have used in the past, you have all of your options for interacting directly with the IDE. The most important ones to note are the green arrow, which represents the Run app option, and the green arrow with a bug behind it, which is the Debug App option. The Debug App option is arguably the one that you use the most in this book.

By default, the left side of the IDE shows the Project window, as shown in Figure 2-7. The Project window enables you to quickly navigate the files within your project. By default, the Project window is set to the Android view (seen just above the Project window display). To change the view, click the word Android and use the drop-down list of options to make the change. I like to keep mine on Project view when I am working.

FIGURE 2-7

On the right side of the IDE (and taking up the largest area) are the Editor tabs (see Figure 2-8). The Editor tabs are where you write and work with your code files.

```
activity_main.xml ×   MainActivity.java ×
package com.jfdimarzio.ideexplorer;

import ...

public class MainActivity extends AppCompatActivity {

    @Override
    protected void onCreate(Bundle savedInstanceState) {
        super.onCreate(savedInstanceState);
        setContentView(R.layout.activity_main);
    }
}
```

FIGURE 2-8

To work on a new file, simply locate the file in the Project window and double-click it to open a new Editor tab that contains that file's code. If you need to create a new file from scratch, right-click the directory into which you want to place your file, and select New ➪ *<File Type>* from the context menu.

Finally, at the bottom of the IDE, you should see a button labeled Android Monitor. Click this button to open the Android Monitor (see Figure 2-9).

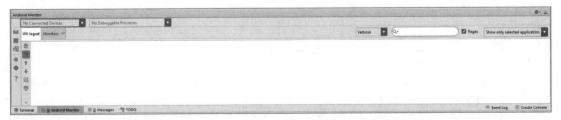

FIGURE 2-9

The Android Monitor automatically displays when you debug an application. It contains a very useful tool called logcat. Logcat displays most of the helpful messages that are output by your application while you are trying to debug it. In future chapters, you will make use of logcat—including writing custom messages to it.

USING CODE COMPLETION

Code completion is an invaluable tool that shows you contextual options for completing the piece of code that you are trying to write. For example, in the editor tab for the `MainActivity.js` file, locate the line that reads

```
setContentView(R.layout.activity_main);
```

Place your cursor after this line and press the Enter key. On the new line, type the letter R, and then type a period, as shown here:

```
R.
```

Android Studio Code Completion should display a list of values that you could use to try to complete the code statement. Figure 2-10 shows what this list might look like. This is important if you are not entirely sure of the spelling of a method call or of how to identify the different method signatures.

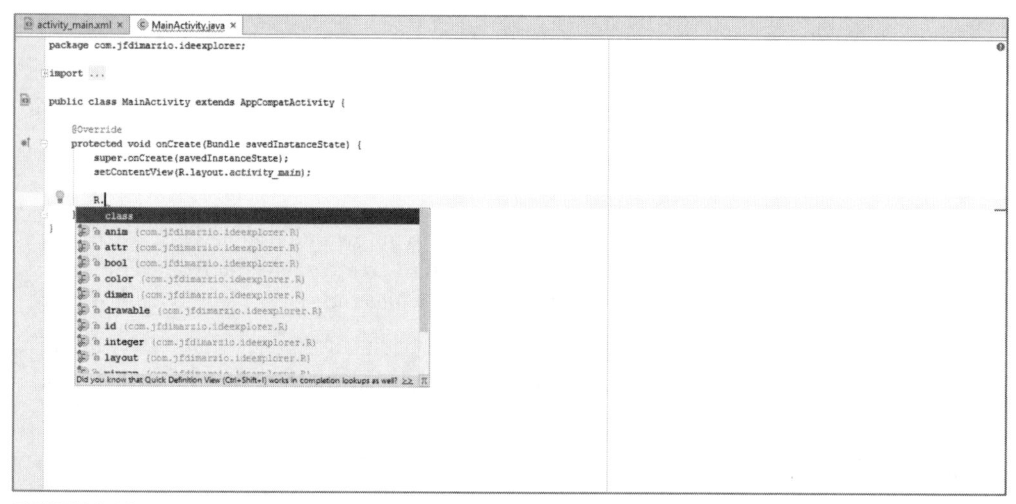

FIGURE 2-10

> ***NOTE*** *If the code completion window does not open, press Ctrl+Space to force it to open. This is the same key combination used in some other IDEs for their versions of code completion.*

You can also use code completion to insert code stubs into your classes. If you are inheriting from a class that has methods you must override, code completion notifies you that there are methods that need to be overridden. With a click, it inserts the stubs of those methods into your application.

Finally, the ability to import packages is one of the Android Studio features and its code completion implementation that you will use most often while navigating the examples in this book.

For example, if you were to attempt to create a variable of a type that belongs to a package that you have not imported, Android Studio recognizes this and underlines the type with a red squiggle. Set the cursor to that line and press Alt+Enter to automatically import the package into a using statement at the top of your code file.

DEBUGGING YOUR APPLICATION

After you have built an application, you need to be able to debug it and see what is going on inside your code. One of the handiest ways to be able to see inside your code it through the use of breakpoints. Breakpoints allow you to pause the execution of your code at specific locations and see what is going on (or what is going wrong). Let's take a look at how to use breakpoints in Android Studio.

Setting Breakpoints

Breakpoints are a mechanism by which you can tell Android Studio to temporarily pause execution of your code, which allows you to examine the condition of your application. This means that you can check on the values of variables in your application while you are debugging it. Also, you can check whether certain lines of code are being executed as expected—or at all.

To tell Android Studio that you want to examine a specific line of code during debugging, you must set a breakpoint at that line. Click the margin of the editor tab next to line of code you want to break at, to set a breakpoint. A red circle is placed in the margin, and the corresponding line is highlighted in red, as shown in Figure 2-11.

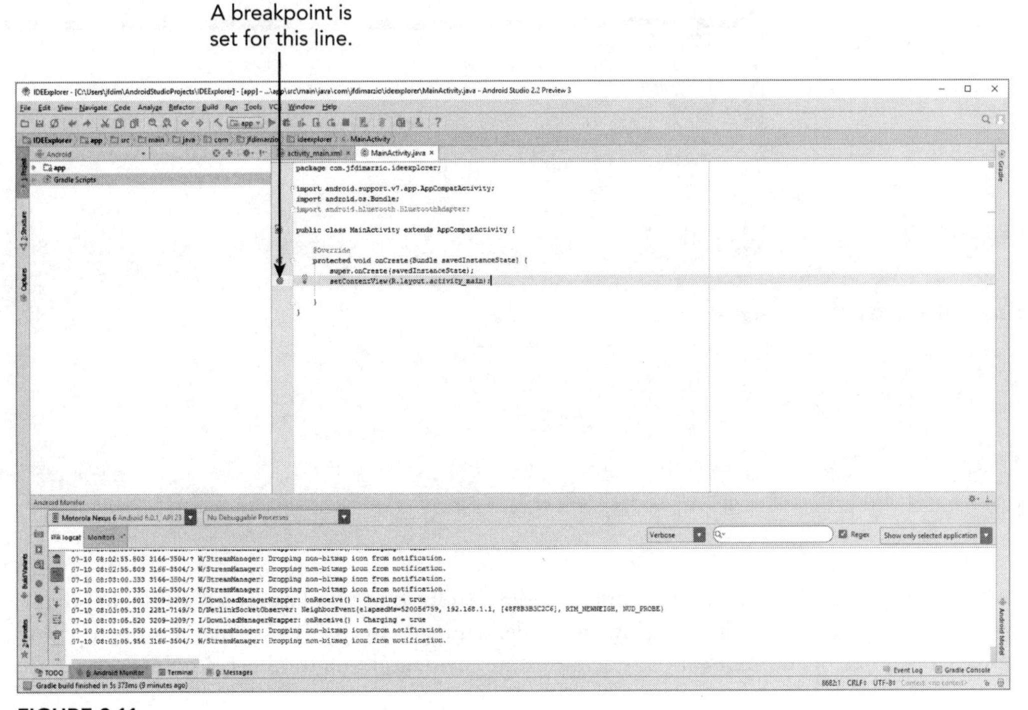
A breakpoint is
set for this line.

FIGURE 2-11

You can also set a breakpoint by placing your cursor in the line of code where you want it to break and clicking Run ➪ Toggle Line Breakpoint. Notice that the term used is *toggle*, which means that any breakpoints you set can be turned off the same way you turn them on. Simply click an existing breakpoint to remove it from your code.

> ***NOTE*** *Android Studio only pauses execution at breakpoints when you debug your application—not when you run it. This means you must use the green arrow with the bug behind it (or select Run ➪ Debug 'app', or press Shift+F9).*

Let's say that you do not know the exact line of code where you want the break to be. You might want to check on the condition of your code when a specific method is called. You can set a method breakpoint by selecting Run ➪ Toggle Method Breakpoint. A method breakpoint is represented by a red circle containing four dots placed at the method signature, as shown in Figure 2-12.

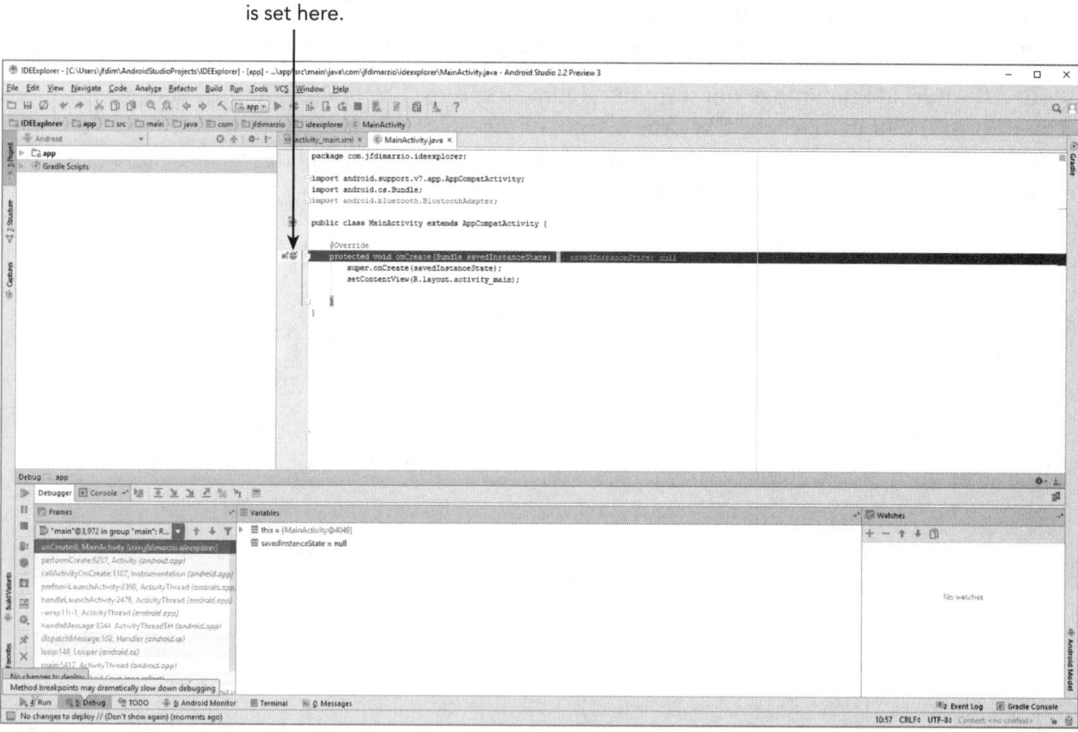

FIGURE 2-12

Notice in the lower left-hand area of Figure 2-12 that Android Studio has issued a warning that method breakpoints can dramatically slow down debugging. This is because method breakpoints do more than simple breakpoints in their default state. By default, method breakpoints are set apart from simple breakpoints. Android Studio pauses execution when the method is hit, and it also automatically sets a corresponding breakpoint and pauses at the end of the method (as shown in Figure 2-13).

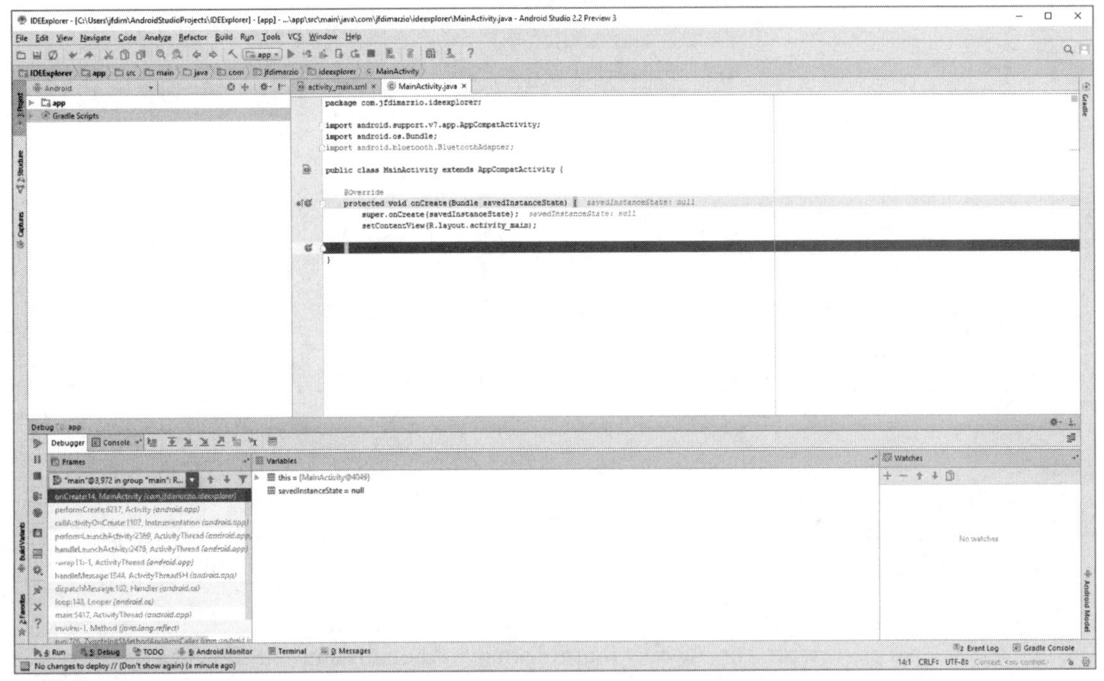

FIGURE 2-13

> ***NOTE*** *Using a method breakpoint is different from setting a simple breakpoint at the signature of a method. You could easily click in the margin of the editor tab at the signature of a method to set a simple breakpoint there. However, this one will get hit when execution enters the method. Also, a method breakpoint automatically pauses when the method is exited.*

Thus far, I've discussed simple and method breakpoints. However, there are two other types of breakpoints that you examine in this section: temporary breakpoints and conditional breakpoints.

Temporary Breakpoints

A temporary breakpoint is useful when you are trying to debug a large loop, or you just want to make sure a line of code is being hit during execution. To set a temporary breakpoint, place your cursor at the location in the code where you want it to break and select Run ➪ Toggle Temporary Line Breakpoint. Notice that a red circle containing a 1 is now placed in the margin (once you set the conditions as shown in Figure 2-14).

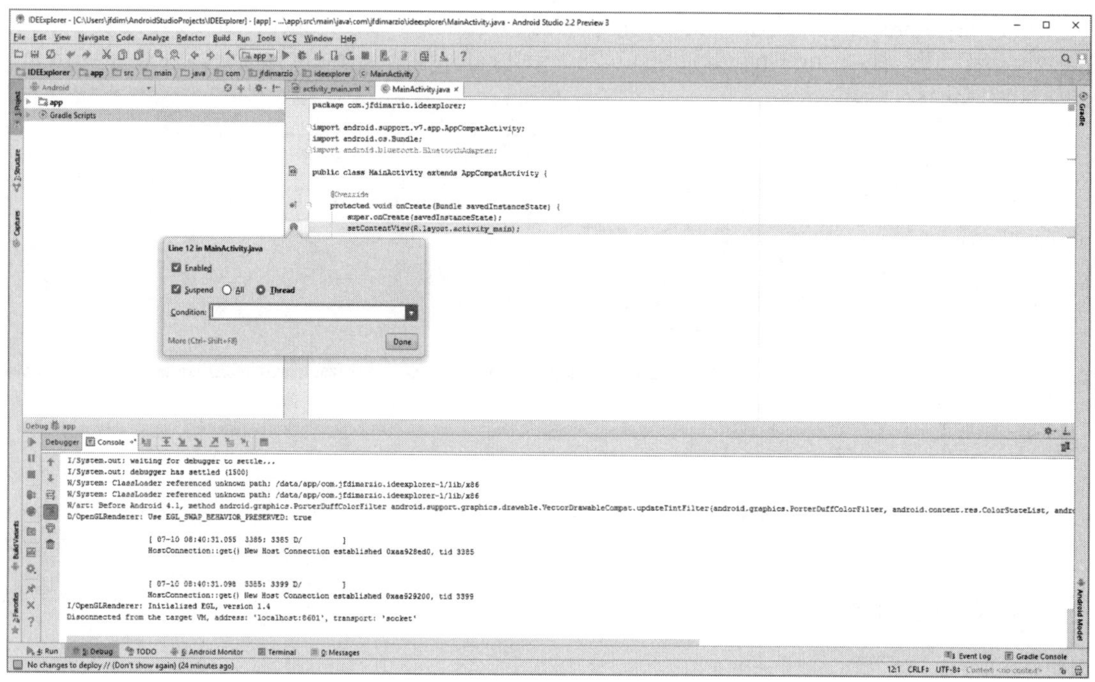

FIGURE 2-14

The 1 in the red circle represents the fact that Android Studio only stops at this breakpoint the first time your code enters it. After that, the line is executed as though there is no breakpoint set. This can be very useful if you want to ensure a line within a loop is being hit, but you don't want to stop at the line every time it is executed.

However, let's say that you want to ensure that a line within a loop is only being called when a specific variable is set to true (or something similarly complex). In such a case, you can use a conditional breakpoint.

Conditional Breakpoints

A condition breakpoint is a breakpoint at which Android Studio only pauses when specific conditions are met. To set a conditional breakpoint, first set a simple breakpoint at the line of code you want to examine, then right-click the simple breakpoint to bring up the condition context menu (refer to Figure 2-14).

From here you can set conditions that tell Android Studio when to pause at a breakpoint. For example, you can tell Android Studio to only pause at a line of code when your variable named foo equals true. You would then set the condition in the breakpoint to

```
foo == true
```

Conditional breakpoints are extremely useful in diagnosing intermittent issues in complex code blocks.

Navigating Paused Code

While in debug mode, Android Studio pauses at any breakpoint that you have set. That is, as long as a breakpoint has been set on a reachable line of code (a line of code that would be executed by system), Android Studio halts execution at that line until you tell it to continue.

When Android Studio hits, and pauses at, a breakpoint, the red circle in the margin next to the corresponding line of code changes to a circle with a check mark (see Figure 2-15).

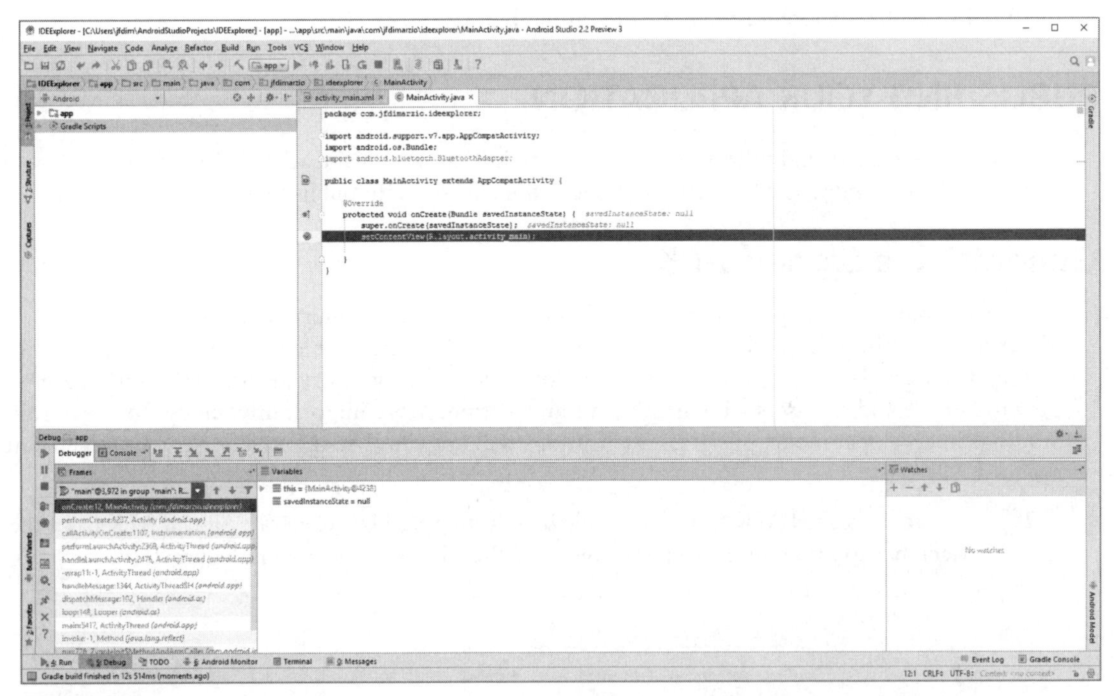

FIGURE 2-15

Once a breakpoint has been hit, the debug window opens at the bottom of Android Studio, as shown in Figure 2-16. The debug window contains many of the tools you use to navigate around your code.

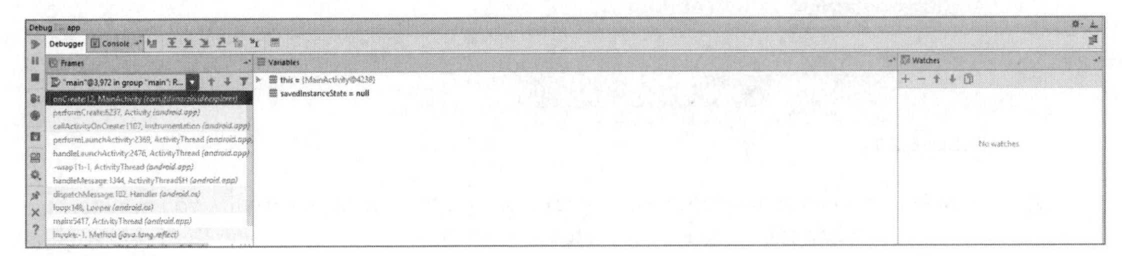

FIGURE 2-16

Notice the navigation buttons located in the menu bar of the debug window. The most commonly used are Step Over and Step Into. Step Over advances you to the line of code that immediately follows the one at which you are currently paused. This means that if you are paused at a method call, and you press Step Over, Android Studio executes the method call without pausing and then pauses again when execution reached the next line. However, what if an exception happens in that method call and execution never reaches the next line of code? For these situations use Step Into.

Step Into follows execution wherever it leads in the code. Therefore, if you are paused at a method call and click Step Into, Android Studio will shift the view to the method call and pause execution at the first line of code within that method. This allows you to then follow the execution of that method line-by-line before it returns to the calling block.

PUBLISHING YOUR APPLICATION

After you have created, and fully debugged, your application, you might want to deploy it to the Google Store for others to enjoy. The following sections outline the steps for publishing your applications.

Generating a Signed APK

To publish your finished application on the Google Play Store, you must generate a signed APK (the Android application package). The APK is the compiled, executable version of your application. Signing it is much like signing your name to a document. The signature identifies the app's developer to Google and the users who install your application. More importantly, unless your Android Studio is in developer mode, unsigned applications will not run. Use the following steps to generate a signed APK:

1. Generate a signed APK from your code by selecting Build ➪ Generate Signed APK from the Menu bar to bring up the Generate Signed APK window as shown in Figure 2-17.

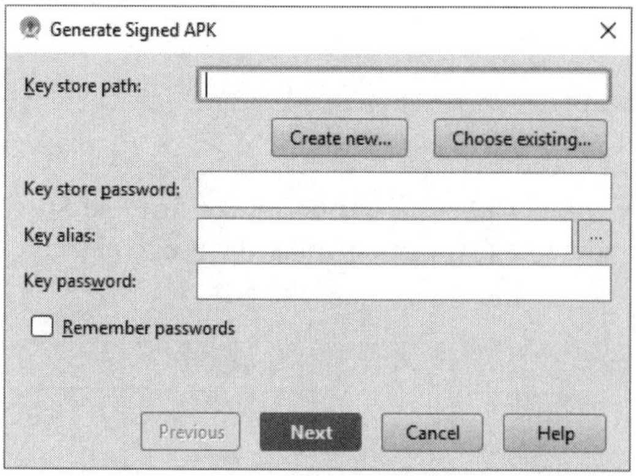

FIGURE 2-17

2. Assuming you have never published an application from Android Studio, you need to create a new key store. Click the Create New button to display the New Key Store window (see Figure 2-18).

3. Fill out all of the information on this form because it pertains to your entity and application.

   Notice that there are two places for a password. These are the passwords for your key store and your key, respectively. Because a key store can hold multiple keys, it requires a separate password than that of the key for a specific app.

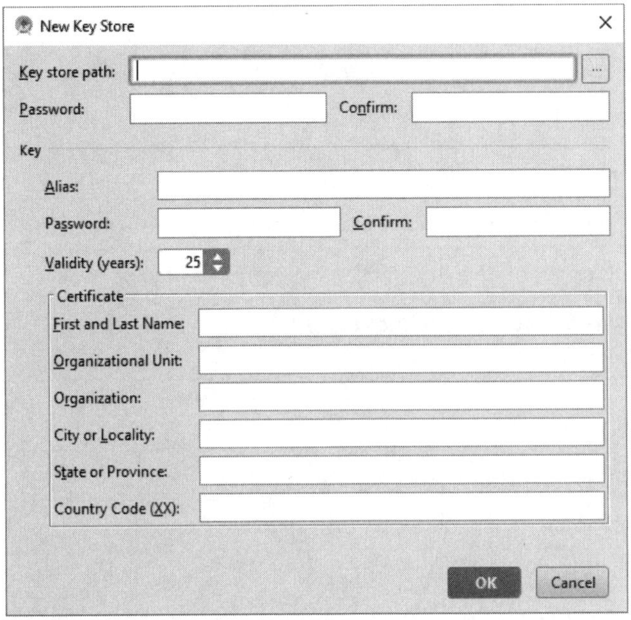

FIGURE 2-18

4. Click OK to return to the Generate Signed APK window.
5. In the Generate Signed APK windows, click Next to review and finish the process.

Now that you have a signed APK, you can upload it to the Google Play Store using the developer console at `https://play.google.com/apps/publish/`.

SUMMARY

Android Studio is a powerful IDE that contains many tools. In this chapter you learned how to navigate the different areas of the Android Studio IDE, such as the Project window and the Editor tabs. You also learned how to set breakpoints and navigate through paused code.

EXERCISES

1. When you are creating a new Android project, for what is the Company Domain field used?
2. For what is the Add an Activity to Mobile screen used?
3. What is Android Code Completion?
4. What is a breakpoint?

You can find answers to the exercises in the appendix.

▶ WHAT YOU LEARNED IN THIS CHAPTER

TOPIC	KEY POINTS
Android Studio IDE	Create a new project
	Name the Java package
	Name the main entry point for your application
Code Completion	Provides contextual information for completing your code
Breakpoints	Paused only while in debug mode
	Simple
	Temporary
	Method
	Conditional

3

Activities, Fragments, and Intents

WHAT YOU WILL LEARN IN THIS CHAPTER

- The life cycles of an activity
- Using fragments to customize your UI
- Applying styles and themes to activities
- How to display activities as dialog windows
- Understanding the concept of intents
- Displaying alerts to the user using notifications

> ***CODE DOWNLOAD*** *The wrox.com code downloads for this chapter are found at* `www.wrox.com/go/beginningandroidprog` *on the Download Code tab. The code is in the chapter 03 download and individually named according to the names throughout the chapter.*

An Android application can have zero or more *activities*. Typically, applications have one or more activities. The main purpose of an activity is to interact with the user. From the moment an activity appears on the screen to the moment it is hidden, it goes through a number of stages. These stages are known as an activity's *life cycle*. Understanding the life cycle of an activity is vital to ensuring that your application works correctly. In addition to activities, Android N also supports *fragments*, a feature that was introduced for tablets in Android 3.0 and for phones in Android 4.0. Think of fragments as "miniature" activities that can be grouped to form an activity. In this chapter, you find out how activities and fragments work together.

Apart from activities, another unique concept in Android is that of an *intent*. An intent is basically the "glue" that enables activities from different applications to work together seamlessly, ensuring that tasks can be performed as though they all belong to one single application. Later in this chapter, you learn more about this very important concept and how you can use it to call built-in applications such as the Browser, Phone, Maps, and more.

UNDERSTANDING ACTIVITIES

This chapter begins by showing you how to create an activity. To create an activity, you create a Java class that extends the `Activity` base class:

```
package com.jfdimarzio.chapter1helloworld;

        import android.support.v7.app.AppCompatActivity;
        import android.os.Bundle;

public class MainActivity extends AppCompatActivity {

    @Override
    protected void onCreate(Bundle savedInstanceState) {
        super.onCreate(savedInstanceState);
        setContentView(R.layout.activity_main);
    }
}
```

Your activity class loads its user interface (UI) component using the XML file defined in your `res/layout` folder. In this example, you would load the UI from the `main.xml` file:

```
        setContentView(R.layout.activity_main);
```

Every activity you have in your application must be declared in your `AndroidManifest.xml` file, like this:

```
<?xml version="1.0" encoding="utf-8"?>
<manifest xmlns:android="http://schemas.android.com/apk/res/android
    package="com.jfdimarzio.chapter1helloworld">

    <application
        android:allowBackup="true"
        android:icon="@mipmap/ic_launcher"
        android:label="@string/app_name"
        android:supportsRtl="true"
        android:theme="@style/AppTheme">
        <activity android:name=".MainActivity">
            <intent-filter>
                <action android:name="android.intent.action.MAIN" />

                <category android:name="android.intent.category.LAUNCHER" />
            </intent-filter>
        </activity>
    </application>

</manifest>
```

The `Activity` base class defines a series of events that govern the life cycle of an activity. Figure 3-1 shows the lifecycle of an `Activity`.

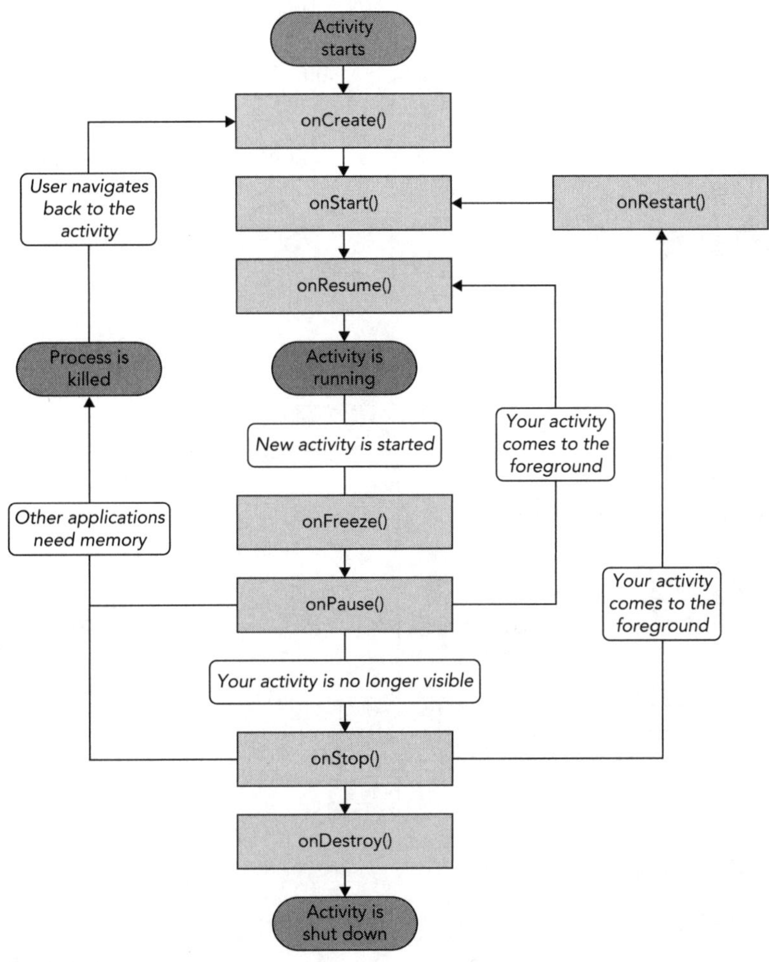

FIGURE 3-1

The `Activity` class defines the following events:

- `onCreate()`—Called when the activity is first created
- `onStart()`—Called when the activity becomes visible to the user
- `onResume()`—Called when the activity starts interacting with the user
- `onPause()`—Called when the current activity is being paused and the previous activity is being resumed
- `onStop()`—Called when the activity is no longer visible to the user

- `onDestroy()`—Called before the activity is destroyed by the system (either manually or by the system to conserve memory)
- `onRestart()`—Called when the activity has been stopped and is restarting again

By default, the activity created for you contains the `onCreate()` event. Within this event handler is the code that helps to display the UI elements of your screen.

Figure 3-2 shows the life cycle of an activity and the various stages it goes through—from when the activity is started until it ends.

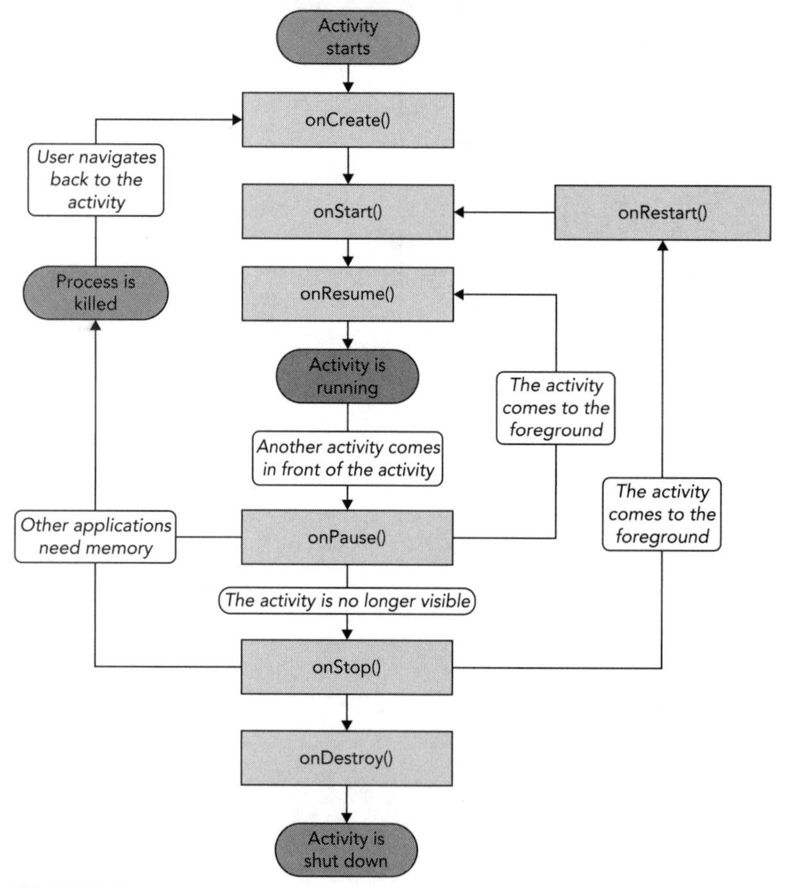

FIGURE 3-2

The best way to understand the various stages of an activity is to create a new project, implement the various events, and then subject the activity to various user interactions.

TRY IT OUT Understanding the Life Cycle of an Activity (Activity101.zip)

1. Using Android Studio, create a new Android project and name it **Activity101**.
2. In the `Activity101Activity.java` file, add the following highlighted statements. (Please note: Throughout this example, be sure to change all references to `"com.jfdimarzio"` to whatever package name your project is using.)

```
package com.jfdimarzio.activity101;

import android.support.v7.app.AppCompatActivity;
import android.os.Bundle;
import android.util.Log;

public class MainActivity extends AppCompatActivity
{
    String tag = "Lifecycle Step";
    @Override
    protected void onCreate(Bundle savedInstanceState)
    {
        super.onCreate(savedInstanceState);
        setContentView(R.layout.activity_main);
        Log.d(tag, "In the onCreate() event");
    }

    public void onStart()
    {
        super.onStart();
        Log.d(tag, "In the onStart() event");
    }

    public void onRestart()
    {
        super.onRestart();
        Log.d(tag, "In the onRestart() event");
    }

    public void onResume()
    {
        super.onResume();
        Log.d(tag, "In the onResume() event");
    }

    public void onPause()
    {
        super.onPause();
        Log.d(tag, "In the onPause() event");
    }
```

```
        public void onStop()
        {
            super.onStop();
            Log.d(tag, "In the onStop() event");
        }

        public void onDestroy()
        {
            super.onDestroy();
            Log.d(tag, "In the onDestroy() event");
        }
    }
```

3. Press Shift+F9 to debug the application, or select Run ➪ Debug. Then select one of your Android Virtual Devices from the pop-up window.

4. When the activity is first loaded, you should see something very similar to the following in the logcat console (see Figure 3-3). If you do not see the logcat console, click Android Monitor at the bottom of the Android Studio window:

```
11-16 06:25:59.396: D/Lifecycle Step(559): In the onCreate() event
11-16 06:25:59.396: D/Lifecycle Step(559): In the onStart() event
11-16 06:25:59.396: D/Lifecycle Step(559): In the onResume() event
```

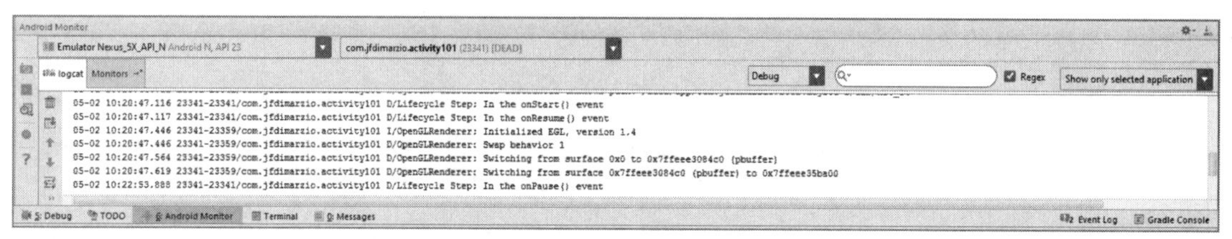

FIGURE 3-3

5. If you click the Back button on the Android emulator, you see the following:

```
11-16 06:29:26.665: D/Lifecycle Step(559): In the onPause() event
11-16 06:29:28.465: D/Lifecycle Step(559): In the onStop() event
11-16 06:29:28.465: D/Lifecycle Step(559): In the onDestroy() event
```

6. Click the Home button, click the `Overview` icon, select the Activity101 application, and observe the following:

```
11-16 06:31:08.905: D/Lifecycle Step(559): In the onCreate() event
11-16 06:31:08.905: D/Lifecycle Step(559): In the onStart() event
11-16 06:31:08.925: D/Lifecycle Step(559): In the onResume() event
```

7. Click the Home button and then click the Phone button on the Android emulator so that the activity is pushed to the background. Observe the output in the logcat window:

```
11-16 06:32:00.585: D/Lifecycle Step(559): In the onPause() event
11-16 06:32:05.015: D/Lifecycle Step(559): In the onStop() event
```

8. Notice that the `onDestroy()` event is not called, indicating that the activity is still in memory. Exit the phone dialer by clicking the Back button. The activity is now visible again. Observe the output in the logcat window:

```
11-16 06:32:50.515: D/Lifecycle(559): In the onRestart() event
11-16 06:32:50.515: D/Lifecycle(559): In the onStart() event
11-16 06:32:50.515: D/Lifecycle(559): In the onResume() event
```

The `onRestart()` event is now fired, followed by the `onStart()` and `onResume()` methods.

How It Works

As you can see from this simple example, an activity is destroyed when you click the Back button. This is crucial to understand because whatever state the activity is currently in will be lost. This means you need to write additional code in your activity to preserve its state when the activity is destroyed (Chapter 4 shows you how). At this point, note that the `onPause()` method is called in both scenarios:

- When an activity is sent to the background
- When a user kills an activity by tapping the Back button

When an activity is started, the `onStart()` and `onResume()`methods are always called, regardless of whether the activity is restored from the background or newly created. When an activity is created for the first time, the `onCreate()` method is called.

From the preceding example, you can derive the following guidelines:

- Use the `onCreate()` method to create and instantiate the objects that you will be using in your application.
- Use the `onResume()` method to start any services or code that needs to run while your activity is in the foreground.
- Use the `onPause()` method to stop any services or code that does not need to run when your activity is not in the foreground.
- Use the `onDestroy()` method to free up resources before your activity is destroyed.

> ***NOTE*** *Even if an application has only one activity and the activity is killed, the application is still running in memory.*

Applying Styles and Themes to an Activity

By default, an activity is themed to the default Android theme. However, there has been a push in recent years to adopt a new theme known as Material. The Material theme has a much more modern and clean look to it.

There are two versions of the Material theme available to Android developers: Material Light and Material Dark. Either of these themes can be applied from the AndroidManifest.xml.

To apply one of the Material themes to an activity, simply modify the <Application> element in the AndroidManifest.xml file by changing the default android:theme attribute. (Please be sure to change all instances of "com.jfdimarzio" to whatever package name your project is using.)

```
<?xml version="1.0" encoding="utf-8"?>
<manifest xmlns:android="http://schemas.android.com/apk/res/android"
    xmlns:tools="http://schemas.android.com/tools"
    package="com.jfdimarzio.activity101">

    <application
        android:allowBackup="true"
        android:icon="@mipmap/ic_launcher"
        android:label="@string/app_name"
        android:supportsRtl="true"
        android:theme="@android:style/Theme.Material">
        <activity android:name=".MainActivity">

            <intent-filter>
                <action android:name="android.intent.action.MAIN" />
                <category android:name="android.intent.category.LAUNCHER" />
            </intent-filter>
        </activity>
    </application>
</manifest>
```

Changing the default theme to @android:style/Theme.Material, as in the highlighted code in the preceding snippet, applies the Material Dark theme and gives your application a darker look as shown in Figure 3-4.

Hiding the Activity Title

You can also hide the title of an activity if desired (such as when you just want to display a status update to the user). To do so, use the requestWindowFeature() method and pass it the Window.FEATURE_NO_TITLE constant, like this:

```
import android.support.v7.app.AppCompatActivity;
import android.os.Bundle;
import android.view.Window;

public class MainActivity extends AppCompatActivity {
    @Override
    protected void onCreate(Bundle savedInstanceState) {
        super.onCreate(savedInstanceState);
        setContentView(R.layout.activity_main);
        requestWindowFeature(Window.FEATURE_NO_TITLE);
    }

}
```

Now you need to change the theme in the AndroidManifest.xml to a theme that has no title bar. Be sure to change all instances of "com.jfdimarzio" to whatever package name your project is using.

```
package com.jfdimarzio.activity101;

<?xml version="1.0" encoding="utf-8"?>
<manifest xmlns:android="http://schemas.android.com/apk/res/android"
    xmlns:tools="http://schemas.android.com/tools"
    package="com.jfdimarzio.activity101">

    <application
        android:allowBackup="true"
        android:icon="@mipmap/ic_launcher"
        android:label="@string/app_name"
        android:supportsRtl="true"
        android:theme="@android:style/Theme.NoTitleBar">
        <activity android:name=".MainActivity">

            <intent-filter>
                <action android:name="android.intent.action.MAIN" />

                <category android:name="android.intent.category.LAUNCHER" />
            </intent-filter>
        </activity>
    </application>

</manifest>
```

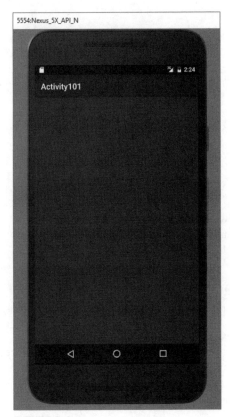

FIGURE 3-4

This hides the title bar, as shown in Figure 3-5.

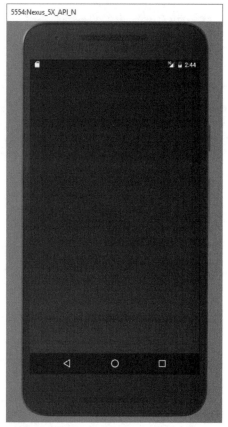

FIGURE 3-5

Displaying a Dialog Window

There are times when you need to display a dialog window to get a confirmation from the user. In this case, you can override the `onCreateDialog()` protected method defined in the `Activity` base class to display a dialog window. The following Try It Out shows you how.

TRY IT OUT Displaying a Dialog Window Using an Activity (Dialog.zip)

1. Using Android Studio, create a new Android project and name it Dialog. When presented with the option, name the main activity `DialogActivity`.

2. Add the following theme in bold to the `AndroidManifest.xml` file. Be sure to change all instances of `"com.jfdimarzio"` to whatever package name your project is using.

```
<?xml version="1.0" encoding="utf-8"?>
<manifest xmlns:android="http://schemas.android.com/apk/res/android"
    package="com.jfdimarzio.dialog" >
```

```
    <application
        android:allowBackup="true"
        android:icon="@mipmap/ic_launcher"
        android:label="@string/app_name"
        android:supportsRtl="true"
        android:theme="@style/AppTheme" >
        <activity
            android:name=".DialogActivity"
            android:label="@string/app_name"
            android:theme="@style/Theme.AppCompat.Dialog" >
            <intent-filter>
                <action android:name="android.intent.action.MAIN" />

                <category android:name="android.intent.category.LAUNCHER" />
            </intent-filter>
        </activity>
    </application>
</manifest>
```

3. Compare your `DialogActivity.java` file to this:

```
package com.jfdimarzio.dialog;

import android.os.Bundle;
import android.support.design.widget.FloatingActionButton;
import android.support.design.widget.Snackbar;
import android.support.v7.app.AppCompatActivity;
import android.support.v7.widget.Toolbar;
import android.view.View;
import android.view.Menu;
import android.view.MenuItem;

public class DialogActivity extends AppCompatActivity {

    @Override
    protected void onCreate(Bundle savedInstanceState) {
        super.onCreate(savedInstanceState);
        setContentView(R.layout.activity_dialog);
        Toolbar toolbar = (Toolbar) findViewById(R.id.toolbar);
        setSupportActionBar(toolbar);

       FloatingActionButton fab = (FloatingActionButton) findViewById(R.id.fab);
        fab.setOnClickListener(new View.OnClickListener() {
            @Override
            public void onClick(View view) {
                Snackbar.make(view, "Replace with your own action",
                  Snackbar.LENGTH_LONG)
                        .setAction("Action", null).show();
            }
        });
    }

    @Override
    public boolean onCreateOptionsMenu(Menu menu) {
        // Inflate the menu; this adds items to the action bar if it is present.
```

```
        getMenuInflater().inflate(R.menu.menu_dialog, menu);
        return true;
    }

    @Override
    public boolean onOptionsItemSelected(MenuItem item) {
        // Handle action bar item clicks here. The action bar will
        // automatically handle clicks on the Home/Up button, so long
        // as you specify a parent activity in AndroidManifest.xml.
        int id = item.getItemId();

        //noinspection SimplifiableIfStatement
        if (id == R.id.action_settings) {
            return true;
        }

        return super.onOptionsItemSelected(item);
    }
}
```

4. Press Shift+F9 to debug the application on the Android emulator. Click the button to display the dialog (see Figure 3-6).

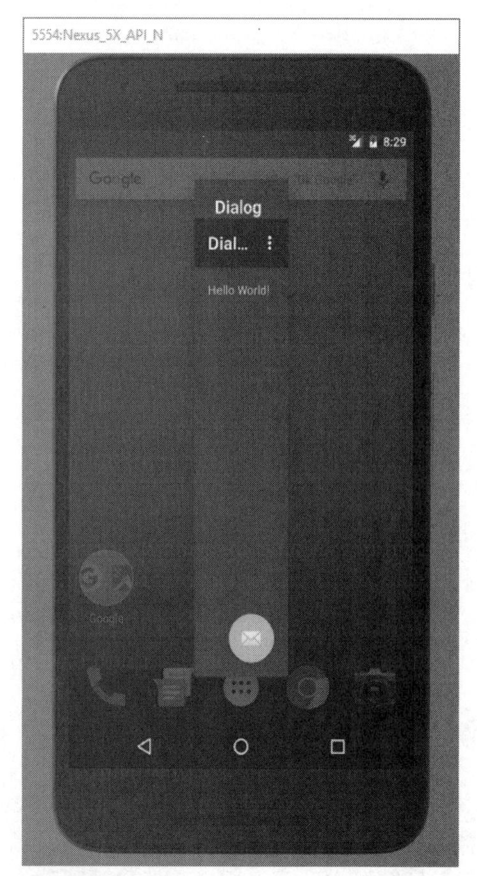

FIGURE 3-6

How It Works

Android uses the `AppCompat.Dialog` theme to draw your standard activity as a free-floating dialog box. It would be very easy to modify this dialog to add some buttons if you needed to provide an OK or Cancel choice.

Notice also that the theme is applied to the Activity, not the project. Therefore, you could have a project with multiple activities, and apply the dialog theme to just one of them.

Displaying a Progress Dialog

One common UI feature in an Android device is the "Please wait" dialog that you typically see when an application is performing a long-running task. For example, the application might be logging in to a server before the user is allowed to use it, or it might be doing a calculation before displaying the result to the user. In such cases, it is helpful to display a dialog, known as a *progress dialog*, so that the user is kept in the loop.

Android provides a `ProgressDialog` class you can call when you want to display a running meter to the user. `ProgressDialog` is easy to call from an activity.

The following Try It Out demonstrates how to display such a dialog.

TRY IT OUT Displaying a Progress (Please Wait) Dialog

1. Using the Activity101 project created earlier in this chapter, make sure you are using the Material theme in the `AndroidManifest.xml` file. Be sure to change all instances of `"com.jfdimarzio"` to whatever package name your project is using.

```
<?xml version="1.0" encoding="utf-8"?>
<manifest xmlns:android="http://schemas.android.com/apk/res/android"
    xmlns:tools="http://schemas.android.com/tools"
    package="com.jfdimarzio.activity101">

    <application
        android:allowBackup="true"
        android:icon="@mipmap/ic_launcher"
        android:label="@string/app_name"
        android:supportsRtl="true"
        android:theme="@android:style/Theme.Material">
        <activity android:name=".MainActivity">

            <intent-filter>
                <action android:name="android.intent.action.MAIN" />

                <category android:name="android.intent.category.LAUNCHER" />
            </intent-filter>
        </activity>
    </application>

</manifest>
```

2. Add the bolded statements from the following code to the `MainActivity.java` file:

```
package com.jfdimarzio.activity101;
import android.app.Activity;
import android.app.ProgressDialog;
import android.os.CountDownTimer;
import android.os.Bundle;


public class MainActivity extends Activity {

    ProgressDialog progressDialog;
    @Override
    protected void onCreate(Bundle savedInstanceState) {
        super.onCreate(savedInstanceState);
        setContentView(R.layout.activity_main);

    }

    public void onStart()
    {
        super.onStart();
         progressDialog = ProgressDialog.show(this,"Please Wait",
            "Processing...",true);
         CountDownTimer timer = new CountDownTimer(3000,1000) {
            @Override
            public void onTick(long millisUntilFinished) {

            }

            @Override
            public void onFinish() {
                progressDialog.dismiss();
            }
        }.start();
    }
}
```

3. Press Shift+F9 to debug the application on the Android emulator. You see the progress dialog, as shown in Figure 3-7. It disappears after three seconds.

How It Works

To create a progress dialog, you create an instance of the `ProgressDialog` class and call its `show()` method:

```
progressDialog = ProgressDialog.show(this,"Please Wait", "Processing...",true);
```

This displays the progress dialog shown in Figure 3-7. Because this is a modal dialog, it will block the UI until it is dismissed. To close the dialog, you create a timer that calls the `dismiss()` method after three seconds. (Chapter 12 covers threads and calling methods that can do extraneous work from a thread while a progress dialog is displayed.)

```
CountDownTimer timer = new CountDownTimer(3000,1000) {
            @Override
            public void onTick(long millisUntilFinished) {
```

```
        }

        @Override
        public void onFinish() {
            progressDialog.dismiss();
        }
    }.start();
```

After the three seconds have elapsed, you dismiss the dialog by calling the `dismiss()` method.

FIGURE 3-7

The next section explains using Intents, which help you navigate between multiple Activities.

LINKING ACTIVITIES USING INTENTS

An Android application can contain zero or more activities. When your application has more than one activity, you often need to navigate from one to another. In Android, you navigate between activities through what is known as an intent.

The best way to understand this very important but somewhat abstract concept is to experience it firsthand and see what it helps you achieve. The following Try It Out shows how to add another activity to an existing project and then navigate between the two activities.

TRY IT OUT Linking Activities with Intents (UsingIntent.zip)

1. Using Android Studio, create a new Android project with an empty Activity named `MainActivity`; name the project **UsingIntent**.
2. Right-click your package name under the `app>>app>>src>>main>>java` folder in the Project Files windows and select New ➪ Java Class
3. Name the new class **SecondActivity** and click OK.
4. Add the bolded statements from the following code to the `AndroidManifest.xml` file. Be sure to change all instances of `"com.jfdimarzio"` to whatever package name your project is using.

```
<?xml version="1.0" encoding="utf-8"?>
<manifest xmlns:android="http://schemas.android.com/apk/res/android"
    package="com.jfdimarzio.usingintent">

    <application
        android:allowBackup="true"
        android:icon="@mipmap/ic_launcher"
        android:label="@string/app_name"
        android:supportsRtl="true"
        android:theme="@style/AppTheme">
        <activity android:name=".MainActivity">
            <intent-filter>
                <action android:name="android.intent.action.MAIN" />

                <category android:name="android.intent.category.LAUNCHER" />
            </intent-filter>
        </activity>
        <activity android:name=".SecondActivity" >
         <intent-filter >
             <action android:name="com.jfdimarzio.usingintent.SecondActivity" />
             <category android:name="android.intent.category.DEFAULT" />
         </intent-filter>
    </activity>
    </application>

</manifest>
```

5. Make a copy of the `activity_main.xml` file (in the `res/layout` folder) by right-clicking it and selecting Copy. Then right-click the `res/layout` folder and select Paste. Name the file activity_second.xml.
6. Modify the `activity_second.xml` file as follows:

```
<?xml version="1.0" encoding="utf-8"?>
<RelativeLayout xmlns:android="http://schemas.android.com/apk/res/android"
    xmlns:tools="http://schemas.android.com/tools"
    android:layout_width="match_parent"
    android:layout_height="match_parent"
```

```
    android:paddingBottom="@dimen/activity_vertical_margin"
    android:paddingLeft="@dimen/activity_horizontal_margin"
    android:paddingRight="@dimen/activity_horizontal_margin"
    android:paddingTop="@dimen/activity_vertical_margin"
    tools:context="com.jfdimarzio.usingintent.SecondActivity">

    <TextView
        android:layout_width="wrap_content"
        android:layout_height="wrap_content"
        android:text="This is the Second Activity!" />
</RelativeLayout>
```

7. In the `SecondActivity.java` file, add the bolded statements from the following code:

```
package com.jfdimarzio.usingintent;

import android.app.Activity;
import android.os.Bundle;

public class SecondActivity extends Activity {
    public void onCreate(Bundle savedInstanceState) {
        super.onCreate(savedInstanceState);
        setContentView(R.layout.activity_second);
    }

}
```

8. Add the bolded lines in the following code to the `activity_main.xml` file:

```
<?xml version="1.0" encoding="utf-8"?>
<RelativeLayout xmlns:android="http://schemas.android.com/apk/res/android"
    xmlns:tools="http://schemas.android.com/tools"
    android:layout_width="match_parent"
    android:layout_height="match_parent"
    android:paddingBottom="@dimen/activity_vertical_margin"
    android:paddingLeft="@dimen/activity_horizontal_margin"
    android:paddingRight="@dimen/activity_horizontal_margin"
    android:paddingTop="@dimen/activity_vertical_margin"
    tools:context="com.jfdimarzio.usingintent.MainActivity">

    <TextView
        android:layout_width="wrap_content"
        android:layout_height="wrap_content"
        android:text="Main Activity!"
        android:id="@+id/textView" />

    <Button
        android:layout_width="wrap_content"
        android:layout_height="wrap_content"
        android:text="Display second activity"
        android:onClick="onClick"
        android:id="@+id/button"
        android:layout_below="@+id/textView"
        android:layout_alignParentStart="true"
        android:layout_marginTop="56dp" />
</RelativeLayout>
```

9. Modify the `MainActivity.java` file as shown in the bolded lines in the following code:

```
package com.jfdimarzio.usingintent;

import android.app.Activity;
import android.content.Intent;
import android.os.Bundle;
import android.view.View;

public class MainActivity extends Activity {

    @Override
    protected void onCreate(Bundle savedInstanceState) {
        super.onCreate(savedInstanceState);
        setContentView(R.layout.activity_main);
    }
    public void onClick(View view) {
        startActivity(new Intent("com.jfdimarzio.usingintent.SecondActivity"));
    }

}
```

10. Press Shift+F9 to debug the application on the Android emulator. When the first activity is loaded, click the button and the second activity also loads (see Figures 3-8 and 3-9).

How It Works

As previously described, an activity is made up of a UI component (for example, `activity_main.xml`) and a class component (for example, `MainActivity.java`). If you want to add another activity to a project, you need to create these two components.

Specifically, you need to add the following to the `AndroidManifest.xml` file:

```
</activity>
        <activity android:name=".SecondActivity" >
        <intent-filter >
            <action android:name="com.jfdimarzio.usingintent.SecondActivity" />
            <category android:name="android.intent.category.DEFAULT" />
        </intent-filter>
</activity>
```

When you add a new activity to the application, be sure to note the following:

- The name (class) of the new activity is `SecondActivity`.
- The intent filter name for the new activity is `<Your Package Name>.SecondActivity`. Other activities that want to call this activity invoke it via this name. Ideally, you should use the reverse domain name of your company as the intent filter name to reduce the chances of another application having the same intent filter name.
- The category for the intent filter is `android.intent.category.DEFAULT`. You need to add this to the intent filter so that this activity can be started by another activity using the `startActivity()` method (more on this shortly).

FIGURE 3-8

FIGURE 3-9

When the Display Second Activity button is clicked, you use the `startActivity()` method to display `SecondActivity` by creating an instance of the `Intent` class and passing it the intent filter name of `SecondActivity` (`net.learn2develop.SecondActivity`):

```
public void onClick(View view) {
    startActivity(new Intent("net.learn2develop.SecondActivity"));
}
```

Activities in Android can be invoked by any application running on the device. For example, you can create a new Android project and then display `SecondActivity` by using its `net.learn2develop.SecondActivity` intent filter. This is one of the fundamental concepts in Android that enables an application to easily invoke another application.

If the activity you want to invoke is defined within the same project, you can rewrite the preceding statement like this:

```
startActivity(new Intent(this, SecondActivity.class));
```

However, this approach is applicable only when the activity you want to display is within the same project as the current activity.

Returning Results from an Intent

The `startActivity()` method invokes another activity but does not return a result to the current activity. For example, you might have an activity that prompts the user for username and password. The information entered by the user in that activity needs to be passed back to the calling activity for further processing. If you need to pass data back from an activity, you should instead use the `startActivityForResult()` method. The following Try It Out demonstrates this.

TRY IT OUT Obtaining a Result from an Activity

1. Using the same project from the previous section, modify the `secondactivity.xml` file to look like the following code. Please be sure to change all references from `"com.jfdimarzio"` to whatever package name your project is using:

```
<?xml version="1.0" encoding="utf-8"?>
<LinearLayout android:orientation="vertical"
    xmlns:android="http://schemas.android.com/apk/res/android"
    xmlns:tools="http://schemas.android.com/tools"
    android:layout_width="match_parent"
    android:layout_height="match_parent"
    android:paddingBottom="@dimen/activity_vertical_margin"
    android:paddingLeft="@dimen/activity_horizontal_margin"
    android:paddingRight="@dimen/activity_horizontal_margin"
    android:paddingTop="@dimen/activity_vertical_margin"
    tools:context="com.jfdimarzio.usingintent.SecondActivity">


    <TextView
        android:layout_width="wrap_content"
        android:layout_height="wrap_content"
        android:text="This is the Second Activity!"
        android:id="@+id/textView2" />

    <TextView
        android:layout_width="wrap_content"
        android:layout_height="wrap_content"
        android:text="Please enter your name"
        android:id="@+id/textView3" />

    <EditText
        android:layout_width="match_parent"
```

```
        android:layout_height="wrap_content"
        android:id="@+id/txtUsername" />

    <Button
        android:layout_width="wrap_content"
        android:layout_height="wrap_content"
        android:text="OK"
        android:onClick="onClick"
        android:id="@+id/button2" />
</LinearLayout>
```

2. Add the bolded statements in the following code to `SecondActivity.java`:

```
package com.jfdimarzio.usingintent;

import android.app.Activity;
import android.content.Intent;
import android.net.Uri;
import android.os.Bundle;
import android.view.View;
import android.widget.EditText;

public class SecondActivity extends Activity {
    public void onCreate(Bundle savedInstanceState) {
        super.onCreate(savedInstanceState);
        setContentView(R.layout.activity_second);
    }
    public void onClick(View view) {
         Intent data = new Intent();
         //---get the EditText view---
         EditText txt_username = (EditText)findViewById(R.id.txtUsername);
         //---set the data to pass back---
         data.setData(Uri.parse( txt_username.getText().toString()));
         setResult(RESULT_OK, data);
         //---closes the activity---
         finish();
    }
}
```

3. Add the bolded statements in the following code to the `MainActivity.java` file:

```
package com.jfdimarzio.usingintent;

import android.app.Activity;
import android.content.Intent;
import android.os.Bundle;
import android.view.View;
import android.widget.Toast;

public class MainActivity extends Activity {
    int request_Code = 1;
    @Override
    protected void onCreate(Bundle savedInstanceState) {
        super.onCreate(savedInstanceState);
```

```
            setContentView(R.layout.activity_main);
        }
        public void onClick(View view) {
            startActivityForResult(new Intent("com.jfdimarzio.usingintent.
              SecondActivity"),request_Code);
        }
        public void onActivityResult(int requestCode, int resultCode, Intent data)
        {
            if (requestCode == request_Code) {
                if (resultCode == RESULT_OK) {
                    Toast.makeText(this,data.getData().toString(),
                       Toast.LENGTH_SHORT).show();
                }
            }
        }
    }
```

4. Press Shift+F9 to debug the application on the Android emulator. When the first activity is loaded, click the button to load `SecondActivity`. Enter your name (see Figures 3-10, 3-11, and 3-12) and click the OK button. The first activity displays the name you have entered using the `Toast` class.

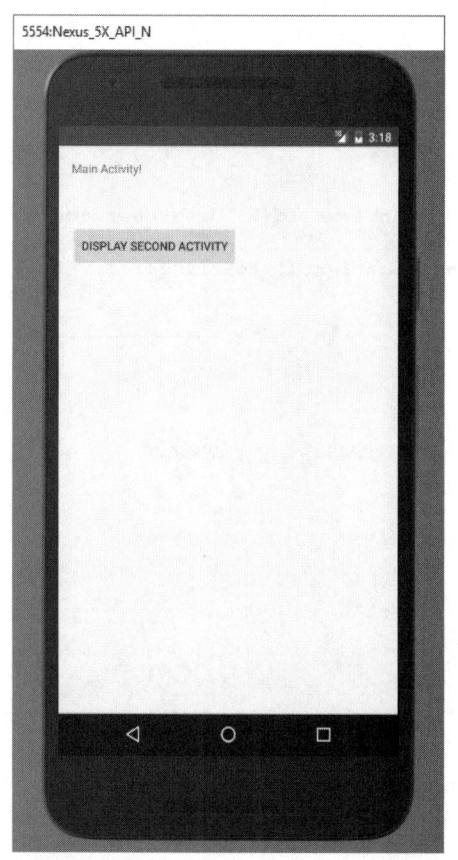

FIGURE 3-10

How It Works

To call an activity and wait for a result to be returned from it, you need to use the `startActivityForResult()` method, like this:

```
startActivityForResult(new Intent("com.jfdimarzio.usingintent.
  SecondActivity"),request_Code);
```

In addition to passing in an `Intent` object, you need to pass in a request code as well. The request code is simply an integer value that identifies an activity you are calling. This is needed because when an activity returns a value, you must have a way to identify it. For example, you might be calling multiple activities at the same time, though some activities might not return immediately (for example, waiting for a reply from a server). When an activity returns, you need this request code to determine which activity is actually returned.

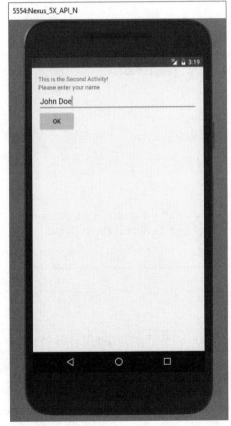

FIGURE 3-11

FIGURE 3-12

> ***NOTE*** *If the request code is set to –1 then calling it using the* `startActivityForResult()` *method is equivalent to calling it using the* `startActivity()` *method. That is, no result is returned.*

In order for an activity to return a value to the calling activity, you use an `Intent` object to send data back via the `setData()` method:

```
Intent data = new Intent();
//---get the EditText view---
EditText txt_username =
    (EditText) findViewById(R.id.txt_username);
//---set the data to pass back---
data.setData(Uri.parse(
    txt_username.getText().toString()));
setResult(RESULT_OK, data);
//---closes the activity---
finish();
```

The `setResult()` method sets a result code (either `RESULT_OK` or `RESULT_CANCELLED`) and the data (an `Intent` object) to be returned back to the calling activity. The `finish()` method closes the activity and returns control to the calling activity.

In the calling activity, you need to implement the `onActivityResult()` method, which is called whenever an activity returns:

```
public void onActivityResult(int requestCode, int resultCode,
Intent data)
{
    if (requestCode == request_Code) {
        if (resultCode == RESULT_OK) {
            Toast.makeText(this,data.getData().toString(),
                Toast.LENGTH_SHORT).show();
        }
    }
}
```

Here, you check for the appropriate request and result codes and display the result that is returned. The returned result is passed in via the `data` argument; and you obtain its details through the `getData()` method.

Passing Data Using an Intent Object

Besides returning data from an activity, it is also common to pass data to an activity. For example, in the previous example, you might want to set some default text in the `EditText` view before the activity is displayed. In this case, you can use the `Intent` object to pass the data to the target activity.

The following Try It Out shows you the various ways in which you can pass data between activities.

TRY IT OUT Passing Data to the Target Activity

1. Using Eclipse, create a new Android project and name it **PassingData**.
2. Add the bolded statements in the following code to the `activity_main.xml` file. Be sure to change all instances of `"com.jfdimarzio"` to whatever package name your project is using.

```
<?xml version="1.0" encoding="utf-8"?>
<LinearLayout android:orientation="vertical"
    xmlns:android="http://schemas.android.com/apk/res/android"
    xmlns:tools="http://schemas.android.com/tools"
    android:layout_width="match_parent"
    android:layout_height="match_parent"
    android:paddingBottom="@dimen/activity_vertical_margin"
    android:paddingLeft="@dimen/activity_horizontal_margin"
    android:paddingRight="@dimen/activity_horizontal_margin"
    android:paddingTop="@dimen/activity_vertical_margin"
    tools:context="com.jfdimarzio.passingdata.MainActivity">


    <Button
        android:layout_width="wrap_content"
        android:layout_height="wrap_content"
        android:text="Click to go to Second Activity"
        android:id="@+id/button"
        android:onClick="onClick"/>
</LinearLayout>
```

3. Add a new XML file to the `res/layout` folder and name it **activity_second.xml**. Populate it as follows:

```
<?xml version="1.0" encoding="utf-8"?>
<LinearLayout android:orientation="vertical"
    xmlns:android="http://schemas.android.com/apk/res/android"
    xmlns:tools="http://schemas.android.com/tools"
    android:layout_width="match_parent"
    android:layout_height="match_parent"
    android:paddingBottom="@dimen/activity_vertical_margin"
    android:paddingLeft="@dimen/activity_horizontal_margin"
    android:paddingRight="@dimen/activity_horizontal_margin"
    android:paddingTop="@dimen/activity_vertical_margin"
    tools:context="com.jfdimarzio.passingdata.MainActivity">


    <TextView
        android:layout_width="wrap_content"
        android:layout_height="wrap_content"
        android:text="Welcome to the Second Activity"
        android:id="@+id/textView" />

    <Button
        android:layout_width="wrap_content"
        android:layout_height="wrap_content"
        android:text="Click to go to Main Activity"
        android:id="@+id/button"
        android:onClick="onClick"/>
</LinearLayout>
```

4. Add a new `Class` file to the package and name it **SecondActivity**. Populate the `SecondActivity.java` file as follows:

```
package com.jfdimarzio.passingdata;
```

```
import android.app.Activity;
import android.content.Intent;
import android.net.Uri;
import android.os.Bundle;
import android.view.View;
import android.widget.Toast;

public class SecondActvity extends Activity {
    @Override
    public void onCreate(Bundle savedInstanceState) {
        super.onCreate(savedInstanceState);
        setContentView(R.layout.activity_second);
        //---get the data passed in using getStringExtra()---
        Toast.makeText(this,getIntent().getStringExtra("str1"),
                Toast.LENGTH_SHORT).show();
        //---get the data passed in using getIntExtra()---
        Toast.makeText(this,Integer.toString(
                getIntent().getIntExtra("age1", 0)),
                Toast.LENGTH_SHORT).show();
        //---get the Bundle object passed in---
        Bundle bundle = getIntent().getExtras();
        //---get the data using the getString()---
        Toast.makeText(this, bundle.getString("str2"),
                Toast.LENGTH_SHORT).show();
        //---get the data using the getInt() method---
        Toast.makeText(this,Integer.toString(bundle.getInt("age2")),
                Toast.LENGTH_SHORT).show();
    }
    public void onClick(View view) {
        //---use an Intent object to return data---
        Intent i = new Intent();
        //---use the putExtra() method to return some
        // value---
        i.putExtra("age3", 45);
        //---use the setData() method to return some value---
        i.setData(Uri.parse("Something passed back to main activity"));
        //---set the result with OK and the Intent object---
        setResult(RESULT_OK, i);
        //---destroy the current activity---
        finish();
    }

}
```

5. Add the bolded statements from the following code to the `AndroidManifest.xml` file:

```
<?xml version="1.0" encoding="utf-8"?>
<manifest xmlns:android="http://schemas.android.com/apk/res/android"
    package="com.jfdimarzio.passingdata">

    <application
        android:allowBackup="true"
        android:icon="@mipmap/ic_launcher"
        android:label="@string/app_name"
        android:supportsRtl="true"
        android:theme="@style/AppTheme">
```

```
        <activity android:name=".MainActivity">
            <intent-filter>
                <action android:name="android.intent.action.MAIN" />

                <category android:name="android.intent.category.LAUNCHER" />
            </intent-filter>
        </activity>
        <activity android:name=".SecondActvity" >
         <intent-filter >
            <action android:name="com.jfdimarzio.passingdata.SecondActivity" />
             <category android:name="android.intent.category.DEFAULT" />
         </intent-filter>

    </activity>
    </application>

</manifest>
```

6. Add the bolded statements from the following code to the `MainActivity.java` file:

```
package com.jfdimarzio.passingdata;

import android.content.Intent;
import android.Activity;
import android.os.Bundle;
import android.view.View;
import android.widget.Toast;

public class MainActivity extends Activity {

    @Override
    protected void onCreate(Bundle savedInstanceState) {
        super.onCreate(savedInstanceState);
        setContentView(R.layout.activity_main);
    }
    public void onClick(View view) {
        Intent i = new
                Intent("com.jfdimarzio.passingdata.SecondActivity");
        //---use putExtra() to add new name/value pairs---
        i.putExtra("str1", "This is a string");
        i.putExtra("age1", 25);
        //---use a Bundle object to add new name/values
        // pairs---
        Bundle extras = new Bundle();
        extras.putString("str2", "This is another string");
        extras.putInt("age2", 35);
        //---attach the Bundle object to the Intent object---
        i.putExtras(extras);
        //---start the activity to get a result back---
        startActivityForResult(i, 1);
    }

    public void onActivityResult(int requestCode,
                                 int resultCode, Intent data)
```

```
        {
            //---check if the request code is 1---
            if (requestCode == 1) {
                //---if the result is OK---
                if (resultCode == RESULT_OK) {
                    //---get the result using getIntExtra()---
                    Toast.makeText(this, Integer.toString(
                            data.getIntExtra("age3", 0)),
                            Toast.LENGTH_SHORT).show();
                    //---get the result using getData()---
                    Toast.makeText(this, data.getData().toString(),
                            Toast.LENGTH_SHORT).show();
                }
            }
        }
    }
```

7. Press Shift+F9 to debug the application on the Android emulator. Click the button on each activity and observe the values displayed.

How It Works

While this application is not visually exciting, it does illustrate some important ways to pass data between activities.

First, you can use the `putExtra()` method of an `Intent` object to add a name/value pair:

```
//---use putExtra() to add new name/value pairs---
i.putExtra("str1", "This is a string");
i.putExtra("age1", 25);
```

The preceding statements add two name/value pairs to the `Intent` object: one of type `string` and one of type `integer`.

Besides using the `putExtra()` method, you can also create a `Bundle` object and then attach it using the `putExtras()` method. Think of a `Bundle` object as a dictionary object—it contains a set of name/value pairs. The following statements create a `Bundle` object and then add two name/value pairs to it. The `Bundle` object is then attached to the `Intent` object:

```
//---use a Bundle object to add new name/values pairs---
Bundle extras = new Bundle();
extras.putString("str2", "This is another string");
extras.putInt("age2", 35);
//---attach the Bundle object to the Intent object---
i.putExtras(extras);
```

To obtain the data sent using the `Intent` object, you first obtain the `Intent` object using the `getIntent()` method. Then, call its `getStringExtra()` method to get the string value set using the `putExtra()` method:

```
//---get the data passed in using getStringExtra()---
Toast.makeText(this,getIntent().getStringExtra("str1"),
        Toast.LENGTH_SHORT).show();
```

In this case, you have to call the appropriate method to extract the name/value pair based on the type of data set. For the integer value, use the `getIntExtra()` method (the second argument is the default value in case no value is stored in the specified name):

```
//---get the data passed in using getIntExtra()---
Toast.makeText(this,Integer.toString(
        getIntent().getIntExtra("age1", 0)),
        Toast.LENGTH_SHORT).show();
```

To retrieve the `Bundle` object, use the `getExtras()` method:

```
//---get the Bundle object passed in---
Bundle bundle = getIntent().getExtras();
```

To get the individual name/value pairs, use the appropriate method. For the string value, use the `getString()` method:

```
//---get the data using the getString()---
Toast.makeText(this, bundle.getString("str2"),
        Toast.LENGTH_SHORT).show();
```

Likewise, use the `getInt()` method to retrieve an integer value:

```
//---get the data using the getInt() method---
Toast.makeText(this,Integer.toString(bundle.getInt("age2")),
        Toast.LENGTH_SHORT).show();
```

Another way to pass data to an activity is to use the `setData()` method (as used in the previous section), like this:

```
//---use the setData() method to return some value---
i.setData(Uri.parse(
        "Something passed back to main activity"));
```

Usually, you use the `setData()` method to set the data on which an `Intent` object is going to operate, such as passing a URL to an `Intent` object so that it can invoke a web browser to view a web page. (For more examples, see the section "Calling Built-In Applications Using Intents," later in this chapter.)

To retrieve the data set using the `setData()` method, use the `getData()` method (in this example `data` is an `Intent` object):

```
//---get the result using getData()---
Toast.makeText(this, data.getData().toString(),
    Toast.LENGTH_SHORT).show();
```

FRAGMENTS

In the previous section, you learned what an activity is and how to use it. In a small-screen device (such as a smartphone), an activity typically fills the entire screen, displaying the various views that make up the user interface of an application. The activity is essentially a container for views. However, when an activity is displayed in a large-screen device, such as on a tablet, it is somewhat out of place. Because the screen is much bigger, all the views in an activity must be arranged to make full use of the increased space, resulting in complex changes to the view hierarchy. A better approach is to have "mini-activities," each containing its own set of views. During runtime, an activity can contain one or more of these mini-activities, depending on the screen orientation in which the device is held. In Android 3.0 and later, these mini-activities are known as *fragments*.

Think of a fragment as another form of activity. You create fragments to contain views, just like activities. Fragments are always embedded in an activity. For example, Figure 3-13 shows two fragments. Fragment 1 might contain a `ListView` showing a list of book titles. Fragment 2 might contain some `TextViews` and `ImageViews` showing some text and images.

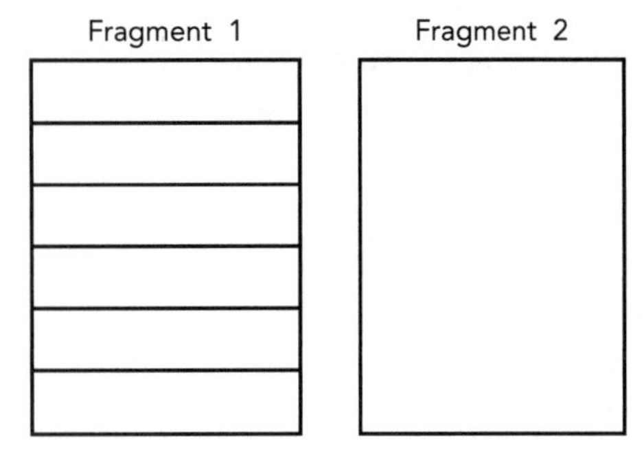

FIGURE 3-13

Now imagine the application is running on an Android tablet (or on an Android smartphone) in portrait mode. In this case, Fragment 1 might be embedded in one activity, whereas Fragment 2 might be embedded in another activity (see Figure 3-14). When users select an item in the list in Fragment 1, Activity 2 is started.

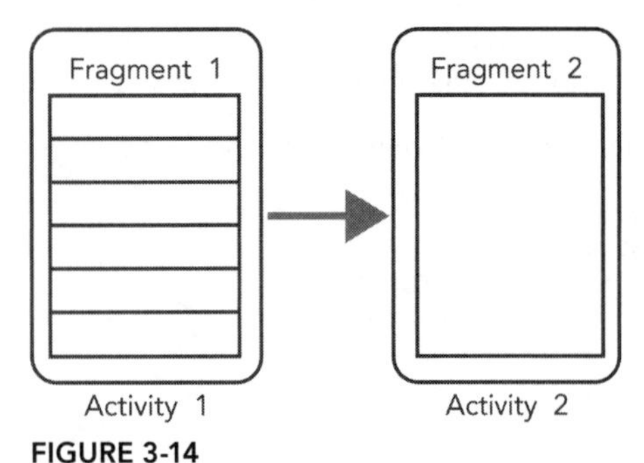

FIGURE 3-14

If the application is now displayed in a tablet in landscape mode, both fragments can be embedded within a single activity, as shown in Figure 3-15.

From this discussion, it becomes apparent that fragments present a versatile way in which you can create the user interface of an Android application. Fragments form the atomic unit of your user interface, and they can be dynamically added (or removed) to activities in order to create the best user experience possible for the target device.

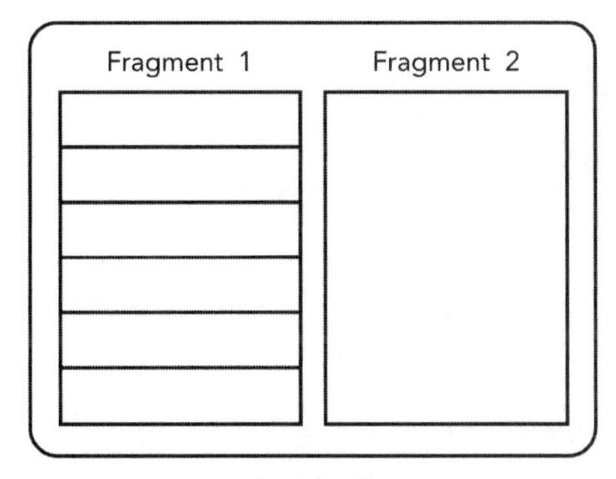

FIGURE 3-15

The following Try It Out shows you the basics of working with fragments.

TRY IT OUT Using Fragments (Fragments.zip)

1. Using Android Studio, create a new Android project and name it **Fragments**.
2. In the `res/layout` folder, add a new layout resource file and name it `fragment1.xml`. Populate it with the following code. Be sure to change all instances of `"com.jfdimarzio"` to whatever package name your project is using.

```
<?xml version="1.0" encoding="utf-8"?>
<LinearLayout
    xmlns:android="http://schemas.android.com/apk/res/android"
    android:orientation="vertical"
    android:layout_width="fill_parent"
    android:layout_height="fill_parent"
    android:background="#00FF00"
    >
<TextView
    android:layout_width="fill_parent"
    android:layout_height="wrap_content"
    android:text="This is fragment #1"
    android:textColor="#000000"
    android:textSize="25sp" />
</LinearLayout>
```

3. Also in the `res/layout` folder, add another new layout resource file and name it `fragment2.xml`. Populate it as follows:

```
<?xml version="1.0" encoding="utf-8"?>
<LinearLayout
    xmlns:android="http://schemas.android.com/apk/res/android"
    android:orientation="vertical"
    android:layout_width="fill_parent"
    android:layout_height="fill_parent"
    android:background="#FFFE00"
    >
```

```
<TextView
    android:layout_width="fill_parent"
    android:layout_height="wrap_content"
    android:text="This is fragment #2"
    android:textColor="#000000"
    android:textSize="25sp" />
</LinearLayout>
```

4. In `activity_main.xml`, add the bolded lines in the following code:

```
<?xml version="1.0" encoding="utf-8"?>
<LinearLayout android:orientation="vertical"
    xmlns:android="http://schemas.android.com/apk/res/android"
    xmlns:tools="http://schemas.android.com/tools"
    android:layout_width="match_parent"
    android:layout_height="match_parent"
    android:paddingBottom="@dimen/activity_vertical_margin"
    android:paddingLeft="@dimen/activity_horizontal_margin"
    android:paddingRight="@dimen/activity_horizontal_margin"
    android:paddingTop="@dimen/activity_vertical_margin"
    tools:context="com.jfdimarzio.fragments.MainActivity">

    <fragment
        android:name="com.jfdimarzio.fragments.Fragment1"
        android:id="@+id/fragment1"
        android:layout_weight="1"
        android:layout_width="fill_parent"
        android:layout_height="match_parent" />
    <fragment
        android:name="com.jfdimarzio.fragments.Fragment2"
        android:id="@+id/fragment2"
        android:layout_weight="1"
        android:layout_width="fill_parent"
        android:layout_height="match_parent" />
</LinearLayout>
```

5. Under the `<Your Package Name>/fragments` package name, add two Java class files and name them `Fragment1.java` and `Fragment2.java`.

6. Add the following code to `Fragment1.java`:

```
package com.jfdimarzio.fragments;

import android.app.Fragment;
import android.os.Bundle;
import android.view.LayoutInflater;
import android.view.View;
import android.view.ViewGroup;
public class Fragment1 extends Fragment {
    @Override
    public View onCreateView(LayoutInflater inflater,
                             ViewGroup container, Bundle savedInstanceState) {
        //---Inflate the layout for this fragment---
        return inflater.inflate(
                R.layout.fragment1, container, false);
    }
}
```

7. Add the following code to `Fragment2.java`:

```
package com.jfdimarzio.fragments;

import android.app.Fragment;
import android.os.Bundle;
import android.view.LayoutInflater;
import android.view.View;
import android.view.ViewGroup;
public class Fragment2 extends Fragment {
    @Override
    public View onCreateView(LayoutInflater inflater,
                             ViewGroup container, Bundle savedInstanceState) {
        //---Inflate the layout for this fragment---
        return inflater.inflate(
                R.layout.fragment2, container, false);
    }
}
```

8. Press Shift+F9 to debug the application on the Android emulator. Figure 3-16 shows the two fragments contained within the activity.

FIGURE 3-16

How It Works

A fragment behaves very much like an activity: It has a Java class and it loads its UI from an XML file. The XML file contains all the usual UI elements that you expect from an activity: `TextView`, `EditText`, `Button`, and so on. The Java class for a fragment needs to extend the `Fragment` base class:

```
public class Fragment1 extends Fragment {
}
```

> ***NOTE** Besides the `Fragment` base class, a fragment can also extend a few other subclasses of the `Fragment` class, such as `DialogFragment`, `ListFragment`, and `PreferenceFragment`. Chapter 6 discusses these types of fragments in more detail.*

To draw the UI for a fragment, you override the `onCreateView()` method. This method needs to return a `View` object, like this:

```
    public View onCreateView(LayoutInflater inflater,
    ViewGroup container, Bundle savedInstanceState) {
        //---Inflate the layout for this fragment---
        return inflater.inflate(
            R.layout.fragment1, container, false);
    }
Here, you use a LayoutInflater object to inflate the UI from the
   specified XML file (R.layout.fragment1 in this case). The
   container argument refers to the parent ViewGroup, which
   is the activity in which you are trying to embed the
   fragment. The savedInstanceState argument enables you
   to restore the fragment to its previously saved state.
To add a fragment to an activity, you use the <fragment> element:
<?xml version="1.0" encoding="utf-8"?>
<LinearLayout xmlns:android="http://schemas.android.com/apk/res
   /android"
    android:layout_width="fill_parent"
    android:layout_height="fill_parent"
    android:orientation="vertical" >
    <fragment
        android:name=" com.jfdimarzio.fragments.Fragment1"
        android:id="@+id/fragment1"
        android:layout_weight="1"
        android:layout_width="fill_parent"
        android:layout_height="match_parent" />
    <fragment
        android:name=" com.jfdimarzio.fragments.Fragment2"
        android:id="@+id/fragment2"
        android:layout_weight="1"
        android:layout_width="fill_parent"
        android:layout_height="match_parent" />
</LinearLayout>
```

Note that each fragment needs a unique identifier. You can assign one via the `android:id` or `android:tag` attribute.

Adding Fragments Dynamically

Although fragments enable you to compartmentalize your UI into various configurable parts, the real power of fragments is realized when you add them dynamically to activities during runtime. In the previous section, you saw how you can add fragments to an activity by modifying the XML file during design time. In reality, it is much more useful if you create fragments and add them to activities during runtime. This enables you to create a customizable user interface for your application. For example, if the application is running on a smartphone, you might fill an activity with a single fragment; if the application is running on a tablet, you might then fill the activity with two or more fragments, as the tablet has much more screen real estate compared to a smartphone.

The following Try It Out shows how you can programmatically add fragments to an activity during runtime.

TRY IT OUT Adding Fragments During Runtime

1. Using the same project created in the previous section, modify the `main.xml` file by commenting out the two `<fragment>` elements. Be sure to change all instances of `"com.jfdimarzio"` to whatever package name your project is using.

```
<?xml version="1.0" encoding="utf-8"?>
<LinearLayout android:orientation="vertical"
    xmlns:android="http://schemas.android.com/apk/res/android"
    xmlns:tools="http://schemas.android.com/tools"
    android:layout_width="match_parent"
    android:layout_height="match_parent"
    android:paddingBottom="@dimen/activity_vertical_margin"
    android:paddingLeft="@dimen/activity_horizontal_margin"
    android:paddingRight="@dimen/activity_horizontal_margin"
    android:paddingTop="@dimen/activity_vertical_margin"
    tools:context="com.jfdimarzio.fragments.MainActivity">
<!--
    <fragment
        android:name="com.jfdimarzio.fragments.Fragment1"
        android:id="@+id/fragment1"
        android:layout_weight="1"
        android:layout_width="fill_parent"
        android:layout_height="match_parent" />
    <fragment
        android:name="com.jfdimarzio.fragments.Fragment2"
        android:id="@+id/fragment2"
        android:layout_weight="1"
        android:layout_width="fill_parent"
        android:layout_height="match_parent" />
-->
</LinearLayout>
```

2. Add the bolded lines in the following code to the `MainActivity.java` file:

```
package com.jfdimarzio.fragments;

import android.app.Activity;
import android.app.FragmentManager;
import android.app.FragmentTransaction;
import android.os.Bundle;
import android.util.DisplayMetrics;

public class MainActivity extends Activity {
    /** Called when the activity is first created. */
    @Override
    public void onCreate(Bundle savedInstanceState) {
        super.onCreate(savedInstanceState);
         FragmentManager fragmentManager = getFragmentManager();
         FragmentTransaction fragmentTransaction =
                 fragmentManager.beginTransaction();
         //---get the current display info---
         DisplayMetrics display = this.getResources().getDisplayMetrics();

         int width = display.widthPixels;
         int height = display.heightPixels;
         if (width> height)
         {
             //---landscape mode---
             Fragment1 fragment1 = new Fragment1();
             // android.R.id.content refers to the content
             // view of the activity
             fragmentTransaction.replace(
                     android.R.id.content, fragment1);
         }
         else
         {
             //---portrait mode---
             Fragment2 fragment2 = new Fragment2();
             fragmentTransaction.replace(
                     android.R.id.content, fragment2);
         }
         fragmentTransaction.commit();
    }
}
```

3. Press Shift + F9 to run the application on the Android emulator. Observe that when the emulator is in portrait mode, Fragment 2 is displayed (see Figure 3-17). If you press Ctrl+Left to change the orientation of the emulator to landscape, Fragment 1 is shown instead (see Figure 3-18).

FIGURE 3-17

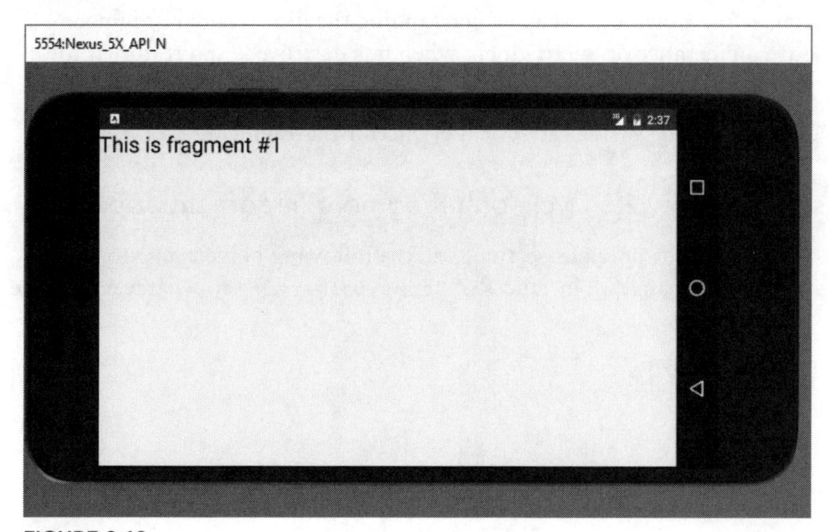

FIGURE 3-18

How It Works

To add fragments to an activity, you use the `FragmentManager` class by first obtaining an instance of it:

```
FragmentManager fragmentManager = getFragmentManager();
```

You also need to use the `FragmentTransaction` class to perform fragment transactions (such as add, remove, or replace) in your activity:

```
FragmentTransaction fragmentTransaction =
        fragmentManager.beginTransaction();
```

In this example, the `WindowManager` is used to determine whether the device is currently in portrait mode or landscape mode. Once that is determined, you can add the appropriate fragment to the activity by creating the fragment. Next, you call the `replace()` method of the `FragmentTransaction` object to add the fragment to the specified view container. In this case, `android.R.id.content` refers to the content view of the activity.

```
//---landscape mode---
Fragment1 fragment1 = new Fragment1();
// android.R.id.content refers to the content
// view of the activity
fragmentTransaction.replace(
        android.R.id.content, fragment1);
```

Using the `replace()` method is essentially the same as calling the `remove()` method followed by the `add()` method of the `FragmentTransaction` object. To ensure that the changes take effect, you need to call the `commit()` method:

```
fragmentTransaction.commit();
```

Life Cycle of a Fragment

Like activities, fragments have their own life cycle. Understanding the life cycle of a fragment enables you to properly save an instance of the fragment when it is destroyed, and restore it to its previous state when it is re-created.

The following Try It Out examines the various states experienced by a fragment.

TRY IT OUT Understanding the Life Cycle of a Fragment (Fragments.zip)

1. Using the same project created in the previous section, add the following bolded code to the `Fragment1.java` file. Be sure to change all instances of `"com.jfdimarzio"` to whatever package name your project is using.

```
package com.jfdimarzio.fragments;
import android.app.Activity;
import android.app.Fragment;
import android.os.Bundle;
import android.util.Log;
```

```
import android.view.LayoutInflater;
import android.view.View;
import android.view.ViewGroup;
public class Fragment1 extends Fragment {
    @Override
    public View onCreateView(LayoutInflater inflater,
    ViewGroup container, Bundle savedInstanceState) {

        Log.d("Fragment 1", "onCreateView");

        //---Inflate the layout for this fragment---
        return inflater.inflate(
            R.layout.fragment1, container, false);
    }

    @Override
    public void onAttach(Activity activity) {
        super.onAttach(activity);
        Log.d("Fragment 1", "onAttach");
    }

    @Override
    public void onCreate(Bundle savedInstanceState) {
        super.onCreate(savedInstanceState);
        Log.d("Fragment 1", "onCreate");
    }
    @Override
    public void onActivityCreated(Bundle savedInstanceState) {
        super.onActivityCreated(savedInstanceState);
        Log.d("Fragment 1", "onActivityCreated");
    }
    @Override
    public void onStart() {
        super.onStart();
        Log.d("Fragment 1", "onStart");
    }
    @Override
    public void onResume() {
        super.onResume();
        Log.d("Fragment 1", "onResume");
    }
    @Override
    public void onPause() {
        super.onPause();
        Log.d("Fragment 1", "onPause");
    }

    @Override
    public void onStop() {
```

```
            super.onStop();
            Log.d("Fragment 1", "onStop");
        }

        @Override
        public void onDestroyView() {
            super.onDestroyView();
            Log.d("Fragment 1", "onDestroyView");
        }
        @Override
        public void onDestroy() {
            super.onDestroy();
            Log.d("Fragment 1", "onDestroy");
        }

        @Override
        public void onDetach() {
            super.onDetach();
            Log.d("Fragment 1", "onDetach");
        }
    }
```

2. Switch the Android emulator to landscape mode by pressing Ctrl+Left.
3. Press Shift+F9 in Android Studio to debug the application on the Android emulator.
4. When the application is loaded on the emulator, the following is displayed in the logcat console in Android Monitor:

```
12-09 04:17:43.436: D/Fragment 1(2995): onAttach
12-09 04:17:43.466: D/Fragment 1(2995): onCreate
12-09 04:17:43.476: D/Fragment 1(2995): onCreateView
12-09 04:17:43.506: D/Fragment 1(2995): onActivityCreated
12-09 04:17:43.506: D/Fragment 1(2995): onStart
12-09 04:17:43.537: D/Fragment 1(2995): onResume
```

5. Click the Home button on the emulator. The following output is displayed in the logcat console:

```
12-09 04:18:47.696: D/Fragment 1(2995): onPause
12-09 04:18:50.346: D/Fragment 1(2995): onStop
```

6. On the emulator, click the Home button and hold it. Launch the application again. This time, the following is displayed:

```
12-09 04:20:08.726: D/Fragment 1(2995): onStart
12-09 04:20:08.766: D/Fragment 1(2995): onResume
```

7. Click the Back button on the emulator. Now you should see the following output:

```
12-09 04:21:01.426: D/Fragment 1(2995): onPause
12-09 04:21:02.346: D/Fragment 1(2995): onStop
```

```
12-09 04:21:02.346: D/Fragment 1(2995): onDestroyView
12-09 04:21:02.346: D/Fragment 1(2995): onDestroy
12-09 04:21:02.346: D/Fragment 1(2995): onDetach
```

How It Works

Like activities, fragments in Android also have their own life cycle. As you have seen, when a fragment is being created, it goes through the following states:

- `onAttach()`
- `onCreate()`
- `onCreateView()`
- `onActivityCreated()`

When the fragment becomes visible, it goes through these states:

- `onStart()`
- `onResume()`

When the fragment goes into the background mode, it goes through these states:

- `onPause()`
- `onStop()`

When the fragment is destroyed (when the activity in which it is currently hosted is destroyed), it goes through the following states:

- `onPause()`
- `onStop()`
- `onDestroyView()`
- `onDestroy()`
- `onDetach()`

Like activities, you can restore an instance of a fragment using a `Bundle` object, in the following states:

- `onCreate()`
- `onCreateView()`
- `onActivityCreated()`

Most of the states experienced by a fragment are similar to those of activities. However, a few new states are specific to fragments:

- `onAttached()`—Called when the fragment has been associated with the activity
- `onCreateView()` Called to create the view for the fragment
- `onActivityCreated()`—Called when the activity's `onCreate()` method has been returned

- onDestroyView()—Called when the fragment's view is being removed
- onDetach()—Called when the fragment is detached from the activity

One of the main differences between activities and fragments is when an activity goes into the background, the activity is placed in the back stack. This allows the activity to be resumed when the user presses the Back button. In the case of fragments, however, they are not automatically placed in the back stack when they go into the background. Rather, to place a fragment into the back stack, you need to explicitly call the addToBackStack() method during a fragment transaction, like this:

```
//---get the current display info---
DisplayMetrics display = this.getResources().getDisplayMetrics();

int width = display.widthPixels;
int height = display.heightPixels;
if (width> height)
{
    //---landscape mode---
    Fragment1 fragment1 = new Fragment1();
    // android.R.id.content refers to the content
    // view of the activity
    fragmentTransaction.replace(
            android.R.id.content, fragment1);
}
else
{
    //---portrait mode---
    Fragment2 fragment2 = new Fragment2();
    fragmentTransaction.replace(
            android.R.id.content, fragment2);
}
//---add to the back stack---
fragmentTransaction.addToBackStack(null);
fragmentTransaction.commit();
```

The preceding code ensures that after the fragment has been added to the activity, the user can click the Back button to remove it.

Interactions Between Fragments

Very often, an activity might contain one or more fragments working together to present a coherent UI to the user. In this case, it is important for fragments to communicate with one another and exchange data. For example, one fragment might contain a list of items (such as postings from an RSS feed). Also, when the user taps on an item in that fragment, details about the selected item might be displayed in another fragment.

The following Try It Out shows how one fragment can access the views contained within another fragment.

TRY IT OUT Communication Between Fragments

1. Using the same project created in the previous section, add the following bolded statement to the `Fragment1.xml` file. Be sure to change all instances of `"com.jfdimarzio"` to whatever package name your project is using.

```
<?xml version="1.0" encoding="utf-8"?>
<LinearLayout
    xmlns:android="http://schemas.android.com/apk/res/android"
    android:orientation="vertical"
    android:layout_width="fill_parent"
    android:layout_height="fill_parent"
    android:background="#00FF00" >
<TextView
    android:id="@+id/lblFragment1"
    android:layout_width="fill_parent"
    android:layout_height="wrap_content"
    android:text="This is fragment #1"
    android:textColor="#000000"
    android:textSize="25sp" />
</LinearLayout>
```

2. Add the following bolded lines to `fragment2.xml`:

```
<?xml version="1.0" encoding="utf-8"?>
<LinearLayout
    xmlns:android="http://schemas.android.com/apk/res/android"
    android:orientation="vertical"
    android:layout_width="fill_parent"
    android:layout_height="fill_parent"
    android:background="#FFFE00" >
<TextView
    android:layout_width="fill_parent"
    android:layout_height="wrap_content"
    android:text="This is fragment #2"
    android:textColor="#000000"
    android:textSize="25sp" />
<Button
    android:id="@+id/btnGetText"
    android:layout_width="wrap_content"
    android:layout_height="wrap_content"
    android:text="Get text in Fragment #1"
    android:textColor="#000000"
    android:onClick="onClick" />
</LinearLayout>
```

3. Return the two fragments to `main.xml`:

```
<?xml version="1.0" encoding="utf-8"?>
<LinearLayout android:orientation="vertical"
    xmlns:android="http://schemas.android.com/apk/res/android"
    xmlns:tools="http://schemas.android.com/tools"
    android:layout_width="match_parent"
    android:layout_height="match_parent"
    android:paddingBottom="@dimen/activity_vertical_margin"
```

```
    android:paddingLeft="@dimen/activity_horizontal_margin"
    android:paddingRight="@dimen/activity_horizontal_margin"
    android:paddingTop="@dimen/activity_vertical_margin"
    tools:context="com.jfdimarzio.fragments.MainActivity">
    <fragment
        android:name="com.jfdimarzio.fragments.Fragment1"
        android:id="@+id/fragment1"
        android:layout_weight="1"
        android:layout_width="fill_parent"
        android:layout_height="match_parent" />
    <fragment
        android:name="com.jfdimarzio.fragments.Fragment2"
        android:id="@+id/fragment2"
        android:layout_weight="1"
        android:layout_width="fill_parent"
        android:layout_height="match_parent" />
</LinearLayout>
```

4. Modify the `MainActivity.java` file by commenting out the code that you added in the earlier sections. It should look like this after modification:

```
public class MainActivity extends Activity {
    /** Called when the activity is first created. */
    @Override
    public void onCreate(Bundle savedInstanceState) {
        super.onCreate(savedInstanceState);
        /*
        FragmentManager fragmentManager = getFragmentManager();
        FragmentTransaction fragmentTransaction =
                fragmentManager.beginTransaction();
        //---get the current display info---
        DisplayMetrics display = this.getResources().getDisplayMetrics();

        int width = display.widthPixels;
        int height = display.heightPixels;
        if (width> height)
        {
            //---landscape mode---
            Fragment1 fragment1 = new Fragment1();
            // android.R.id.content refers to the content
            // view of the activity
            fragmentTransaction.replace(
                    android.R.id.content, fragment1);
        }
        else
        {
            //---portrait mode---
            Fragment2 fragment2 = new Fragment2();
            fragmentTransaction.replace(
                    android.R.id.content, fragment2);
        }
        fragmentTransaction.commit();
        */
    }
}
```

5. Add the following bolded statements to the `Fragment2.java` file:

```
package com.jfdimarzio.fragments;
import android.app.Fragment;
import android.os.Bundle;
import android.view.LayoutInflater;
import android.view.View;
import android.view.ViewGroup;
import android.widget.Button;
import android.widget.TextView;
import android.widget.Toast;
public class Fragment2 extends Fragment {
    @Override
    public View onCreateView(LayoutInflater inflater,
    ViewGroup container, Bundle savedInstanceState) {
        //---Inflate the layout for this fragment---
        return inflater.inflate(
            R.layout.fragment2, container, false);
    }

    @Override
    public void onStart() {
        super.onStart();
        //---Button view---
        Button btnGetText = (Button)
            getActivity().findViewById(R.id.btnGetText);
        btnGetText.setOnClickListener(new View.OnClickListener() {
            public void onClick(View v) {
                TextView lbl = (TextView)
                    getActivity().findViewById(R.id.lblFragment1);
                Toast.makeText(getActivity(), lbl.getText(),
                    Toast.LENGTH_SHORT).show();
            }
        });
    }
}
```

6. Press Shift+F9 to debug the application on the Android emulator. In the second fragment on the right, click the button. You should see the `Toast` class displaying the text `This is fragment #1`.

How It Works

Because fragments are embedded within activities, you can obtain the activity in which a fragment is currently embedded by first using the `getActivity()` method and then using the `findViewById()` method to locate the view(s) contained within the fragment:

```
TextView lbl = (TextView)
    getActivity().findViewById(R.id.lblFragment1);
Toast.makeText(getActivity(), lbl.getText(),
    Toast.LENGTH_SHORT).show();
```

The `getActivity()` method returns the activity with which the current fragment is currently associated.

Alternatively, you can also add the following method to the `MainActivity.java` file:

```
public void onClick(View v) {
    TextView lbl = (TextView)
        findViewById(R.id.lblFragment1);
    Toast.makeText(this, lbl.getText(),
        Toast.LENGTH_SHORT).show();
}
```

Understanding the Intent Object

So far, you have seen the use of the `Intent` object to call other activities. This is a good time to recap and gain a more detailed understanding of how the `Intent` object performs its magic.

First, you learned that you can call another activity by passing its action to the constructor of an `Intent` object:

```
startActivity(new Intent("com.jfdimarzio.SecondActivity"));
```

The action (in this example `"com.jfdimarzio.SecondActivity"`) is also known as the *component name*. This is used to identify the target activity/application that you want to invoke. You can also rewrite the component name by specifying the class name of the activity if it resides in your project, like this:

```
startActivity(new Intent(this, SecondActivity.class));
```

You can also create an `Intent` object by passing in an action constant and data, such as the following:

```
Intent i = new
        Intent(android.content.Intent.ACTION_VIEW,
               Uri.parse("http://www.amazon.com"));
startActivity(i);
```

The action portion defines what you want to do, whereas the data portion contains the data for the target activity to act upon. You can also pass the data to the `Intent` object using the `setData()` method:

```
Intent i = new
        Intent("android.intent.action.VIEW");
i.setData(Uri.parse("http://www.amazon.com"));
```

In this example, you indicate that you want to view a web page with the specified URL. The Android OS will look for all activities that are able to satisfy your request. This process is known as *intent resolution*. The next section discusses in more detail how your activities can be the target of other activities.

For some intents, there is no need to specify the data. For example, to select a contact from the Contacts application, you specify the action and then indicate the MIME type using the `setType()` method:

```
Intent i = new
    Intent(android.content.Intent.ACTION_PICK);
i.setType(ContactsContract.Contacts.CONTENT_TYPE);
```

> **NOTE** *Chapter 9 discusses how to use the Contacts application from within your application.*

The `setType()` method explicitly specifies the MIME data type to indicate the type of data to return. The MIME type for `ContactsContract.Contacts.CONTENT_TYPE` is `"vnd.android.cursor.dir/contact"`.

Besides specifying the action, the data, and the type, an `Intent` object can also specify a category. A category groups activities into logical units so that Android can use those activities for further filtering. The next section discusses categories in more detail.

To summarize, an `Intent` object can contain the following information:

- Action
- Data
- Type
- Category

Using Intent Filters

Earlier, you saw how an activity can invoke another activity using the `Intent` object. In order for other activities to invoke your activity, you need to specify the action and category within the `<intent-filter>` element in the `AndroidManifest.xml` file, like this:

```
<intent-filter >
       <action android:name="com.jfdimarzio.SecondActivity" />
       <category android:name="android.intent.category.DEFAULT" />
</intent-filter>
```

This is a very simple example in which one activity calls another using the `"com.jfdimarzio.SecondActivity"` action.

DISPLAYING NOTIFICATIONS

So far, you have been using the `Toast` class to display messages to the user. While the `Toast` class is a handy way to show users alerts, it is not persistent. It flashes on the screen for a few seconds and then disappears. If it contains important information, users may easily miss it if they are not looking at the screen.

For messages that are important, you should use a more persistent method. In this case, you should use the `NotificationManager` to display a persistent message at the top of the device, commonly known as the *status bar* (sometimes also referred to as the *notification bar*). The following Try It Out demonstrates how.

TRY IT OUT Displaying Notifications on the Status Bar (Notifications.zip)

1. Using Android Studio, create a new Android project and name it **Notifications**.
2. Add a new class file named `NotificationView` to the package. In addition, add a new `notification.xml` layout resource file to the `res/layout` folder.
3. Populate the `notification.xml` file as follows. Be sure to change all instances of `"com.jfdimarzio"` to whatever package name your project is using)

```
<?xml version="1.0" encoding="utf-8"?>
<LinearLayout xmlns:android="http://schemas.android.com/apk/res/android"
    android:orientation="vertical" android:layout_width="match_parent"
    android:layout_height="match_parent">
    <TextView
        android:layout_width="fill_parent"
        android:layout_height="wrap_content"
        android:text="Here are the details for the notification..." />
</LinearLayout>
```

4. Populate the `NotificationView.java` file as follows:

```
package com.jfdimarzio.notifications;

import android.app.Activity;
import android.app.NotificationManager;
import android.os.Bundle;

public class NotificationView extends Activity {

    @Override
    public void onCreate(Bundle savedInstanceState)
    {
        super.onCreate(savedInstanceState);
        setContentView(R.layout.notification);
```

```
        //---look up the notification manager service---
        NotificationManager nm = (NotificationManager)
                getSystemService(NOTIFICATION_SERVICE);
        //---cancel the notification that we started---
        nm.cancel(getIntent().getExtras().getInt("notificationID"));
    }

}
```

5. Add the following statements in bold to the `AndroidManifest.xml` file:

```
<?xml version="1.0" encoding="utf-8"?>
<manifest xmlns:android="http://schemas.android.com/apk/res/android"
    package="com.jfdimarzio.notifications">
    <uses-permission android:name="android.permission.VIBRATE"/>
    <application
        android:allowBackup="true"
        android:icon="@mipmap/ic_launcher"
        android:label="@string/app_name"
        android:supportsRtl="true"
        android:theme="@style/AppTheme">
        <activity android:name=".MainActivity">
            <intent-filter>
                <action android:name="android.intent.action.MAIN" />

                <category android:name="android.intent.category.LAUNCHER" />
            </intent-filter>
        </activity>
        <activity android:name=".NotificationView"
             android:label="Details of notification">
             <intent-filter>
                 <action android:name="android.intent.action.MAIN" />
                 <category android:name="android.intent.category.DEFAULT" />
             </intent-filter>
         </activity>
    </application>

</manifest>
```

6. Add the following statements in bold to the `activity_main.xml` file:

```
<?xml version="1.0" encoding="utf-8"?>
<RelativeLayout xmlns:android="http://schemas.android.com/apk/res/android"
    xmlns:tools="http://schemas.android.com/tools"
    android:layout_width="match_parent"
    android:layout_height="match_parent"
    android:paddingBottom="@dimen/activity_vertical_margin"
    android:paddingLeft="@dimen/activity_horizontal_margin"
    android:paddingRight="@dimen/activity_horizontal_margin"
    android:paddingTop="@dimen/activity_vertical_margin"
    tools:context="com.jfdimarzio.notifications.MainActivity">

    <Button
        android:id="@+id/btn_displaynotif"
```

```
        android:layout_width="fill_parent"
        android:layout_height="wrap_content"
        android:text="Display Notification"
        android:onClick="onClick"/>
</RelativeLayout>
```

7. Add the following statements in bold to the `MainActivity.java` file:

```
package com.jfdimarzio.notifications;

import android.app.Activity;
import android.app.NotificationManager;
import android.app.PendingIntent;
import android.content.Intent;
import android.os.Bundle;
import android.support.v4.app.NotificationCompat;
import android.view.View;

public class MainActivity extends Activity {
    int notificationID = 1;
    @Override
    protected void onCreate(Bundle savedInstanceState) {
        super.onCreate(savedInstanceState);
        setContentView(R.layout.activity_main);
    }
    public void onClick(View view) {
        displayNotification();
    }

    protected void displayNotification()
    {
        //---PendingIntent to launch activity if the user selects
        // this notification---
        Intent i = new Intent(this, NotificationView.class);
        i.putExtra("notificationID", notificationID);
        PendingIntent pendingIntent = PendingIntent.getActivity(this, 0, i, 0);
        NotificationManager nm = (NotificationManager)getSystemService
          (NOTIFICATION_SERVICE);
        NotificationCompat.Builder notifBuilder;
        notifBuilder = new NotificationCompat.Builder(this)
                .setSmallIcon(R.mipmap.ic_launcher)
                .setContentTitle("Meeting Reminder")
                .setContentText("Reminder: Meeting starts in 5 minutes");
        nm.notify(notificationID, notifBuilder.build());
    }
}
```

8. Press Shift+F9 to debug the application on the Android emulator.
9. Click the Display Notification button and a notification ticker text (set in the constructor of the `Notification` object) displays on the status bar.
10. Click and drag the status bar down to reveal the notification details set using the `setLatestEventInfo()` method of the `Notification` object (see Figure 3-19).

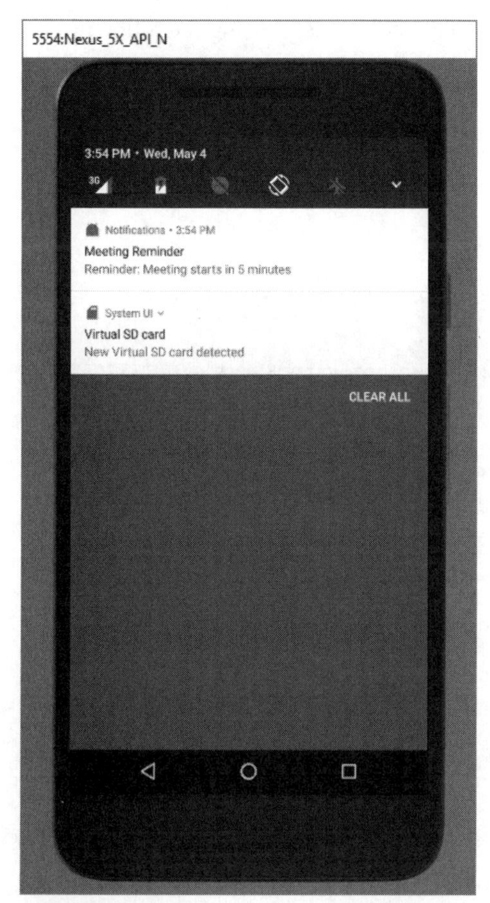

FIGURE 3-19

How It Works

To display a notification, you first created an `Intent` object to point to the `NotificationView` class:

```
Intent i = new Intent(this, NotificationView.class);
i.putExtra("notificationID", notificationID);
```

This intent is used to launch another activity when the user selects a notification from the list. In this example, you added a name/value pair to the `Intent` object so that you can tag the notification ID, identifying the notification to the target activity. Later, you will use this ID to dismiss the notification.

You also need to create a `PendingIntent` object. A `PendingIntent` object helps you to perform an action on your application's behalf, often at a later time, regardless of whether your application is running. In this case, you initialized it as follows:

```
PendingIntent pendingIntent =
    PendingIntent.getActivity(this, 0, i, 0);
```

The `getActivity()` method retrieves a `PendingIntent` object and you set it using the following arguments:

- **context**—Application context
- **request code**—Request code for the intent
- **intent**—The intent for launching the target activity
- **flags**—The flags in which the activity is to be launched

You then obtain an instance of the `NotificationManager` class and create an instance of the `NotificationCompat.Builder` class:

```
NotificationManager nm = (NotificationManager)getSystemService(NOTIFICATION
  _SERVICE);
 NotificationCompat.Builder notifBuilder;
 notifBuilder = new NotificationCompat.Builder(this)
         .setSmallIcon(R.mipmap.ic_launcher)
         .setContentTitle("Meeting Reminder")
         .setContentText("Reminder: Meeting starts in 5 minutes");
```

The `NotificationCompat.Builder` class enables you to specify the notification's main information.

Finally, to display the notification you use the `notify()` method:

```
nm.notify(notificationID, notifBuilder.build());
```

SUMMARY

This chapter first provided a detailed look at how activities and fragments work and the various forms in which you can display them. You also learned how to display dialog windows using activities.

The second part of this chapter demonstrated a very important concept in Android—the intent. The intent is the "glue" that enables different activities to be connected, and it is a vital concept to understand when developing for the Android platform.

EXERCISES

1. To create an activity, you create a Java class that extends what base class?
2. What attribute of the Application element is used to specify the theme?
3. What method do you override when displaying a dialog?
4. What is used to navigate between activities?
5. What method should you use if you plan on receiving information back from an activity?

You can find answers to the exercises in the appendix.

▶ WHAT YOU LEARNED IN THIS CHAPTER

TOPIC	KEY CONCEPTS
Creating an activity	All activities must be declared in the `AndroidManifest.xml` file.
Key life cycle of an activity	When an activity is started, the `onStart()` and `onResume()` events are always called. When an activity is killed or sent to the background, the `onPause()` event is always called.
Displaying an activity as a dialog	Use the `showDialog()` method and implement the `onCreateDialog()` method.
Fragments	Fragments are "mini-activities" that you can add or remove from activities.
Manipulating fragments programmatically	You need to use the `FragmentManager` and `FragmentTransaction` classes when adding, removing, or replacing fragments during runtime.
Life cycle of a fragment	Similar to that of an activity—you save the state of a fragment in the `onPause()` event, and restore its state in one of the following events: `onCreate()`, `onCreateView()`, or `onActivityCreated()`.
Intent	The "glue" that connects different activities.
Calling an activity	Use the `startActivity()` or `startActivityForResult()` method.
Passing data to an activity	Use the `Bundle` object.
Components in an `Intent` object	An `Intent` object can contain the following: action, data, type, and category.
Displaying notifications	Use the `NotificationManager` class.

Getting to Know the Android User Interface

WHAT YOU WILL LEARN IN THIS CHAPTER

- How ViewGroups and Layouts can be used to lay out your views and organize your application screen
- How to adapt and manage changes in screen orientation
- How to create the UI programmatically
- How to listen for UI notifications

> ***CODE DOWNLOAD*** *The wrox.com code downloads for this chapter are found at* `www.wrox.com/go/beginningandroidprog` *on the Download Code tab. The code is in the chapter 04 download and individually named according to the names throughout the chapter.*

Chapter 3 discusses activities and their life cycles. An activity is a means by which users interact with the application. However, an activity by itself does not have a presence on the screen. Instead, it has to draw the screen using *views* and *ViewGroups*. In this chapter, you find out how to create user interfaces (UIs) in Android and how users interact with the UIs. In addition, you discover how to handle changes in screen orientation on your Android devices.

UNDERSTANDING THE COMPONENTS OF A SCREEN

As explained in Chapter 3, the basic unit of an Android application is an *activity*, which displays the UI of your application. The activity may contain widgets such as buttons, labels, textboxes, and so on. Typically, you define your UI using an XML file (for example, the `activity_main.xml` file located in the `res/layout` folder of your project), which looks similar to what is shown in here.

```
<?xml version="1.0" encoding="utf-8"?>
<android.support.design.widget.CoordinatorLayout
xmlns:android="http://schemas.android.com/apk/res/android"
    xmlns:app="http://schemas.android.com/apk/res-auto"
    xmlns:tools="http://schemas.android.com/tools"
    android:layout_width="match_parent"
    android:layout_height="match_parent"
    android:fitsSystemWindows="true"
    tools:context="com.jfdimarzio.helloworld.MainActivity">

    <android.support.design.widget.AppBarLayout
        android:layout_width="match_parent"
        android:layout_height="wrap_content"
        android:theme="@style/AppTheme.AppBarOverlay">

        <android.support.v7.widget.Toolbar
            android:id="@+id/toolbar"
            android:layout_width="match_parent"
            android:layout_height="?attr/actionBarSize"
            android:background="?attr/colorPrimary"
            app:popupTheme="@style/AppTheme.PopupOverlay" />

    </android.support.design.widget.AppBarLayout>

    <include layout="@layout/content_main" />

    <android.support.design.widget.FloatingActionButton
        android:id="@+id/fab"
        android:layout_width="wrap_content"
        android:layout_height="wrap_content"
        android:layout_gravity="bottom|end"
        android:layout_margin="@dimen/fab_margin"
        android:src="@android:drawable/ic_dialog_email" />

</android.support.design.widget.CoordinatorLayout>
```

During runtime, you load the XML UI in the `onCreate()` method handler in your `Activity` class, using the `setContentView()` method of the `Activity` class:

```
    @Override
    public void onCreate(Bundle savedInstanceState) {
        super.onCreate(savedInstanceState);
        setContentView(R.layout.main);
    }
```

During compilation, each element in the XML file is compiled into its equivalent Android GUI (Graphical User Interface) class, with attributes represented by methods. The Android system then creates the activity's UI when the activity is loaded.

> ***NOTE*** *Although it is always easier to build your UI using an XML file, sometimes you need to build your UI dynamically during runtime (for example, when writing games). Hence, it is also possible to create your UI entirely using code. Later in this chapter is an example showing how to create a UI using code.*

Views and ViewGroups

An activity contains *views* and *ViewGroups*. A view is a widget that has an appearance on screen. Examples of views are buttons, labels, and text boxes. A view derives from the base class `android.view.View`.

> ***NOTE*** *Chapters 5 and 6 discuss the various common views in Android.*

One or more views can be grouped into a ViewGroup. A ViewGroup (which is itself a special type of view) provides the layout in which you can order the appearance and sequence of views. Examples of ViewGroups include `RadioGroup` and `ScrollView`. A ViewGroup derives from the base class `android.view.ViewGroup`.

Another type of ViewGroup is a `Layout`. A `Layout` is another container that derives from `android.view.ViewGroup` and is used as a container for other views. However, whereas the purpose of a ViewGroup is to group views logically—such as a group of buttons with a similar purpose—a `Layout` is used to group and arrange views visually on the screen. The `Layouts` available to you in Android are as follows:

- `FrameLayout`
- `LinearLayout (Horizontal)`
- `LinearLayout (Vertical)`
- `TableLayout`
- `TableRow`
- `GridLayout`
- `RelativeLayout`

The following sections describe each of these `Layouts` in more detail.

> ***NOTE*** *One of the great things about Android development, is that you can mix and match multiple Layouts to create a truly unique control layout for your application.*

FrameLayout

The `FrameLayout` is the most basic of the Android layouts. `FrameLayouts` are built to hold one view. As with all things related to development, there is no hard rule that `FrameLayouts` can't be used to hold multiple views. However, there is a reason why `FrameLayouts` were built the way they were.

Given that there are myriad screen sizes and resolutions, you have little control over the specifications of the devices that install your application. Therefore, when your application is resized and reformatted to fit any number of different devices you want to make sure it still looks as close to your initial design as possible.

The `FrameLayout` is used to help you control the stacking of single views as the screen is resized. In the following Try It Out, you add a `TextView` to a `FrameLayout` in your `HelloWorld` application.

TRY IT OUT Place a TextView Within a FrameLayout

Using the HelloWorld project you created in Chapters 1 and 2, create a new layout resource file for your application, add a `FrameLayout` to the new layout resource, and finally place a `TextView` within the `FrameLayout`.

1. Open the HelloWorld project in Android Studio.
2. Right-click the `res/layout` folder and add a new layout resource file. Name the file **framelayout_example.xml**.
4. Using the design panel, drag the `FrameLayout` and place it anywhere on the device screen.
5. Using the design panel, drag a `Plain TextView` and place it in the `FrameLayout`.
6. Type some text into the `Plain TextView`.

How It Works

The `FrameLayout` displays the `Plain TextView` as a free-floating control. The original purpose of the `FrameLayout` was to hold a single element. However, it can be used to hold more.

LinearLayout (Horizontal) and LinearLayout (Vertical)

The `LinearLayout` arranges views in a single column or a single row. Child views can be arranged either horizontally or vertically, which explains the need for two different layouts—one for horizontal rows of views and one for vertical columns of views.

> ***NOTE*** *`LinearLayout (Horizontal)` and `LinearLayout (Vertical)` are actually the same layout with one property changed. Later in this section, you find out how the `android:orientation` property of the `LinearLayout` controls if the application has a horizontal or vertical flow.*

To see how `LinearLayout` works, consider the following elements typically contained in the `activity_main.xml` file:

```
<?xml version="1.0" encoding="utf-8"?>
<LinearLayout xmlns:android="http://schemas.android.com/apk/res/android"
    android:layout_width="fill_parent"
    android:layout_height="fill_parent"
    android:orientation="vertical" >
    <TextView
        android:layout_width="fill_parent"
        android:layout_height="wrap_content"
        android:text="@string/hello" />
</LinearLayout>
```

In the `activity_main.xml` file, observe that the root element is `<LinearLayout>` and it has a `<TextView>` element contained within it. The `<LinearLayout>` element controls the order in which the views contained within it appear.

Each view and ViewGroup has a set of common attributes, some of which are described in Table 4-1.

TABLE 4-1: Common Attributes Used in Views and ViewGroups

ATTRIBUTE	DESCRIPTION
`layout_width`	Specifies the width of the view or ViewGroup
`layout_height`	Specifies the height of the view or ViewGroup
`layout_marginTop`	Specifies extra space on the top side of the view or ViewGroup
`layout_marginBottom`	Specifies extra space on the bottom side of the view or ViewGroup
`layout_marginLeft`	Specifies extra space on the left side of the view or ViewGroup
`layout_marginRight`	Specifies extra space on the right side of the view or ViewGroup
`layout_gravity`	Specifies how child views are positioned
`layout_weight`	Specifies how much of the extra space in the layout should be allocated to the view
`layout_x`	Specifies the x-coordinate of the view or ViewGroup
`layout_y`	Specifies the y-coordinate of the view or ViewGroup

> ***NOTE*** *Some of these attributes are applicable only when a view is in a specific ViewGroup. For example, the* `layout_weight` *and* `layout_gravity` *attributes are applicable only when a view is in either a* `LinearLayout` *or a* `TableLayout`.

For example, the width of the `<TextView>` element fills the entire width of its parent (which is the screen in this case) using the `fill_parent` constant. Its height is indicated by the `wrap_content` constant, which means that its height is the height of its content (in this case, the text contained within it). If you don't want the `<TextView>` view to occupy the entire row, you can set its `layout_width` attribute to `wrap_content`, like this:

```
<TextView
        android:layout_width="wrap_content"
        android:layout_height="wrap_content"
        android:text="@string/hello" />
```

The preceding code sets the width of the view to be equal to the width of the text contained within it. Consider the layout in the next code snippet, which shows two views with their width explicitly stated as a measurement, and their heights set to the height of their contents.

```
<?xml version="1.0" encoding="utf-8"?>
<LinearLayout xmlns:android="http://schemas.android.com/apk/res/android"
    android:layout_width="fill_parent"
    android:layout_height="fill_parent"
    android:orientation="vertical" >
<TextView
    android:layout_width="100dp"
    android:layout_height="wrap_content"
    android:text="@string/hello" />
<Button
    android:layout_width="160dp"
    android:layout_height="wrap_content"
    android:text="Button"
    android:onClick="onClick" />
</LinearLayout>
```

UNITS OF MEASUREMENT

When specifying the size of an element on an Android UI, you should be aware of the following units of measurement:

- `dp`—Density-independent pixel. 1 `dp` is equivalent to one pixel on a 160 dpi screen. This is the recommended unit of measurement when you're specifying the dimension of views in your layout. The 160 dpi screen is the baseline density assumed by Android. You can specify either `dp` or `dip` when referring to a density-independent pixel.
- `sp`—Scale-independent pixel. This is similar to `dp` and is recommended for specifying font sizes.

- `pt`—Point. A point is defined to be 1/72 of an inch, based on the physical screen size.
- `px`—Pixel. Corresponds to actual pixels on the screen. Using this unit is not recommended, as your UI might not render correctly on devices with a different screen resolution.

Here, you set the width of both the `TextView` and `Button` views to an absolute value. In this case, the width for the `TextView` is set to 100 density-independent pixels wide, and the `Button` to 160 density-independent pixels wide. Before you see how the views look on different screens with different pixel densities, it is important to understand how Android recognizes screens of varying sizes and densities.

Figure 4-1 shows the screen of the Nexus 5 (from the emulator). It has a 5-inch screen (diagonally), with a screen width of 2.72 inches. Its resolution is 1080 (width) × 1920 (height) pixels. The pixel density of a screen varies according to screen size and resolution.

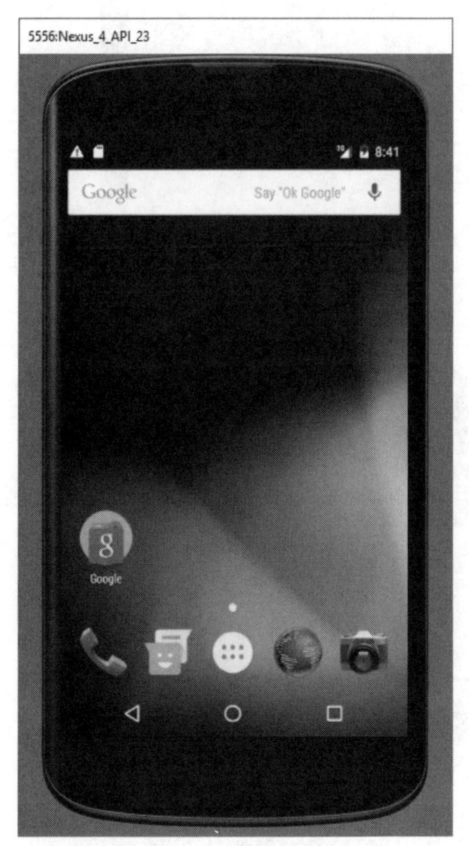

FIGURE 4-1

To test how the views defined in the XML file look when displayed on screens of different densities, create two Android Virtual Devices (AVDs) with different screen resolutions and abstracted LCD densities. Figure 4-2 shows an AVD with 1080 × 1920 resolution and LCD density of 480.

Figure 4-3 shows another AVD with 768 × 1280 resolution and LCD density of 320.

Using the `dp` unit ensures that your views are always displayed in the right proportion regardless of the screen density. Android automatically scales the size of the view depending on the density of the screen.

FIGURE 4-2

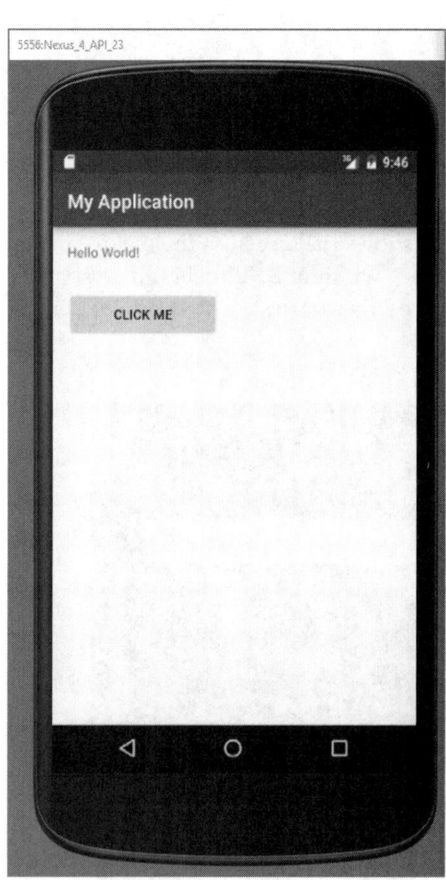

FIGURE 4-3

HOW TO CONVERT DP TO PX

The formula for converting `dp` to `px` (pixels) is as follows:

Actual pixels = `dp` * (dpi / 160), where dpi is either 120, 160, 240, or 320.

Therefore, in the case of the `Button` on a 235 dpi screen, its actual width is 160 * (240/160) = 240 `px`. When run on the 180 dpi emulator (regarded as a 160 dpi device), its actual pixel width is now 160 * (160/160) = 160 `px`. In this case, one `dp` is equivalent to one `px`.

To prove that this is indeed correct, you can use the `getWidth()` method of a `View` object to get its width in pixels:

```
public void onClick(View view) {
    Toast.makeText(this,
        String.valueOf(view.getWidth()),
        Toast.LENGTH_LONG).show();
}
```

What if instead of using `dp` you now specify the size using pixels (`px`)?

```
<TextView
    android:layout_width="100px"
    android:layout_height="wrap_content"
    android:text="@string/hello" />
<Button
    android:layout_width="160px"
    android:layout_height="wrap_content"
    android:text="Click Me"
    android:onClick="onClick"/>
```

Figure 4-4 shows how the `Label` and `Button` appear on a 480 dpi screen. Figure 4-5 shows the same views on a 320 dpi screen. In this case, Android does not perform any conversion because all the sizes are specified in pixels. If you use pixels for view sizes, the views appear smaller on a device with a high dpi screen than a screen with a lower dpi (assuming screen sizes are the same).

FIGURE 4-4

FIGURE 4-5

The preceding example also specifies that the orientation of the layout is vertical:

```
<LinearLayout xmlns:android="http://schemas.android.com/apk/res/android"
    android:layout_width="fill_parent"
    android:layout_height="fill_parent"
    android:orientation="vertical" >
```

The default orientation layout is horizontal, so if you omit the `android:orientation` attribute, the views appear as shown in Figure 4-6.

FIGURE 4-6

In `LinearLayout`, you can apply the `layout_weight` and `layout_gravity` attributes to views contained within it, as the modifications to `activity_main.xml` in the following code snippet show:

```
<?xml version="1.0" encoding="utf-8"?>
<LinearLayout xmlns:android="http://schemas.android.com/apk/res/android"
    android:layout_width="fill_parent"
    android:layout_height="fill_parent"
    android:orientation="vertical" >
```

```
<Button
android:layout_width="160dp"
    android:layout_height="0dp"
    android:text="Button"
    android:layout_gravity="left"
    android:layout_weight="1" />
<Button
android:layout_width="160dp"
    android:layout_height="0dp"
    android:text="Button"
    android:layout_gravity="center"
    android:layout_weight="2" />
<Button
android:layout_width="160dp"
    android:layout_height="0dp"
    android:text="Button"
    android:layout_gravity="right"
    android:layout_weight="3" />
    </LinearLayout>
```

Figure 4-7 shows the positioning of the views as well as their heights. The `layout_gravity` attribute indicates the positions the views should gravitate toward, whereas the `layout_weight` attribute specifies the distribution of available space. In the preceding example, the three buttons occupy about 16.6 percent (1/(1+2+3) * 100), 33.3 percent (2/(1+2+3) * 100), and 50 percent (3/(1+2+3) * 100) of the available height, respectively.

> ***NOTE*** *The height of each button is set to 0* `dp` *because the layout orientation is vertical.*

If you change the orientation of the `LinearLayout` to horizontal (as shown in the following code snippet), you need to change the width of each view to 0 `dp`. The views display as shown in Figure 4-8:

```
<LinearLayout xmlns:android="http://schemas.android.com/apk/res/android"
    android:layout_width="fill_parent"
    android:layout_height="fill_parent"
    android:orientation="horizontal" >
<Button
    android:layout_width="0dp"
    android:layout_height="wrap_content"
    android:text="Button"
    android:layout_gravity="left"
    android:layout_weight="1" />
<Button
    android:layout_width="0dp"
    android:layout_height="wrap_content"
```

```
        android:text="Button"
        android:layout_gravity="center_horizontal"
        android:layout_weight="2" />
    <Button
        android:layout_width="0dp"
        android:layout_height="wrap_content"
        android:text="Button"
        android:layout_gravity="right"
        android:layout_weight="3" />
</LinearLayout>
```

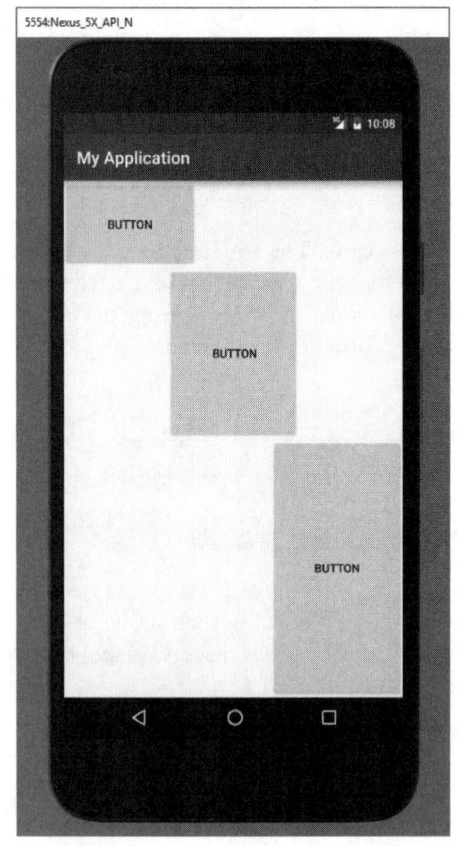

FIGURE 4-7

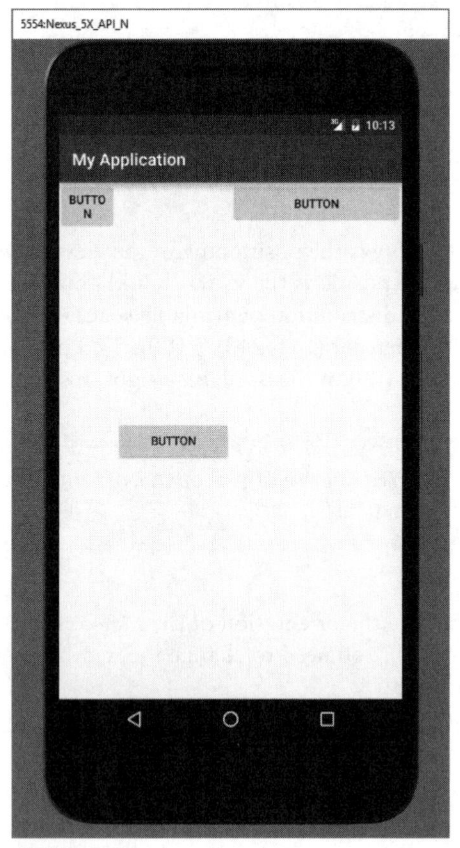

FIGURE 4-8

In the following Try It Out, you combine multiple `LinearLayouts` to create an L-shaped configuration of views.

TRY IT OUT Combine Two LinearLayouts with Different Orientations

Use two `LinearLayouts`, one with a vertical orientation and one with a horizontal orientation to place three `TextViews` and three `Buttons` in the configuration shown in Figure 4-9.

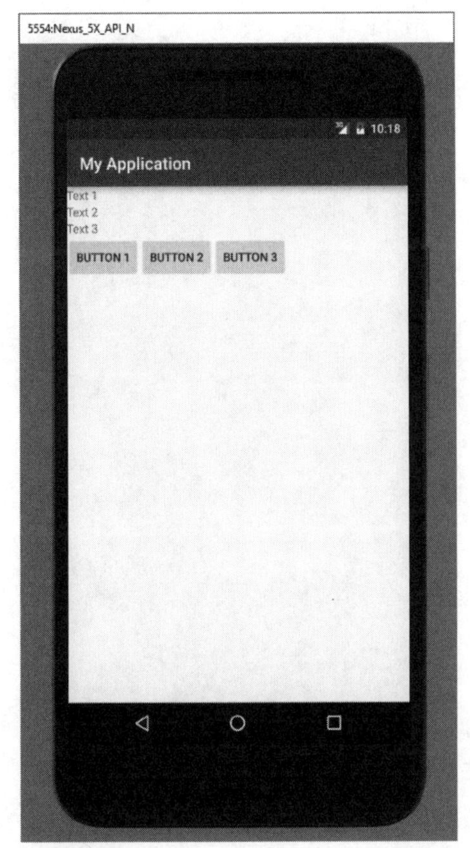

FIGURE 4-9

1. Create a new layout resource file named `linearlayouts_example.xml`. By default, this new file will be created with a `LinearLayout` (Vertical).
2. Place three stacked `TextViews` in a single column within the `LinearLayout`.
3. Place a `LinearLayout` (Horizontal) under the third `TextView`.
4. Place three buttons in a row within the `LinearLayout` (Horizontal).

How It Works

Layouts can be combined in many different configurations to produce almost any look imaginable. In this example, you use a vertical and a horizontal `LinearLayout` to create an L-shaped layout. Your finished `.xml` file should look like this:

```
<?xml version="1.0" encoding="utf-8"?>
<LinearLayout xmlns:android="http://schemas.android.com/apk/res/android"
    android:layout_width="fill_parent"
```

```
    android:layout_height="fill_parent"
    android:orientation="vertical" >

    <TextView
        android:layout_width="wrap_content"
        android:layout_height="wrap_content"
        android:text="Text 1"
        android:id="@+id/textView" />

    <TextView
        android:layout_width="wrap_content"
        android:layout_height="wrap_content"
        android:text="Text 2"
        android:id="@+id/textView2" />

    <TextView
        android:layout_width="wrap_content"
        android:layout_height="wrap_content"
        android:text="Text 3"
        android:id="@+id/textView3" />

    <LinearLayout
        android:orientation="horizontal"
        android:layout_width="match_parent"
        android:layout_height="wrap_content">

        <Button
            android:layout_width="wrap_content"
            android:layout_height="wrap_content"
            android:text="Button 1"
            android:id="@+id/button" />

        <Button
            android:layout_width="wrap_content"
            android:layout_height="wrap_content"
            android:text="Button 2"
            android:id="@+id/button2" />

        <Button
            android:layout_width="wrap_content"
            android:layout_height="wrap_content"
            android:text="Button 3"
            android:id="@+id/button3" />
    </LinearLayout>
</LinearLayout>
```

TableLayout

The `TableLayout` Layout groups views into rows and columns. You use the `<TableRow>` element to designate a row in the table. Each row can contain one or more views. Each view you place within a row forms a cell. The width of each column is determined by the largest width of each cell in that column.

Consider the content of `activity_main.xml` shown here:

```
<TableLayout
    xmlns:android="http://schemas.android.com/apk/res/android"
    android:layout_height="fill_parent"
    android:layout_width="fill_parent" >
    <TableRow>
        <TextView
            android:text="User Name:"
            android:width ="120dp"
            />
        <EditText
            android:id="@+id/txtUserName"
            android:width="200dp" />
    </TableRow>
    <TableRow>
        <TextView
            android:text="Password:"
            />
        <EditText
            android:id="@+id/txtPassword"
            android:inputType="textPassword"
            />
    </TableRow>
    <TableRow>
        <TextView />
        <CheckBox android:id="@+id/chkRememberPassword"
            android:layout_width="fill_parent"
            android:layout_height="wrap_content"
            android:text="Remember Password"
            />
    </TableRow>
    <TableRow>
        <Button
            android:id="@+id/buttonSignIn"
            android:text="Log In" />
    </TableRow>
</TableLayout>
```

Figure 4-10 shows how the preceding code appears when rendered on the Android emulator.

> ***NOTE*** *In the preceding example, there are two columns and four rows in the* `TableLayout`*. The cell directly under the Password* `TextView` *is populated with a* `<TextView/>` *empty element. If you don't do this, the Remember Password check box will appear under the Password* `TextView`*, as shown in Figure 4-11.*

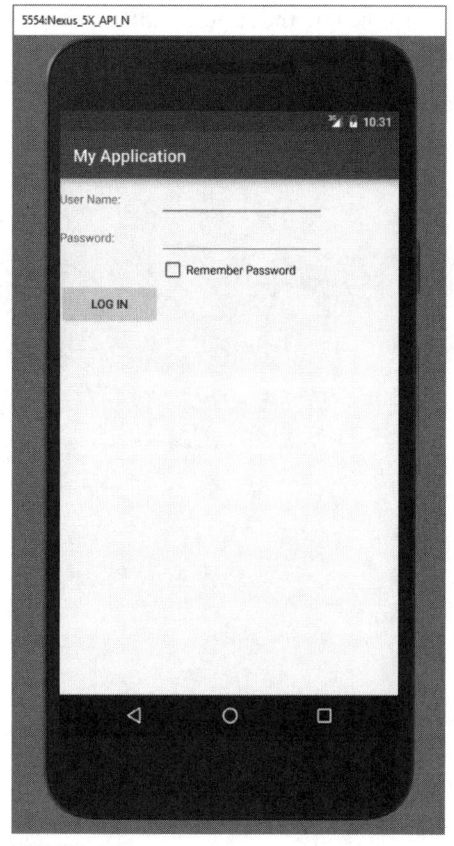

FIGURE 4-10

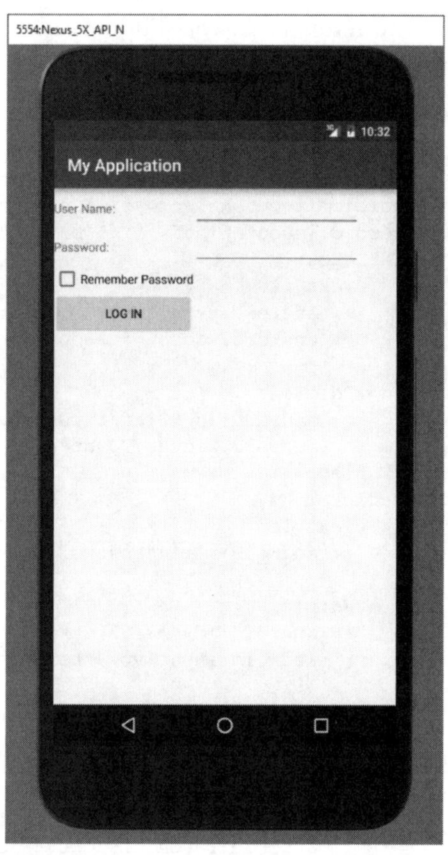

FIGURE 4-11

RelativeLayout

The `RelativeLayout` layout enables you to specify how child views are positioned relative to each other. Consider the following `activity_main.xml` file:

```
<?xml version="1.0" encoding="utf-8"?>
<RelativeLayout
    android:id="@+id/RLayout"
    android:layout_width="fill_parent"
    android:layout_height="fill_parent"
    xmlns:android="http://schemas.android.com/apk/res/android" >

    <TextView
        android:id="@+id/lblComments"
        android:layout_width="wrap_content"
        android:layout_height="wrap_content"
        android:text="Comments"
        android:layout_alignParentTop="true"
        android:layout_alignParentStart="true" />
```

```
        <EditText
            android:id="@+id/txtComments"
            android:layout_width="fill_parent"
            android:layout_height="170dp"
            android:textSize="18sp"
            android:layout_alignStart="@+id/lblComments"
            android:layout_below="@+id/lblComments"
            android:layout_centerHorizontal="true" />

        <Button
            android:id="@+id/btnSave"
            android:layout_width="125dp"
            android:layout_height="wrap_content"
            android:text="Save"
            android:layout_below="@+id/txtComments"
            android:layout_alignEnd="@+id/txtComments" />

        <Button
            android:id="@+id/btnCancel"
            android:layout_width="124dp"
            android:layout_height="wrap_content"
            android:text="Cancel"
            android:layout_below="@+id/txtComments"
            android:layout_alignStart="@+id/txtComments" />
    </RelativeLayout>
```

Notice that each view embedded within the `RelativeLayout` has attributes that enable it to align with another view. These attributes are as follows:

- `layout_alignParentTop`
- `layout_alignParentStart`
- `layout_alignStart`
- `layout_alignEnd`
- `layout_below`
- `layout_centerHorizontal`

The value for each of these attributes is the ID for the view that you are referencing. The preceding XML UI creates the screen shown in Figure 4-12.

FrameLayout

The `FrameLayout` layout is a placeholder on screen that you can use to display a single view. Views that you add to a `FrameLayout` are always anchored to the top left of the layout. Consider the following content in `main.xml`:

```
<?xml version="1.0" encoding="utf-8"?>
<RelativeLayout
    android:id="@+id/RLayout"
    android:layout_width="fill_parent"
```

```
    android:layout_height="fill_parent"
    xmlns:android="http://schemas.android.com/apk/res/android" >
    <TextView
        android:id="@+id/lblComments"
        android:layout_width="wrap_content"
        android:layout_height="wrap_content"
        android:text="Hello, Android!"
        android:layout_alignParentTop="true"
        android:layout_alignParentStart="true" />
    <FrameLayout
        android:layout_width="wrap_content"
        android:layout_height="wrap_content"
        android:layout_alignStart="@+id/lblComments"
        android:layout_below="@+id/lblComments"
        android:layout_centerHorizontal="true" >
        <ImageView
            android:src="@mipmap/butterfly"
        android:layout_width="wrap_content"
        android:layout_height="wrap_content" />
    </FrameLayout>
</RelativeLayout>
```

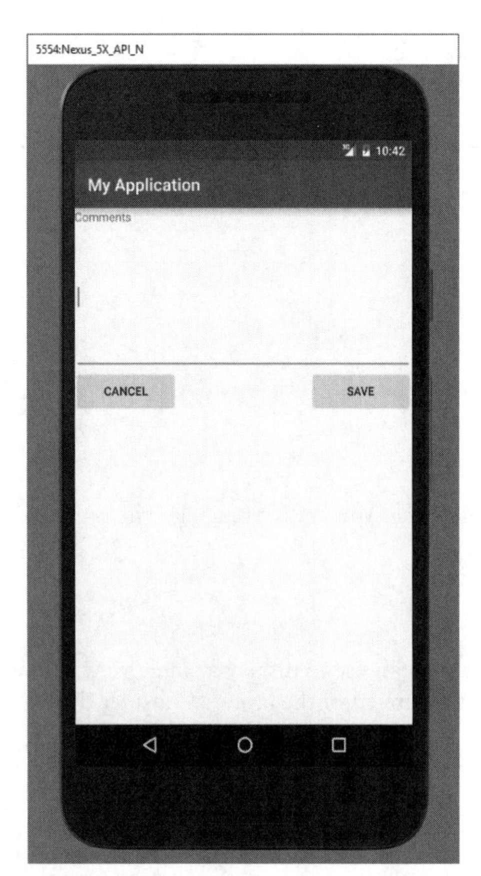

FIGURE 4-12

Here, you have a `FrameLayout` within a `RelativeLayout`. Within the `FrameLayout`, you embed an `ImageView`. The UI is shown in Figure 4-13.

FIGURE 4-13

> ***NOTE*** *This example assumes that the* `res/mipmap-hdpi` *folder has an image named* `butterfly.png`.

If you add another view (such as a `Button` view) within the `FrameLayout`, the view overlaps the previous view (see Figure 4-14):

```
<?xml version="1.0" encoding="utf-8"?>
<RelativeLayout
    android:id="@+id/RLayout"
    android:layout_width="fill_parent"
    android:layout_height="fill_parent"
    xmlns:android="http://schemas.android.com/apk/res/android" >
    <TextView
```

```
        android:id="@+id/lblComments"
        android:layout_width="wrap_content"
        android:layout_height="wrap_content"
        android:text="Hello, Android!"
        android:layout_alignParentTop="true"
        android:layout_alignParentStart="true" />
    <FrameLayout
        android:layout_width="wrap_content"
        android:layout_height="wrap_content"
        android:layout_alignStart="@+id/lblComments"
        android:layout_below="@+id/lblComments"
        android:layout_centerHorizontal="true" >
        <ImageView
            android:src="@mipmap/butterfly"
        android:layout_width="wrap_content"
        android:layout_height="wrap_content" />
        <Button
            android:layout_width="124dp"
            android:layout_height="wrap_content"
            android:text="Print Picture" />
    </FrameLayout>
```

FIGURE 4-14

> ***NOTE*** *You can add multiple views to a* `FrameLayout`*, but each is stacked on top of the previous one. This is when you want to animate a series of images, with only one visible at a time.*

ScrollView

A `ScrollView` is a special type of `FrameLayout` in that it enables users to scroll through a list of views that occupy more space than the physical display. The `ScrollView` can contain only one child view or ViewGroup, which normally is a `LinearLayout`.

> ***NOTE*** *Do not use a* `ListView` *(discussed in Chapter 5) with the* `ScrollView`*. The* `ListView` *is designed for showing a list of related information and is optimized for dealing with large lists.*

The following `main.xml` content shows a `ScrollView` containing a `LinearLayout`, which in turn contains some `Button` and `EditText` views:

```
<ScrollView
    android:layout_width="fill_parent"
    android:layout_height="fill_parent"
    xmlns:android="http://schemas.android.com/apk/res/android" >

    <LinearLayout
        android:layout_width="fill_parent"
        android:layout_height="wrap_content"
        android:orientation="vertical" >
        <Button
            android:id="@+id/button1"
            android:layout_width="fill_parent"
            android:layout_height="wrap_content"
            android:text="Button 1" />
        <Button
            android:id="@+id/button2"
            android:layout_width="fill_parent"
            android:layout_height="wrap_content"
            android:text="Button 2" />
        <Button
            android:id="@+id/button3"
            android:layout_width="fill_parent"
            android:layout_height="wrap_content"
            android:text="Button 3" />
        <EditText
            android:id="@+id/txt"
            android:layout_width="fill_parent"
            android:layout_height="600dp" />
```

```
        <Button
            android:id="@+id/button4"
            android:layout_width="fill_parent"
            android:layout_height="wrap_content"
            android:text="Button 4" />
        <Button
            android:id="@+id/button5"
            android:layout_width="fill_parent"
            android:layout_height="wrap_content"
            android:text="Button 5" />
    </LinearLayout>
</ScrollView>
```

If you load the preceding code on the Android emulator, you see something like what's shown in Figure 4-15.

FIGURE 4-15

Because the `EditText` automatically gets the focus, it fills up the entire activity (as the height was set to 600dp). To prevent it from getting the focus, add the following two bolded attributes to the `<LinearLayout>` element:

```
    <LinearLayout
        android:layout_width="fill_parent"
```

```
android:layout_height="wrap_content"
android:orientation="vertical"
 android:focusable="true"
 android:focusableInTouchMode="true" >
```

Now you are able to view the buttons and scroll through the list of views (see Figure 4-16).

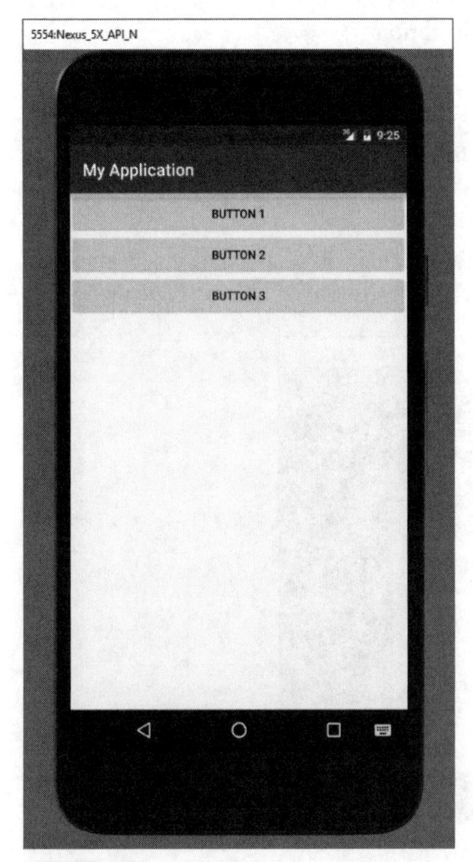

FIGURE 4-16

Sometimes you might want `EditText` to automatically get the focus, but you do not want the soft input panel (keyboard) to appear automatically (which happens on a real device). To prevent the keyboard from appearing, add the following bolded attribute to the `<activity>` element in the `AndroidManifest.xml` file:

```
<activity
    android:label="@string/app_name"
    android:name=".LayoutsActivity"
    android:windowSoftInputMode="stateHidden" >
    <intent-filter >
        <action android:name="android.intent.action.MAIN" />
        <category android:name="android.intent.category.LAUNCHER" />
    </intent-filter>
</activity>
```

ADAPTING TO DISPLAY ORIENTATION

One of the key features of modern smartphones is their ability to switch screen orientation, and Android is no exception. Android supports two screen orientations: *portrait* and *landscape*. By default, when you change the display orientation of your Android device, the current activity automatically redraws its content in the new orientation. This is because the `onCreate()` method of the activity is fired whenever there is a change in display orientation.

> **NOTE** *When you change the orientation of your Android device, your current activity is actually destroyed and then re-created.*

However, when the views are redrawn, they may be drawn in their original locations (depending on the layout selected). Figure 4-17 shows the previous example displayed in landscape mode.

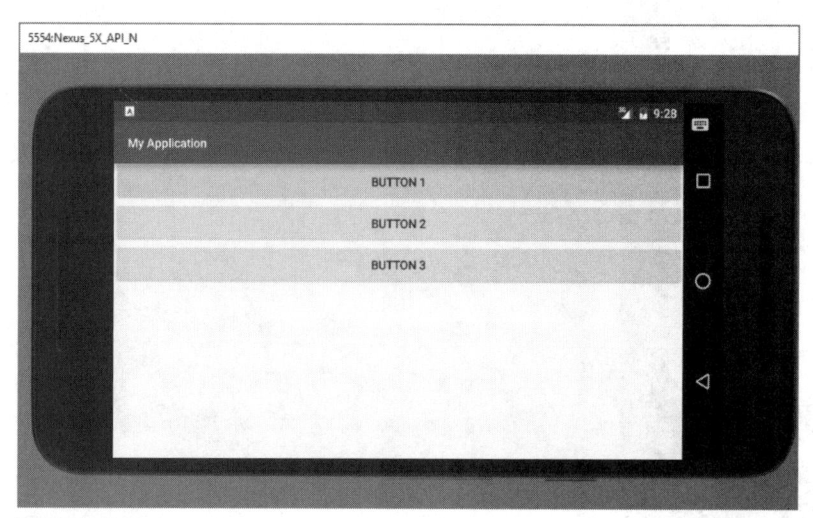

FIGURE 4-17

In general, you can employ two techniques to handle changes in screen orientation:

- **Anchoring**—The easiest way is to "anchor" your views to the four edges of the screen. When the screen orientation changes, the views can anchor neatly to the edges.
- **Resizing and repositioning**—Whereas anchoring and centralizing are simple techniques to ensure that views can handle changes in screen orientation, the ultimate technique is resizing each and every view according to the current screen orientation.

Anchoring Views

Anchoring can be easily achieved by using `RelativeLayout`. Consider the following `main.xml` file, which contains five `Button` views embedded within the `<RelativeLayout>` element:

```
<RelativeLayout
    android:layout_width="fill_parent"
    android:layout_height="fill_parent"
    xmlns:android="http://schemas.android.com/apk/res/android">
    <Button
        android:id="@+id/button1"
        android:layout_width="wrap_content"
        android:layout_height="wrap_content"
        android:text="Top Left"
        android:layout_alignParentStart="true"
        android:layout_alignParentTop="true" />
    <Button
        android:id="@+id/button2"
        android:layout_width="wrap_content"
        android:layout_height="wrap_content"
        android:text="Top Right"
        android:layout_alignParentTop="true"
        android:layout_alignParentEnd="true" />
    <Button
        android:id="@+id/button3"
        android:layout_width="wrap_content"
        android:layout_height="wrap_content"
        android:text="Bottom Left"
        android:layout_alignParentStart="true"
        android:layout_alignParentBottom="true" />
    <Button
        android:id="@+id/button4"
        android:layout_width="wrap_content"
        android:layout_height="wrap_content"
        android:text="Bottom Right"
        android:layout_alignParentEnd="true"
        android:layout_alignParentBottom="true" />
    <Button
        android:id="@+id/button5"
        android:layout_width="fill_parent"
        android:layout_height="wrap_content"
        android:text="Middle"
        android:layout_centerVertical="true"
        android:layout_centerHorizontal="true" />
</RelativeLayout>
```

Note the following attributes found in the various `Button` views:

- `layout_alignParentStart`—Aligns the view to the left of the parent view
- `layout_alignParentEnd`—Aligns the view to the right of the parent view

- `layout_alignParentTop`—Aligns the view to the top of the parent view
- `layout_alignParentBottom`—Aligns the view to the bottom of the parent view
- `layout_centerVertical`—Centers the view vertically within its parent view
- `layout_centerHorizontal`—Centers the view horizontally within its parent view

Figure 4-18 shows the activity when viewed in portrait mode.

When the screen orientation changes to landscape mode, the four buttons are aligned to the four edges of the screen, and the center button is centered in the middle of the screen with its width fully stretched (see Figure 4-19).

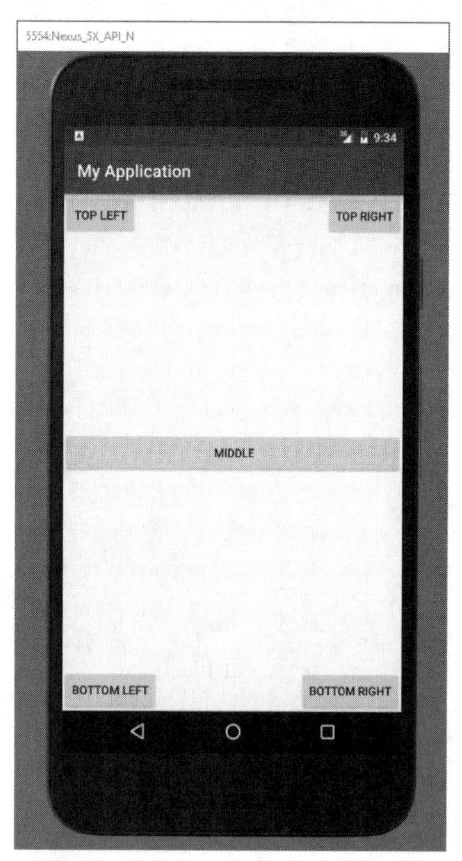

FIGURE 4-18

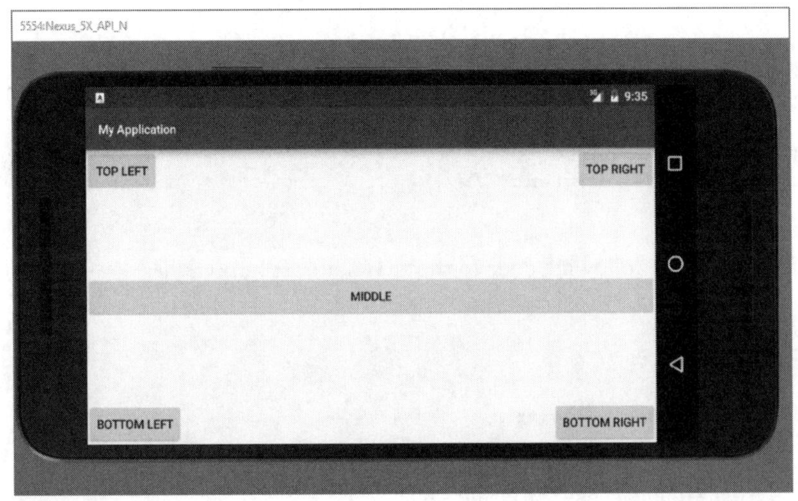

FIGURE 4-19

MANAGING CHANGES TO SCREEN ORIENTATION

Now that you have looked at screen orientation changes, let's explore what happens to an activity's state when the device changes orientation.

The following Try It Out demonstrates the behavior of an activity when the device changes orientation.

TRY IT OUT Understanding Activity Behavior When Orientation Changes (Orientations.zip)

1. Using Android Studio, create a new Android project and name it **Orientations**.
2. Add the bolded statements in the following code to the `activity_main.xml` file:

```
<?xml version="1.0" encoding="utf-8"?>
<LinearLayout xmlns:android="http://schemas.android.com/apk/res/android"
    android:layout_width="fill_parent"
    android:layout_height="fill_parent"
    android:orientation="vertical" >
```

```
<EditText
    android:id="@+id/txtField1"
    android:layout_width="fill_parent"
    android:layout_height="wrap_content" />
<EditText
    android:layout_width="fill_parent"
    android:layout_height="wrap_content" />
</LinearLayout>
```

3. Add the bolded statements in in the following code to the `MainActivity.java` file:

```
import android.app.Activity;
import android.os.Bundle;
import android.util.Log;

public class MainActivity extends Activity {

    @Override
    protected void onCreate(Bundle savedInstanceState) {
        super.onCreate(savedInstanceState);
        setContentView(R.layout.activity_main);
        Log.d("StateInfo", "onCreate");
    }

    @Override
    public void onStart() {
        Log.d("StateInfo", "onStart");
        super.onStart();
    }
    @Override
    public void onResume() {
        Log.d("StateInfo", "onResume");
        super.onResume();
    }
    @Override
    public void onPause() {
        Log.d("StateInfo", "onPause");
        super.onPause();
    }
    @Override
    public void onStop() {
        Log.d("StateInfo", "onStop");
        super.onStop();
    }
    @Override
    public void onDestroy() {
        Log.d("StateInfo", "onDestroy");
        super.onDestroy();
    }
```

```
        @Override
        public void onRestart() {
            Log.d("StateInfo", "onRestart");
            super.onRestart();
        }
    }
```

4. Press Shift+F9 to debug the application on the Android emulator.
5. Enter some text into the two `EditText` views (see Figure 4-20).

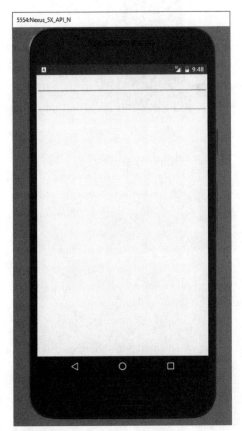

FIGURE 4-20

6. Change the orientation of the Android emulator by pressing Ctrl+Left. Figure 4-21 shows the emulator in landscape mode. Note that the text in the first `EditText` view is still visible, while the second `EditText` view is now empty.

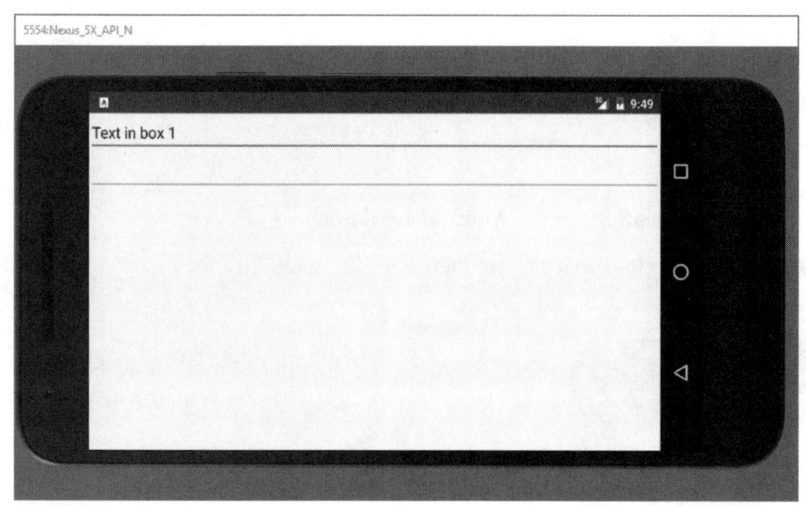

FIGURE 4-21

7. Observe the output in the logcat console. You should see something like this:

```
12-15 12:27:20.747: D/StateInfo(557): onCreate
12-15 12:27:20.747: D/StateInfo(557): onStart
12-15 12:27:20.747: D/StateInfo(557): onResume
...
12-15 12:39:37.846: D/StateInfo(557): onPause
12-15 12:39:37.846: D/StateInfo(557): onStop
12-15 12:39:37.866: D/StateInfo(557): onDestroy
12-15 12:39:38.206: D/StateInfo(557): onCreate
12-15 12:39:38.216: D/StateInfo(557): onStart
12-15 12:39:38.257: D/StateInfo(557): onResume
```

How It Works

From the output shown in the logcat console, it is apparent that when the device changes orientation, the activity is destroyed:

```
12-15 12:39:37.846: D/StateInfo(557): onPause
12-15 12:39:37.846: D/StateInfo(557): onStop
12-15 12:39:37.866: D/StateInfo(557): onDestroy
```

It is then re-created:

```
12-15 12:39:38.206: D/StateInfo(557): onCreate
12-15 12:39:38.216: D/StateInfo(557): onStart
12-15 12:39:38.257: D/StateInfo(557): onResume
```

It is important to understand this behavior because you need to ensure that you take the necessary steps to preserve the state of your activity before it changes orientation. For example, your activity might have variables containing values needed for some calculations in the activity. For any activity, you should save whatever state you need to save in the `onPause()` method, which is fired every time the activity changes orientation. The following section demonstrates the different ways to save this state information.

Another important behavior to understand is that only views that are named (via the `android:id` attribute) in an activity have their state persisted when the activity they are contained in is destroyed. For example, the user might change orientation while entering some text into an `EditText` view. When this happens, any text inside the `EditText` view is persisted and restored automatically when the activity is re-created. Conversely, if you do not name the `EditText` view using the `android:id` attribute, the activity isn't able to persist the text currently contained within it.

Persisting State Information During Changes in Configuration

So far, you have learned that changing screen orientation destroys an activity and re-creates it. Keep in mind that when an activity is re-created, its current state might be lost. When an activity is killed, it fires one or both of the following methods:

- `onPause()`—This method is always fired whenever an activity is killed or pushed into the background.
- `onSaveInstanceState()`—This method is also fired whenever an activity is about to be killed or put into the background (just like the `onPause()` method). However, unlike the `onPause()` method, the `onSaveInstanceState()` method is not fired when an activity is being unloaded from the stack (such as when the user pressed the back button) because there is no need to restore its state later.

In short, to preserve the state of an activity, you could always implement the `onPause()` method and then use your own ways to preserve the state of your activity, such as using a database, internal or external file storage, and so on.

If you simply want to preserve the state of an activity so that it can be restored later when the activity is re-created (such as when the device changes orientation), a much simpler way is to implement the `onSaveInstanceState()` method, as it provides a `Bundle` object as an argument so that you can use it to save your activity's state. The following code shows that you can save the string `ID` into the `Bundle` object during the `onSaveInstanceState()` method:

```
@Override
public void onSaveInstanceState(Bundle outState) {
    //---save whatever you need to persist---
    outState.putString("ID", "1234567890");
    super.onSaveInstanceState(outState);
}
```

When an activity is re-created, the `onCreate()` method is first fired, followed by the `onRestoreInstanceState()` method, which enables you to retrieve the state that you saved previously in the `onSaveInstanceState()` method through the `Bundle` object in its argument:

```
        @Override
        public void onRestoreInstanceState(Bundle savedInstanceState) {
            super.onRestoreInstanceState(savedInstanceState);
            //---retrieve the information persisted earlier---
            String ID = savedInstanceState.getString("ID");
        }
    }
```

> **NOTE** *When screen orientation changes, this change is part of what is known as a configuration change, which causes your current activity to be destroyed.*

Detecting Orientation Changes

Sometimes you need to know the device's current orientation during runtime. To determine that, you can use the `getResources()` method. The following code snippet demonstrates how you can programmatically detect the current orientation of your activity:

```
        @Override
        protected void onCreate(Bundle savedInstanceState) {
            super.onCreate(savedInstanceState);
            setContentView(R.layout.activity_main);

            if(getResources().getConfiguration().orientation == Configuration
    .ORIENTATION_LANDSCAPE){
                Log.d("StateInfo", "Landscape");
            }else if(getResources().getConfiguration().orientation == Configuration
    .ORIENTATION_PORTRAIT){
                Log.d("StateInfo", "Portrait");
            }
        }
```

The `getConfiguration()` method contains an orientation object representing the screen of the device. You can then test this against the Configuration set of constants to determine the orientation.

Controlling the Orientation of the Activity

Occasionally, you might want to ensure that your application is displayed in only a certain orientation. For example, you may be writing a game that should be viewed only in landscape mode. In this case, you can programmatically force a change in orientation using the `setRequestOrientation()` method of the `Activity` class:

```
    import android.content.pm.ActivityInfo;
        @Override
        public void onCreate(Bundle savedInstanceState) {
            super.onCreate(savedInstanceState);
            setContentView(R.layout.main);
```

```
            //---change to landscape mode---
            setRequestedOrientation(ActivityInfo.SCREEN_ORIENTATION_LANDSCAPE);
        }
```

To change to portrait mode, use the `ActivityInfo.SCREEN_ORIENTATION_PORTRAIT` constant.

Besides using the `setRequestOrientation()` method, you can also use the `android:screenOrientation` attribute on the `<activity>` element in `AndroidManifest.xml` as follows to constrain the activity to a certain orientation:

```
<?xml version="1.0" encoding="utf-8"?>
<manifest xmlns:android="http://schemas.android.com/apk/res/android"
    package="com.jfdimarzio.orientations">

    <application
        android:allowBackup="true"
        android:icon="@mipmap/ic_launcher"
        android:label="@string/app_name"
        android:supportsRtl="true"
        android:theme="@style/AppTheme">
        <activity android:name=".MainActivity"
            android:screenOrientation="landscape" >
            <intent-filter>
                <action android:name="android.intent.action.MAIN" />

                <category android:name="android.intent.category.LAUNCHER" />
            </intent-filter>
        </activity>
    </application>

</manifest>
```

The preceding example constrains the activity to a certain orientation (landscape in this case) and prevents the activity from being destroyed; that is, the activity will not be destroyed and the `onCreate()` method will not be fired again when the orientation of the device changes.

Following are two other values that you can specify in the `android:screenOrientation` attribute:

- `portrait`—Portrait mode
- `sensor`—Based on the accelerometer (default)

UTILIZING THE ACTION BAR

Besides fragments, another feature of Android is the Action Bar. In place of the traditional title bar located at the top of the device's screen, the Action Bar displays the application icon and the activity title. Optionally, on the right side of the Action Bar are action items. The next section discusses action items in more detail.

The following Try It Out shows how you can programmatically hide or display the Action Bar.

TRY IT OUT Showing and Hiding the Action Bar

1. Using Android Studio, create a new Android project and name it **MyActionBar**.
2. When prompted, select a Basic Activity as the template.
3. Press Shift+F9 to debug the application on the Android emulator. You should see the application and its Action Bar located at the top of the screen. The Action Bar contains the application icon and the application name MyActionBar as shown in Figure 4-22.

FIGURE 4-22

4. To hide the Action Bar, remove the bolded line from the `MainActivity.java` file:

```
import android.os.Bundle;
import android.support.design.widget.FloatingActionButton;
import android.support.design.widget.Snackbar;
import android.support.v7.app.AppCompatActivity;
```

```
import android.support.v7.widget.Toolbar;
import android.view.View;
import android.view.Menu;
import android.view.MenuItem;

public class MainActivity extends AppCompatActivity {

    @Override
    protected void onCreate(Bundle savedInstanceState) {
        super.onCreate(savedInstanceState);
        setContentView(R.layout.activity_main);
        Toolbar toolbar = (Toolbar) findViewById(R.id.toolbar);
        setSupportActionBar(toolbar);

        FloatingActionButton fab = (FloatingActionButton) findViewById(R.id.fab);
        fab.setOnClickListener(new View.OnClickListener() {
            @Override
            public void onClick(View view) {
                Snackbar.make(view, "Replace with your own action"
      , Snackbar.LENGTH_LONG)
                        .setAction("Action", null).show();
            }
        });
    }

    @Override
    public boolean onCreateOptionsMenu(Menu menu) {
        // Inflate the menu; this adds items to the action bar if it is present.
        getMenuInflater().inflate(R.menu.menu_main, menu);
        return true;
    }

    @Override
    public boolean onOptionsItemSelected(MenuItem item) {
        // Handle action bar item clicks here. The action bar will
        // automatically handle clicks on the Home/Up button, so long
        // as you specify a parent activity in AndroidManifest.xml.
        int id = item.getItemId();

        //noinspection SimplifiableIfStatement
        if (id == R.id.action_settings) {
            return true;
        }

        return super.onOptionsItemSelected(item);
    }
}
```

5. Press Shift+F9 to debug the application on the Android emulator again. This time, the Action Bar is not displayed (see Figure 4-23).

FIGURE 4-23

How It Works

The `setSupportActionBar()` method writes your Action Bar to the screen. The Action Bar can be an instance of a Tool Bar. In this case, Android has created an empty Tool Bar for you and then has set that Tool Bar to the Action Bar.

Adding Action Items to the Action Bar

Besides displaying the application icon and the activity title on the left of the Action Bar, you can also display additional items on the Action Bar. These additional items are called action items. *Action items* are shortcuts to some of the commonly performed operations in your application. For example, you might be building an RSS reader application, in which case some of the action items might be Refresh Feed, Delete Feed, and Add New Feed.

The following Try It Out shows how you can add action items to the Action Bar.

TRY IT OUT Adding Action Items

1. Using the MyActionBar project created in the previous section, modify the `MyActionBarActivity.java` file to appear as follows:

```
import android.os.Bundle;
import android.support.design.widget.FloatingActionButton;
import android.support.design.widget.Snackbar;
import android.support.v7.app.AppCompatActivity;
import android.support.v7.widget.Toolbar;
import android.view.View;
import android.view.Menu;
import android.view.MenuItem;
import android.widget.Toast;

public class MainActivity extends AppCompatActivity {

    @Override
    protected void onCreate(Bundle savedInstanceState) {
        super.onCreate(savedInstanceState);
        setContentView(R.layout.activity_main);
        Toolbar toolbar = (Toolbar) findViewById(R.id.toolbar);
        setSupportActionBar(toolbar);

        FloatingActionButton fab = (FloatingActionButton) findViewById(R.id.fab);
        fab.setOnClickListener(new View.OnClickListener() {
            @Override
            public void onClick(View view) {
                Snackbar.make(view,
"Replace with your own action", Snackbar.LENGTH_LONG)
                        .setAction("Action", null).show();
            }
        });
    }

    @Override
    public boolean onCreateOptionsMenu(Menu menu) {
        // Inflate the menu; this adds items to the action bar if it is present.
        //getMenuInflater().inflate(R.menu.menu_main, menu);
        CreateMenu(menu);
        return true;
    }
    private void CreateMenu(Menu menu)
    {
        MenuItem mnu1 = menu.add(0, 0, 0, "Item 1");
        {
            mnu1.setIcon(R.mipmap.ic_launcher);
            mnu1.setShowAsAction(MenuItem.SHOW_AS_ACTION_IF_ROOM);
        }
        MenuItem mnu2 = menu.add(0, 1, 1, "Item 2");
        {
            mnu2.setIcon(R.mipmap.ic_launcher);
```

```
            mnu2.setShowAsAction(MenuItem.SHOW_AS_ACTION_IF_ROOM);
        }
        MenuItem mnu3 = menu.add(0, 2, 2, "Item 3");
        {
            mnu3.setIcon(R.mipmap.ic_launcher);
            mnu3.setShowAsAction(MenuItem.SHOW_AS_ACTION_IF_ROOM);
        }
        MenuItem mnu4 = menu.add(0, 3, 3, "Item 4");
        {
            mnu4.setShowAsAction(MenuItem.SHOW_AS_ACTION_IF_ROOM);
        }
        MenuItem mnu5 = menu.add(0, 4, 4,"Item 5");
        {
            mnu5.setShowAsAction(MenuItem.SHOW_AS_ACTION_IF_ROOM);
        }
    }

    private boolean MenuChoice(MenuItem item)
    {
        switch (item.getItemId()) {
            case 0:
                Toast.makeText(this, "You clicked on Item 1",
                        Toast.LENGTH_LONG).show();
                return true;
            case 1:
                Toast.makeText(this, "You clicked on Item 2",
                        Toast.LENGTH_LONG).show();
                return true;
            case 2:
                Toast.makeText(this, "You clicked on Item 3",
                        Toast.LENGTH_LONG).show();
                return true;
            case 3:
                Toast.makeText(this, "You clicked on Item 4",
                        Toast.LENGTH_LONG).show();
                return true;
            case 4:
                Toast.makeText(this, "You clicked on Item 5",
                        Toast.LENGTH_LONG).show();
                return true;
        }
        return false;
    }


    @Override
    public boolean onOptionsItemSelected(MenuItem item) {
        // Handle action bar item clicks here. The action bar will
        // automatically handle clicks on the Home/Up button, so long
        // as you specify a parent activity in AndroidManifest.xml.
```

```
            int id = item.getItemId();

            //noinspection SimplifiableIfStatement
            if (id == R.id.action_settings) {
                return true;
            }

            return MenuChoice(item);
        }
    }
```

2. Press Shift+F9 to debug the application on the Android emulator. Observe the menu items on the right side of the Action Bar (see Figure 4-24). If you click the Menu button on the emulator, you see the rest of the menu items (see Figure 4-25). This is known as the *overflow menu*. On devices that do not have the Menu button, an overflow menu is represented by an icon with an arrow.
3. Clicking each menu item causes the `Toast` class to display the name of the menu item selected (see Figure 4-26).

FIGURE 4-24

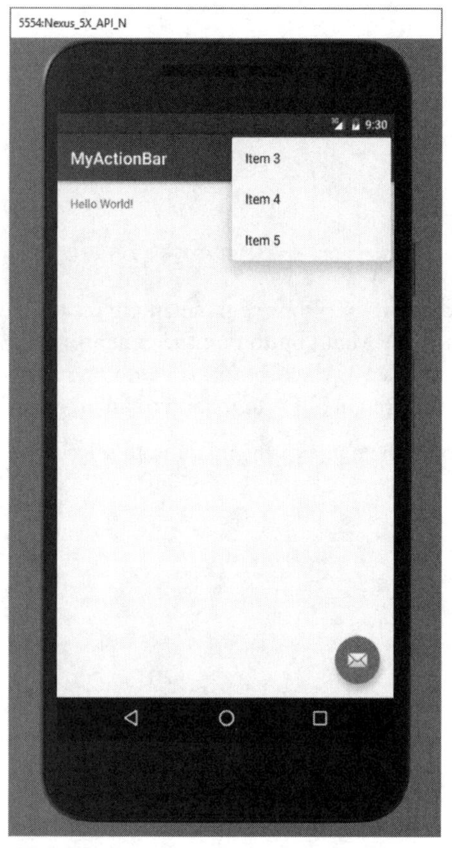

FIGURE 4-25

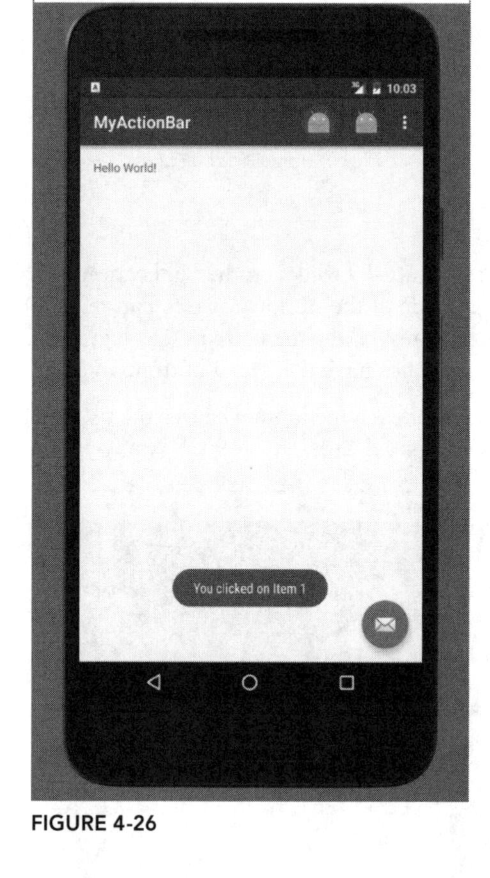

FIGURE 4-26

4. Press Control+Left to change the display orientation of the emulator to landscape mode. You now see five action items (three with icons and one with text) on the Action Bar, as shown in Figure 4-27.

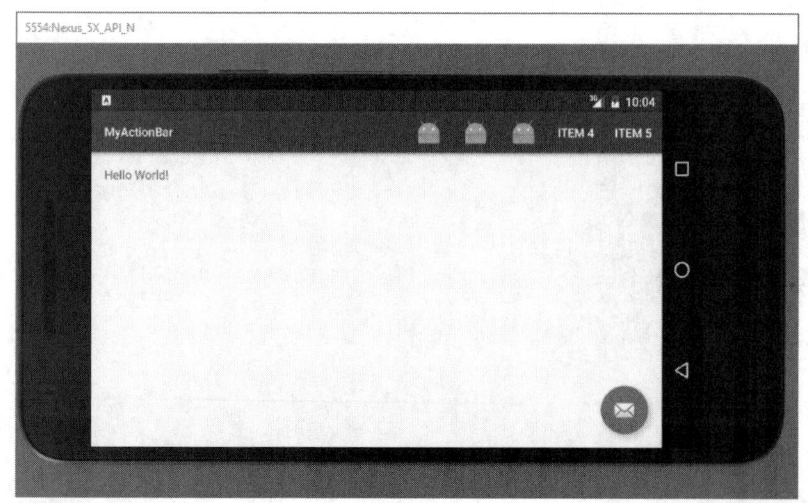

FIGURE 4-27

How It Works

The Action Bar populates its action items by calling the `onCreateOptionsMenu()` method of an activity:

```
@Override
public boolean onCreateOptionsMenu(Menu menu) {
    super.onCreateOptionsMenu(menu);
    CreateMenu(menu);
    return true;
}
```

In the preceding example, you called the `CreateMenu()` method to display a list of menu items:

```
private void CreateMenu(Menu menu)
    {
        MenuItem mnu1 = menu.add(0, 0, 0, "Item 1");
        {
            mnu1.setIcon(R.mipmap.ic_launcher);
            mnu1.setShowAsAction(MenuItem.SHOW_AS_ACTION_IF_ROOM);
        }
        MenuItem mnu2 = menu.add(0, 1, 1, "Item 2");
        {
            mnu2.setIcon(R.mipmap.ic_launcher);
            mnu2.setShowAsAction(MenuItem.SHOW_AS_ACTION_IF_ROOM);
        }
        MenuItem mnu3 = menu.add(0, 2, 2, "Item 3");
        {
            mnu3.setIcon(R.mipmap.ic_launcher);
            mnu3.setShowAsAction(MenuItem.SHOW_AS_ACTION_IF_ROOM);
        }
        MenuItem mnu4 = menu.add(0, 3, 3, "Item 4");
        {
            mnu4.setShowAsAction(MenuItem.SHOW_AS_ACTION_IF_ROOM);
        }
        MenuItem mnu5 = menu.add(0, 4, 4,"Item 5");
        {
            mnu5.setShowAsAction(MenuItem.SHOW_AS_ACTION_IF_ROOM);
        }
    }
```

To make the menu item appear as an action item, you call its `setShowAsAction()` method using the `SHOW_AS_ACTION_IF_ROOM` constant. This tells the Android device to display the menu item as an action item if there is room for it.

When a menu item is selected by the user, the `onOptionsItemSelected()` method is called:

```
@Override
public boolean onOptionsItemSelected(MenuItem item)
{
     return MenuChoice(item);
}
```

Here, you call the self-defined `MenuChoice()` method to check which menu item was clicked and then display a message:

```
private boolean MenuChoice(MenuItem item)
{
    switch (item.getItemId()) {
    case 0:
        Toast.makeText(this, "You clicked on Item 1",
            Toast.LENGTH_LONG).show();
        return true;
    case 1:
        Toast.makeText(this, "You clicked on Item 2",
            Toast.LENGTH_LONG).show();
        return true;
    case 2:
        Toast.makeText(this, "You clicked on Item 3",
            Toast.LENGTH_LONG).show();
        return true;
    case 3:
        Toast.makeText(this, "You clicked on Item 4",
            Toast.LENGTH_LONG).show();
        return true;
    case 4:
        Toast.makeText(this, "You clicked on Item 5",
            Toast.LENGTH_LONG).show();
        return true;
    }
    return false;
}
```

CREATING THE USER INTERFACE PROGRAMMATICALLY

So far, all the UIs you have seen in this chapter are created using XML. As mentioned earlier, besides using XML you can also create the UI using code. This approach is useful if your UI needs to be dynamically generated during runtime. For example, suppose you are building a cinema ticket reservation system and your application displays the seats of each cinema using buttons. In this case, you need to dynamically generate the UI based on the cinema selected by the user.

The following Try It Out demonstrates the code needed to dynamically build the UI in your activity.

TRY IT OUT Creating the UI via Code (UICode.zip)

1. Using Android Studio, create a new Android project and name it **UICode**.
2. In the `MainActivity.java` file, add the bold statements in the following code:

```
import android.support.v7.app.AppCompatActivity;
import android.os.Bundle;
import android.support.v7.widget.LinearLayoutCompat;
import android.widget.Button;
import android.widget.LinearLayout;
import android.widget.TextView;
```

```
public class MainActivity extends AppCompatActivity {

    @Override
    protected void onCreate(Bundle savedInstanceState) {
        super.onCreate(savedInstanceState);
        LinearLayoutCompat.LayoutParams params =
                new LinearLayoutCompat.LayoutParams(
                        LinearLayoutCompat.LayoutParams.WRAP_CONTENT,
                        LinearLayoutCompat.LayoutParams.WRAP_CONTENT);
        //---create a layout---
        LinearLayout layout = new LinearLayout(this);
        layout.setOrientation(LinearLayout.VERTICAL);
        //---create a textview---
        TextView tv = new TextView(this);
        tv.setText("This is a TextView");
        tv.setLayoutParams(params);
        //---create a button---
        Button btn = new Button(this);
        btn.setText("This is a Button");
        btn.setLayoutParams(params);

        //---adds the textview---
        layout.addView(tv);
        //---adds the button---
        layout.addView(btn);
        //---create a layout param for the layout---
        LinearLayoutCompat.LayoutParams layoutParam =
                new LinearLayoutCompat.LayoutParams(
                        LinearLayoutCompat.LayoutParams.WRAP_CONTENT,
                        LinearLayoutCompat.LayoutParams.WRAP_CONTENT );
        this.addContentView(layout, layoutParam);

    }
}
```

3. Press Shift+F9 to debug the application on the Android emulator. Figure 4-28 shows the activity.

How It Works

In this example, you first commented out the `setContentView()` statement so that it does not load the UI from the `activity_main.xml` file.

You then created a `LayoutParams` object to specify the layout parameter that can be used by other views (which you will create next):

```
//---create a layout param for the layout---
LinearLayoutCompat.LayoutParams layoutParam =
        new LinearLayoutCompat.LayoutParams(
                LinearLayoutCompat.LayoutParams.WRAP_CONTENT,
                LinearLayoutCompat.LayoutParams.WRAP_CONTENT );
```

You also created a `LinearLayout` object to contain all the views in your activity:

```
//---create a layout---
LinearLayout layout = new LinearLayout(this);
layout.setOrientation(LinearLayout.VERTICAL);
```

FIGURE 4-28

Next, you created a `TextView` and a `Button` view:

```
//---create a textview---
TextView tv = new TextView(this);
tv.setText("This is a TextView");
tv.setLayoutParams(params);
//---create a button---
Button btn = new Button(this);
btn.setText("This is a Button");
btn.setLayoutParams(params);
```

You then added them to the `LinearLayout` object:

```
//---adds the textview---
layout.addView(tv);
//---adds the button---
layout.addView(btn);
```

You also created a `LayoutParams` object to be used by the `LinearLayout` object:

```
//---create a layout param for the layout---
LinearLayout.LayoutParams layoutParam =
    new LinearLayout.LayoutParams(
```

```
LayoutParams.FILL_PARENT,
LayoutParams.WRAP_CONTENT );
```

Finally, you added the `LinearLayout` object to the activity:

```
this.addContentView(layout, layoutParam);
```

As you can see, using code to create the UI is quite a laborious affair. Hence, you should dynamically generate your UI using code only when necessary.

LISTENING FOR UI NOTIFICATIONS

Users interact with your UI at two levels: the activity level and the view level. At the activity level, the `Activity` class exposes methods that you can override. Some common methods that you can override in your activities include the following:

- `onKeyDown`—Called when a key was pressed and not handled by any of the views contained within the activity
- `onKeyUp`—Called when a key was released and not handled by any of the views contained within the activity
- `onMenuItemSelected`—Called when a panel's menu item has been selected by the user (covered in Chapter 6)
- `onMenuOpened`—Called when a panel's menu is opened by the user (covered in Chapter 6)

SUMMARY

In this chapter, you have learned how user interfaces are created in Android. You have also learned about the different layouts that you can use to position the views in your Android UI. Because Android devices support more than one screen orientation, you need to take special care to ensure that your UI can adapt to changes in screen orientation.

EXERCISES

1. What is the difference between the `dp` unit and the `px` unit? Which one should you use to specify the dimension of a view?
2. Why is the `AbsoluteLayout` not recommended for use?
3. What is the difference between the `onPause()` method and the `onSaveInstanceState()` method?
4. Name the three methods you can override to save an activity's state. In what instances should you use the various methods?
5. How do you add action items to the Action Bar?

You can find answers to the exercises in the appendix.

▶ WHAT YOU LEARNED IN THIS CHAPTER

TOPIC	KEY CONCEPTS
`LinearLayout`	Arranges views in a single column or single row.
`AbsoluteLayout`	Enables you to specify the exact location of its children.
`TableLayout`	Groups views into rows and columns.
`RelativeLayout`	Enables you to specify how child views are positioned relative to each other.
`FrameLayout`	A placeholder on screen that you can use to display a single view.
`ScrollView`	A special type of `FrameLayout` in that it enables users to scroll through a list of views that occupy more space than the physical display allows.
Unit of Measure	Use `dp` for specifying the dimension of views and `sp` for font size.
Two ways to adapt to changes in orientation	Anchoring, and resizing and repositioning.
Using different XML files for different orientations	Use the `layout` folder for portrait UI, and `layout-land` for landscape UI.
Three ways to persist activity state	Use the `onPause()` method. Use the `onSaveInstanceState()` method. Use the `onRetainNonConfigurationInstance()` method.
Getting the dimension of the current device	Use the `WindowManager` class's `getDefaultDisplay()` method.
Constraining the activity's orientation	Use the `setRequestOrientation()` method or the `android:screenOrientation` attribute in the `AndroidManifest.xml` file.
Action Bar	Replaces the traditional title bar for older versions of Android.
Action items	Action items are displayed on the right of the Action Bar. They are created just like options menus.
Application icon	Usually used to return to the "home" activity of an application. It is advisable to use the `Intent` object with the `Intent.FLAG_ACTIVITY_CLEAR_TOP` flag.

5

Designing Your User Interface with Views

WHAT YOU WILL LEARN IN THIS CHAPTER

- How to use the basic views in Android to design your user interface
- How to use the picker views to display lists of items
- How to use the list views to display lists of items
- How to use specialized fragments

> ***CODE DOWNLOAD*** *The wrox.com code downloads for this chapter are found at* `www.wrox.com/go/beginningandroidprog` *on the Download Code tab. The code is in the chapter 05 download and individually named according to the names throughout the chapter.*

In the previous chapter, you learned about the various layouts that you can use to position your views in an activity. You also learned about the techniques you can use to adapt to different screen resolutions and sizes. This chapter gives you a look at the various views that you can use to design the user interface (UI) for your applications.

In particular, the chapter covers the following ViewGroups:

- **Basic views**—Commonly used views, such as the `TextView`, `EditText`, and `Button` views
- **Picker views**—Views that enable users to select from a list, such as the `TimePicker` and `DatePicker` views

- **List views**—Views that display a long list of items, such as the `ListView` and the `SpinnerView` views
- **Specialized fragments**—Special fragments that perform specific functions

Subsequent chapters cover the other views not covered in this chapter, such as the analog and digital clock views and other views for displaying graphics, and so on.

USING BASIC VIEWS

To get started, this section explores some of the basic views that you can use to design the UI of your Android applications:

- `TextView`
- `EditText`
- `Button`
- `ImageButton`
- `CheckBox`
- `ToggleButton`
- `RadioButton`
- `RadioGroup`

These basic views enable you to display text information, as well as perform some basic selection. The following sections explore all these views in more detail.

TextView View

When you create a new Android project, Android Studio always creates the `activity_main.xml` file (located in the `res/layout` folder), which contains a `<TextView>` element:

```
<?xml version="1.0" encoding="utf-8"?>
<LinearLayout xmlns:android="http://schemas.android.com/apk/res/android"
    android:layout_width="fill_parent"
    android:layout_height="fill_parent"
    android:orientation="vertical" >
    <TextView
        android:layout_width="fill_parent"
        android:layout_height="wrap_content"
        android:text="@string/hello" />

</LinearLayout>
```

You use the `TextView` view to display text to the user. This is the most basic view and one that you will frequently use when you develop Android applications. If you need to allow users to edit the text displayed, you should use the subclass of `TextView`—`EditText`—which is discussed in the next section.

> **NOTE** *In some other platforms,* `TextView` *is commonly known as the Label View. Its sole purpose is to display text on the screen, and it is read only—the user cannot enter any text into a label.*

Button, ImageButton, EditText, CheckBox, ToggleButton, RadioButton, and RadioGroup Views

Besides the `TextView` view, which you will likely use the most often, there are some other basic views that you will find yourself frequently using:

- `Button`—Represents a push-button widget.
- `ImageButton`—Similar to the `Button` view, except that it also displays an image.
- `EditText`—A subclass of the `TextView` view, which allows users to edit its text content.
- `CheckBox`—A special type of button that has two states: checked or unchecked.
- `RadioGroup` and `RadioButton`—The `RadioButton` has two states: either checked or unchecked. A `RadioGroup` is used to group one or more `RadioButton` views, thereby allowing only one `RadioButton` to be checked within the `RadioGroup`.
- `ToggleButton`—Displays checked/unchecked states using a light indicator.

The following Try It Out provides details about how these views work.

TRY IT OUT Using the Basic Views (BasicViews1.zip)

1. Using Android Studio, create an Android project and name it **BasicViews1**.
2. Modify the `activity_main.xml` file located in the `res/layout` folder by adding the following elements shown in bold:

```
<?xml version="1.0" encoding="utf-8"?>
<LinearLayout xmlns:android="http://schemas.android.com/apk/res/android"
    android:layout_width="fill_parent"
    android:layout_height="fill_parent"
    android:orientation="vertical" >

<Button android:id="@+id/btnSave"
    android:layout_width="fill_parent"
    android:layout_height="wrap_content"
    android:text="save" />
<Button android:id="@+id/btnOpen"
    android:layout_width="wrap_content"
```

```
        android:layout_height="wrap_content"
        android:text="Open" />
    <ImageButton android:id="@+id/btnImg1"
        android:layout_width="fill_parent"
        android:layout_height="wrap_content"
        android:src="@mipmap/ic_launcher" />
    <EditText android:id="@+id/txtName"
        android:layout_width="fill_parent"
        android:layout_height="wrap_content" />
    <CheckBox android:id="@+id/chkAutosave"
        android:layout_width="fill_parent"
        android:layout_height="wrap_content"
        android:text="Autosave" />
    <CheckBox android:id="@+id/star"
        style="?android:attr/starStyle"
        android:layout_width="wrap_content"
        android:layout_height="wrap_content" />
    <RadioGroup android:id="@+id/rdbGp1"
        android:layout_width="fill_parent"
        android:layout_height="wrap_content"
        android:orientation="vertical" >

        <RadioButton android:id="@+id/rdb1"
            android:layout_width="fill_parent"
            android:layout_height="wrap_content"
            android:text="Option 1" />
        <RadioButton android:id="@+id/rdb2"
            android:layout_width="fill_parent"
            android:layout_height="wrap_content"
            android:text="Option 2" />
    </RadioGroup>
    <ToggleButton android:id="@+id/toggle1"
        android:layout_width="wrap_content"
        android:layout_height="wrap_content" />
    </LinearLayout>
```

3. To see the views in action, debug the project in Android Studio by pressing Shift+F9. Figure 5-1 shows the various views displayed in the Android emulator.
4. Click each of the views and note how they vary in look and feel. Figure 5-2 shows the following changes to the view:
    - The first `CheckBox` view (Autosave) is checked.
    - The second `CheckBox` View (star) is selected.
    - The second `RadioButton` (Option 2) is selected.
    - The `ToggleButton` is turned on.

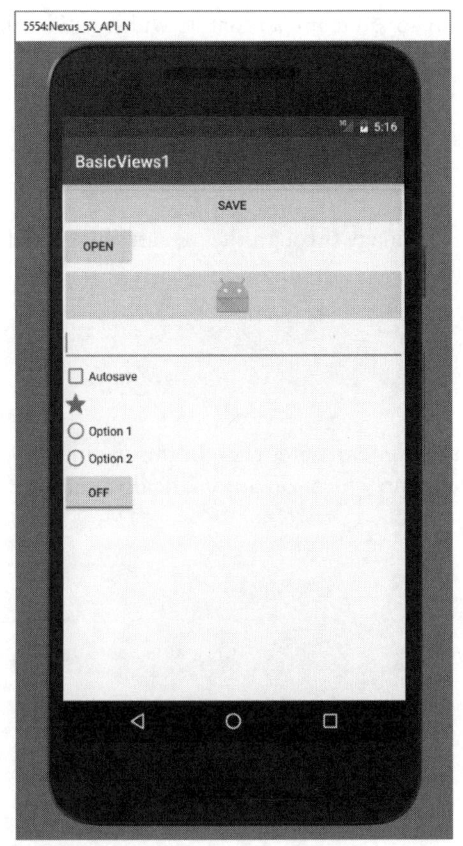

FIGURE 5-1

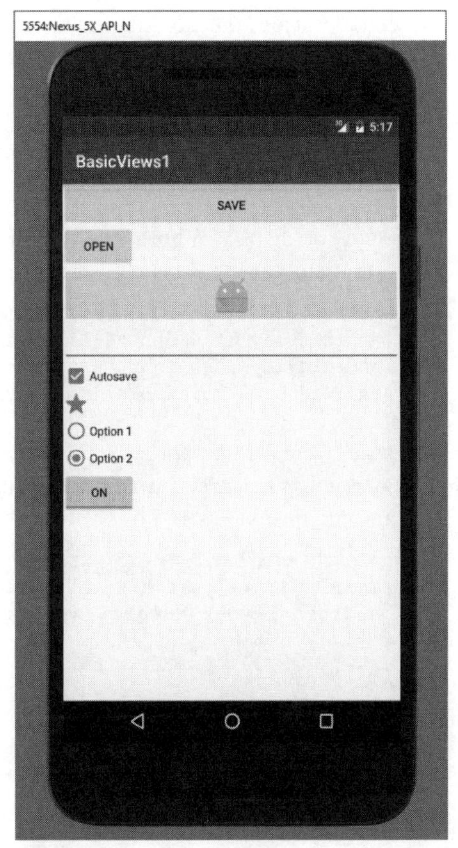

FIGURE 5-2

How It Works

So far, all the views are relatively straightforward. The views are listed using the `<LinearLayout>` element, so they are stacked on top of each other when they are displayed in the activity.

For the first `Button`, the `layout_width` attribute is set to `fill_parent`, which makes its width occupy the entire width of the screen:

```
<Button android:id="@+id/btnSave"
    android:layout_width="fill_parent"
    android:layout_height="wrap_content"
    android:text="save" />
```

For the second Button, the `layout_width` attribute is set to `wrap_content` so that its width will be the width of its content—specifically, the text that is displayed (for example, Open):

```
<Button android:id="@+id/btnOpen"
    android:layout_width="wrap_content"
    android:layout_height="wrap_content"
    android:text="Open" />
```

The `ImageButton` displays a button with an image. You set the image through the `src` attribute. In this code, note that an image has been used for the application icon:

```
<ImageButton android:id="@+id/btnImg1"
    android:layout_width="fill_parent"
    android:layout_height="wrap_content"
    android:src="@drawable/ic_launcher" />
```

The `EditText` view displays a rectangular region in which the user can enter text. In this example, `layout_height` has been set to `wrap_content` so that the text entry location automatically adjusts to fit the amount of text entered by the user (see Figure 5-3).

```
<EditText android:id="@+id/txtName"
    android:layout_width="fill_parent"
    android:layout_height="wrap_content" />
```

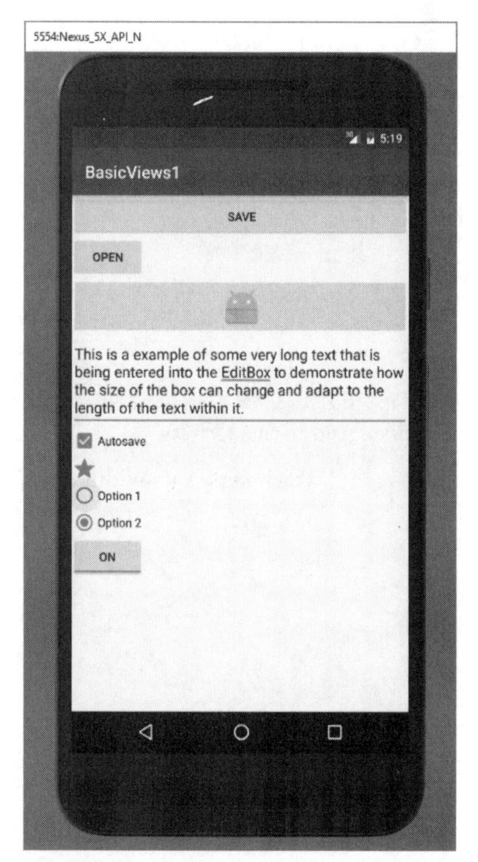

FIGURE 5-3

The CheckBox displays a check box that users can tap to check or uncheck:

```
<CheckBox android:id="@+id/chkAutosave"
    android:layout_width="fill_parent"
    android:layout_height="wrap_content"
    android:text="Autosave" />
```

If you do not like the default look of the CheckBox, you can apply a style attribute so that the check mark is replaced by another image, such as a star:

```
<CheckBox android:id="@+id/star"
    style="?android:attr/starStyle"
    android:layout_width="wrap_content"
    android:layout_height="wrap_content" />
```

The format for the value of the style attribute is as follows:

```
?[package:][type:]name
```

The RadioGroup encloses two RadioButtons. This is important because radio buttons are usually used to present multiple options to the user for selection. When a RadioButton in a RadioGroup is selected, all other RadioButtons are automatically unselected:

```
<RadioGroup android:id="@+id/rdbGp1"
    android:layout_width="fill_parent"
    android:layout_height="wrap_content"
    android:orientation="vertical" >

    <RadioButton android:id="@+id/rdb1"
        android:layout_width="fill_parent"
        android:layout_height="wrap_content"
        android:text="Option 1" />
    <RadioButton android:id="@+id/rdb2"
        android:layout_width="fill_parent"
        android:layout_height="wrap_content"
        android:text="Option 2" />
</RadioGroup>
```

Notice that the RadioButtons are listed vertically, one on top of another. If you want to list them horizontally, you need to change the orientation attribute to horizontal. You would also need to ensure that the layout_width attribute of the RadioButton views are set to wrap_content:

```
<RadioGroup android:id="@+id/rdbGp1"
    android:layout_width="fill_parent"
    android:layout_height="wrap_content"
    android:orientation="horizontal" >
    <RadioButton android:id="@+id/rdb1"
        android:layout_width="wrap_content"
        android:layout_height="wrap_content"
        android:text="Option 1" />
    <RadioButton android:id="@+id/rdb2"
        android:layout_width="wrap_content"
        android:layout_height="wrap_content"
        android:text="Option 2" />
</RadioGroup>
```

Figure 5-4 shows the `RadioButton` views displayed horizontally.

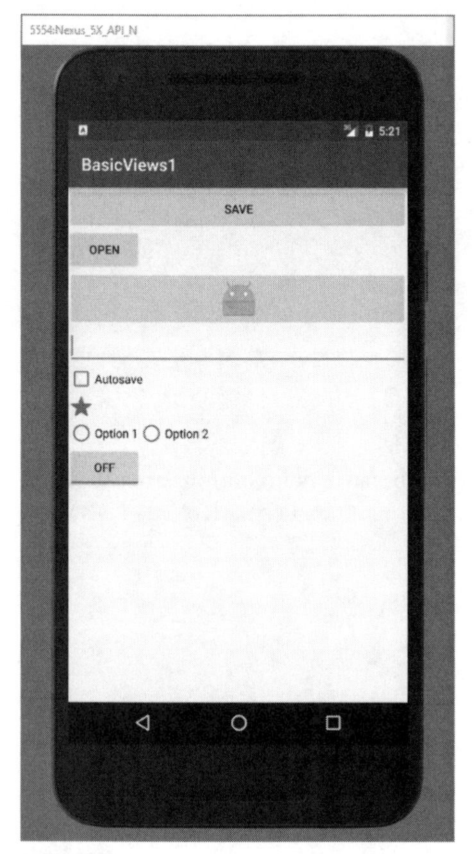

FIGURE 5-4

The `ToggleButton` displays a rectangular button that users can toggle on and off by clicking:

```
<ToggleButton android:id="@+id/toggle1"
    android:layout_width="wrap_content"
    android:layout_height="wrap_content" />
```

One thing that has been consistent throughout this example is that each view has the `id` attribute set to a particular value, such as in the case of the `Button`:

```
<Button android:id="@+id/btnSave"
    android:layout_width="fill_parent"
    android:layout_height="wrap_content"
    android:text="@string/save" />
```

The `id` attribute is an identifier for a view, which allows it to be retrieved using the `View.findViewById()` or `Activity.findViewById()` methods.

Now that you have seen what the various views for an activity look like, the following Try It Out demonstrates how you can programmatically control them.

TRY IT OUT Handling View Events

1. Using the BasicViews1 project you created in the previous Try It Out, modify the `MainActivity.java` file by adding the following bolded statements:

```
import android.support.v7.app.AppCompatActivity;
import android.os.Bundle;
import android.view.View;
import android.widget.Button;
import android.widget.CheckBox;
import android.widget.RadioButton;
import android.widget.RadioGroup;
import android.widget.Toast;
import android.widget.ToggleButton;

public class MainActivity extends AppCompatActivity {

    @Override
    protected void onCreate(Bundle savedInstanceState) {
        super.onCreate(savedInstanceState);
        setContentView(R.layout.activity_main);
        //---Button view---
        Button btnOpen = (Button) findViewById(R.id.btnOpen);
        btnOpen.setOnClickListener(new View.OnClickListener() {
            public void onClick(View v) {
                DisplayToast("You have clicked the Open button");
            }
        });
        //---Button view---
        Button btnSave = (Button) findViewById(R.id.btnSave);
        btnSave.setOnClickListener(new View.OnClickListener()
        {
            public void onClick(View v) {
                DisplayToast("You have clicked the Save button");
            }
        });
        //---CheckBox---
        CheckBox checkBox = (CheckBox) findViewById(R.id.chkAutosave);
        checkBox.setOnClickListener(new View.OnClickListener()
        {
            public void onClick(View v) {
                if (((CheckBox)v).isChecked())
                    DisplayToast("CheckBox is checked");
                else
                    DisplayToast("CheckBox is unchecked");
            }
        });
        //---RadioButton---
        RadioGroup radioGroup = (RadioGroup) findViewById(R.id.rdbGp1);
        radioGroup.setOnCheckedChangeListener(
```

```
        new RadioGroup.OnCheckedChangeListener()
            {
                public void onCheckedChanged(RadioGroup group, int checkedId) {
                    RadioButton rb1 = (RadioButton) findViewById(R.id.rdb1);
                    if (rb1.isChecked()) {
                        DisplayToast("Option 1 checked!");
                    } else {
                        DisplayToast("Option 2 checked!");
                    }
                }
            });
            //---ToggleButton---
            ToggleButton toggleButton =
                    (ToggleButton) findViewById(R.id.toggle1);
            toggleButton.setOnClickListener(new View.OnClickListener()
            {
                public void onClick(View v) {
                    if (((ToggleButton)v).isChecked())
                        DisplayToast("Toggle button is On");
                    else
                        DisplayToast("Toggle button is Off");
                }
            });
        }
        private void DisplayToast(String msg)
        {
            Toast.makeText(getBaseContext(), msg,
                    Toast.LENGTH_SHORT).show();
        }
    }
```

2. Press Shift+F9 to debug the project on the Android emulator.
3. Click each of the views and observe the message displayed in the Toast window.

How It Works

To handle the events fired by each view, you first must programmatically locate the view that you created during the `onCreate()` event. You do so using the `findViewById()` method (belonging to the `Activity` base class). You supply the `findViewById()` method with the ID of the view:

```
//---Button view---
Button btnOpen = (Button) findViewById(R.id.btnOpen);
```

The `setOnClickListener()` method registers a callback to be invoked later when the view is clicked:

```
btnOpen.setOnClickListener(new View.OnClickListener() {
    public void onClick(View v) {
        displayToast("You have clicked the Open button");
    }
});
```

The `onClick()` method is called when the view is clicked.

To determine the state of the CheckBox, you must typecast the argument of the onClick() method to a CheckBox and then verify its isChecked() method to see if it is checked:

```
CheckBox checkBox = (CheckBox) findViewById(R.id.chkAutosave);
checkBox.setOnClickListener(new View.OnClickListener()
{
    public void onClick(View v) {
        if (((CheckBox)v).isChecked())
            DisplayToast("CheckBox is checked");
        else
            DisplayToast("CheckBox is unchecked");
    }
});
```

For the RadioButton, you need to use the setOnCheckedChangeListener() method on the RadioGroup to register a callback to be invoked when the checked RadioButton changes in this group. The following code will work for two radio buttons, as in a yes/no selection on a form:

```
//---RadioButton---
RadioGroup radioGroup = (RadioGroup) findViewById(R.id.rdbGp1);
radioGroup.setOnCheckedChangeListener(new OnCheckedChangeListener()
{
    public void onCheckedChanged(RadioGroup group, int checkedId) {
        RadioButton rb1 = (RadioButton) findViewById(R.id.rdb1);
        if (rb1.isChecked()) {
            DisplayToast("Option 1 checked!");
        } else {
            DisplayToast("Option 2 checked!");
        }
    }
});
```

When a RadioButton is selected, the onCheckedChanged() method is fired. Within it, locate individual RadioButton views and then call each isChecked() method to determine which RadioButton is selected. Alternatively, the onCheckedChanged() method contains a second argument that contains a unique identifier of the selected RadioButton.

The ToggleButton works just like the CheckBox.

So far, to handle the events on the views, you first had to get a reference to the view and then register a callback to handle the event. However, there is another way to handle view events. Using the Button as an example, you can add an attribute called onClick:

```
<Button android:id="@+id/btnSave"
    android:layout_width="fill_parent"
    android:layout_height="wrap_content"
    android:text="@string/save"
    android:onClick="btnSaved_clicked"/>
```

The onClick attribute specifies the click event of the button. The value of this attribute is the name of the event handler. Therefore, to handle the button's click event, you simply create a method called btnSaved_clicked, as shown in the following example (note that the method must have a single parameter of type View):

```
public class BasicViews1Activity extends Activity {

    public void btnSaved_clicked (View view) {
        DisplayToast("You have clicked the Save button1");
    }

    /** Called when the activity is first created. */
    @Override
    public void onCreate(Bundle savedInstanceState) {
        super.onCreate(savedInstanceState);
        setContentView(R.layout.main);
        //...
    }
    private void DisplayToast(String msg)
    {
        Toast.makeText(getBaseContext(), msg,
                Toast.LENGTH_SHORT).show();
    }
}
```

If you compare the onClick approach to the callback method discussed previously, you'll see this is much simpler. Which method you use is really up to you, but this book mostly uses the onClick approach.

ProgressBar View

The ProgressBar view provides visual feedback about some ongoing tasks, such as when you are performing a task in the background. For example, you might be downloading some data from the web and need to update the user about the status of the download. In this case, the ProgressBar view is a good choice. The following activity demonstrates how to use the ProgressBar view.

TRY IT OUT Using the ProgressBar View (BasicViews2.zip)

1. Using Android Studio, create an Android project and name it **BasicViews2**.
2. Modify the activity_main.xml file located in the res/layout folder by adding the following code in bold:

```
<?xml version="1.0" encoding="utf-8"?>
<LinearLayout xmlns:android="http://schemas.android.com/apk/res/android"
    android:layout_width="fill_parent"
    android:layout_height="fill_parent"
    android:orientation="vertical" >
<ProgressBar android:id="@+id/progressbar"
    android:layout_width="wrap_content"
    android:layout_height="wrap_content" />
</LinearLayout>
```

3. In the `MainActivity.java` file, add the following bolded statements:

```
import android.os.Handler;
import android.support.v7.app.AppCompatActivity;
import android.os.Bundle;
import android.view.View;
import android.widget.ProgressBar;

public class MainActivity extends AppCompatActivity {
    static int progress;
    ProgressBar progressBar;
    int progressStatus = 0;
    Handler handler = new Handler();
    /** Called when the activity is first created. */
    @Override
    public void onCreate(Bundle savedInstanceState) {
        super.onCreate(savedInstanceState);
        setContentView(R.layout.activity_main);

        progress = 0;
        progressBar = (ProgressBar) findViewById(R.id.progressbar);
        //---do some work in background thread---
        new Thread(new Runnable()
        {
            public void run()
            {
                //---do some work here---
                while (progressStatus < 10)
                {
                    progressStatus = doSomeWork();
                }
                //---hides the progress bar---
                handler.post(new Runnable()
                {
                    public void run()
                    {
                        //---0 - VISIBLE; 4 - INVISIBLE; 8 - GONE---
                        progressBar.setVisibility(View.GONE);
                    }
                });
            }
            //---do some long running work here---
            private int doSomeWork()
            {
                try {
                    //---simulate doing some work---
                    Thread.sleep(500);
                } catch (InterruptedException e)
                {
                    e.printStackTrace();
                }
                return ++progress;
            }
        }).start();
    }
}
```

4. Press Shift+F9 to debug the project on the Android emulator. Figure 5-5 shows the `ProgressBar` animating. After about five seconds, it disappears.

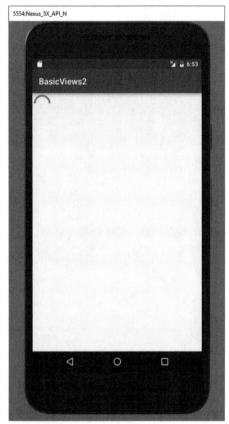

FIGURE 5-5

How It Works

The default mode of the `ProgressBar` view is indeterminate—that is, it shows a cyclic animation. This mode is useful for tasks that do not have specific completion times, such as when you are sending some data to a web service and waiting for the server to respond. If you simply put the `<ProgressBar>` element in your `main.xml` file, it continuously displays a spinning icon. It is your responsibility to stop it when your background task has completed.

The code added to the `MainActivity.java` file shows how you can spin off a background thread to simulate performing some long-running tasks. To do so, use the `Thread` class with a `Runnable` object. The `run()` method starts the execution of the thread, which in this case calls the `doSomeWork()` method to simulate doing some work. When the simulated work is done (after about five seconds), use a `Handler` object to send a message to the thread to dismiss the `ProgressBar`:

```
//---do some work in background thread---
new Thread(new Runnable()
{
```

```
            public void run()
            {
                //---do some work here---
                while (progressStatus < 10)
                {
                    progressStatus = doSomeWork();
                }
                //---hides the progress bar---
                handler.post(new Runnable()
                {
                    public void run()
                    {
                        //---0 - VISIBLE; 4 - INVISIBLE; 8 - GONE---
                        progressBar.setVisibility(View.GONE);
                    }
                });
            }
            //---do some long running work here---
            private int doSomeWork()
            {
                try {
                    //---simulate doing some work---
                    Thread.sleep(500);
                } catch (InterruptedException e)
                {
                    e.printStackTrace();
                }
                return ++progress;
            }
        }).start();
```

When the task is completed, hide the `ProgressBar` by setting its `Visibility` property to `View.GONE` (value `8`). There are two differences between the `INVISIBLE` constant and the `GONE` constant:

- `INVISIBLE` constant simply hides the `ProgressBar` (the region occupied by the `ProgressBar` is still taking up space in the activity).
- `GONE` constant removes the `ProgressBar` view from the activity and does not take up any space.

The next Try It Out shows how you can change the look of the `ProgressBar`.

TRY IT OUT Customizing the ProgressBar View

1. Using the BasicViews2 project created in the previous Try It Out, modify the `activity_main.xml` file as shown here:

```
<?xml version="1.0" encoding="utf-8"?>
<LinearLayout xmlns:android="http://schemas.android.com/apk/res/android"
    android:layout_width="fill_parent"
    android:layout_height="fill_parent"
    android:orientation="vertical" >
<ProgressBar android:id="@+id/progressbar"
```

```
    android:layout_width="wrap_content"
    android:layout_height="wrap_content"
    style="@android:style/Widget.ProgressBar.Horizontal" />
</LinearLayout>
```

2. Modify the `MainActivity.java` file by adding the following bolded statements:

```
import android.os.Handler;
import android.support.v7.app.AppCompatActivity;
import android.os.Bundle;
import android.view.View;
import android.widget.ProgressBar;

public class MainActivity extends AppCompatActivity {
    static int progress;
    ProgressBar progressBar;
    int progressStatus = 0;
    Handler handler = new Handler();
    /** Called when the activity is first created. */
    @Override
    public void onCreate(Bundle savedInstanceState) {
        super.onCreate(savedInstanceState);
        setContentView(R.layout.activity_main);

        progress = 0;
        progressBar = (ProgressBar) findViewById(R.id.progressbar);
        progressBar.setMax(200);

        //---do some work in background thread---
        new Thread(new Runnable()
        {
            public void run()
            {
                //---do some work here---
                while (progressStatus < 100)
                 {
                     progressStatus = doSomeWork();
                     //---Update the progress bar---
                     handler.post(new Runnable()
                     {
                         public void run() {
                             progressBar.setProgress(progressStatus);
                         }
                     });
                 }
                 //---hides the progress bar---
                 handler.post(new Runnable()
                 {
                     public void run()
                     {
                         //---0 - VISIBLE; 4 - INVISIBLE; 8 - GONE---
                         progressBar.setVisibility(View.GONE);
                     }
                 });
```

```
            }
            //---do some long running work here---
            private int doSomeWork()
            {
                try {
                    //---simulate doing some work---
                    Thread.sleep(500);
                } catch (InterruptedException e)
                {
                    e.printStackTrace();
                }
                return ++progress;
            }
        }).start();
    }
}
```

3. Press Shift+F9 to debug the project on the Android emulator.
4. Figure 5-6 shows the `ProgressBar` displaying the progress. The `ProgressBar` disappears when the progress reaches 50 percent.

FIGURE 5-6

How It Works

To make the `ProgressBar` display horizontally, simply set its `style` attribute to `@android:style/Widget.ProgressBar.Horizontal`:

```
<ProgressBar android:id="@+id/progressbar"
    android:layout_width="wrap_content"
    android:layout_height="wrap_content"
    style="@android:style/Widget.ProgressBar.Horizontal" />
```

To display the progress, call its `setProgress()` method, passing in an integer indicating its progress:

```
//---Update the progress bar---
handler.post(new Runnable()
{
    public void run() {
        progressBar.setProgress(progressStatus);
    }
});
```

In this example, set the range of the `ProgressBar` from 0 to 200 (via the `setMax()` method). This causes the `ProgressBar` to stop and then disappear when it is halfway through (because you only continue to call the `doSomeWork()` method as long as the `progressStatus` is less than 100). To ensure that the `ProgressBar` disappears only when the progress reaches 100%, either set the maximum value to 100 or modify the `while` loop to stop when the `progressStatus` reaches 200, like this:

```
//---do some work here---
while (progressStatus < 200)
```

Besides the horizontal style for the `ProgressBar` that you have used for this example, you can also use the following constants:

- `Widget.ProgressBar.Horizontal`
- `Widget.ProgressBar.Small`
- `Widget.ProgressBar.Large`
- `Widget.ProgressBar.Inverse`
- `Widget.ProgressBar.Small.Inverse`
- `Widget.ProgressBar.Large.Inverse`

AutoCompleteTextView View

The `AutoCompleteTextView` is a view that is similar to `EditText` (in fact it is a subclass of `EditText`), except that it automatically shows a list of completion suggestions while the user is typing. The following Try It Out shows how to use the `AutoCompleteTextView` to automatically help users complete the text entry.

TRY IT OUT Using the AutoCompleteTextView (BasicViews3.zip)

1. Using Android Studio, create an Android project and name it **BasicViews3**.
2. Modify the `activity_main.xml` file located in the `res/layout` folder as shown here in bold:

```
<?xml version="1.0" encoding="utf-8"?>
<LinearLayout xmlns:android="http://schemas.android.com/apk/res/android"
    android:layout_width="fill_parent"
    android:layout_height="fill_parent"
    android:orientation="vertical" >
<TextView
    android:layout_width="fill_parent"
    android:layout_height="wrap_content"
    android:text="Name of President" />
<AutoCompleteTextView android:id="@+id/txtCountries"
    android:layout_width="fill_parent"
    android:layout_height="wrap_content" />
</LinearLayout>
```

3. Add the following bolded statements to the `MainActivity.java` file:

```
import android.support.v7.app.AppCompatActivity;
import android.os.Bundle;

public class MainActivity extends AppCompatActivity {
    String[] presidents = {
            "Dwight D. Eisenhower",
            "John F. Kennedy",
            "Lyndon B. Johnson",
            "Richard Nixon",
            "Gerald Ford",
            "Jimmy Carter",
            "Ronald Reagan",
            "George H. W. Bush",
            "Bill Clinton",
            "George W. Bush",
            "Barack Obama"
    };
    /** Called when the activity is first created. */
    @Override
    public void onCreate(Bundle savedInstanceState) {
        super.onCreate(savedInstanceState);
        setContentView(R.layout.activity_main);

        ArrayAdapter<String> adapter = new ArrayAdapter<String>(this,
                android.R.layout.simple_dropdown_item_1line, presidents);
        AutoCompleteTextView textView = (AutoCompleteTextView)
                findViewById(R.id.txtCountries);
        textView.setThreshold(3);
        textView.setAdapter(adapter);
    }
}
```

4. Press Shift+F9 to debug the application on the Android emulator. As shown in Figure 5-7, a list of matching names appears as you type into the `AutoCompleteTextView` field.

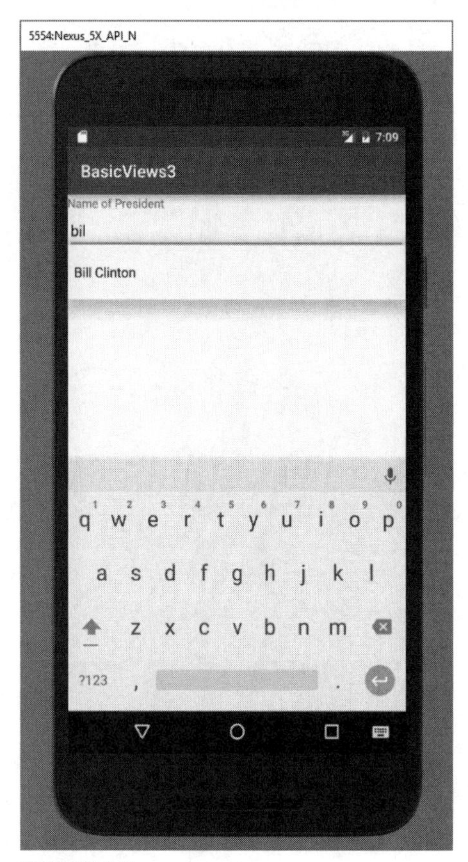

FIGURE 5-7

How It Works

In the `BasicViews3Activity` class, you first create a `String` array containing a list of presidents' names:

```
String[] presidents = {
        "Dwight D. Eisenhower",
        "John F. Kennedy",
        "Lyndon B. Johnson",
        "Richard Nixon",
        "Gerald Ford",
        "Jimmy Carter",
        "Ronald Reagan",
        "George H. W. Bush",
        "Bill Clinton",
```

```
            "George W. Bush",
            "Barack Obama"
        };
```

The ArrayAdapter object manages the array of strings that are displayed by the AutoCompleteTextView. In the preceding example, you set the AutoCompleteTextView to display in the simple_dropdown_item_1line mode:

```
ArrayAdapter<String> adapter = new ArrayAdapter<String>(this,
    android.R.layout.simple_dropdown_item_1line, presidents);
```

The setThreshold() method sets the minimum number of characters the user must type before the suggestions appear as a drop-down menu:

```
textView.setThreshold(3);
```

The list of suggestions to display for the AutoCompleteTextView is obtained from the ArrayAdapter object:

```
textView.setAdapter(adapter);
```

USING PICKER VIEWS

Selecting a date and time is one of the common tasks you need to perform in a mobile application. Android supports this functionality through the TimePicker and DatePicker views. The following sections demonstrate how to use these views in your activity.

TimePicker View

The TimePicker view enables users to select a time of the day, in either 24-hour mode or AM/PM mode. The following Try It Out shows you how to use the TimePicker in the latest version of the Android SDK. When you are creating the project for this sample, be sure that you choose an SDK that is level 23 or greater.

TRY IT OUT Using the TimePicker View (BasicViews4.zip)

1. Using Android Studio, create an Android project and name it **BasicViews4**.
2. Modify the activity_main.xml file located in the res/layout folder by adding the following bolded lines:

```
<?xml version="1.0" encoding="utf-8"?>
<LinearLayout xmlns:android="http://schemas.android.com/apk/res/android"
    android:layout_width="fill_parent"
    android:layout_height="fill_parent"
    android:orientation="vertical" >
<TimePicker android:id="@+id/timePicker"
    android:layout_width="wrap_content"
```

```
        android:layout_height="wrap_content" />
    <Button android:id="@+id/btnSet"
        android:layout_width="wrap_content"
        android:layout_height="wrap_content"
        android:text="I am all set!"
        android:onClick="onClick" />
</LinearLayout>
```

3. Press Shift+F9 to debug the application on the Android emulator. Figure 5-8 shows the `TimePicker` in action. You can use the numeric keypad or the time widget on the screen to change the hour and minute.

FIGURE 5-8

4. Back in Android Studio, add the following bolded statements to the `MainActivity.java` file:

```
import android.support.v7.app.AppCompatActivity;
import android.os.Bundle;
import android.view.View;
import android.widget.TimePicker;
import android.widget.Toast;

public class MainActivity extends AppCompatActivity {
    TimePicker timePicker;
```

```
    /** Called when the activity is first created. */
    @Override
    public void onCreate(Bundle savedInstanceState) {
        super.onCreate(savedInstanceState);
        setContentView(R.layout.activity_main);

        timePicker = (TimePicker) findViewById(R.id.timePicker);
        timePicker.setIs24HourView(true);
    }

    public void onClick(View view) {
        Toast.makeText(getBaseContext(),
                "Time selected:" +
                timePicker.getHour() +
        ":" + timePicker.getMinute(),
                Toast.LENGTH_SHORT).show();
    }
}
```

5. Press Shift+F9 to debug the application on the Android emulator. This time, the `TimePicker` is displayed in the 24-hour format. Clicking the `Button` displays the time that you have set in the `TimePicker` (see Figure 5-9).

FIGURE 5-9

How It Works

The TimePicker displays a standard UI to enable users to set a time. By default, it displays the time in the AM/PM format. If you want to display the time in the 24-hour format, you can use the setIs24HourView() method.

To programmatically get the time set by the user, use the getHour() and getMinute() methods:

```
public void onClick(View view) {
        Toast.makeText(getBaseContext(),
                "Time selected:" +
                timePicker.getHour() +
        ":" + timePicker.getMinute(),
                Toast.LENGTH_SHORT).show();
    }
```

> ***NOTE*** *The* getHour() *method always returns the hour in 24-hour format (that is, a value from 0 to 23).*

Although you can display the TimePicker in an activity, it's better to display it in a dialog window because after the time is set, the window disappears and doesn't take up any space in an activity. The following Try It Out demonstrates how to do it.

TRY IT OUT Using a Dialog to Display the TimePicker View

1. Using the BasicViews4 project created in the previous Try It Out, modify the MainActivity.java file as shown here:

```
import android.app.TimePickerDialog;
import android.support.v7.app.AppCompatActivity;
import android.os.Bundle;
import android.widget.TimePicker;
import java.util.Calendar;

public class MainActivity extends AppCompatActivity {

TimePickerDialog.OnTimeSetListener dialogListener = new TimePickerDialog
.OnTimeSetListener() {
    @Override
    public void onTimeSet(TimePicker timePicker, int i, int i1) {

    }
};
    Calendar cal = Calendar.getInstance();

    @Override
    public void onCreate(Bundle savedInstanceState) {
        super.onCreate(savedInstanceState);
        setContentView(R.layout.activity_main);
```

```
        showTimeDialog();
    }


    public void showTimeDialog(){
        new TimePickerDialog(MainActivity.this,dialogListener, cal.get(Calendar.HOUR_
    OF_DAY), cal.get(Calendar.MINUTE), false).show(); {};
    }


}
```

2. Modify the `activity_main.xml` to look as follows:

```
<?xml version="1.0" encoding="utf-8"?>
<LinearLayout xmlns:android="http://schemas.android.com/apk/res/android"
    android:layout_width="fill_parent"
    android:layout_height="fill_parent"
    android:orientation="vertical" >

</LinearLayout>
```

3. Press Shift+F9 to debug the application on the Android emulator. When the activity is loaded, you can see the `TimePicker` displayed in a dialog window (see Figure 5-10).

FIGURE 5-10

How It Works

To display a dialog window, you use the `showTimeDialog()` method:

```
showTimeDialog();
```

When the `showTimeDialog()` method is called, it creates a new instance of the `TimePickerDialog` class, passing it the current context, the callback, the initial hour and minute. It also determines whether the `TimePicker` should be displayed in 24-hour format.

```
public void showTimeDialog(){
        new TimePickerDialog(MainActivity.this,dialogListener, cal.get(Calendar.HOUR_
OF_DAY), cal.get(Calendar.MINUTE), false).show();
        {

        };
    }
```

DatePicker View

Another view that is similar to the `TimePicker` is the `DatePicker`. Using the `DatePicker`, you can enable users to select a particular date on the activity. The following Try It Out shows you how to use the `DatePicker`.

TRY IT OUT Using the DatePicker View

1. Using the BasicViews4 project created earlier, modify the `activity_main.xml` file as shown here:

```
<?xml version="1.0" encoding="utf-8"?>
<LinearLayout xmlns:android="http://schemas.android.com/apk/res/android"
    android:layout_width="fill_parent"
    android:layout_height="fill_parent"
    android:orientation="vertical" >
<Button android:id="@+id/btnSet"
    android:layout_width="wrap_content"
    android:layout_height="wrap_content"
    android:text="I am all set!"
    android:onClick="onClick" />
<DatePicker android:id="@+id/datePicker"
    android:layout_width="wrap_content"
    android:layout_height="wrap_content" />
<TimePicker android:id="@+id/timePicker"
    android:layout_width="wrap_content"
    android:layout_height="wrap_content" />
</LinearLayout>
```

2. Add the following bolded statements to the `MainActivity.java` file:

```
import android.app.TimePickerDialog;
import android.icu.text.SimpleDateFormat;
import android.support.v7.app.AppCompatActivity;
import android.os.Bundle;
```

```
import android.view.View;
import android.widget.DatePicker;
import android.widget.TimePicker;
import android.widget.Toast;

import java.util.Date;

public class MainActivity extends AppCompatActivity {
    TimePicker timePicker;
    DatePicker datePicker;

    int hour, minute;

    /** Called when the activity is first created. */
    @Override
    public void onCreate(Bundle savedInstanceState) {
        super.onCreate(savedInstanceState);
        setContentView(R.layout.activity_main);
        timePicker = (TimePicker) findViewById(R.id.timePicker);
        timePicker.setIs24HourView(true);

        datePicker = (DatePicker) findViewById(R.id.datePicker);
    }

    private TimePickerDialog.OnTimeSetListener mTimeSetListener =
            new TimePickerDialog.OnTimeSetListener()
            {
                public void onTimeSet(
                        TimePicker view, int hourOfDay, int minuteOfHour)
                {
                    hour = hourOfDay;
                    minute = minuteOfHour;

                    SimpleDateFormat timeFormat = new SimpleDateFormat("hh:mm aa");
                    Date date = new Date();
                    String strDate = timeFormat.format(date);

                    Toast.makeText(getBaseContext(),
                            "You have selected " + strDate,
                            Toast.LENGTH_SHORT).show();
                }
            };
    public void onClick(View view) {
        Toast.makeText(getBaseContext(),
                "Date selected:" + (datePicker.getMonth() + 1) +
                        "/" + datePicker.getDayOfMonth() +
                        "/" + datePicker.getYear() + "\n" +
                        "Time selected:" + timePicker.getHour() +
                        ":" + timePicker.getMinute(),
                Toast.LENGTH_SHORT).show();
    }
}
```

3. Press Shift+F9 to debug the application on the Android emulator. After the date is set, clicking the `Button` displays the date set (see Figure 5-11).

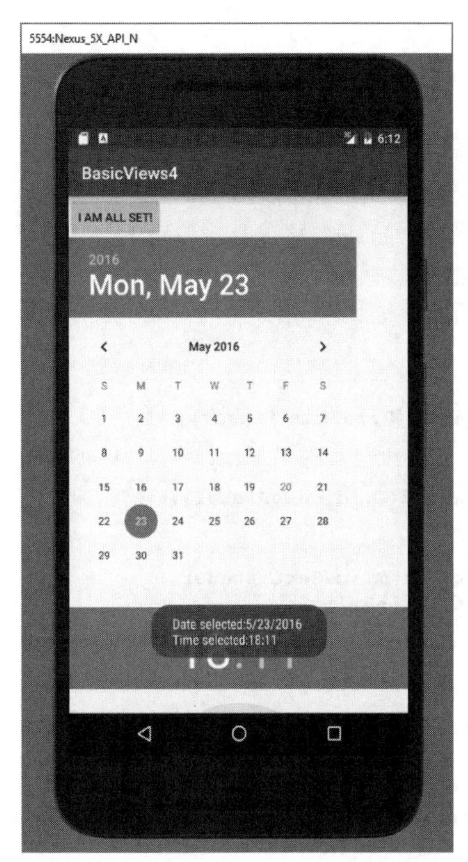

FIGURE 5-11

How It Works

As with the `TimePicker`, you call the `getMonth()`, `getDayOfMonth()`, and `getYear()` methods to get the month, day, and year, respectively:

```
"Date selected:" + (datePicker.getMonth() + 1) +
"/" + datePicker.getDayOfMonth() +
"/" + datePicker.getYear() + "\n" +
```

Note that the `getMonth()` method returns 0 for January, 1 for February, and so on. This means you need to increment the result of this method by one to get the corresponding month number.

Like the `TimePicker`, you can also display the `DatePicker` in a dialog window.

USING LIST VIEWS TO DISPLAY LONG LISTS

List views are views that enable you to display a long list of items. In Android, there are two types of list views: `ListView` and `SpinnerView`. Both are useful for displaying long lists of items. The Try It Outs in this section show them in action.

ListView View

The `ListView` displays a list of items in a vertically scrolling list. The following Try It Out demonstrates how to display a list of items using the `ListView`.

TRY IT OUT Displaying a Long List of Items Using the ListView (BasicViews5.zip)

1. Using Android Studio, create an Android project and name it **BasicViews5**.
2. Modify the `MainActivity.java` file by inserting the bolded statements shown here:

```
import android.app.ListActivity;
import android.os.Bundle;
import android.view.View;
import android.widget.ArrayAdapter;
import android.widget.ListView;
import android.widget.Toast;

public class MainActivity extends ListActivity {
    String[] presidents = {
            "Dwight D. Eisenhower",
            "John F. Kennedy",
            "Lyndon B. Johnson",
            "Richard Nixon",
            "Gerald Ford",
            "Jimmy Carter",
            "Ronald Reagan",
            "George H. W. Bush",
            "Bill Clinton",
            "George W. Bush",
            "Barack Obama"
    };

    /** Called when the activity is first created. */
    @Override
    public void onCreate(Bundle savedInstanceState) {
        super.onCreate(savedInstanceState);

        setListAdapter(new ArrayAdapter<String>(this,
                android.R.layout.simple_list_item_1, presidents));
    }

    public void onListItemClick(
            ListView parent, View v, int position, long id)
```

```
        {
            Toast.makeText(this,
                    "You have selected " + presidents[position],
                    Toast.LENGTH_SHORT).show();
        }
    }
```

3. Press Shift+F9 to debug the application on the Android emulator. Figure 5-12 shows the activity displaying the list of presidents' names.

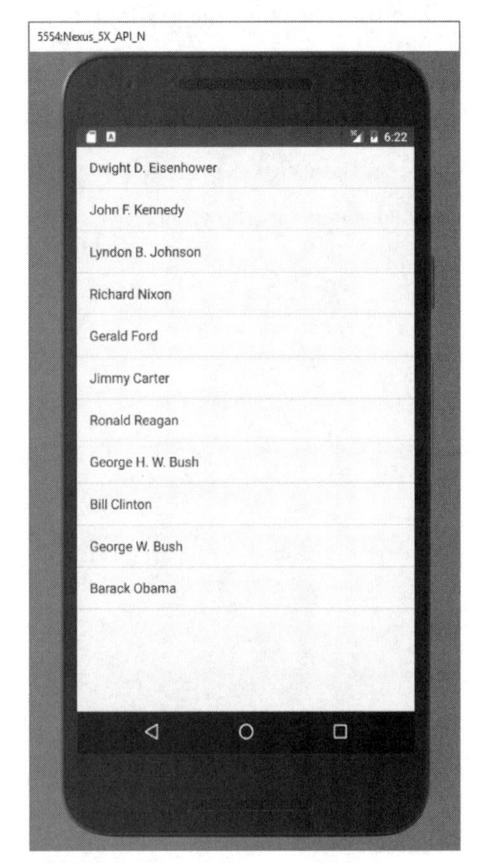

FIGURE 5-12

4. Click an item. A message containing the item selected is displayed.

How It Works

The first thing to notice in this example is that the `MainActivity` class extends the `ListActivity` class. The `ListActivity` class extends the `Activity` class and displays a list of items by binding to a data source. Also note there is no need to modify the `activity_main.xml` file to include the `ListView` because the `ListActivity` class itself contains a `ListView`. With the `onCreate()` method, you don't need to call the `setContentView()` method to load the UI from the `main.xml` file:

```
//---no need to call this---
//setContentView(R.layout.activity_main);
```

In the `onCreate()` method, you use the `setListAdapter()` method to programmatically fill the entire screen of the activity with a `ListView`. The `ArrayAdapter` object manages the array of strings that are displayed by the `ListView`. In the preceding example, you set the `ListView` to display in the `simple_list_item_1` mode:

```
setListAdapter(new ArrayAdapter<String>(this,
    android.R.layout.simple_list_item_1, presidents));
```

The `onListItemClick()` method is fired whenever an item in the `ListView` has been clicked:

```
public void onListItemClick(
ListView parent, View v, int position, long id)
{
    Toast.makeText(this,
        "You have selected " + presidents[position],
        Toast.LENGTH_SHORT).show();
}
```

Here, you simply display the name of the president selected using the `Toast` class.

Customizing the ListView

The `ListView` is a versatile view that you can further customize. The following Try It Out shows how to allow multiple items in the `ListView` to be selected and how to enable filtering support.

TRY IT OUT Enabling Filtering and Multi-Item Support in the ListView

1. Using the BasicViews5 project created in the previous section, add the following bolded statements to the `MainActivity.java` file:

```
public void onCreate(Bundle savedInstanceState) {
        super.onCreate(savedInstanceState);

        ListView lstView = getListView();
        lstView.setChoiceMode(ListView.CHOICE_MODE_MULTIPLE);
        lstView.setTextFilterEnabled(true);
        setListAdapter(new ArrayAdapter<String>(this,
                android.R.layout.simple_list_item_checked, presidents));
    }
```

2. Press Shift+F9 to debug the application on the Android emulator. You can now click each item to display the check icon next to it (see Figure 5-13).

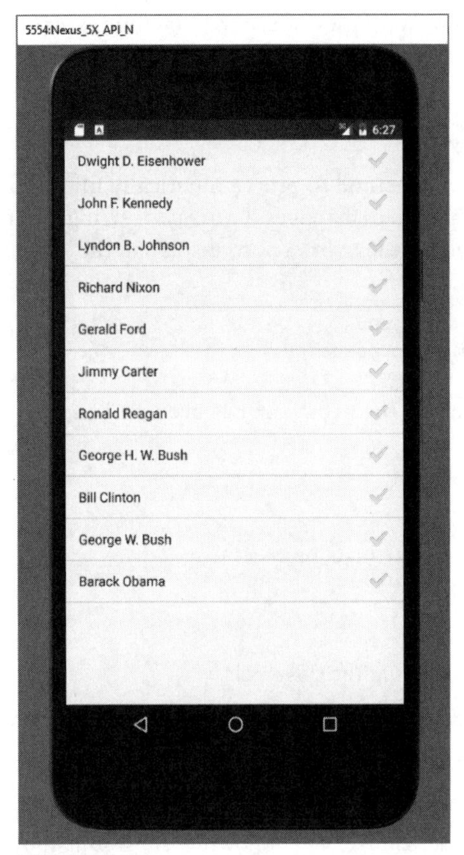

FIGURE 5-13

How It Works

To programmatically get a reference to the `ListView` object, use the `getListView()` method, which fetches the `ListActivity`'s list view. This is necessary so that you can programmatically modify the behavior of the `ListView`. In this case, you used the `setChoiceMode()` method to specify how the `ListView` should handle a user's click. For this example, set the `setChoiceMode()` to `ListView.CHOICE_MODE_MULTIPLE`, which allows the user to select multiple items:

```
ListView lstView = getListView();
lstView.setChoiceMode(ListView.CHOICE_MODE_MULTIPLE);
```

A very cool feature of the `ListView` is its support for filtering. When you enable filtering through the `setTextFilterEnabled()` method, users can type on the keypad and the `ListView` automatically filters the items to match what was typed:

```
lstView.setTextFilterEnabled(true);
```

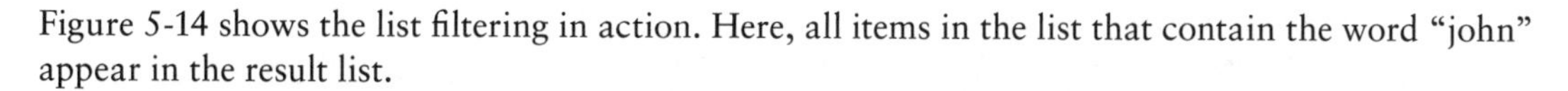

Figure 5-14 shows the list filtering in action. Here, all items in the list that contain the word “john” appear in the result list.

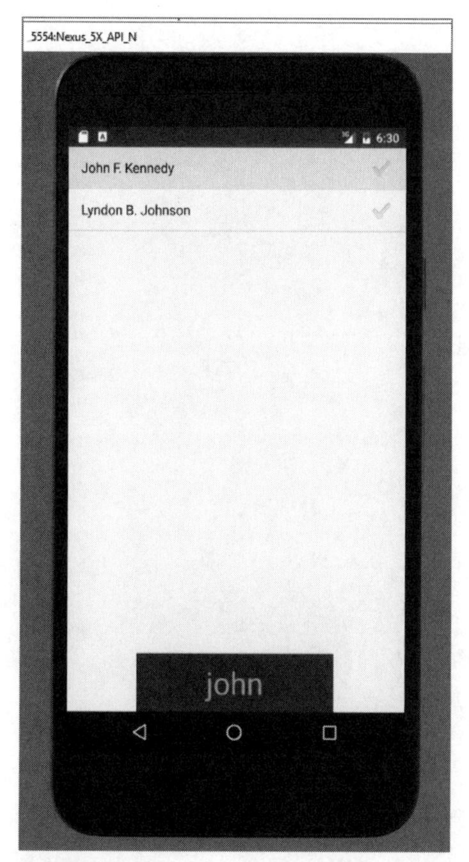

FIGURE 5-14

Although the previous example shows that the list of presidents’ names is stored in an array, in a real-life application it is recommended that you either retrieve them from a database or at least store them in the `strings.xml` file. The following Try It Out shows you how.

TRY IT OUT Storing Items in the strings.xml File

1. Using the BasicViews5 project created earlier, add the following bolded lines to the `strings.xml` file located in the `res/values` folder:

```
<?xml version="1.0" encoding="utf-8"?>
<resources>
    <string name="hello">Hello World, BasicViews5Activity!</string>
    <string name="app_name">BasicViews5</string>
```

```
    <string-array name="presidents_array">
        <item>Dwight D. Eisenhower</item>
        <item>John F. Kennedy</item>
        <item>Lyndon B. Johnson</item>
        <item>Richard Nixon</item>
        <item>Gerald Ford</item>
        <item>Jimmy Carter</item>
        <item>Ronald Reagan</item>
        <item>George H. W. Bush</item>
        <item>Bill Clinton</item>
        <item>George W. Bush</item>
        <item>Barack Obama</item>
    </string-array>
</resources>
```

2. Modify the `MainActivity.java` file as shown in bold:

```
import android.app.ListActivity;
import android.os.Bundle;
import android.view.View;
import android.widget.ArrayAdapter;
import android.widget.ListView;
import android.widget.Toast;

public class MainActivity extends ListActivity {
    String[] presidents;

    /** Called when the activity is first created. */
    @Override
    public void onCreate(Bundle savedInstanceState) {
        super.onCreate(savedInstanceState);

        ListView lstView = getListView();
        lstView.setChoiceMode(ListView.CHOICE_MODE_MULTIPLE);
        lstView.setTextFilterEnabled(true);
        presidents =
                getResources().getStringArray(R.array.presidents_array);
        setListAdapter(new ArrayAdapter<String>(this,
                android.R.layout.simple_list_item_checked, presidents));
    }

    public void onListItemClick(
            ListView parent, View v, int position, long id)
    {
        Toast.makeText(this,
                "You have selected " + presidents[position],
                Toast.LENGTH_SHORT).show();
    }
}
```

3. Press Shift+F9 to debug the application on the Android emulator. You should see the same list of names that appeared in the previous Try It Out.

How It Works

With the names now stored in the `strings.xml` file, you can retrieve it programmatically in the `BasicViews5Activity.java` file using the `getResources()` method:

```
presidents =
        getResources().getStringArray(R.array.presidents_array);
```

In general, you can programmatically retrieve resources bundled with your application using the `getResources()` method.

This example demonstrated how to make items in a `ListView` selectable. At the end of the selection process, how do you know which item or items are selected? The following Try It Out shows you how.

TRY IT OUT Checking Which Items Are Selected

1. Using the BasicViews5 project again, add the following bolded lines to the `activity_main.xml` file:

```
<?xml version="1.0" encoding="utf-8"?>
<LinearLayout xmlns:android="http://schemas.android.com/apk/res/android"
    android:layout_width="fill_parent"
    android:layout_height="fill_parent"
    android:orientation="vertical" >

<Button
    android:id="@+id/btn"
    android:layout_width="fill_parent"
    android:layout_height="wrap_content"
    android:text="Show selected items"
    android:onClick="onClick"/>
<ListView
    android:id="@+id/android:list"
    android:layout_width="wrap_content"
    android:layout_height="wrap_content" />
</LinearLayout>
```

2. Add the following bolded lines to the `MainActivity.java` file:

```
import android.app.ListActivity;
import android.os.Bundle;
import android.view.View;
import android.widget.ArrayAdapter;
import android.widget.ListView;
import android.widget.Toast;

public class MainActivity extends ListActivity {
    String[] presidents;
```

```
    /** Called when the activity is first created. */
    @Override
    public void onCreate(Bundle savedInstanceState) {
        super.onCreate(savedInstanceState);

        setContentView(R.layout.activity_main);
        ListView lstView = getListView();
        lstView.setChoiceMode(ListView.CHOICE_MODE_MULTIPLE);
        lstView.setTextFilterEnabled(true);
        presidents =
                getResources().getStringArray(R.array.presidents_array);
        setListAdapter(new ArrayAdapter<String>(this,
                android.R.layout.simple_list_item_checked, presidents));
    }

    public void onListItemClick(
            ListView parent, View v, int position, long id)
    {
        Toast.makeText(this,
                "You have selected " + presidents[position],
                Toast.LENGTH_SHORT).show();
    }

    public void onClick(View view) {
        ListView lstView = getListView();

        String itemsSelected = "Selected items: \n";
        for (int i=0; i<lstView.getCount(); i++) {
            if (lstView.isItemChecked(i)) {
                itemsSelected += lstView.getItemAtPosition(i) + "\n";
            }
        }
        Toast.makeText(this, itemsSelected, Toast.LENGTH_LONG).show();
    }
}
```

3. Press Shift+F9 to debug the application on the Android emulator. Click a few items and then click the Show Selected Items button (see Figure 5-15). The list of names selected is displayed.

How It Works

In the previous section's exercise, you saw how to populate a `ListView` that occupies the entire activity. In that example, there is no need to add a `ListView` element to the `activity_main.xml` file. In this example, you saw how a `ListView` can partially fill an activity. To do that, you add a `ListView` element with the `id` attribute set to `@+id/android:list`:

```
<ListView
    android:id="@+id/android:list"
    android:layout_width="wrap_content"
    android:layout_height="wrap_content" />
```

You then load the content of the activity using the `setContentView()` method (previously commented out):

```
setContentView(R.layout.main);
```

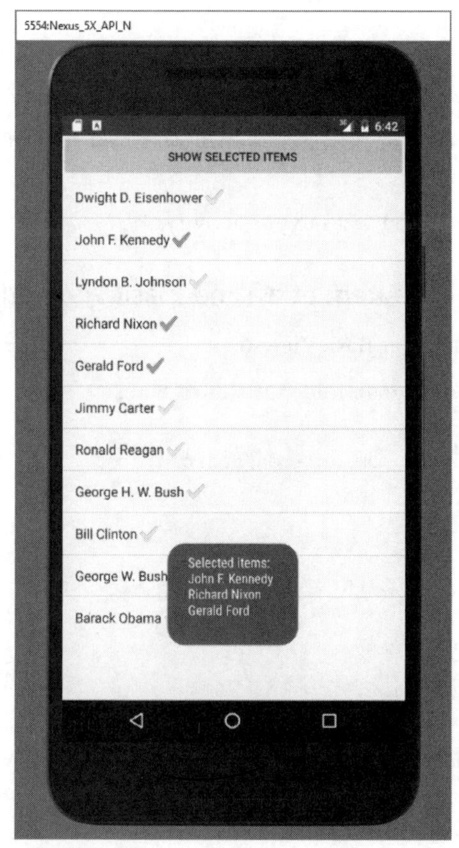

FIGURE 5-15

To find out which items in the `ListView` have been checked, use the `isItemChecked()` method:

```
ListView lstView = getListView();
String itemsSelected = "Selected items: \n";
for (int i=0; i<lstView.getCount(); i++) {
    if (lstView.isItemChecked(i)) {
        itemsSelected += lstView.getItemAtPosition(i) + "\n";
    }
}
Toast.makeText(this, itemsSelected, Toast.LENGTH_LONG).show();
```

The `getItemAtPosition()` method returns the name of the item at the specified position.

> ***NOTE*** *So far, all the examples show how to use the* `ListView` *inside a* `ListActivity`. *This is not absolutely necessary; you can also use the* `ListView` *inside an* `Activity`. *To programmatically refer to the* `ListView`, *you use the* `findViewByID()` *method instead of the* `getListView()` *method. Also, the* `id` *attribute of the* `<ListView>` *element can use the* `@+id/<view_name>` *format.*

Using the Spinner View

The `ListView` displays a long list of items in an activity, but you might want the user interface to display other views, meaning you do not have the additional space for a full-screen view, such as the `ListView`. In such cases, you should use the `SpinnerView`. The `SpinnerView` displays one item at a time from a list and enables users to choose from them.

The following Try It Out shows how you can use the `SpinnerView` in your activity.

TRY IT OUT Using the SpinnerView to Display One Item at a Time (BasicView6.zip)

1. Using Android Studio, create an Android project and name it **BasicViews6**.
2. Modify the `activity_main.xml` file located in the `res/layout` folder as shown here:

```
<?xml version="1.0" encoding="utf-8"?>
<LinearLayout xmlns:android="http://schemas.android.com/apk/res/android"
    android:layout_width="fill_parent"
    android:layout_height="fill_parent"
    android:orientation="vertical" >
<Spinner
    android:id="@+id/spinner1"
    android:layout_width="wrap_content"
    android:layout_height="wrap_content"
    android:drawSelectorOnTop="true" />
</LinearLayout>
```

3. Add the following bolded lines to the `strings.xml` file located in the `res/values` folder:

```
<resources>
    <string name="hello">Hello World, BasicViews6Activity!</string>
    <string name="app_name">BasicViews6</string>
    <string-array name="presidents_array">
        <item>Dwight D. Eisenhower</item>
        <item>John F. Kennedy</item>
        <item>Lyndon B. Johnson</item>
        <item>Richard Nixon</item>
        <item>Gerald Ford</item>
        <item>Jimmy Carter</item>
        <item>Ronald Reagan</item>
        <item>George H. W. Bush</item>
        <item>Bill Clinton</item>
        <item>George W. Bush</item>
        <item>Barack Obama</item>
    </string-array>
</resources>
```

4. Add the following bolded statements to the `MainActivity.java` file:

```
import android.support.v7.app.AppCompatActivity;
import android.os.Bundle;
```

```
import android.view.View;
import android.widget.AdapterView;
import android.widget.ArrayAdapter;
import android.widget.Spinner;
import android.widget.Toast;

public class MainActivity extends AppCompatActivity {
    String[] presidents;
    /** Called when the activity is first created. */
    @Override
    public void onCreate(Bundle savedInstanceState) {
        super.onCreate(savedInstanceState);
        setContentView(R.layout.activity_main);
        presidents =
                getResources().getStringArray(R.array.presidents_array);
        Spinner s1 = (Spinner) findViewById(R.id.spinner1);
        ArrayAdapter<String> adapter = new ArrayAdapter<String>(this,
                android.R.layout.simple_spinner_item, presidents);
        s1.setAdapter(adapter);
        s1.setOnItemSelectedListener(new AdapterView.OnItemSelectedListener()
        {
            @Override
            public void onItemSelected(AdapterView<?> arg0,
                                       View arg1, int arg2, long arg3)
            {
                int index = arg0.getSelectedItemPosition();
                Toast.makeText(getBaseContext(),
                        "You have selected item : " + presidents[index],
                        Toast.LENGTH_SHORT).show();
            }
            @Override
            public void onNothingSelected(AdapterView<?> arg0) { }
        });
    }
}
```

5. Press Shift+F9 to debug the application on the Android emulator. Click `SpinnerView` and you see a pop-up displaying the list of presidents' names (see Figure 5-16). Clicking an item displays a message showing the selected item.

How It Works

The `onNothingSelected()` method is fired when the user presses the back button, which dismisses the list of items displayed. In this case, nothing is selected so you do not need to do anything.

Instead of displaying the items in the `ArrayAdapter` as a simple list, you can display them using radio buttons. To do so, modify the second parameter in the constructor of the `ArrayAdapter` class:

```
ArrayAdapter<String> adapter = new ArrayAdapter<String>(this,
        android.R.layout.simple_list_item_single_choice, presidents);
```

This causes the items to be displayed as a list of radio buttons (see Figure 5-17).

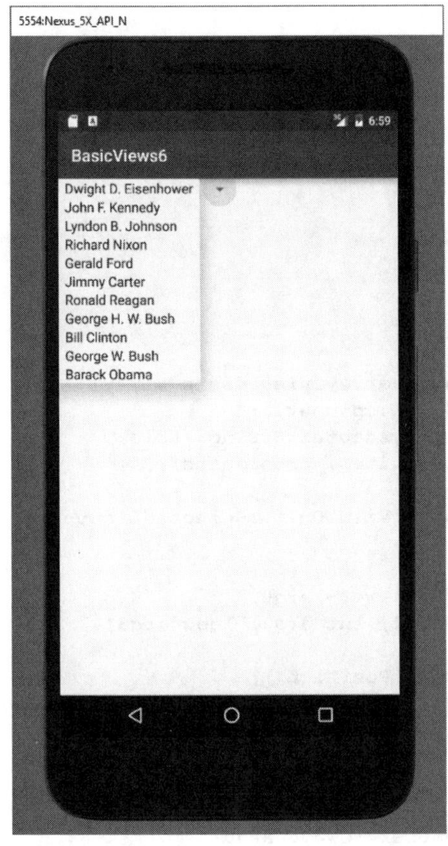

FIGURE 5-16

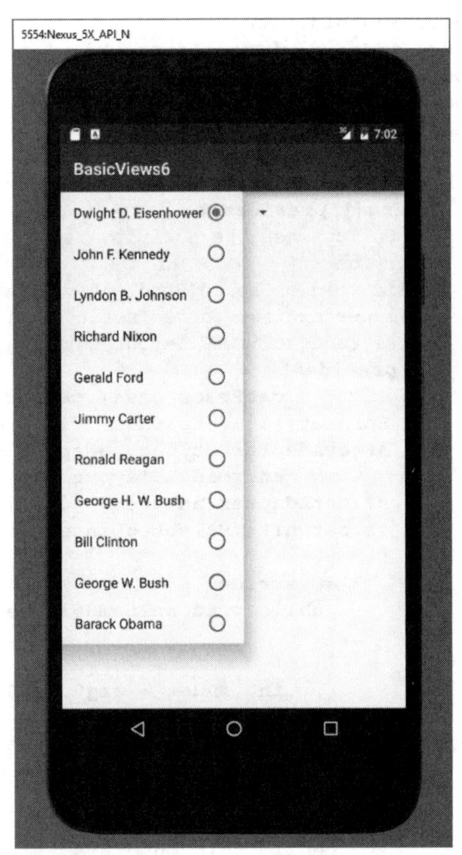

FIGURE 5-17

UNDERSTANDING SPECIALIZED FRAGMENTS

Chapter 3 discusses the fragment feature that was added in Android 3. Fragments allow you to customize the user interface of your Android application by dynamically rearranging fragments to fit within an activity. This enables you to build applications that run on devices with different screen sizes.

As you have learned, fragments are really "mini-activities" that have their own life cycles. To create a fragment, you need a class that extends the `Fragment` base class. In addition to the `Fragment` base class, you can also extend from some other subclasses of the `Fragment` base class to create more specialized fragments. The following sections discuss the three subclasses of `Fragment`:

- `ListFragment`
- `DialogFragment`
- `PreferenceFragment`

Using a ListFragment

A list fragment is a fragment that contains a `ListView`, which displays a list of items from a data source, such as an array or a `Cursor`. A list fragment is useful because it's common to have one fragment that contains a list of items (such as a list of RSS postings), and another fragment that displays details about the selected posting. To create a list fragment, you need to extend the `ListFragment` base class.

The following Try It Out shows you how to get started with a list fragment.

TRY IT OUT Creating and Using a List Fragment (ListFragmentExample.zip)

1. Using Android Studio, create an Android project and name it **ListFragmentExample**.
2. Modify the `activity_main.xml` file as shown in bold. (Please replace instances of `com.jfdimarzio` with references your project's package:

```
<?xml version="1.0" encoding="utf-8"?>
<LinearLayout xmlns:android="http://schemas.android.com/apk/res/android"
    android:layout_width="fill_parent"
    android:layout_height="fill_parent"
    android:orientation="horizontal" >
    <fragment
        android:name="com.jfdimarzio.listfragmentexample.Fragment1"
        android:id="@+id/fragment1"
        android:layout_weight="0.5"
        android:layout_width="0dp"
        android:layout_height="200dp" />
    <fragment
        android:name="com.jfdimarzio.listfragmentexample.Fragment1"
        android:id="@+id/fragment2"
        android:layout_weight="0.5"
        android:layout_width="0dp"
        android:layout_height="300dp" />
</LinearLayout>
```

3. Add an XML file to the `res/layout` folder and name it **fragment1.xml**.
4. Populate the `fragment1.xml` as follows:

```
<?xml version="1.0" encoding="utf-8"?>
<LinearLayout xmlns:android="http://schemas.android.com/apk/res/android"
    android:orientation="vertical"
    android:layout_width="fill_parent"
    android:layout_height="fill_parent">
    <ListView
        android:id="@id/android:list"
        android:layout_width="match_parent"
        android:layout_height="match_parent"
        android:layout_weight="1"
        android:drawSelectorOnTop="false"/>
</LinearLayout>
```

5. Add a Java Class file to the package and name it **Fragment1**.

6. Populate the `Fragment1.java` file as follows:

```
import android.app.ListFragment;
import android.os.Bundle;
import android.view.LayoutInflater;
import android.view.View;
import android.view.ViewGroup;
import android.widget.ArrayAdapter;
import android.widget.ListView;
import android.widget.Toast;
public class Fragment1 extends ListFragment {
    String[] presidents = {
        "Dwight D. Eisenhower",
        "John F. Kennedy",
        "Lyndon B. Johnson",
        "Richard Nixon",
        "Gerald Ford",
        "Jimmy Carter",
        "Ronald Reagan",
        "George H. W. Bush",
        "Bill Clinton",
        "George W. Bush",
        "Barack Obama"
    };
    @Override
    public View onCreateView(LayoutInflater inflater,
    ViewGroup container, Bundle savedInstanceState) {
        return inflater.inflate(R.layout.fragment1, container, false);
    }
    @Override
    public void onCreate(Bundle savedInstanceState) {
        super.onCreate(savedInstanceState);
        setListAdapter(new ArrayAdapter<String>(getActivity(),
            android.R.layout.simple_list_item_1, presidents));
    }

    public void onListItemClick(ListView parent, View v,
    int position, long id)
    {
        Toast.makeText(getActivity(),
            "You have selected " + presidents[position],
            Toast.LENGTH_SHORT).show();
    }
}
```

7. Press Shift+F9 to debug the application on the Android emulator. Figure 5-18 shows the two list fragments displaying the two lists of presidents' names.

8. Click any of the items in the two `ListView` views, and you see a message (see Figure 5-19).

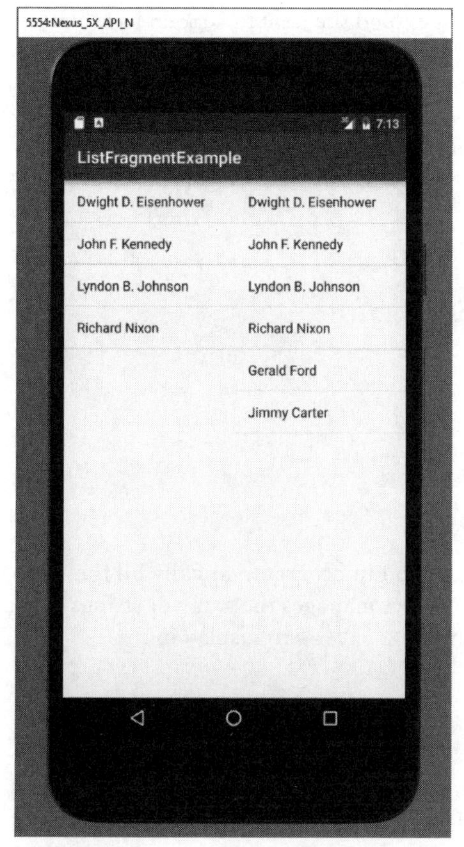

FIGURE 5-18

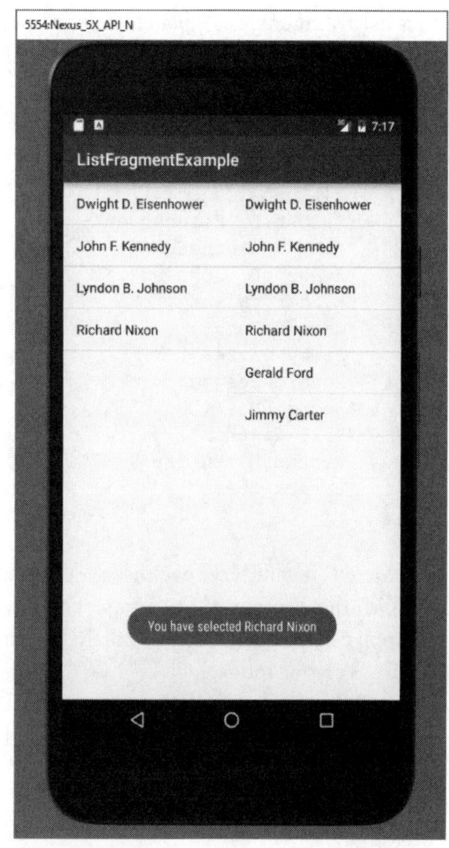

FIGURE 5-19

How It Works

First, create the XML file for the fragment by adding a `ListView` element:

```
<?xml version="1.0" encoding="utf-8"?>
<LinearLayout xmlns:android="http://schemas.android.com/apk/res/android"
    android:orientation="vertical"
    android:layout_width="fill_parent"
    android:layout_height="fill_parent">
    <ListView
        android:id="@id/android:list"
        android:layout_width="match_parent"
        android:layout_height="match_parent"
        android:layout_weight="1"
        android:drawSelectorOnTop="false"/>
</LinearLayout>
```

To create a list fragment, the Java class for the fragment must extend the `ListFragment` base class:

```
public class Fragment1 extends ListFragment {
}
```

You then declare an array to contain the list of presidents' names in your activity:

```
    String[] presidents = {
        "Dwight D. Eisenhower",
        "John F. Kennedy",
        "Lyndon B. Johnson",
        "Richard Nixon",
        "Gerald Ford",
        "Jimmy Carter",
        "Ronald Reagan",
        "George H. W. Bush",
        "Bill Clinton",
        "George W. Bush",
        "Barack Obama"
    };
```

In the `onCreate()` event, you use the `setListAdapter()` method to programmatically fill the `ListView` with the content of the array. The `ArrayAdapter` object manages the array of strings that are displayed by the `ListView`. In this example, you set the `ListView` to display in the `simple_list_item_1` mode:

```
    @Override
    public void onCreate(Bundle savedInstanceState) {
        super.onCreate(savedInstanceState);
        setListAdapter(new ArrayAdapter<String>(getActivity(),
            android.R.layout.simple_list_item_1, presidents));
    }
```

The `onListItemClick()` method is fired whenever an item in the `ListView` is clicked:

```
    public void onListItemClick(ListView parent, View v,
    int position, long id)
    {
        Toast.makeText(getActivity(),
            "You have selected " + presidents[position],
            Toast.LENGTH_SHORT).show();
    }
```

Finally, you add two fragments to the activity. Note the height of each fragment:

```
<?xml version="1.0" encoding="utf-8"?>
<LinearLayout xmlns:android="http://schemas.android.com/apk/res/android"
    android:layout_width="fill_parent"
    android:layout_height="fill_parent"
    android:orientation="horizontal" >
<fragment
    android:name="net.learn2develop.ListFragmentExample.Fragment1"
    android:id="@+id/fragment1"
    android:layout_weight="0.5"
    android:layout_width="0dp"
    android:layout_height="200dp" />
```

```
<fragment
    android:name="net.learn2develop.ListFragmentExample.Fragment1"
    android:id="@+id/fragment2"
    android:layout_weight="0.5"
    android:layout_width="0dp"
    android:layout_height="300dp" />
</LinearLayout>
```

Using a DialogFragment

A dialog fragment floats on top of an activity and is displayed modally. Dialog fragments are useful when you need to obtain the user's response before continuing with execution. To create a dialog fragment, you must extend the `DialogFragment` base class.

The following Try It Out shows how to create a dialog fragment.

TRY IT OUT Creating and Using a Dialog Fragment (DialogFragmentExample.zip)

1. Using Android Studio, create an Android project and name it **DialogFragmentExample.**
2. Add a Java Class file under the package and name it **Fragment1**.
3. Populate the `Fragment1.java` file as follows:

```
import android.app.AlertDialog;
import android.app.Dialog;
import android.app.DialogFragment;
import android.content.DialogInterface;
import android.os.Bundle;

public class Fragment1 extends DialogFragment {
    static Fragment1 newInstance(String title) {
        Fragment1 fragment = new Fragment1();
        Bundle args = new Bundle();
        args.putString("title", title);
        fragment.setArguments(args);
        return fragment;
    }
    @Override
    public Dialog onCreateDialog(Bundle savedInstanceState) {
        String title = getArguments().getString("title");
        return new AlertDialog.Builder(getActivity())
                .setIcon(R.mipmap.ic_launcher)
                .setTitle(title)
                .setPositiveButton("OK",
                        new DialogInterface.OnClickListener() {
                            public void onClick(DialogInterface dialog,
                                                int whichButton) {
                                ((MainActivity)
                                        getActivity()).doPositiveClick();
```

```
                            }
                        })
                .setNegativeButton("Cancel",
                        new DialogInterface.OnClickListener() {
                            public void onClick(DialogInterface dialog,
                                                int whichButton) {
                                ((MainActivity)
                                        getActivity()).doNegativeClick();
                            }
                        }).create();
    }
}
```

4. Populate the `MainActivity.java` file as shown here in bold:

```
import android.support.v7.app.AppCompatActivity;
import android.os.Bundle;
import android.util.Log;

public class MainActivity extends AppCompatActivity {

    @Override
    protected void onCreate(Bundle savedInstanceState) {
        super.onCreate(savedInstanceState);
        setContentView(R.layout.activity_main);
        Fragment1 dialogFragment = Fragment1.newInstance(
                "Are you sure you want to do this?");
         dialogFragment.show(getFragmentManager(), "dialog");
    }

    public void doPositiveClick() {
        //---perform steps when user clicks on OK---
        Log.d("DialogFragmentExample", "User clicks on OK");
    }
    public void doNegativeClick() {
        //---perform steps when user clicks on Cancel---
        Log.d("DialogFragmentExample", "User clicks on Cancel");
    }
}
```

5. Press Shift+F9 to debug the application on the Android emulator. Figure 5-20 shows the fragment displayed as an alert dialog. Click either OK or Cancel and observe the message displayed.

How It Works

To create a dialog fragment, your Java class first must extend the `DialogFragment` base class:

```
public class Fragment1 extends DialogFragment {
}
```

In this example, you create an alert dialog, which is a dialog window that displays a message with optional buttons. Within the `Fragment1` class, define the `newInstance()` method:

```
    static Fragment1 newInstance(String title) {
        Fragment1 fragment = new Fragment1();
```

```
            Bundle args = new Bundle();
            args.putString("title", title);
            fragment.setArguments(args);
            return fragment;
        }
```

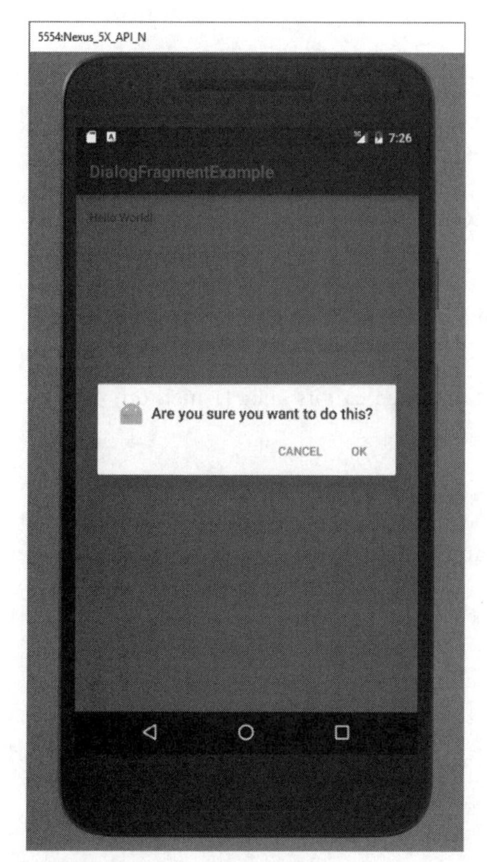

FIGURE 5-20

The `newInstance()` method allows a new instance of the fragment to be created. Also, this method accepts an argument specifying the string (`title`) to display in the alert dialog. The `title` is then stored in a `Bundle` object for use later.

Next, you define the `onCreateDialog()` method, which is called after `onCreate()` and before `onCreateView()`:

```
    public Dialog onCreateDialog(Bundle savedInstanceState) {
            String title = getArguments().getString("title");
            return new AlertDialog.Builder(getActivity())
                    .setIcon(R.mipmap.ic_launcher)
                    .setTitle(title)
                    .setPositiveButton("OK",
```

```
                    new DialogInterface.OnClickListener() {
                        public void onClick(DialogInterface dialog,
                                                int whichButton) {
                            ((MainActivity)
                                    getActivity()).doPositiveClick();
                        }
                    })
                .setNegativeButton("Cancel",
                    new DialogInterface.OnClickListener() {
                        public void onClick(DialogInterface dialog,
                                                int whichButton) {
                            ((MainActivity)
                                    getActivity()).doNegativeClick();
                        }
                    }).create();
}
```

Here, you create an alert dialog with two buttons: OK and Cancel. The string to be displayed in the alert dialog is obtained from the `title` argument saved in the `Bundle` object.

To display the dialog fragment, you create an instance of it and then call its `show()` method:

```
Fragment1 dialogFragment = Fragment1.newInstance(
        "Are you sure you want to do this?");
    dialogFragment.show(getFragmentManager(), "dialog");
```

Also , you implement two methods, `doPositiveClick()` and `doNegativeClick()`, to handle the user clicking the OK or Cancel buttons, respectively:

```
public void doPositiveClick() {
    //---perform steps when user clicks on OK---
    Log.d("DialogFragmentExample", "User clicks on OK");
}
public void doNegativeClick() {
    //---perform steps when user clicks on Cancel---
    Log.d("DialogFragmentExample", "User clicks on Cancel");
}
```

Using a PreferenceFragment

Typically, in your Android applications you provide preferences for users to personalize the application. For example, you might allow users to save the login credentials that they use to access their web resources. Also, you could save information, such as how often the feeds must be refreshed (for example, in an RSS reader application), and so on. In Android, you can use the `PreferenceActivity` base class to display an activity for the user to edit the preferences. In Android 3.0 and later, you can use the `PreferenceFragment` class to do the same thing.

The following Try It Out shows you how to create and use a preference fragment in Android 3 and 4.

TRY IT OUT Creating and Using a Preference Fragment (PreferenceFragmentExample.zip)

1. Using Android Studio, create an Android project and name it **PreferenceFragmentExample.**
2. Create a new `xml` directory under the `res` folder and then add a new XML resource file to it. Name the XML file **preferences.xml.**
3. Populate the `preferences.xml` file as follows:

```
<?xml version="1.0" encoding="utf-8"?>
<PreferenceScreen
    xmlns:android="http://schemas.android.com/apk/res/android">
    <PreferenceCategory android:title="Category 1">
        <CheckBoxPreference
            android:title="Checkbox"
            android:defaultValue="false"
            android:summary="True of False"
            android:key="checkboxPref" />
        </PreferenceCategory>

    <PreferenceCategory android:title="Category 2">
        <EditTextPreference
            android:name="EditText"
            android:summary="Enter a string"
            android:defaultValue="[Enter a string here]"
            android:title="Edit Text"
            android:key="editTextPref" />
        <RingtonePreference
            android:name="Ringtone Preference"
            android:summary="Select a ringtone"
            android:title="Ringtones"
            android:key="ringtonePref" />
        <PreferenceScreen
            android:title="Second Preference Screen"
            android:summary=
                "Click here to go to the second Preference Screen"
            android:key="secondPrefScreenPref">
            <EditTextPreference
                android:name="EditText"
                android:summary="Enter a string"
                android:title="Edit Text (second Screen)"
                android:key="secondEditTextPref" />
        </PreferenceScreen>
    </PreferenceCategory>

</PreferenceScreen>
```

4. Add a Java Class file to the package and name it **Fragment1.**
5. Populate the `Fragment1.java` file as follows:

```
import android.os.Bundle;
import android.preference.PreferenceFragment;
```

```
public class Fragment1 extends PreferenceFragment {
    @Override
    public void onCreate(Bundle savedInstanceState) {
        super.onCreate(savedInstanceState);
        //---load the preferences from an XML file---
        addPreferencesFromResource(R.xml.preferences);
    }
}
```

6. Modify the `MainActivity.java` file as shown in bold:

```
import android.app.FragmentManager;
import android.app.FragmentTransaction;
import android.support.v7.app.AppCompatActivity;
import android.os.Bundle;

public class MainActivity extends AppCompatActivity {

    @Override
    protected void onCreate(Bundle savedInstanceState) {
        super.onCreate(savedInstanceState);
        setContentView(R.layout.activity_main);

        FragmentManager fragmentManager = getFragmentManager();
        FragmentTransaction fragmentTransaction =
                fragmentManager.beginTransaction();
        Fragment1 fragment1 = new Fragment1();
        fragmentTransaction.replace(android.R.id.content, fragment1);
        fragmentTransaction.addToBackStack(null);
        fragmentTransaction.commit();

    }
}
```

7. Press Shift+F9 to debug the application on the Android emulator. Figure 5-21 shows the preference fragment displaying the list of preferences that the user can modify.
8. When the Edit Text preference is clicked, a pop-up is displayed (see Figure 5-22).
9. Clicking Edit Text (Second Screen) causes a second preference screen to be displayed (see Figure 5-23).
10. To dismiss the preference fragment, click the Back button on the emulator.

> ***NOTE*** *Chapter 7 describes how to retrieve the values saved in a preference file.*

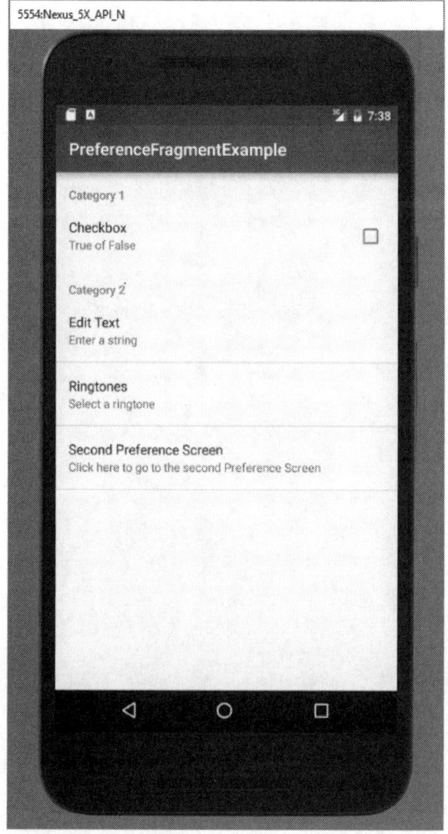

FIGURE 5-21

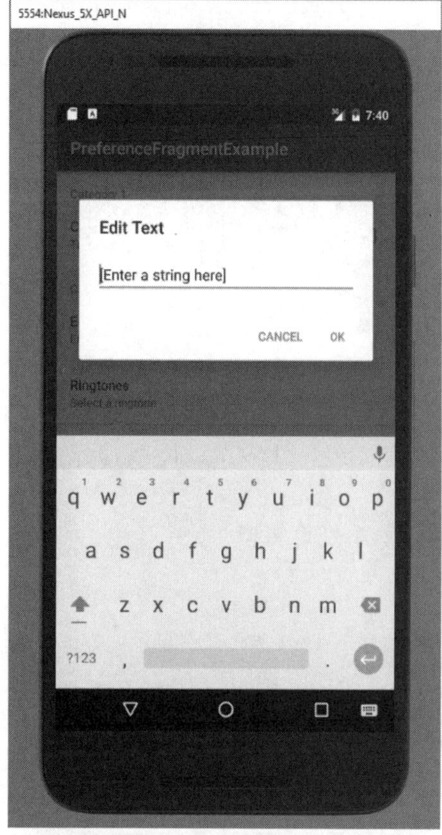

FIGURE 5-22

How It Works

To create a list of preferences in your Android application, you first need to create the `preferences.xml` file and populate it with the various XML elements. This XML file defines the various items that you want to persist in your application.

To create the preference fragment, you must extend the `PreferenceFragment` base class:

```
public class Fragment1 extends PreferenceFragment {
}
```

To load the preferences file in the preference fragment, use the `addPreferencesFromResource()` method:

```
    @Override
    public void onCreate(Bundle savedInstanceState) {
```

```
        super.onCreate(savedInstanceState);
        //---load the preferences from an XML file---
        addPreferencesFromResource(R.xml.preferences);
    }
```

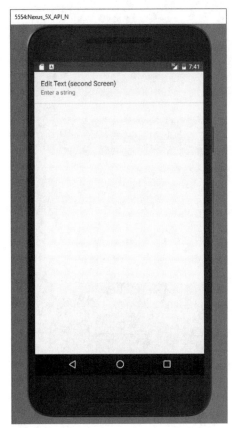

FIGURE 5-23

To display the preference fragment in your activity, you can make use of the `FragmentManager` and the `FragmentTransaction` classes:

```
FragmentManager fragmentManager = getFragmentManager();
FragmentTransaction fragmentTransaction =
    fragmentManager.beginTransaction();
Fragment1 fragment1 = new Fragment1();
fragmentTransaction.replace(android.R.id.content, fragment1);
fragmentTransaction.addToBackStack(null);
fragmentTransaction.commit();
```

You need to add the preference fragment to the back stack using the `addToBackStack()` method so that the user can dismiss the fragment by clicking the Back button.

SUMMARY

This chapter provided a look at some of the commonly used views in an Android application. Although it is not possible to exhaustively examine each view in detail, the views you learned about here should provide a good foundation for designing your Android application's user interface, regardless of its requirements.

EXERCISES

1. How do you programmatically determine whether a `RadioButton` is checked?

2. How do you access the string resource stored in the `strings.xml` file?

3. Write the code snippet to obtain the current date.

4. Name the three specialized fragments you can use in your Android application and describe their uses.

You can find answers to the exercises in the appendix.

▶ WHAT YOU LEARNED IN THIS CHAPTER

TOPIC	KEY CONCEPTS
TextView	<TextView android:layout_width="fill_parent" android:layout_height="wrap_content" android:text="@string/hello" />
Button	<Button android:id="@+id/btnSave" android:layout_width="fill_parent" android:layout_height="wrap_content" android:text="Save" />
ImageButton	<ImageButton android:id="@+id/btnImg1" android:layout_width="fill_parent" android:layout_height="wrap_content" android:src="@drawable/icon" />
EditText	<EditText android:id="@+id/txtName" android:layout_width="fill_parent" android:layout_height="wrap_content" />
CheckBox	<CheckBox android:id="@+id/chkAutosave" android:layout_width="fill_parent" android:layout_height="wrap_content" android:text="Autosave" />
RadioGroup and RadioButton	<RadioGroup android:id="@+id/rdbGp1" android:layout_width="fill_parent" android:layout_height="wrap_content" android:orientation="vertical" > <RadioButton android:id="@+id/rdb1" android:layout_width="fill_parent" android:layout_height="wrap_content" android:text="Option 1" /> <RadioButton android:id="@+id/rdb2" android:layout_width="fill_parent" android:layout_height="wrap_content" android:text="Option 2" /> </RadioGroup>

TOPIC	KEY CONCEPTS
ToggleButton	<ToggleButton android:id="@+id/toggle1" android:layout_width="wrap_content"
ProgressBar	<ProgressBar android:id="@+id/progressbar" android:layout_width="wrap_content" android:layout_height="wrap_content" />
AutoCompleteTextBox	<AutoCompleteTextView android:id="@+id/txtCountries" android:layout_width="fill_parent" android:layout_height="wrap_content" />
TimePicker	<TimePicker android:id="@+id/timePicker" android:layout_width="wrap_content" android:layout_height="wrap_content" />
DatePicker	<DatePicker android:id="@+id/datePicker" android:layout_width="wrap_content" android:layout_height="wrap_content" />
Spinner	<Spinner android:id="@+id/spinner1" android:layout_width="wrap_content" android:layout_height="wrap_content" android:drawSelectorOnTop="true" />
Specialized fragment types	ListFragment, DialogFragment, and PreferenceFragment

Displaying Pictures and Menus with Views

WHAT YOU WILL LEARN IN THIS CHAPTER

- How to use the ImageSwitcher, GridView, and ImageView views to display images
- How to display options menus and context menus
- How to display web content using the WebView view

CODE DOWNLOAD The wrox.com code downloads for this chapter are found at `www.wrox.com/go/beginningandroidprog` on the Download Code tab. The code is in the chapter 06 download and individually named according to the names throughout the chapter.

In the previous chapter, you learned about the various views that you can use to build the user interface of your Android application. This chapter continues your exploration of the other views that you can use to create robust and compelling applications.

In particular, you find out how to work with views that enable you to display images. Also, you see how to create option and context menus in your Android application. This chapter ends with a discussion of some helpful views that enable users to display the current time and web content.

USING IMAGE VIEWS TO DISPLAY PICTURES

So far, all the views you have seen are used to display text information. However, you can use the `ImageView`, `ImageSwitcher`, and `GridView` views for displaying images.

The following sections discuss each view in detail.

ImageView View

The `ImageView` is a view that shows images on the device screen. The following Try It Out shows you how to use the `ImageView` view to display an image.

TRY IT OUT Using the Image View (Gallery.zip)

1. Using Android Studio, create a new Android project and name it **Image**.
2. Add an image to your project under the `res/mipmap` folder as shown in Figure 6-1. (The image I used in this example is `butterfly.png` from `http://jfdimarzio.com/butterfly.png.`) Please note that you must be in project view to drag and drop images into the `res/mipmap` folder.

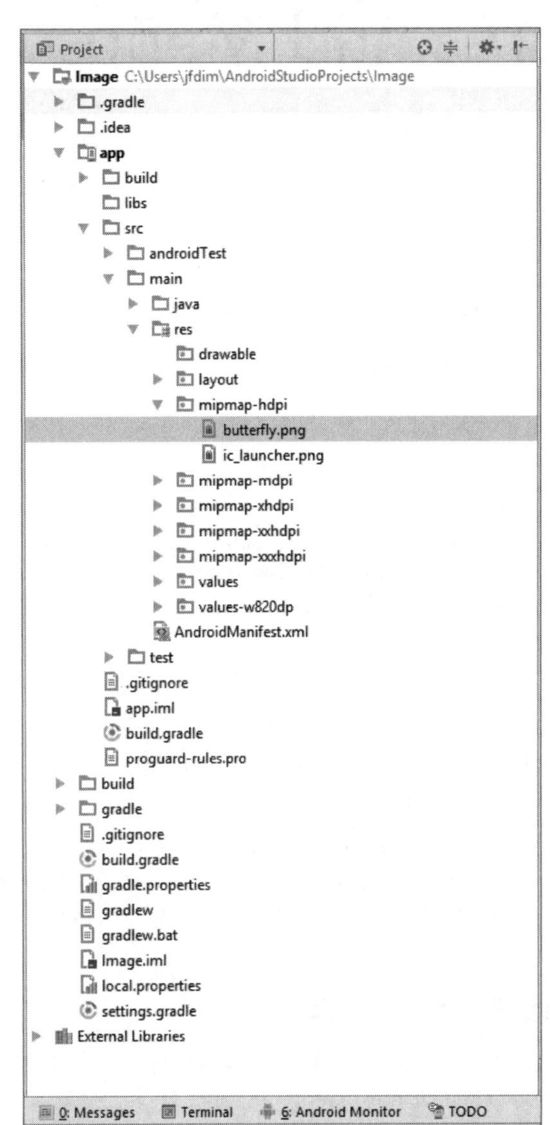

FIGURE 6-1

3. Modify the `activity_main.xml` file as shown in bold:

```
<?xml version="1.0" encoding="utf-8"?>
<LinearLayout xmlns:android="http://schemas.android.com/apk/res/android"
    xmlns:app="http://schemas.android.com/apk/res-auto"
    xmlns:tools="http://schemas.android.com/tools"
    android:id="@+id/activity_main"
    android:layout_width="wrap_content"
    android:layout_height="match_parent"
    tools:context="com.jfdimarzio.image.MainActivity">

    <android.support.v7.widget.AppCompatImageView
        android:layout_width="match_parent"
        android:layout_height="match_parent"
        android:src="@mipmap/butterfly" />

</LinearLayout>
```

4. Press Shift+F9 to debug the application on the Android emulator. Figure 6-2 shows the image displayed in the `Image` view.

FIGURE 6-2

How It Works

You first add the `ImageView` view to `activity_main.xml`. Then you associate that `ImageView` with an image from the `res/mipmap` folder. This allows you to view that image on the device screen.

ImageSwitcher

The previous section demonstrated how to use the `ImageView` to display an image. However, sometimes you don't want an image to appear abruptly when the user opens the view. For example, you might want to apply some animation to an image when it transitions from one image to another. In this case, you need to use the `ImageSwitcher`. The following Try It Out shows you how.

TRY IT OUT Using the ImageSwitcher View (ImageSwitcher.zip)

1. Using Android Studio, create a new Android project and name it **ImageSwitcher**.
2. Modify the `activity_main.xml` file by adding the following bolded statements. Please be sure to change all instances of `com.jfdimarzio` to reflect the package you use in your project:

```
<?xml version="1.0" encoding="utf-8"?>
<RelativeLayout xmlns:android="http://schemas.android.com/apk/res/android"
    xmlns:tools="http://schemas.android.com/tools"
    android:layout_width="match_parent"
    android:layout_height="match_parent"
    android:paddingBottom="@dimen/activity_vertical_margin"
    android:paddingLeft="@dimen/activity_horizontal_margin"
    android:paddingRight="@dimen/activity_horizontal_margin"
    android:paddingTop="@dimen/activity_vertical_margin"
    tools:context="com.jfdimarzio.imageswitcher.MainActivity">
    <Button
        android:text="View Windows"
        android:layout_width="wrap_content"
        android:layout_height="wrap_content"
        android:id="@+id/button2"
        />

    <ImageSwitcher
        android:layout_width="match_parent"
        android:layout_height="match_parent"
        android:layout_alignParentStart="true"
        android:layout_below="@+id/button2"
        android:id="@+id/imageSwitcher">
    </ImageSwitcher>

    <Button
        android:text="View Butterfly"
        android:layout_width="wrap_content"
        android:layout_height="wrap_content"
        android:id="@+id/button"
```

```
        android:layout_alignParentTop="true"
        android:layout_alignParentEnd="true"
        />
</RelativeLayout>
```

3. Add two images to your `res/mipmap` folder (as you did in the previous Try It Out). For this example, I added an image named `butterfly.png` and an image named `windows.jpg`.

4. Add the following bolded statements to the `MainActivity.java` file:

```
import android.support.v7.app.ActionBar;
import android.support.v7.app.AppCompatActivity;
import android.os.Bundle;
import android.view.View;
import android.view.animation.AnimationUtils;
import android.widget.Button;
import android.widget.ImageSwitcher;
import android.widget.ImageView;
import android.widget.Toast;
import android.widget.ViewSwitcher;

public class MainActivity extends AppCompatActivity {
    private ImageSwitcher imgSwitcher;
    private Button btnViewWindows,btnViewButterfly;

    @Override
    protected void onCreate(Bundle savedInstanceState) {
        super.onCreate(savedInstanceState);
        setContentView(R.layout.activity_main);

        imgSwitcher = (ImageSwitcher) findViewById(R.id.imageSwitcher);
        imgSwitcher.setInAnimation(AnimationUtils.loadAnimation(this,
                android.R.anim.fade_in));
        imgSwitcher.setOutAnimation(AnimationUtils.loadAnimation(this,
                android.R.anim.fade_out));

        btnViewWindows = (Button) findViewById(R.id.button2);
        btnViewButterfly = (Button) findViewById(R.id.button);

        imgSwitcher.setFactory(new ViewSwitcher.ViewFactory() {
            @Override
            public View makeView() {
                ImageView myView = new ImageView(getApplicationContext());
                myView.setScaleType(ImageView.ScaleType.FIT_CENTER);
                myView.setLayoutParams(new ImageSwitcher.LayoutParams(
    ActionBar.LayoutParams.WRAP_CONTENT, ActionBar.LayoutParams.WRAP_CONTENT));
                return myView;
            }
        });
        btnViewWindows.setOnClickListener(new View.OnClickListener() {
            @Override
            public void onClick(View v) {
                Toast.makeText(getApplicationContext()
```

```
, "View Windows",Toast.LENGTH_LONG).show();
                imgSwitcher.setImageResource(R.mipmap.windows);
            }
        });

        btnViewButterfly.setOnClickListener(new View.OnClickListener() {
            @Override
            public void onClick(View v) {
                Toast.makeText(getApplicationContext(), "View Butterfly"
,Toast.LENGTH_LONG).show();
                imgSwitcher.setImageResource(R.mipmap.butterfly);
            }
        });
    }
}
```

5. Press Shift+F9 to debug the application on the Android emulator. Figure 6-3 shows the `ImageSwitcher` and `Button` views, with no images loaded.

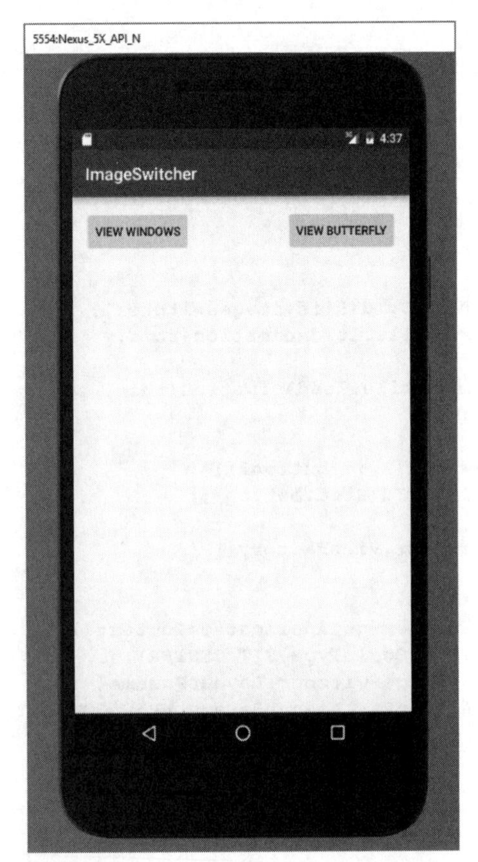

FIGURE 6-3

6. Click the View Windows button. You see the windows image and a `Toast` indicating that the image is being viewed, as shown in Figure 6-4.

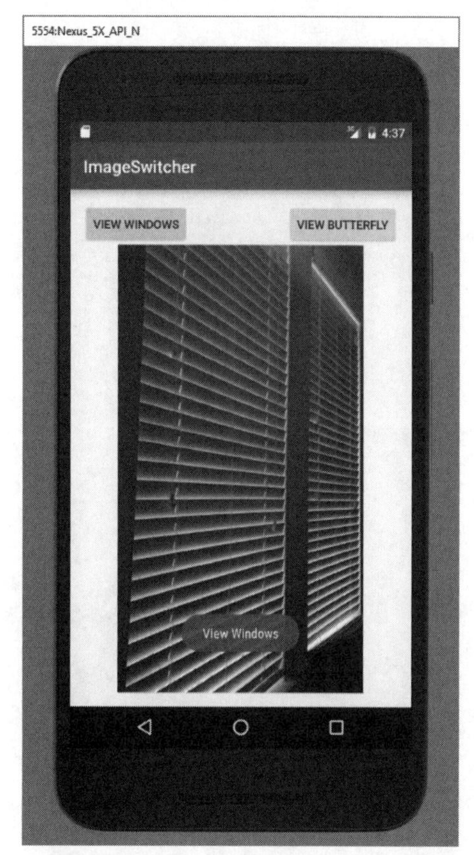

FIGURE 6-4

7. Click the View Butterfly button. You see a fade-out and a fade-in animation from the windows image to the butterfly image. You also see a `Toast` indicating that the image is being viewed (as shown in Figure 6-5).

How It Works

To use the `ImageSwitcher` view, you need to implement the `ViewFactory` interface, which creates the views for use with the `ImageSwitcher` view. For this, you need to implement the `makeView()` method:

```
imgSwitcher.setFactory(new ViewSwitcher.ViewFactory() {
            @Override
            public View makeView() {
                ImageView myView = new ImageView(getApplicationContext());
```

```
                myView.setScaleType(ImageView.ScaleType.FIT_CENTER);
                myView.setLayoutParams(new ImageSwitcher.LayoutParams(
    ActionBar.LayoutParams.WRAP_CONTENT, ActionBar.LayoutParams.WRAP_CONTENT));
                return myView;
            }
        });
```

FIGURE 6-5

This method creates a new `View` to be added in the `ImageSwitcher` view, which in this case is an `ImageView`.

In the `onCreate()` method, you get a reference to the `ImageSwitcher` view and set the animation, specifying how images should "fade" in and out of the view.

Finally, when an image is selected from the `Gallery` view, the image is displayed in the `ImageSwitcher` view:

```
protected void onCreate(Bundle savedInstanceState) {
        super.onCreate(savedInstanceState);
        setContentView(R.layout.activity_main);
```

```
        imgSwitcher = (ImageSwitcher) findViewById(R.id.imageSwitcher);
        imgSwitcher.setInAnimation(AnimationUtils.loadAnimation(this,
                android.R.anim.fade_in));
        imgSwitcher.setOutAnimation(AnimationUtils.loadAnimation(this,
                android.R.anim.fade_out));

        btnViewWindows = (Button) findViewById(R.id.button2);
        btnViewButterfly = (Button) findViewById(R.id.button);

    ...
}
```

In this example, when an image is selected in the `Gallery` view, it appears by "fading" in. When the next image is selected, the current image fades out. If you want the image to slide in from the left and slide out to the right when another image is selected, try the following animation:

```
imageSwitcher.setInAnimation(AnimationUtils.loadAnimation(this,
        android.R.anim.slide_in_left));
imageSwitcher.setOutAnimation(AnimationUtils.loadAnimation(this,
        android.R.anim.slide_out_right));
```

GridView

The `GridView` shows items in a two-dimensional scrolling grid. You can use the `GridView` together with an `ImageView` to display a series of images. The following Try It Out demonstrates how.

TRY IT OUT Using the GridView View (Grid.zip)

1. Using Android Studio, create a new Android project and name it **Grid**.
2. Drag and drop a series of images into the `res/mipmap` folder (see step 3 in the previous Try It Out for the images).
3. Populate the `activity_main.xml` file with the following content:

```
<?xml version="1.0" encoding="utf-8"?>
<android.support.constraint.ConstraintLayout xmlns:android=
    "http://schemas.android.com/apk/res/android"
    xmlns:app="http://schemas.android.com/apk/res-auto"
    xmlns:tools="http://schemas.android.com/tools"
    android:id="@+id/activity_main"
    android:layout_width="match_parent"
    android:layout_height="match_parent"
    tools:context="com.jfdimarzio.grid.MainActivity"
    tools:layout_editor_absoluteX="0dp"
    tools:layout_editor_absoluteY="81dp">

        <GridView
        android:layout_width="384dp"
        android:layout_height="511dp"
        tools:layout_editor_absoluteX="0dp"
```

```
        tools:layout_editor_absoluteY="0dp"
        app:layout_constraintLeft_toLeftOf="@+id/activity_main"
        tools:layout_constraintLeft_creator="0"
        app:layout_constraintTop_toTopOf="@+id/activity_main"
        tools:layout_constraintTop_creator="0"
        app:layout_constraintRight_toRightOf="@+id/activity_main"
        tools:layout_constraintRight_creator="0"
        app:layout_constraintBottom_toBottomOf="@+id/activity_main"
        tools:layout_constraintBottom_creator="0"
        android:id="@+id/gridview" />

</android.support.constraint.ConstraintLayout>
```

4. Add the following bolded statements to the `MainActivity.java` file:

```
import android.content.Context;
import android.support.v7.app.AppCompatActivity;
import android.os.Bundle;
import android.view.View;
import android.view.ViewGroup;
import android.widget.AdapterView;
import android.widget.BaseAdapter;
import android.widget.GridView;
import android.widget.ImageView;
import android.widget.Toast;

public class MainActivity extends AppCompatActivity {
    //---the images to display---
    Integer[] imageIDs = {
            R.mipmap.butterfly,
            R.mipmap.windows,
            R.mipmap.ic_launcher
    };

    @Override
    protected void onCreate(Bundle savedInstanceState) {
        super.onCreate(savedInstanceState);
        setContentView(R.layout.activity_main);

        GridView gridView = (GridView) findViewById(R.id.gridview);
        gridView.setAdapter(new ImageAdapter(this));
        gridView.setOnItemClickListener(new AdapterView.OnItemClickListener()
        {
            public void onItemClick(AdapterView parent,
                                    View v, int position, long id)
            {
                Toast.makeText(getBaseContext(),
                        "pic" + (position + 1) + " selected",
                Toast.LENGTH_SHORT).show();
            }
        });
    }

    public class ImageAdapter extends BaseAdapter
```

```
    {
        private Context context;
        public ImageAdapter(Context c)
        {
            context = c;
        }
        //---returns the number of images---
        public int getCount() {
            return imageIDs.length;
        }
        //---returns the item---
        public Object getItem(int position) {
            return position;
        }
        //---returns the ID of an item---
        public long getItemId(int position) {
            return position;
        }
        //---returns an ImageView view---
        public View getView(int position, View convertView,
                            ViewGroup parent)
        {
            ImageView imageView;
            if (convertView == null) {
                imageView = new ImageView(context);
                imageView.setLayoutParams(new
                        GridView.LayoutParams(150, 150));
                imageView.setScaleType(
                        ImageView.ScaleType.CENTER_CROP);
                imageView.setPadding(5, 5, 5, 5);
            } else {
                imageView = (ImageView) convertView;
            }
            imageView.setImageResource(imageIDs[position]);
            return imageView;
        }
    }
}
```

5. Press Shift+F9 to debug the application on the Android emulator. Figure 6-6 shows the `GridView` displaying all the images.

How It Works

Like the `ImageSwitcher` example, you first implement the `ImageAdapter` class and then bind it to the `GridView`:

```
GridView gridView = (GridView) findViewById(R.id.gridview);
gridView.setAdapter(new ImageAdapter(this));
gridView.setOnItemClickListener(new OnItemClickListener()
{
    public void onItemClick(AdapterView parent,
    View v, int position, long id)
```

```
            {
                Toast.makeText(getBaseContext(),
                        "pic" + (position + 1) + " selected",
                        Toast.LENGTH_SHORT).show();
            }
        });
```

FIGURE 6-6

When an image is selected, you display a `Toast` message indicating the selected image.

Within the `getView()` method, you can specify the size of the images. You can also specify how images are spaced in the `GridView` by setting the padding for each image:

```
        //---returns an ImageView view---
        public View getView(int position, View convertView,
        ViewGroup parent)
        {
            ImageView imageView;
            if (convertView == null) {
                imageView = new ImageView(context);
                imageView.setLayoutParams(new
```

```
                GridView.LayoutParams(85, 85));
            imageView.setScaleType(
                ImageView.ScaleType.CENTER_CROP);
            imageView.setPadding(5, 5, 5, 5);
        } else {
            imageView = (ImageView) convertView;
        }
        imageView.setImageResource(imageIDs[position]);
        return imageView;
    }
}
```

USING MENUS WITH VIEWS

Menus are useful for displaying additional options that are not directly visible on the main user interface (UI) of an application. There are two main types of menus in Android:

- **Options menu**—This menu displays information related to the current activity. In Android, you activate the options menu by pressing the Menu button.
- **Context menu**—This menu displays information related to a particular view on an activity. In Android, you tap and hold a context menu to activate it.

Creating the Helper Methods

Before you go ahead and create your options and context menus, you need to create two helper methods. One creates a list of items to show inside a menu, whereas the other handles the event that is fired when the user selects an item inside the menu.

TRY IT OUT Creating the Menu Helper Methods (Menus.zip)

1. Using Android Studio, create a new Android project and name it **Menus**.
2. In the `MainActivity.java` file, add the following bolded statements:

```
import android.support.v7.app.AppCompatActivity;
import android.os.Bundle;
import android.view.Menu;
import android.view.MenuItem;
import android.widget.Toast;

public class MainActivity extends AppCompatActivity {

    @Override
    protected void onCreate(Bundle savedInstanceState) {
        super.onCreate(savedInstanceState);
        setContentView(R.layout.activity_main);
    }
```

```
    private void createMenu(Menu menu) {
        MenuItem mnu1 = menu.add(0, 0, 0, "Item 1");
        {
            mnu1.setAlphabeticShortcut('a');
        }
        MenuItem mnu2 = menu.add(0, 1, 1, "Item 2");
        {
            mnu2.setAlphabeticShortcut('b');
        }
        MenuItem mnu3 = menu.add(0, 2, 2, "Item 3");
        {
            mnu3.setAlphabeticShortcut('c');
        }
        MenuItem mnu4 = menu.add(0, 3, 3, "Item 4");
        {
            mnu4.setAlphabeticShortcut('d');
        }
        menu.add(0, 4, 4, "Item 5");
        menu.add(0, 5, 5, "Item 6");
        menu.add(0, 6, 6, "Item 7");
    }

    private boolean MenuChoice(MenuItem item) {
        switch (item.getItemId()) {
            case 0:
                Toast.makeText(this, "You clicked on Item 1",
                        Toast.LENGTH_LONG).show();
                return true;
            case 1:
                Toast.makeText(this, "You clicked on Item 2",
                        Toast.LENGTH_LONG).show();
                return true;
            case 2:
                Toast.makeText(this, "You clicked on Item 3",
                        Toast.LENGTH_LONG).show();
                return true;
            case 3:
                Toast.makeText(this, "You clicked on Item 4",
                        Toast.LENGTH_LONG).show();
                return true;
            case 4:
                Toast.makeText(this, "You clicked on Item 5",
                        Toast.LENGTH_LONG).show();
                return true;
            case 5:
                Toast.makeText(this, "You clicked on Item 6",
                        Toast.LENGTH_LONG).show();
                return true;
            case 6:
                Toast.makeText(this, "You clicked on Item 7",
                        Toast.LENGTH_LONG).show();
                return true;
        }
        return false;
    }
}
```

How It Works

The preceding example creates two methods:

- `createMenu()`
- `menuChoice()`

The `createMenu()` method adds a series of menu items to a `Menu` argument.

To add a menu item to the menu, you create an instance of the `MenuItem` class and use the `Menu` object's `add()` method:

```
MenuItem mnu1 = menu.add(0, 0, 0, "Item 1");
{
    mnu1.setAlphabeticShortcut('a');
    mnu1.setIcon(R.mipmap.ic_launcher);
}
```

The four arguments of the `add()` method are

- `groupId`—The group identifier of which the menu item should be a part. Use 0 if an item is not in a group.
- `itemId`—A unique item ID.
- `order`—The order in which the item should be displayed.
- `title`—The text to display for the menu item.

You can use the `setAlphabeticShortcut()` method to assign a shortcut key to the menu item so that users can select an item by pressing a key on the keyboard. The `setIcon()` method sets an image to be displayed on the menu item.

The `menuChoice()` method takes a `MenuItem` argument and checks its ID to determine the menu item that is selected. It then displays a `Toast` message to let the user know which menu item was selected.

Options Menu

You are now ready to modify the application to display the options menu when the user presses the Menu key on the Android device.

TRY IT OUT Displaying an Options Menu

1. Using the same project created in the previous section, add the following bolded statements to the `MainActivity.java` file:

```
import android.support.v7.app.AppCompatActivity;
import android.os.Bundle;
import android.view.Menu;
import android.view.MenuItem;
import android.widget.Toast;
```

```
public class MainActivity extends AppCompatActivity {

    @Override
    protected void onCreate(Bundle savedInstanceState) {
        super.onCreate(savedInstanceState);
        setContentView(R.layout.activity_main);
    }

    @Override
    public boolean onCreateOptionsMenu(Menu menu) {
        super.onCreateOptionsMenu(menu);
        createMenu(menu);
        return true;
    }

    @Override
    public boolean onOptionsItemSelected(MenuItem item)
    {
        return menuChoice(item);
    }


    private void createMenu(Menu menu) {
        MenuItem mnu1 = menu.add(0, 0, 0, "Item 1");
        {
            mnu1.setAlphabeticShortcut('a');
        }
        MenuItem mnu2 = menu.add(0, 1, 1, "Item 2");
        {
            mnu2.setAlphabeticShortcut('b');
        }
        MenuItem mnu3 = menu.add(0, 2, 2, "Item 3");
        {
            mnu3.setAlphabeticShortcut('c');
        }
        MenuItem mnu4 = menu.add(0, 3, 3, "Item 4");
        {
            mnu4.setAlphabeticShortcut('d');
        }
        menu.add(0, 4, 4, "Item 5");
        menu.add(0, 5, 5, "Item 6");
        menu.add(0, 6, 6, "Item 7");
    }

    private boolean menuChoice(MenuItem item) {
        switch (item.getItemId()) {
            case 0:
                Toast.makeText(this, "You clicked on Item 1",
                        Toast.LENGTH_LONG).show();
```

```
                return true;
            case 1:
                Toast.makeText(this, "You clicked on Item 2",
                        Toast.LENGTH_LONG).show();
                return true;
            case 2:
                Toast.makeText(this, "You clicked on Item 3",
                        Toast.LENGTH_LONG).show();
                return true;
            case 3:
                Toast.makeText(this, "You clicked on Item 4",
                        Toast.LENGTH_LONG).show();
                return true;
            case 4:
                Toast.makeText(this, "You clicked on Item 5",
                        Toast.LENGTH_LONG).show();
                return true;
            case 5:
                Toast.makeText(this, "You clicked on Item 6",
                        Toast.LENGTH_LONG).show();
                return true;
            case 6:
                Toast.makeText(this, "You clicked on Item 7",
                        Toast.LENGTH_LONG).show();
                return true;
        }
        return false;
    }
}
```

2. Press Shift+F9 to debug the application on the Android emulator. Figure 6-7 shows the options menu that displays when you click the Menu button. To select a menu item, either click an individual item or use its shortcut key (A to D, and applicable only to the first four items).

How It Works

To display the options menu for your activity, you need to implement two methods in your activity:

- `onCreateOptionsMenu()`
- `onOptionsItemSelected()`

The `onCreateOptionsMenu()` method is called when the Menu button is pressed. In this case, you call the `createMenu()` helper method to display the options menu.

When a menu item is selected, the `onOptionsItemSelected()` method is called. In this case, you call the `menuChoice()` method to display the menu item selected (and perform whatever action is appropriate).

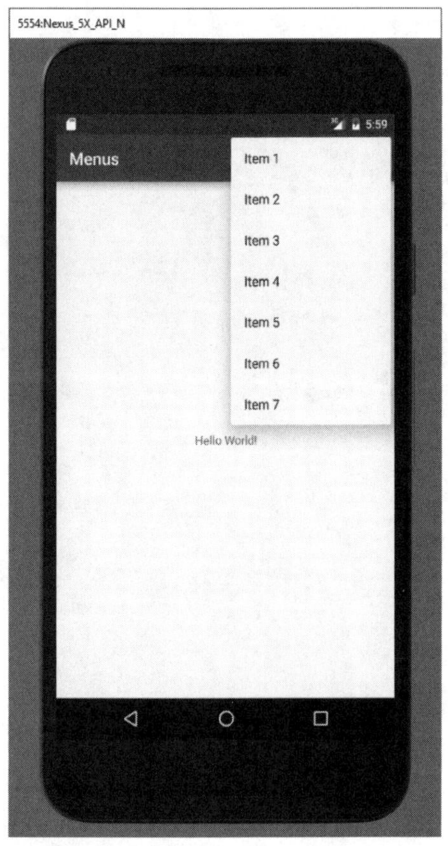

FIGURE 6-7

Take note of the look and feel of the options menu in different versions of Android. Starting with Honeycomb, the options menu items do not have icons and display all menu items in a scrollable list. Prior to Honeycomb, no more than five menu items are displayed. Additional menu items are part of the More menu item that represents the rest of the menu items.

Context Menu

The previous section showed how the options menu is displayed when the user presses the Menu button. In addition to the options menu, you can also display a context menu. A context menu is usually associated with a view on an activity. A context menu is displayed when the user taps and holds an item. For example, if the user taps a `Button` view and holds it for a few seconds, a context menu can be displayed.

If you want to associate a context menu with a view on an activity, you need to call the `setOnCreateContextMenuListener()` method of that particular view. The following Try It Out shows how you can associate a context menu with a `Button` view.

TRY IT OUT Displaying a Context Menu (Menus.zip)

1. Using the same project from the previous example, add the following bolded statements to the `activity_main.xml` file:

```
<?xml version="1.0" encoding="utf-8"?>
<android.support.constraint.ConstraintLayout xmlns:android=
    "http://schemas.android.com/apk/res/android"
    xmlns:app="http://schemas.android.com/apk/res-auto"
    xmlns:tools="http://schemas.android.com/tools"
    android:id="@+id/activity_main"
    android:layout_width="match_parent"
    android:layout_height="match_parent"
    tools:context="com.jfdimarzio.menus.MainActivity"
    tools:layout_editor_absoluteX="0dp"
    tools:layout_editor_absoluteY="81dp">

    <TextView
        android:layout_width="wrap_content"
        android:layout_height="wrap_content"
        android:text="Hello World!"
        tools:layout_editor_absoluteX="154dp"
        tools:layout_editor_absoluteY="247dp"
        app:layout_constraintLeft_toLeftOf="@+id/activity_main"
        tools:layout_constraintLeft_creator="0"
        app:layout_constraintTop_toTopOf="@+id/activity_main"
        tools:layout_constraintTop_creator="0"
        app:layout_constraintRight_toRightOf="@+id/activity_main"
        tools:layout_constraintRight_creator="0"
        app:layout_constraintBottom_toBottomOf="@+id/activity_main"
        tools:layout_constraintBottom_creator="0" />

    <Button
        android:text="Button"
        android:layout_width="wrap_content"
        android:layout_height="wrap_content"
        tools:layout_editor_absoluteX="148dp"
        tools:layout_editor_absoluteY="102dp"
        android:id="@+id/button"
        app:layout_constraintLeft_toLeftOf="@+id/activity_main"
        tools:layout_constraintLeft_creator="0"
        app:layout_constraintRight_toRightOf="@+id/activity_main"
        tools:layout_constraintRight_creator="0" />

</android.support.constraint.ConstraintLayout>
```

2. Add the following bolded statements to the `MenusActivity.java` file:

```
import android.os.Bundle;
import android.view.ContextMenu;
import android.view.Menu;
import android.view.MenuItem;
import android.view.View;
import android.widget.Button;
import android.widget.Toast;

public class MainActivity extends AppCompatActivity {

    @Override
    protected void onCreate(Bundle savedInstanceState) {
        super.onCreate(savedInstanceState);
        setContentView(R.layout.activity_main);

        Button btn = (Button) findViewById(R.id.button);
        btn.setOnCreateContextMenuListener(this);
    }

    @Override
    public void onCreateContextMenu(ContextMenu menu, View view,
                                    ContextMenu.ContextMenuInfo menuInfo)
    {
         super.onCreateContextMenu(menu, view, menuInfo);
         createMenu(menu);
    }


    @Override
    public boolean onCreateOptionsMenu(Menu menu) {
        super.onCreateOptionsMenu(menu);
        createMenu(menu);
        return true;
    }

    @Override
    public boolean onOptionsItemSelected(MenuItem item)
    {
        return menuChoice(item);
    }


    private void createMenu(Menu menu) {
        MenuItem mnu1 = menu.add(0, 0, 0, "Item 1");
        {
            mnu1.setAlphabeticShortcut('a');
        }
        MenuItem mnu2 = menu.add(0, 1, 1, "Item 2");
        {
            mnu2.setAlphabeticShortcut('b');
```

```
        }
        MenuItem mnu3 = menu.add(0, 2, 2, "Item 3");
        {
            mnu3.setAlphabeticShortcut('c');
        }
        MenuItem mnu4 = menu.add(0, 3, 3, "Item 4");
        {
            mnu4.setAlphabeticShortcut('d');
        }
        menu.add(0, 4, 4, "Item 5");
        menu.add(0, 5, 5, "Item 6");
        menu.add(0, 6, 6, "Item 7");
    }

    private boolean menuChoice(MenuItem item) {
        switch (item.getItemId()) {
            case 0:
                Toast.makeText(this, "You clicked on Item 1",
                        Toast.LENGTH_LONG).show();
                return true;
            case 1:
                Toast.makeText(this, "You clicked on Item 2",
                        Toast.LENGTH_LONG).show();
                return true;
            case 2:
                Toast.makeText(this, "You clicked on Item 3",
                        Toast.LENGTH_LONG).show();
                return true;
            case 3:
                Toast.makeText(this, "You clicked on Item 4",
                        Toast.LENGTH_LONG).show();
                return true;
            case 4:
                Toast.makeText(this, "You clicked on Item 5",
                        Toast.LENGTH_LONG).show();
                return true;
            case 5:
                Toast.makeText(this, "You clicked on Item 6",
                        Toast.LENGTH_LONG).show();
                return true;
            case 6:
                Toast.makeText(this, "You clicked on Item 7",
                        Toast.LENGTH_LONG).show();
                return true;
        }
        return false;
    }
}
```

3. Press Shift+F9 to debug the application on the Android emulator. Figure 6-8 shows the context menu that displays when you click and hold the `Button` view.

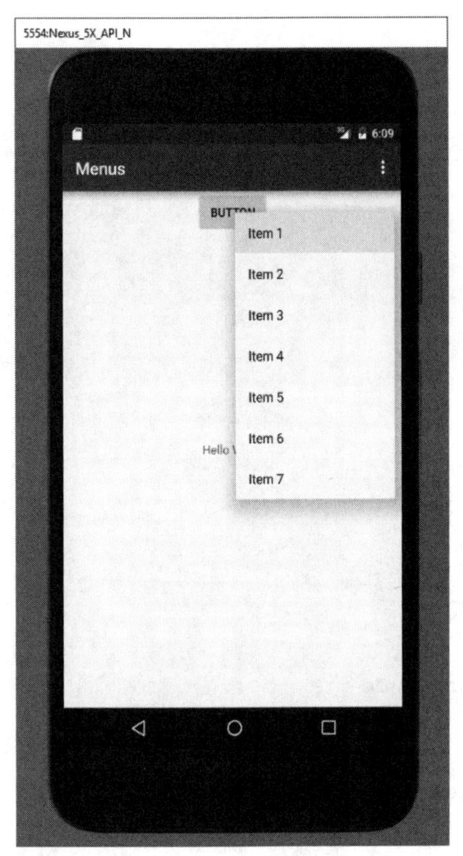

FIGURE 6-8

How It Works

In the preceding example, you call the `setOnCreateContextMenuListener()` method of the `Button` view to associate it with a context menu.

When the user taps and holds the `Button` view, the `onCreateContextMenu()` method is called. In this method, you call the `createMenu()` method to display the context menu.

Similarly, when an item inside the context menu is selected, the `onContextItemSelected()` method is called, where you call the `menuChoice()` method to display a message to the user.

Notice that the shortcut keys for the menu items do not work. To enable the shortcuts keys, you need to call the `setQuertyMode()` method of the `Menu` object, like this:

```
private void createMenu(Menu menu)
{
    menu.setQwertyMode(true);
    MenuItem mnu1 = menu.add(0, 0, 0, "Item 1");
```

```
        {
            mnu1.setAlphabeticShortcut('a');
        }
        //...
    }
```

USING WEBVIEW

Aside from the standard views that you have seen up to this point, the Android SDK provides some additional views that make your applications much more interesting. This section explains more about the `WebView`.

WebView

The `WebView` enables you to embed a web browser in your activity. This is very useful if your application needs to embed some web content, such as maps from some other providers, and so on. The following Try It Out shows how you can programmatically load the content of a web page and display it in your activity.

TRY IT OUT Using the WebView View (WebView.zip)

1. Using Android Studio, create a new Android project and name it **WebView**.
2. Add the following bolded statements to the `activity_main.xml` file:

```
<?xml version="1.0" encoding="utf-8"?>
<android.support.constraint.ConstraintLayout xmlns:android=
    "http://schemas.android.com/apk/res/android"
    xmlns:app="http://schemas.android.com/apk/res-auto"
    xmlns:tools="http://schemas.android.com/tools"
    android:id="@+id/activity_main"
    android:layout_width="match_parent"
    android:layout_height="match_parent"
    tools:context="com.jfdimarzio.webview.MainActivity"
    tools:layout_editor_absoluteX="0dp"
    tools:layout_editor_absoluteY="81dp">

    <WebView
        android:layout_width="384dp"
        android:layout_height="511dp"
        tools:layout_editor_absoluteX="0dp"
        tools:layout_editor_absoluteY="0dp"
        app:layout_constraintLeft_toLeftOf="@+id/activity_main"
        tools:layout_constraintLeft_creator="0"
        app:layout_constraintTop_toTopOf="@+id/activity_main"
        tools:layout_constraintTop_creator="0"
```

```
        app:layout_constraintRight_toRightOf="@+id/activity_main"
        tools:layout_constraintRight_creator="0"
        app:layout_constraintBottom_toBottomOf="@+id/activity_main"
        tools:layout_constraintBottom_creator="0"
        android:id="@+id/webview" />

</android.support.constraint.ConstraintLayout>
```

3. In the `MainActivity.java` file, add the following bolded statements:

```
import android.support.v7.app.AppCompatActivity;
import android.os.Bundle;
import android.webkit.WebSettings;
import android.webkit.WebView;

public class MainActivity extends AppCompatActivity {

    @Override
    protected void onCreate(Bundle savedInstanceState) {
        super.onCreate(savedInstanceState);
        setContentView(R.layout.activity_main);

        WebView wv = (WebView) findViewById(R.id.webview);

        WebSettings webSettings = wv.getSettings();
        webSettings.setBuiltInZoomControls(true);
        wv.loadUrl(
                "http://chart.apis.google.com/chart" +
                        "?chs=300x225" +
                        "&cht=v" +
                        "&chco=FF6342,ADDE63,63C6DE" +
                        "&chd=t:100,80,60,30,30,30,10" +
                        "&chdl=A|B|C");
    }
}
```

4. In the `app/manifests/AndroidManifest.xml` file, add the following permission (shown in bold):

```
<?xml version="1.0" encoding="utf-8"?>
<manifest xmlns:android="http://schemas.android.com/apk/res/android"
    package="com.jfdimarzio.webview">
    <uses-permission android:name="android.permission.INTERNET"/>
    <application
        android:allowBackup="true"
        android:icon="@mipmap/ic_launcher"
        android:label="@string/app_name"
        android:supportsRtl="true"
        android:theme="@style/AppTheme">
        <activity android:name=".MainActivity">
            <intent-filter>
                <action android:name="android.intent.action.MAIN" />
```

```
                <category android:name="android.intent.category.LAUNCHER" />
            </intent-filter>
        </activity>
    </application>

</manifest>
```

5. Press Shift+F9 to debug the application on the Android emulator. Figure 6-9 shows the content of the `WebView`.

FIGURE 6-9

How It Works

To use the `WebView` to load a web page, you use the `loadUrl()` method and pass a URL to it, like this:

```
wv.loadUrl(
    "http://chart.apis.google.com/chart" +
    "?chs=300x225" +
    "&cht=v" +
```

```
            "&chco=FF6342,ADDE63,63C6DE" +
            "&chd=t:100,80,60,30,30,30,10" +
            "&chdl=A|B|C");
```

To display the built-in zoom controls, you need to first get the `WebSettings` property from the `WebView` and then call its `setBuiltInZoomControls()` method:

```
WebSettings webSettings = wv.getSettings();
webSettings.setBuiltInZoomControls(true);
```

> ***NOTE*** *Although most Android devices support multitouch screens, the built-in zoom controls are useful for zooming your web content when testing your application on the Android emulator.*

SUMMARY

In this chapter, you have taken a look at the various views that enable you to display images: `Gallery`, `ImageView`, `ImageSwitcher`, and `GridView`. Also, you learned about the difference between options menus and context menus, and how to display both in your application. Finally, you learned about the `WebView`, which displays the content of a web page.

EXERCISES

1. What is the purpose of the `ImageSwitcher`?
2. Name the two methods you need to override when implementing an options menu in your activity.
3. Name the two methods you need to override when implementing a context menu in your activity.

You can find answers to the exercises in the appendix.

▶ WHAT YOU LEARNED IN THIS CHAPTER

TOPIC	KEY CONCEPTS
ImageView	<ImageView android:id="@+id/image1" android:layout_width="320px" android:layout_height="250px" android:scaleType="fitXY" />
Using the **ImageSwitcher** view	Performs animation when switching between images
ImageSwitcher	<ImageSwitcher android:id="@+id/switcher1" android:layout_width="fill_parent" android:layout_height="fill_parent" android:layout_alignParentLeft="true" android:layout_alignParentRight="true" android:layout_alignParentBottom="true" />
Using the **GridView**	Shows items in a two-dimensional scrolling grid
GridView	<GridView android:id="@+id/gridview" android:layout_width="fill_parent" android:layout_height="fill_parent" android:numColumns="auto_fit" android:verticalSpacing="10dp" android:horizontalSpacing="10dp" android:columnWidth="90dp" android:stretchMode="columnWidth" android:gravity="center" />
WebView	<WebView android:id="@+id/webview1" android:layout_width="wrap_content" android:layout_height="wrap_content" />

7

Data Persistence

WHAT YOU WILL LEARN IN THIS CHAPTER

- How to save simple data using the SharedPreferences object
- How to enable users to modify preferences using a PreferenceActivity class
- How to write and read files in internal and external storage
- How to create and use a SQLite database

> ***CODE DOWNLOAD*** *The wrox.com code downloads for this chapter are found at* `www.wrox.com/go/beginningandroidprog` *on the Download Code tab. The code is in the chapter 07 download and individually named according to the names throughout the chapter.*

This chapter describes how to persist data in your Android applications. Persisting data is an important topic in application development because users typically expect to reuse data in the future. For Android, there are primarily three basic ways of persisting data:

- A lightweight mechanism known as *shared preferences* to save small chunks of data
- Traditional file systems
- A relational database management system through the support of SQLite databases

The techniques discussed in this chapter enable applications to create and access their own private data. Chapter 8 shows you how to share data across applications.

SAVING AND LOADING USER PREFERENCES

Android provides the `SharedPreferences` object to help you save simple application data. For example, your application may have an option that enables users to specify the font size used in your application. In this case, your application needs to remember the size set by the user so that the size is set appropriately each time the app is opened. You have several options for saving this type of preference:

- **Save data to a file**—You can save the data to a file, but you have to perform some file management routines, such as writing the data to the file, indicating how many characters to read from it, and so on. Also, if you have several pieces of information to save, such as text size, font name, preferred background color, and so on, then the task of writing to a file becomes more onerous.
- **Writing text to a database**—An alternative to writing to a text file is to use a database. However, saving simple data to a database is overkill, both from a developer's point of view and in terms of the application's run-time performance.
- **Using the `SharedPreferences` object**—The `SharedPreferences` object, however, saves data through the use of name/value pairs. For example, specify a name for the data you want to save, and then both it and its value will be saved automatically to an XML file.

Accessing Preferences Using an Activity

In the following Try It Out, you see how to use the `SharedPreferences` object to store application data. You also find out how the stored application data can be modified directly by the user through a special type of activity provided by the Android OS.

TRY IT OUT Saving Data Using the SharedPreferences Object (SharedPreferences.zip)

1. Using Android Studio, create an Android project and name it **UsingPreferences.**
2. Create a new subdirectory in the res directory and name it **xml.** In this newly created directory, add a file and name it **myapppreferences.xml** (see Figure 7-1).

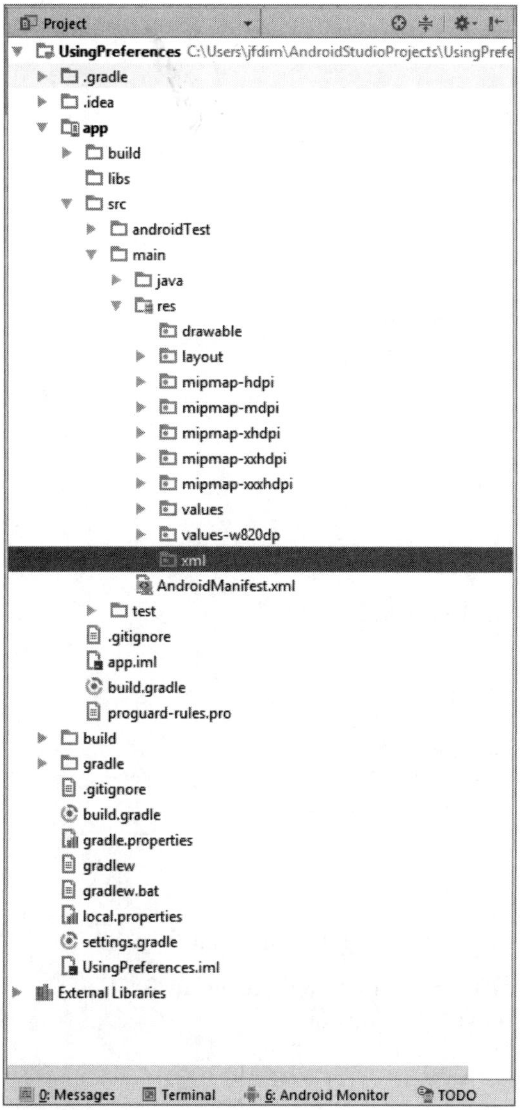

Project
UsingPreferences C:\Users\jfdim\AndroidStudioProjects\UsingPrefe
.gradle
.idea
app
build
libs
src
androidTest
main
java
res
drawable
layout
mipmap-hdpi
mipmap-mdpi
mipmap-xhdpi
mipmap-xxhdpi
mipmap-xxxhdpi
values
values-w820dp
xml
AndroidManifest.xml
test
.gitignore
app.iml
build.gradle
proguard-rules.pro
build
gradle
.gitignore
build.gradle
gradle.properties
gradlew
gradlew.bat
local.properties
settings.gradle
UsingPreferences.iml
External Libraries
0: Messages
Terminal
6: Android Monitor
TODO

FIGURE 7-1

3. Populate the myapppreferences.xml file as follows:

```
<?xml version="1.0" encoding="utf-8"?>
<PreferenceScreen
    xmlns:android="http://schemas.android.com/apk/res/android">
    <PreferenceCategory android:title="Category 1">
        <CheckBoxPreference
            android:title="Checkbox"
            android:defaultValue="false"
            android:summary="True or False"
            android:key="checkboxPref" />
        </PreferenceCategory>
    <PreferenceCategory android:title="Category 2">
        <EditTextPreference
            android:summary="Enter a string"
            android:defaultValue="[Enter a string here]"
            android:title="Edit Text"
            android:key="editTextPref" />
        <RingtonePreference
            android:summary="Select a ringtone"
            android:title="Ringtones"
            android:key="ringtonePref" />
        <PreferenceScreen
            android:title="Second Preference Screen"
            android:summary=
                "Click here to go to the second Preference Screen"
            android:key="secondPrefScreenPref" >
            <EditTextPreference
                android:summary="Enter a string"
                android:title="Edit Text (second Screen)"
                android:key="secondEditTextPref" />
        </PreferenceScreen>
    </PreferenceCategory>
</PreferenceScreen>
```

4. Create another XML file in the res/xml folder and name it **prefheaders.xml.**

5. Populate the prefheaders.xml file as follows. Please be sure to replace instances of com.jfdimarzio with the package name used in your project:

```
<?xml version="1.0" encoding="utf-8"?>
<preference-headers
    xmlns:android="http://schemas.android.com/apk/res/android">

    <header android:fragment=
    "com.jfdimarzio.usingpreferences.AppPreferenceActivity$PrefFragment"
        android:title="Preferences"
        android:summary="Sample preferences" />
</preference-headers>
```

6. Under the app/java/< package name>, add a new Class file and name it **AppPreferenceActivity.**

7. Populate the AppPreferenceActivity.java file as follows:

```
import android.os.Bundle;
import android.preference.PreferenceActivity;
import android.preference.PreferenceFragment;
```

```
import android.preference.PreferenceManager;

import java.util.List;

public class AppPreferenceActivity extends PreferenceActivity {

    @Override
    public void onCreate(Bundle savedInstanceState) {
        super.onCreate(savedInstanceState);
    }

    @Override
    public void onBuildHeaders(List<Header> target) {
        loadHeadersFromResource(R.xml.prefheaders, target);
    }

    @Override
    protected boolean isValidFragment(String fragmentName) {
        return true;
    }

    public static class PrefFragment extends PreferenceFragment {
        @Override
        public void onCreate(Bundle savedInstanceState) {
            super.onCreate(savedInstanceState);

            PreferenceManager.setDefaultValues(getActivity(),
                    R.xml.myapppreferences, false);
            // Load the preferences from an XML resource
            addPreferencesFromResource(R.xml.myapppreferences);
        }
    }

}
```

8. In the `AndroidManifest.xml` file, add the new entry for the `AppPreferenceActivity` class. Please be sure to replace instances of `com.jfdimarzio` with the package name used in your project:

```
<?xml version="1.0" encoding="utf-8"?>
<manifest xmlns:android="http://schemas.android.com/apk/res/android"
    package="com.jfdimarzio.usingpreferences">

    <application
        android:allowBackup="true"
        android:icon="@mipmap/ic_launcher"
        android:label="@string/app_name"
        android:supportsRtl="true"
        android:theme="@style/AppTheme">
        <activity
            android:name="com.jfdimarzio.usingpreferences.MainActivity"
            android:label="@string/app_name" >
            <intent-filter>
                <action android:name="android.intent.action.MAIN" />

                <category android:name="android.intent.category.LAUNCHER" />
            </intent-filter>
```

```
        </activity>
        <activity
            android:name="com.jfdimarzio.usingpreferences.
AppPreferenceActivity"
            android:label="@string/app_name" >
            <intent-filter>
                <action android:name="com.jfdimarzio.AppPreferenceActivity" />

                <category android:name="android.intent.category.DEFAULT" />
            </intent-filter>
        </activity>
    </application>
</manifest>
```

9. In the `activity_main.xml` file, add the following bolded code (replacing the existing `TextView`). Please be sure to replace instances of `com.jfdimarzio` with the package name used in your project:

```
<?xml version="1.0" encoding="utf-8"?>
<android.support.constraint.ConstraintLayout xmlns:android=
    "http://schemas.android.com/apk/res/android"
    xmlns:app="http://schemas.android.com/apk/res-auto"
    xmlns:tools="http://schemas.android.com/tools"
    android:id="@+id/activity_main"
    android:layout_width="match_parent"
    android:layout_height="match_parent"
    tools:context="com.jfdimarzio.usingpreferences.MainActivity">


    <Button
        android:text="Load Preferences Screen"
        android:layout_width="310dp"
        android:layout_height="wrap_content"
        android:id="@+id/btnPreferences"
        app:layout_constraintLeft_toLeftOf="@+id/activity_main"
        android:layout_marginStart="40dp"
        app:layout_constraintTop_toTopOf="@+id/activity_main"
        android:layout_marginTop="16dp"
        app:layout_constraintRight_toRightOf="@+id/activity_main"
        android:layout_marginEnd="16dp"
        app:layout_constraintBottom_toBottomOf="@+id/activity_main"
        android:layout_marginBottom="16dp"
        app:layout_constraintVertical_bias="0.0"
        android:onClick="onClickLoad"/>

    <Button
        android:text="Display Preferences Values"
        android:layout_width="310dp"
        android:layout_height="wrap_content"
        android:id="@+id/btnDisplayValues"
        app:layout_constraintLeft_toLeftOf="@+id/btnPreferences"
        app:layout_constraintTop_toBottomOf="@+id/btnPreferences"
```

```
            android:layout_marginTop="16dp"
            app:layout_constraintRight_toRightOf="@+id/btnPreferences"
            android:onClick="onClickDisplay"/>

        <EditText
            android:layout_width="310dp"
            android:layout_height="wrap_content"
            android:inputType="textPersonName"
            android:ems="10"
            android:id="@+id/editText"
            app:layout_constraintLeft_toLeftOf="@+id/btnPreferences"
            app:layout_constraintTop_toBottomOf="@+id/btnDisplayValues"
            android:layout_marginTop="16dp"
            app:layout_constraintRight_toRightOf="@+id/btnPreferences" />

        <Button
            android:text="Modify Preferences Values"
            android:layout_width="fill_parent"
            android:layout_height="wrap_content"
            android:id="@+id/btnModifyValues"
            app:layout_constraintLeft_toLeftOf="@+id/btnDisplayValues"
            app:layout_constraintTop_toBottomOf="@+id/editText"
            android:layout_marginTop="16dp"
            app:layout_constraintRight_toRightOf="@+id/btnDisplayValues"
            android:onClick="onClickModify" />
</android.support.constraint.ConstraintLayout>
```

10. Add the following bolded lines to the `MainActivity.java` file: Please be sure to replace instances of `com.jfdimarzio` with the package name used in your project:

```
import android.support.v7.app.AppCompatActivity;
import android.content.Intent;
import android.os.Bundle;
import android.view.View;
public class MainActivity extends AppCompatActivity {
    /** Called when the activity is first created. */
    @Override
    public void onCreate(Bundle savedInstanceState) {
        super.onCreate(savedInstanceState);
        setContentView(R.layout.activity_main);
    }

    public void onClickLoad(View view) {
        Intent i = new Intent("com.jfdimarzio.AppPreferenceActivity");
        startActivity(i);
    }
}
```

11. Press Shift+F9 to debug the application on the Android emulator.

12. Click the Load Preferences Screen button to see the Preference Headers screen.

13. Click the Preferences Headers to see the Preferences Screen, as shown in Figure 7-2.

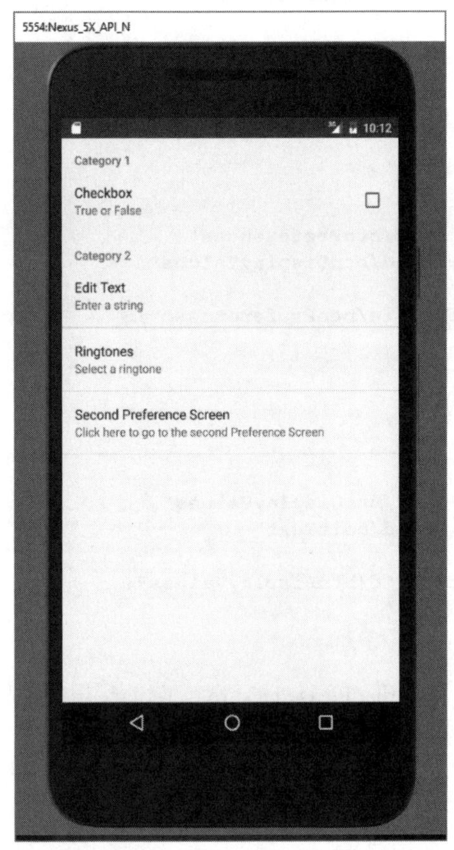

FIGURE 7-2

13. Clicking the Checkbox item toggles the check box's value between checked and unchecked. Note the two categories: Category 1 and Category 2.
14. Click the Edit Text item and enter some values as shown in Figure 7-3. Click OK to dismiss the dialog.

15. Click the Ringtones item to select either the default ringtone or silent mode (see Figure 7-4). If you test the application on a real Android device, you can select from a more comprehensive list of ringtones.

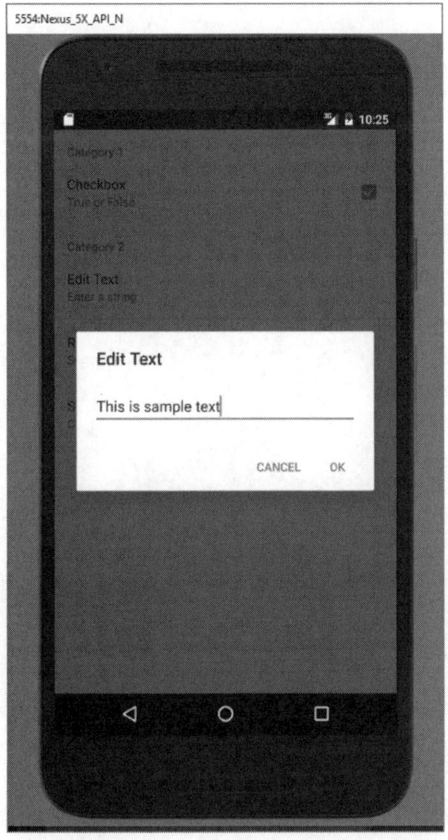

FIGURE 7-3

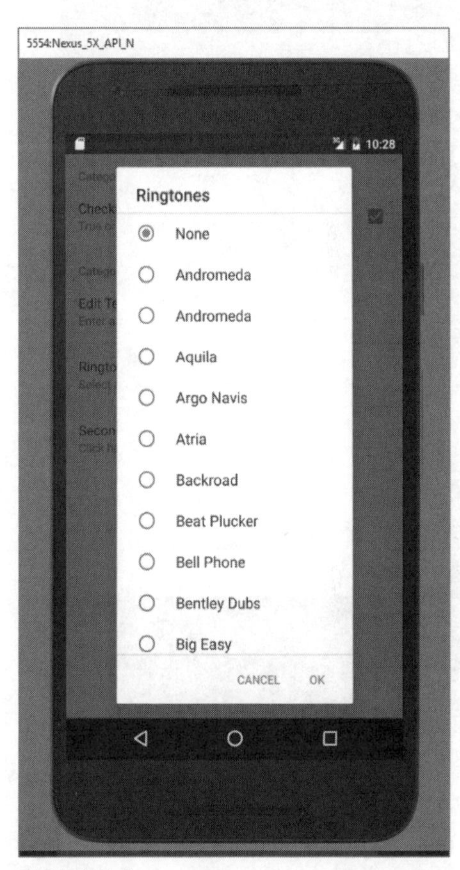

FIGURE 7-4

16. Click the Second Preference Screen item to navigate to the next screen (see Figure 7-5).

FIGURE 7-5

17. Click the Back button to go back to the previous screen. To dismiss the preferences screen, you also click the Back button.

How It Works

You first create an XML file named `myapppreferences.xml` to store the types of preferences you want to save for your application:

```
<?xml version="1.0" encoding="utf-8"?>
<PreferenceScreen
    xmlns:android="http://schemas.android.com/apk/res/android">
    <PreferenceCategory android:title="Category 1">
        <CheckBoxPreference
            android:title="Checkbox"
            android:defaultValue="false"
            android:summary="True or False"
            android:key="checkboxPref" />
        </PreferenceCategory>
    <PreferenceCategory android:title="Category 2">
        <EditTextPreference
```

```
            android:summary="Enter a string"
            android:defaultValue="[Enter a string here]"
            android:title="Edit Text"
            android:key="editTextPref" />
        <RingtonePreference
            android:summary="Select a ringtone"
            android:title="Ringtones"
            android:key="ringtonePref" />
        <PreferenceScreen
            android:title="Second Preference Screen"
            android:summary=
                "Click here to go to the second Preference Screen"
            android:key="secondPrefScreenPref" >
            <EditTextPreference
                android:summary="Enter a string"
                android:title="Edit Text (second Screen)"
                android:key="secondEditTextPref" />
        </PreferenceScreen>
    </PreferenceCategory>
</PreferenceScreen>
```

In the preceding snippet, you created the following:

- Two preference categories for grouping different types of preferences
- Two check box preferences with keys named `checkboxPref` and `secondEditTextPref`
- A ringtone preference with a key named `ringtonePref`
- A preference screen to contain additional preferences

The `android:key` attribute specifies the key that you can programmatically reference in your code to set or retrieve the value of that particular preference.

To get the operating system (OS) to display all these preferences for users to edit, you create an activity that extends the `PreferenceActivity` base class, and then call a PreferenceFragment. The PreferenceFragment loads the `prefheaders.xml` and calls the `addPreferencesFromResource()` method to load the XML file containing the preferences:

```
public class AppPreferenceActivity extends PreferenceActivity {

    @Override
    public void onCreate(Bundle savedInstanceState) {
        super.onCreate(savedInstanceState);
    }

    @Override
    public void onBuildHeaders(List<Header> target) {
        loadHeadersFromResource(R.xml.prefheaders, target);
    }

    @Override
    protected boolean isValidFragment(String fragmentName) {
        return true;
    }
```

```
        public static class PrefFragment extends PreferenceFragment {
            @Override
            public void onCreate(Bundle savedInstanceState) {
                super.onCreate(savedInstanceState);

                PreferenceManager.setDefaultValues(getActivity(),
                        R.xml.myapppreferences, false);
                // Load the preferences from an XML resource
                addPreferencesFromResource(R.xml.myapppreferences);
            }
        }
    }
```

The `PreferenceActivity` class is a specialized type of activity that displays a hierarchy of preferences to the user.

To display the activity for the preferences, you invoke it using an `Intent` object:

```
        public void onClickLoad(View view) {
            Intent i = new Intent("com.jfdimarzio.AppPreferenceActivity");
            startActivity(i);
        }
```

All the changes made to the preferences are automatically persisted to an XML file in the `shared_prefs` folder of the application.

Programmatically Retrieving and Modifying the Preferences Values

In the previous section, you saw how the `PreferenceActivity` class both enables developers to easily create preferences and enables users to modify them during runtime. To make use of these preferences in your application, you use the `SharedPreferences` class. The following Try It Out shows you how.

TRY IT OUT Retrieving and Modifying Preferences

1. Using the same project created in the previous section, add the following bolded lines to the `MainActivity.java` file. Please be sure to replace instances of `com.jfdimarzio` with the package name used in your project:

```
import android.support.v7.app.AppCompatActivity;
import android.os.Bundle;
```

```
import android.view.View;
import android.widget.EditText;
import android.widget.Toast;

public class MainActivity extends AppCompatActivity {

    @Override
    protected void onCreate(Bundle savedInstanceState) {
        super.onCreate(savedInstanceState);
        setContentView(R.layout.activity_main);
    }
    public void onClickLoad(View view) {
        Intent i = new Intent("com.jfdimarzio.AppPreferenceActivity");
        startActivity(i);
    }
    public void onClickDisplay(View view) {
        SharedPreferences appPrefs =
                getSharedPreferences(
"com.jfdimarzio.usingpreferences_preferences", MODE_PRIVATE);
        DisplayText(appPrefs.getString("editTextPref", ""));
    }
    public void onClickModify(View view) {
        SharedPreferences appPrefs =
                getSharedPreferences(
"com.jfdimarzio.usingpreferences_preferences", MODE_PRIVATE);
        SharedPreferences.Editor prefsEditor = appPrefs.edit();
        prefsEditor.putString("editTextPref",
                ((EditText) findViewById(R.id.editText)).getText().toString());
        prefsEditor.commit();
    }
    private void DisplayText(String str) {
        Toast.makeText(getBaseContext(), str, Toast.LENGTH_LONG).show();
    }

}
```

2. Press Shift+F9 to rerun the application on the Android emulator. Clicking the Display Preferences Values button displays the value shown in Figure 7-6.
3. Enter a string in the `EditText` view and click the Modify Preferences Values button (see Figure 7-7).

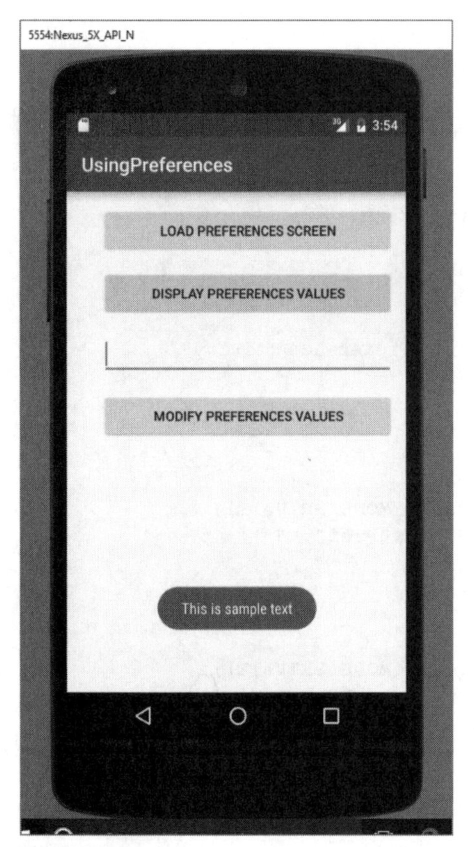

FIGURE 7-6

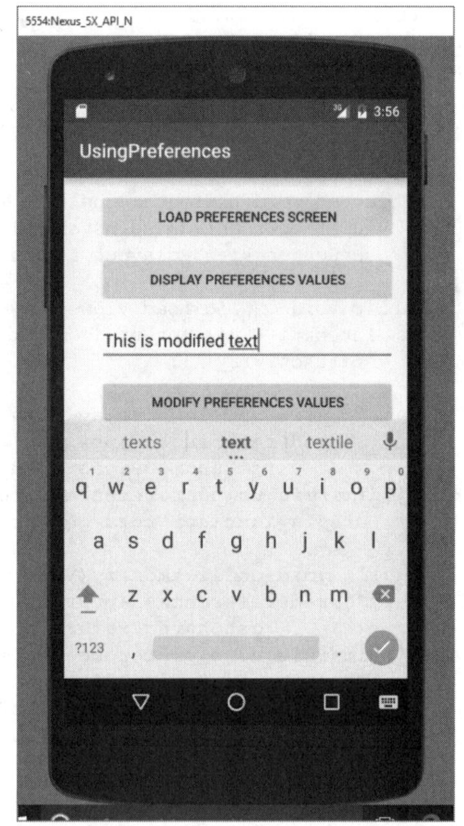

FIGURE 7-7

4. Now click the Display Preferences Values button again. Note that the new value is saved (see Figure 7-8).

How It Works

In the `onClickDisplay()` method, you first used the `getSharedPreferences()` method to obtain an instance of the `SharedPreferences` class. You do so by specifying the name of the XML file (in this case it is "`<PackageName>.usingpreferences_preferences`," using the format: *`<PackageName>_preferences`*). To retrieve a string preference, you used the `getString()` method, passing it the key to the preference that you want to retrieve:

```
public void onClickDisplay(View view) {
        SharedPreferences appPrefs =
                getSharedPreferences("com.jfdimarzio.usingpreferences_preferences",
                        MODE_PRIVATE);
        DisplayText(appPrefs.getString("editTextPref", ""));
    }
```

The MODE_PRIVATE constant indicates that the preference file can be opened only by the application that created it.

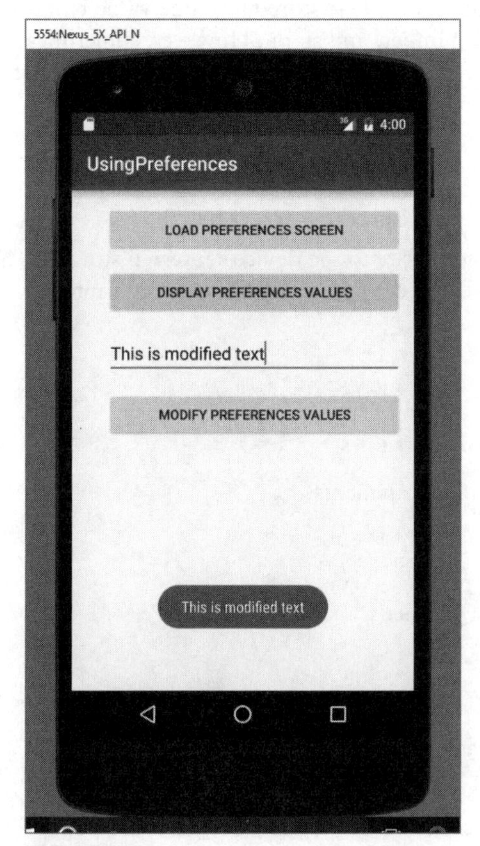

FIGURE 7-8

In the onClickModify() method, create a SharedPreferences.Editor object through the edit() method of the SharedPreferences object. To change the value of a string preference, use the putString() method. To save the changes to the preferences file, use the commit() method:

```
public void onClickModify(View view) {
        SharedPreferences appPrefs =
                getSharedPreferences("com.jfdimarzio.usingpreferences_preferences",
                        MODE_PRIVATE);
        SharedPreferences.Editor prefsEditor = appPrefs.edit();
        prefsEditor.putString("editTextPref",
                ((EditText) findViewById(R.id.editText)).getText().toString());
        prefsEditor.commit();
    }
```

PERSISTING DATA TO FILES

The `SharedPreferences` object enables you to store data that is best stored as name/value pairs—for example, user ID, birth date, gender, driver's license number, and so on. However, sometimes you might prefer to use the traditional file system to store your data. For example, you might want to store the text of poems you want to display in your applications. In Android, you can use the classes in the `java.io` package to do so.

Saving to Internal Storage

The first way to save files in your Android application is to write to the device's internal storage. The following Try It Out demonstrates how to save a string entered by the user to the device's internal storage.

TRY IT OUT Saving Data to Internal Storage (Files.zip)

1. Using Android Studio, create an Android project and name it **Files**.
2. In the `activity_main.xml` file, add the following bolded statements:

```
<?xml version="1.0" encoding="utf-8"?>
<android.support.constraint.ConstraintLayout xmlns:android=
    "http://schemas.android.com/apk/res/android"
    xmlns:app="http://schemas.android.com/apk/res-auto"
    xmlns:tools="http://schemas.android.com/tools"
    android:id="@+id/activity_main"
    android:layout_width="match_parent"
    android:layout_height="match_parent"
    tools:context="com.jfdimarzio.files.MainActivity">

    <TextView
        android:text="Please enter some text."
        android:layout_width="245dp"
        android:layout_height="wrap_content"
        android:id="@+id/textView"
        app:layout_constraintLeft_toLeftOf="@+id/activity_main"
       app:layout_constraintTop_toTopOf="@+id/activity_main"
        android:layout_marginTop="16dp"
        app:layout_constraintRight_toRightOf="@+id/activity_main"
        app:layout_constraintBottom_toTopOf="@+id/editText"
        android:layout_marginBottom="8dp"
        app:layout_constraintVertical_bias="0.28" />

    <EditText
        android:layout_width="241dp"
        android:layout_height="wrap_content"
        android:inputType="text"
        android:ems="10"
        tools:layout_editor_absoluteY="82dp"
        android:id="@+id/editText"
        app:layout_constraintLeft_toLeftOf="@+id/activity_main"
```

```
        app:layout_constraintRight_toRightOf="@+id/activity_main"
        app:layout_constraintTop_toBottomOf="@+id/textView"
        android:layout_marginTop="136dp"/>

    <Button
        android:text="Save"
        android:layout_width="240dp"
        android:layout_height="wrap_content"
        android:id="@+id/btnSave"
        app:layout_constraintLeft_toLeftOf="@+id/activity_main"
        android:layout_marginStart="16dp"
        app:layout_constraintTop_toBottomOf="@+id/editText"
        android:layout_marginTop="136dp"
        app:layout_constraintRight_toRightOf="@+id/activity_main"
        android:layout_marginEnd="16dp"
        android:onClick="onClickSave" />

    <Button
        android:text="Load"
        android:layout_width="241dp"
        android:layout_height="wrap_content"
        android:id="@+id/btnLoad"
        app:layout_constraintLeft_toLeftOf="@+id/activity_main"
        android:layout_marginStart="16dp"
        app:layout_constraintTop_toBottomOf="@+id/editText"
        android:layout_marginTop="48dp"
        app:layout_constraintRight_toRightOf="@+id/activity_main"
        android:layout_marginEnd="16dp"
        android:onClick="onClickLoad" />

</android.support.constraint.ConstraintLayout>
```

3. In the `MainActivity.java` file, add the following bolded statements:

```
import android.os.Bundle;
import android.support.v7.app.AppCompatActivity;
import android.view.View;
import android.widget.EditText;
import android.widget.Toast;

import java.io.FileInputStream;
import java.io.FileOutputStream;
import java.io.IOException;
import java.io.InputStreamReader;
import java.io.OutputStreamWriter;

public class MainActivity extends AppCompatActivity {
    EditText textBox;
    static final int READ_BLOCK_SIZE = 100;

    @Override
    protected void onCreate(Bundle savedInstanceState) {
        super.onCreate(savedInstanceState);
```

```
        setContentView(R.layout.activity_main);

        textBox = (EditText) findViewById(R.id.editText);
    }

    public void onClickSave(View view) {
        String str = textBox.getText().toString();
        try {
            FileOutputStream fOut = openFileOutput("textfile.txt",
MODE_PRIVATE);
            OutputStreamWriter osw = new OutputStreamWriter(fOut);
            //---write the string to the file---
            try {
                osw.write(str);
            } catch (IOException e) {
                e.printStackTrace();
            }
            osw.flush();
            osw.close();
            //---display file saved message---
            Toast.makeText(getBaseContext(),
      "File saved successfully!", Toast.LENGTH_SHORT).show();
            //---clears the EditText---
            textBox.setText("");
        } catch (IOException ioe) {
            ioe.printStackTrace();
        }
    }

    public void onClickLoad(View view) {
        try {
            FileInputStream fIn = openFileInput("textfile.txt");
            InputStreamReader isr = new InputStreamReader(fIn);
            char[] inputBuffer = new char[READ_BLOCK_SIZE];
            String s = "";
            int charRead;
            while ((charRead = isr.read(inputBuffer)) > 0) {
                //---convert the chars to a String---
                String readString =
                        String.copyValueOf(inputBuffer, 0,
                                charRead);
                s += readString;
                inputBuffer = new char[READ_BLOCK_SIZE];
            }
            //---set the EditText to the text that has been
            // read---
            textBox.setText(s);
            Toast.makeText(getBaseContext(), "File loaded successfully!",
                    Toast.LENGTH_SHORT).show();
        } catch (IOException ioe) {
            ioe.printStackTrace();
        }
    }
}
```

4. Press Shift+F9 to debug the application on the Android emulator.
5. Type some text into the `EditText` view (see Figure 7-9) and then click the Save button.

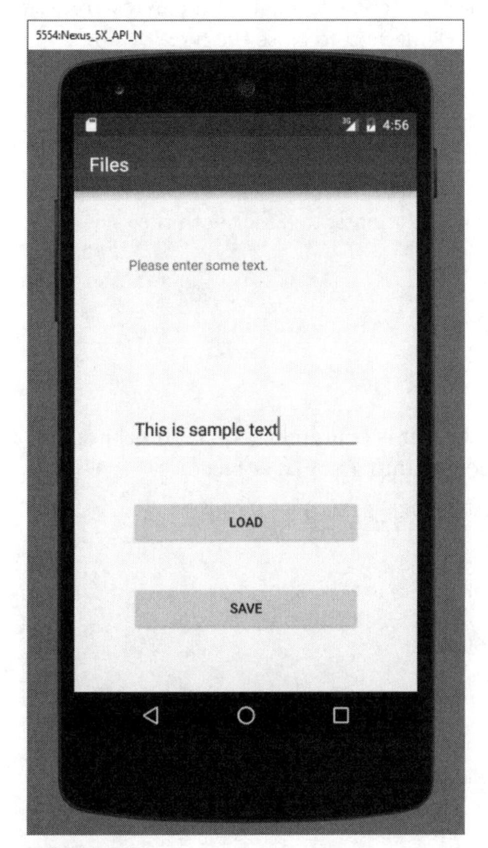

FIGURE 7-9

6. If the file is saved successfully, you see the `Toast` class displaying the "File saved successfully!" message. The text in the `EditText` view should disappear.
7. Click the Load button and you should see the string appearing in the `EditText` view again. This confirms that the text is saved correctly.

How It Works

To save text into a file, you use the `FileOutputStream` class. The `openFileOutput()` method opens a named file for writing, with the mode specified. In this example, you use the `MODE_PRIVATE` constant to indicate that the file is readable by all other applications:

```
FileOutputStream fOut = openFileOutput("textfile.txt", MODE_PRIVATE);
```

To convert a character stream into a byte stream, you use an instance of the `OutputStreamWriter` class, by passing it an instance of the `FileOutputStream` object:

```
OutputStreamWriter osw = new
        OutputStreamWriter(fOut);
```

You then use its `write()` method to write the string to the file. To ensure that all the bytes are written to the file, use the `flush()` method. Finally, use the `close()` method to close the file:

```
//---write the string to the file---
osw.write(str);
osw.flush();
osw.close();
```

7. To read the content of a file, you use the `FileInputStream` class, together with the `InputStreamReader` class:

```
FileInputStream fIn =
        openFileInput("textfile.txt");
InputStreamReader isr = new
        InputStreamReader(fIn);
```

Because you do not know the size of the file to read, the content is read in blocks of 100 characters into a buffer (character array). The characters read are then copied into a `String` object:

```
char[] inputBuffer = new char[READ_BLOCK_SIZE];
String s = "";
int charRead;
while ((charRead = isr.read(inputBuffer))>0)
{
    //---convert the chars to a String---
    String readString =
            String.copyValueOf(inputBuffer, 0,
                    charRead);
    s += readString;
    inputBuffer = new char[READ_BLOCK_SIZE];
}
```

The `read()` method of the `InputStreamReader` object checks the number of characters read and returns –1 if the end of the file is reached.

Saving to External Storage (SD Card)

The previous section showed how you can save your files to the internal storage of your Android device. Sometimes, it would be useful to save them to external storage (such as an SD card) because of its larger capacity, as well as the capability to share the files easily with other users (by removing the SD card and passing it to somebody else). You can use the following steps to save files to external storage:

1. Using the project created in the previous section as the example (saving text entered by the user to the SD card), modify the `onClick()` method of the Save button as shown in bold here:

```
import java.io.File;
import java.io.FileInputStream;
import java.io.FileOutputStream;
import java.io.IOException;
import java.io.InputStreamReader;
import java.io.OutputStreamWriter;
import android.app.Activity;
import android.os.Bundle;
import android.os.Environment;
import android.view.View;
import android.widget.EditText;
import android.widget.Toast;
    public void onClickSave(View view) {
        String str = textBox.getText().toString();
        try
        {
            //---SD Card Storage---
            File sdCard = Environment.getExternalStorageDirectory();
            File directory = new File (sdCard.getAbsolutePath() +
                "/MyFiles");
            directory.mkdirs();
            File file = new File(directory, "textfile.txt");
            FileOutputStream fOut = new FileOutputStream(file);
            /*
            FileOutputStream fOut =
                    openFileOutput("textfile.txt",
                            MODE_WORLD_READABLE);
            */

            OutputStreamWriter osw = new
                    OutputStreamWriter(fOut);
            //---write the string to the file---
            osw.write(str);
            osw.flush();
            osw.close();
            //---display file saved message---
            Toast.makeText(getBaseContext(),
                    "File saved successfully!",
                    Toast.LENGTH_SHORT).show();
            //---clears the EditText---
            textBox.setText("");
        }
        catch (IOException ioe)
        {
            ioe.printStackTrace();
        }
    }
```

2. The preceding code uses the `getExternalStorageDirectory()` method to return the full path to the external storage. Typically, it should return the "`/sdcard`" path for a real device, and "`/mnt/sdcard`" for an Android emulator. However, you should never try to hardcode the path to the SD card, as manufacturers may choose to assign a different path name to the SD card. Be sure to use the `getExternalStorageDirectory()` method to return the full path to the SD card.
3. You then create a directory called `MyFiles` in the SD card.
4. Finally, you save the file into this directory.
5. To load the file from the external storage, modify the `onClickLoad()` method for the Load button:

```
public void onClickLoad(View view) {
    try
    {
        //---SD Storage---
        File sdCard = Environment.getExternalStorageDirectory();
        File directory = new File (sdCard.getAbsolutePath() +
            "/MyFiles");
        File file = new File(directory, "textfile.txt");
        FileInputStream fIn = new FileInputStream(file);
        InputStreamReader isr = new InputStreamReader(fIn);
        /*
        FileInputStream fIn =
                openFileInput("textfile.txt");
        InputStreamReader isr = new
                InputStreamReader(fIn);
        */

        char[] inputBuffer = new char[READ_BLOCK_SIZE];
        String s = "";
        int charRead;
        while ((charRead = isr.read(inputBuffer))>0)
        {
            //---convert the chars to a String---
            String readString =
                    String.copyValueOf(inputBuffer, 0,
                            charRead);
            s += readString;
            inputBuffer = new char[READ_BLOCK_SIZE];
        }
        //---set the EditText to the text that has been
        // read---
        textBox.setText(s);
        Toast.makeText(getBaseContext(),
                "File loaded successfully!",
```

```
                    Toast.LENGTH_SHORT).show();
        }
        catch (IOException ioe) {
            ioe.printStackTrace();
        }
    }
```

6. Note that in order to write to the external storage, you need to add the `WRITE_EXTERNAL_STORAGE` permission in your `AndroidManifest.xml` file:

```
<?xml version="1.0" encoding="utf-8"?>
<manifest xmlns:android="http://schemas.android.com/apk/res/android"
    package="com.jfdimarzio.Files"
    android:versionCode="1"
    android:versionName="1.0" >
    <uses-sdk android:minSdkVersion="14" />
    <uses-permission android:name=
"android.permission.WRITE_EXTERNAL_STORAGE" />

    <application
        android:icon="@drawable/ic_launcher"
        android:label="@string/app_name" >
        <activity
            android:label="@string/app_name"
            android:name=".FilesActivity" >
            <intent-filter >
                <action android:name="android.intent.action.MAIN" />
                <category android:name="android.intent.category.LAUNCHER" />
            </intent-filter>
        </activity>
    </application>
</manifest>
```

Choosing the Best Storage Option

The previous sections described three main ways to save data in your Android applications: the `SharedPreferences` object, internal storage, and external storage. Which one should you use in your applications? Here are some guidelines:

- If you have data that can be represented using name/value pairs, then use the `SharedPreferences` object. For example, if you want to store user preference data such as username, background color, date of birth, or last login date, then the `SharedPreferences` object is the ideal way to store this data. Moreover, you don't really have to do much to store data this way. Simply use the `SharedPreferences` object to store and retrieve it.
- If you need to store ad-hoc data then using the internal storage is a good option. For example, your application (such as an RSS reader) might need to download images from the

web for display. In this scenario, saving the images to internal storage is a good solution. You might also need to persist data created by the user, such as when you have an application that enables users to take notes and save them for later use. In both of these scenarios, using the internal storage is a good choice.

- There are times when you need to share your application data with other users. For example, you might create an Android application that logs the coordinates of the locations that a user has been to, and subsequently, you want to share all this data with other users. In this scenario, you can store your files on the SD card of the device so that users can easily transfer the data to other devices (and computers) for use later.

CREATING AND USING DATABASES

So far, all the techniques you have seen are useful for saving simple sets of data. For saving relational data, using a database is much more efficient. For example, if you want to store the test results of all the students in a school, it is much more efficient to use a database to represent them because you can use database querying to retrieve the results of specific students. Moreover, using databases enables you to enforce data integrity by specifying the relationships between different sets of data.

Android uses the SQLite database system. The database that you create for an application is only accessible to itself; other applications will not be able to access it.

In this section, you find out how to programmatically create a SQLite database in your Android application. For Android, the SQLite database that you create programmatically in an application is always stored in the `/data/data/<package_name>/databases` folder.

Creating the DBAdapter Helper Class

A good practice for dealing with databases is to create a helper class to encapsulate all the complexities of accessing the data so that it is transparent to the calling code. For this section, you create a helper class called `DBAdapter`, which creates, opens, closes, and uses a SQLite database.

In this example, you are going to create a database named `MyDB` containing one table named `contacts`. This table has three columns: `_id`, `name`, and `email`.

TRY IT OUT Creating the Database Helper Class (Databases.zip)

1. Using Android Studio, create an Android project and name it **Databases**.
2. Add a new Java Class file to the package and name it **DBAdapter** (see Figure 7-10).

FIGURE 7-10

3. Add the following bolded statements to the `DBAdapter.java` file:

```
import android.content.ContentValues;
import android.content.Context;
```

```
import android.database.Cursor;
import android.database.SQLException;
import android.database.sqlite.SQLiteDatabase;
import android.database.sqlite.SQLiteOpenHelper;
import android.util.Log;

public class DBAdapter {
    static final String KEY_ROWID = "_id";
    static final String KEY_NAME = "name";
    static final String KEY_EMAIL = "email";
    static final String TAG = "DBAdapter";
    static final String DATABASE_NAME = "MyDB";
    static final String DATABASE_TABLE = "contacts";
    static final int DATABASE_VERSION = 1;
    static final String DATABASE_CREATE =
            "create table contacts (_id integer primary key autoincrement, "
                    + "name text not null, email text not null);";
    final Context context;
    DatabaseHelper DBHelper;
    SQLiteDatabase db;

    public DBAdapter(Context ctx)
    {
        this.context = ctx;
        DBHelper = new DatabaseHelper(context);
    }
    private static class DatabaseHelper extends SQLiteOpenHelper
    {
        DatabaseHelper(Context context)
        {
            super(context, DATABASE_NAME, null, DATABASE_VERSION);
        }
        @Override
        public void onCreate(SQLiteDatabase db)
        {
            try {
                db.execSQL(DATABASE_CREATE);
            } catch (SQLException e) {
                e.printStackTrace();
            }
        }
        @Override
        public void onUpgrade(SQLiteDatabase db, int oldVersion, int newVersion)
        {
            Log.w(TAG, "Upgrading database from version " + oldVersion + " to "
                    + newVersion + ", which will destroy all old data");
            db.execSQL("DROP TABLE IF EXISTS contacts");
            onCreate(db);
        }
    }
    //---opens the database---
    public DBAdapter open() throws SQLException
```

```
    {
        db = DBHelper.getWritableDatabase();
        return this;
    }
    //---closes the database---
    public void close()
    {
        DBHelper.close();
    }
    //---insert a contact into the database---
    public long insertContact(String name, String email)
    {
        ContentValues initialValues = new ContentValues();
        initialValues.put(KEY_NAME, name);
        initialValues.put(KEY_EMAIL, email);
        return db.insert(DATABASE_TABLE, null, initialValues);
    }
    //---deletes a particular contact---
    public boolean deleteContact(long rowId)
    {
        return db.delete(DATABASE_TABLE, KEY_ROWID + "=" + rowId, null) > 0;
    }
    //---retrieves all the contacts---
    public Cursor getAllContacts()
    {
        return db.query(DATABASE_TABLE, new String[] {KEY_ROWID, KEY_NAME,
                KEY_EMAIL}, null, null, null, null, null);
    }
    //---retrieves a particular contact---
    public Cursor getContact(long rowId) throws SQLException
    {
        Cursor mCursor =
                db.query(true, DATABASE_TABLE, new String[] {KEY_ROWID,
                                KEY_NAME, KEY_EMAIL},
     KEY_ROWID + "=" + rowId, null,
                        null, null, null, null);
        if (mCursor != null) {
            mCursor.moveToFirst();
        }
        return mCursor;
    }
    //---updates a contact---
    public boolean updateContact(long rowId, String name, String email)
    {
        ContentValues args = new ContentValues();
        args.put(KEY_NAME, name);
        args.put(KEY_EMAIL, email);
        return db.update(DATABASE_TABLE, args, KEY_ROWID + "=" + rowId, null) >
0;
    }
}
```

How It Works

You first define several constants to contain the various fields for the table that you are going to create in your database:

```
static final String KEY_ROWID = "_id";
static final String KEY_NAME = "name";
static final String KEY_EMAIL = "email";
static final String TAG = "DBAdapter";
static final String DATABASE_NAME = "MyDB";
static final String DATABASE_TABLE = "contacts";
static final int DATABASE_VERSION = 1;
static final String DATABASE_CREATE =
    "create table contacts (_id integer primary key autoincrement, "
    + "name text not null, email text not null);";
```

In particular, the `DATABASE_CREATE` constant contains the SQL statement for creating the `contacts` table within the `MyDB` database.

Within the `DBAdapter` class, you also add a private class that extends the `SQLiteOpenHelper` class. `SQLiteOpenHelper` is a helper class in Android to manage database creation and version management. In particular, you must override the `onCreate()` and `onUpgrade()` methods:

```
private static class DatabaseHelper extends SQLiteOpenHelper
{
    DatabaseHelper(Context context)
    {
        super(context, DATABASE_NAME, null, DATABASE_VERSION);
    }
    @Override
    public void onCreate(SQLiteDatabase db)
    {
        try {
            db.execSQL(DATABASE_CREATE);
        } catch (SQLException e) {
            e.printStackTrace();
        }
    }
    @Override
    public void onUpgrade(SQLiteDatabase db, int oldVersion, int newVersion)
    {
        Log.w(TAG, "Upgrading database from version " + oldVersion + " to "
                + newVersion + ", which will destroy all old data");
        db.execSQL("DROP TABLE IF EXISTS contacts");
        onCreate(db);
    }
}
```

The `onCreate()` method creates a new database if the required database is not present. The `onUpgrade()` method is called when the database needs to be upgraded. This is achieved by checking the value defined in the `DATABASE_VERSION` constant. For this implementation of the `onUpgrade()` method, you simply drop the table and create it again.

You can then define the various methods for opening and closing the database, as well as the methods for adding/editing/deleting rows in the table:

```
//---opens the database---
public DBAdapter open() throws SQLException
{
    db = DBHelper.getWritableDatabase();
    return this;
}
//---closes the database---
public void close()
{
    DBHelper.close();
}
//---insert a contact into the database---
public long insertContact(String name, String email)
{
    ContentValues initialValues = new ContentValues();
    initialValues.put(KEY_NAME, name);
    initialValues.put(KEY_EMAIL, email);
    return db.insert(DATABASE_TABLE, null, initialValues);
}
//---deletes a particular contact---
public boolean deleteContact(long rowId)
{
    return db.delete(DATABASE_TABLE, KEY_ROWID + "=" + rowId, null) > 0;
}
//---retrieves all the contacts---
public Cursor getAllContacts()
{
    return db.query(DATABASE_TABLE, new String[] {KEY_ROWID, KEY_NAME,
            KEY_EMAIL}, null, null, null, null, null);
}
//---retrieves a particular contact---
public Cursor getContact(long rowId) throws SQLException
{
    Cursor mCursor =
            db.query(true, DATABASE_TABLE, new String[] {KEY_ROWID,
            KEY_NAME, KEY_EMAIL}, KEY_ROWID + "=" + rowId, null,
            null, null, null, null);
    if (mCursor != null) {
        mCursor.moveToFirst();
    }
    return mCursor;
}
//---updates a contact---
public boolean updateContact(long rowId, String name, String email)
{
    ContentValues args = new ContentValues();
    args.put(KEY_NAME, name);
    args.put(KEY_EMAIL, email);
    return db.update(DATABASE_TABLE, args, KEY_ROWID + "=" + rowId, null) > 0;
}
```

Notice that Android uses the `Cursor` class as a return value for queries. Think of the `Cursor` as a pointer to the result set from a database query. Using `Cursor` enables Android to more efficiently manage rows and columns as needed.

You use a `ContentValues` object to store name/value pairs. Its `put()` method enables you to insert keys with values of different data types.

To create a database in your application using the `DBAdapter` class, you create an instance of the `DBAdapter` class:

```
public DBAdapter(Context ctx)
{
    this.context = ctx;
    DBHelper = new DatabaseHelper(context);
}
```

The constructor of the `DBAdapter` class will then create an instance of the `DatabaseHelper` class to create a new database:

```
DatabaseHelper(Context context)
{
    super(context, DATABASE_NAME, null, DATABASE_VERSION);
}
```

Using the Database Programmatically

With the `DBAdapter` helper class created, you are now ready to use the database. In the following sections, you will learn how to perform the regular CRUD (create, read, update and delete) operations commonly associated with databases.

Adding Contacts

The following Try It Out demonstrates how you can add a contact to the table.

TRY IT OUT Adding Contacts to a Table (Databases.zip)

1. Using the same project created earlier, add the following bolded statements to the `MainActivity.java` file:

```
import android.support.v7.app.AppCompatActivity;
import android.os.Bundle;

public class MainActivity extends AppCompatActivity {

    @Override
    protected void onCreate(Bundle savedInstanceState) {
        super.onCreate(savedInstanceState);
        setContentView(R.layout.activity_main);

        DBAdapter db = new DBAdapter(this);
```

```
        //---add a contact---
        db.open();
        long id = db.insertContact("Jennifer Ann",
"jenniferann@jfdimarzio.com");
        id = db.insertContact("Oscar Diggs", "oscar@oscardiggs.com");
        db.close();
    }
}
```

2. Press Shift+F9 to debug the application on the Android emulator.

How It Works

In this example, you create an instance of the `DBAdapter` class:

```
DBAdapter db = new DBAdapter(this);
```

The `insertContact()` method returns the ID of the inserted row. If an error occurs during the operation, it returns –1.

Retrieving All the Contacts

To retrieve all the contacts in the `contacts` table, use the `getAllContacts()` method of the `DBAdapter` class, as the following Try It Out shows.

TRY IT OUT Retrieving All Contacts from a Table (Databases.zip)

1. Using the same project created earlier, add the following bolded statements to the `MainActivity.java` file:

```
import android.database.Cursor;
import android.support.v7.app.AppCompatActivity;
import android.os.Bundle;
import android.widget.Toast;

public class MainActivity extends AppCompatActivity {

    @Override
    protected void onCreate(Bundle savedInstanceState) {
        super.onCreate(savedInstanceState);
        setContentView(R.layout.activity_main);

        DBAdapter db = new DBAdapter(this);
        //---add a contact---
        db.open();
        long id = db.insertContact("Jennifer Ann", "jenniferann@jfdimarzio.com");
        id = db.insertContact("Oscar Diggs", "oscar@oscardiggs.com");
        db.close();
        db.open();
        Cursor c = db.getAllContacts();
        if (c.moveToFirst())
```

```
        {
            do {
                DisplayContact(c);
            } while (c.moveToNext());
        }
        db.close();
    }

    public void DisplayContact(Cursor c)
    {
        Toast.makeText(this,
                "id: " + c.getString(0) + "\n" +
        "Name: " + c.getString(1) + "\n" +
        "Email:  " + c.getString(2),
            Toast.LENGTH_LONG).show();
    }
}
```

2. Press Shift+F9 to debug the application on the Android emulator. Figure 7-11 shows the `Toast` class displaying the contacts retrieved from the database.

FIGURE 7-11

How It Works

The `getAllContacts()` method of the `DBAdapter` class retrieves all the contacts stored in the database. The result is returned as a `Cursor` object. To display all the contacts, you first need to call the `moveToFirst()` method of the `Cursor` object. If it succeeds (which means at least one row is available), then you display the details of the contact using the `DisplayContact()` method. To move to the next contact, call the `moveToNext()` method of the `Cursor` object.

Retrieving a Single Contact

To retrieve a single contact using its ID, call the `getContact()` method of the `DBAdapter` class, as the following Try It Out shows.

TRY IT OUT Retrieving a Contact from a Table (Databases.zip)

1. Using the same project created earlier, add the following bolded statements to the `MainActivity.java` file:

```
@Override
public void onCreate(Bundle savedInstanceState) {
    super.onCreate(savedInstanceState);
    setContentView(R.layout.main);
    DBAdapter db = new DBAdapter(this);
    /*
    //---add a contact---
    ...
    //--get all contacts---
    ...
    db.close();
    */

    //---get a contact---
    db.open();
    Cursor c = db.getContact(2);
     if (c.moveToFirst())
         DisplayContact(c);
     else
         Toast.makeText(this, "No contact found", Toast.LENGTH_LONG).show();
     db.close();
}
```

2. Press Shift+F9 to debug the application on the Android emulator. The details of the second contact are displayed using the `Toast` class.

How It Works

The `getContact()` method of the `DBAdapter` class retrieves a single contact using its ID. You pass in the ID of the contact. In this case, you pass in an ID of 2 to indicate that you want to retrieve the second contact:

```
Cursor c = db.getContact(2);
```

The result is returned as a `Cursor` object. If a row is returned, you display the details of the contact using the `DisplayContact()` method. Otherwise, you display a message using the `Toast` class.

Updating a Contact

To update a particular contact, call the `updateContact()` method in the `DBAdapter` class by passing the ID of the contact you want to update, as the following Try It Out shows.

TRY IT OUT Updating a Contact in a Table (Databases.zip)

1. Using the same project created earlier, add the following bolded statements to the `MainActivity.java` file:

```
    @Override
    public void onCreate(Bundle savedInstanceState) {
        super.onCreate(savedInstanceState);
        setContentView(R.layout.main);
        DBAdapter db = new DBAdapter(this);
        /*
        //---add a contact---
        ...
        //--get all contacts---
        ...
        //---get a contact---
        ...
        db.close();
        */

        //---update contact---
        db.open();
         if (db.updateContact(1, "Oscar Diggs", "oscar@oscardiggs.com"))
             Toast.makeText(this, "Update successful.",
Toast.LENGTH_LONG).show();
         else
             Toast.makeText(this, "Update failed.", Toast.LENGTH_LONG).show();
         db.close();
    }
```

2. Press Shift+F9 to debug the application on the Android emulator. A message is displayed if the update is successful.

How It Works

The `updateContact()` method in the `DBAdapter` class updates a contact's details by using the ID of the contact you want to update. It returns a Boolean value, indicating whether the update was successful.

Deleting a Contact

To delete a contact, use the `deleteContact()` method in the `DBAdapter` class by passing the ID of the contact you want to update, as the following Try It Out shows.

TRY IT OUT Deleting a Contact from a Table (Databases.zip)

1. Using the same project created earlier, add the following bolded statements to the `MainActivity.java` file:

```
@Override
public void onCreate(Bundle savedInstanceState) {
    super.onCreate(savedInstanceState);
    setContentView(R.layout.main);
    DBAdapter db = new DBAdapter(this);
    /*
    //---add a contact---
    ...
    //--get all contacts---
    ...
    //---get a contact---
    ...
    //---update contact---
    ...
    db.close();
    */

    //---delete a contact---
    db.open();
    if (db.deleteContact(1))
        Toast.makeText(this, "Delete successful.",
Toast.LENGTH_LONG).show();
    else
        Toast.makeText(this, "Delete failed.", Toast.LENGTH_LONG).show();
    db.close();
}
```

2. Press Shift+F9 to debug the application on the Android emulator. A message is displayed if the deletion was successful.

How It Works

The `deleteContact()` method in the `DBAdapter` class deletes a contact using the ID of the contact you want to delete. It returns a Boolean value, indicating whether the deletion was successful.

Upgrading the Database

Sometimes, after creating and using the database, you might need to add additional tables, change the schema of the database, or add columns to your tables. In this case, you need to migrate your existing data from the old database to a newer one.

To upgrade the database, change the `DATABASE_VERSION` constant to a value higher than the previous one. For example, if its previous value was 1, change it to 2:

```
public class DBAdapter {
    static final String KEY_ROWID = "_id";
    static final String KEY_NAME = "name";
    static final String KEY_EMAIL = "email";
```

```
static final String TAG = "DBAdapter";
static final String DATABASE_NAME = "MyDB";
static final String DATABASE_TABLE = "contacts";
static final int DATABASE_VERSION = 2;
```

> ***NOTE*** *Before you run this example, be sure to comment out the block of delete statements described in the previous section. If you don't, the deletion fails because the table in the database is dropped (deleted).*

When you run the application one more time, you see the following message in the logcat window of Android Studio:

```
DBAdapter(8705): Upgrading database from version 1 to 2, which
will destroy all old data
```

For simplicity, simply drop the existing table and create a new one. In real life, you usually back up your existing table and then copy it over to the new table.

SUMMARY

In this chapter, you were introduced to the different ways to save persistent data to your Android device. For simple unstructured data, using the `SharedPreferences` object is the ideal solution. If you need to store bulk data then consider using the traditional file system. Finally, for structured data, it is more efficient to store it in a relational database management system. For this, Android provides the SQLite database, which you can access easily using the APIs exposed.

Note that for the `SharedPreferences` object and the SQLite database, the data is accessible only by the application that creates it. In other words, it is not shareable. If you need to share data among different applications, you need to create a *content provider*. Content providers are discussed in more detail in Chapter 8.

EXERCISES

1. How do you display the preferences of your application using an activity?

2. Name the method that enables you to obtain the external storage path for an Android device.

3. What method is called when a database needs to be upgraded?

You can find answers to the exercises in the appendix.

▶ WHAT YOU LEARNED IN THIS CHAPTER

TOPIC	KEY CONCEPTS
Saving simple user data	Use the `SharedPreferences` object.
Sharing data among activities in the same application	Use the `getSharedPreferences()` method.
Saving to a file	Use the `FileOutputStream` and `OutputStreamReader` classes.
Reading from a file	Use the `FileInputStream` and `InputStreamReader` classes.
Saving to external storage	Use the `getExternalStorageDirectory()` method to return the path to the external storage.
Accessing files in the `res/raw folder`	Use the `openRawResource()` method in the `Resources` object (obtained via the `getResources()` method).
Creating a database helper class	Extend the `SQLiteOpenHelper` class.

8

Content Providers

WHAT YOU WILL LEARN IN THIS CHAPTER

- What content providers are
- How to use a content provider in Android
- How to create and use your own content provider

> ***CODE DOWNLOAD*** *The wrox.com code downloads for this chapter are found at* `www.wrox.com/go/beginningandroidprog` *on the Download Code tab. The code is in the chapter 08 download and individually named according to the names throughout the chapter.*

The previous chapter explains the various ways to persist data—using shared preferences, files, as well as SQLite databases. Although using the database approach is the recommended way to save structured and complex data, sharing data is a challenge because the database is accessible to only the package that created it.

This chapter explains Android's way of sharing data through the use of *content providers*. You find out how to use the built-in content providers, as well as implement your own content providers to share data across packages.

SHARING DATA IN ANDROID

In Android, using a content provider is the recommended way to share data across packages. Think of a content provider as a data store. How it stores its data is not relevant to the application using it. However, the way in which packages can access the data stored in it using a consistent programming interface is important. A content provider behaves very much like a database—you can query it, edit its content, and add or delete content. However, unlike a database, a content provider can use different ways to store its data. The data can be stored in a database, in files, or even over a network.

Android ships with many useful content providers, including the following:

- **Browser**—Stores data such as browser bookmarks, browser history, and so on
- **CallLog**—Stores data such as missed calls, call details, and so on
- **Contacts**—Stores contact details
- **MediaStore**—Stores media files such as audio, video, and images
- **Settings**—Stores the device's settings and preferences

Besides the many built-in content providers, you can also create your own content providers.

To query a content provider, you specify the query string in the form of a Uniform Resource Identifier (URI), with an optional specifier for a particular row. Here's the format of the query URI:

```
<standard_prefix>://<authority>/<data_path>/<id>
```

The various parts of the URI are as follows:

- The *standard prefix* for content providers is always `content://`.

  The *authority* specifies the name of the content provider. An example would be `contacts` for the built-in Contacts content provider. For third-party content providers, this could be the fully qualified name, such as `com.wrox.provider` or `com.jfdimarzio.provider`.
- The *data path* specifies the kind of data requested. For example, if you are getting all the contacts from the Contacts content provider then the data path would be `people`, and the URI would look like this: `content://contacts/people`.
- The *id* specifies the specific record requested. For example, if you are looking for contact number 2 in the Contacts content provider, the URI would look like this: `content://contacts/people/2`.

Table 8-1 shows some examples of query strings.

TABLE 8-1: Example Query Strings

QUERY STRING	DESCRIPTION
`content://media/internal/images`	Returns a list of the internal images on the device
`content://media/external/images`	Returns a list of the images stored on the external storage (for example, SD card) on the device
`content://call_log/calls`	Returns a list of calls registered in the Call Log
`content://browser/bookmarks`	Returns a list of bookmarks stored in the browser

USING A CONTENT PROVIDER

The best way to understand content providers is to actually use one. The following Try It Out shows how you can use a content provider from within your Android application.

TRY IT OUT Using the Contacts Content Provider (Provider.zip)

1. Using Android Studio, create a new Android project and name it Provider.
2. Add the following bolded statements to the `activity_main.xml` file. Be sure to change all instances of `com.jfdimarzio` to your package name:

```
<?xml version="1.0" encoding="utf-8"?>
<android.support.constraint.ConstraintLayout xmlns:android=
    "http://schemas.android.com/apk/res/android"
    xmlns:app="http://schemas.android.com/apk/res-auto"
    xmlns:tools="http://schemas.android.com/tools"
    android:id="@+id/activity_main"
    android:layout_width="match_parent"
    android:layout_height="match_parent"
    tools:context="com.jfdimarzio.provider.MainActivity">


    <TextView
        android:text="TextView"
        android:layout_width="0dp"
        android:layout_height="60dp"
        android:id="@+id/contactName"
        app:layout_constraintLeft_toLeftOf="@+id/activity_main"
        android:layout_marginStart="63dp"
```

```
        tools:layout_constraintLeft_creator="1"
        app:layout_constraintRight_toRightOf="@+id/activity_main"
        android:layout_marginEnd="63dp"
        tools:layout_constraintRight_creator="1"
        app:layout_constraintBottom_toTopOf="@+id/contactID"
        android:layout_marginBottom="40dp"
        tools:layout_constraintBottom_creator="1" />

    <TextView
        android:text="TextView"
        android:layout_width="0dp"
        android:layout_height="64dp"
        android:id="@+id/contactID"
        app:layout_constraintLeft_toLeftOf="@+id/activity_main"
        android:layout_marginStart="63dp"
        tools:layout_constraintLeft_creator="1"
        app:layout_constraintRight_toRightOf="@+id/activity_main"
        android:layout_marginEnd="63dp"
        tools:layout_constraintRight_creator="1"
        app:layout_constraintBottom_toBottomOf="@+id/activity_main"
        android:layout_marginBottom="56dp"
        tools:layout_constraintBottom_creator="1" />

    <ListView
        android:layout_height="0dp"
        android:id="@android:id/list"
        android:layout_width="wrap_content"
        app:layout_constraintLeft_toLeftOf="@+id/activity_main"
        app:layout_constraintTop_toTopOf="@+id/activity_main"
        tools:layout_constraintTop_creator="1"
        app:layout_constraintRight_toRightOf="@+id/activity_main"
        app:layout_constraintBottom_toTopOf="@+id/contactName"
        android:layout_marginBottom="5dp"
        tools:layout_constraintBottom_creator="1" />
</android.support.constraint.ConstraintLayout>
```

3. In the `MainActivity.java` class, code the following:

```
import android.Manifest;
import android.app.ListActivity;
import android.content.pm.PackageManager;
import android.database.Cursor;
import android.net.Uri;
import android.provider.ContactsContract;
import android.support.v4.app.ActivityCompat;
import android.support.v4.content.ContextCompat;
import android.support.v4.content.CursorLoader;
import android.support.v4.widget.CursorAdapter;
import android.support.v4.widget.SimpleCursorAdapter;
import android.os.Bundle;
import android.widget.Toast;

public class MainActivity extends ListActivity {
    final private int REQUEST_READ_CONTACTS = 123;
    @Override
```

```
protected void onCreate(Bundle savedInstanceState) {
    super.onCreate(savedInstanceState);
    setContentView(R.layout.activity_main);

    if (ContextCompat.checkSelfPermission(this,
            Manifest.permission.READ_CONTACTS)
            != PackageManager.PERMISSION_GRANTED) {

        ActivityCompat.requestPermissions(this,
                new String[]{Manifest.permission.READ_CONTACTS},
                REQUEST_READ_CONTACTS);
    } else{
        ListContacts();
    }


    }
@Override
public void onRequestPermissionsResult(int requestCode
, String[] permissions, int[] grantResults) {
    switch (requestCode) {
        case REQUEST_READ_CONTACTS:
            if (grantResults[0] == PackageManager.PERMISSION_GRANTED) {

                ListContacts();

            } else {
                Toast.makeText(MainActivity.this
, "Permission Denied", Toast.LENGTH_SHORT).show();
            }
            break;
        default:
            super.onRequestPermissionsResult(requestCode
, permissions, grantResults);
    }
}
protected void ListContacts(){
    Uri allContacts = Uri.parse("content://contacts/people");
    Cursor c;
    CursorLoader cursorLoader = new CursorLoader(
            this,
            allContacts,
            null,
            null,
            null,
            null);
    c = cursorLoader.loadInBackground();

    String[] columns = new String[]{
            ContactsContract.Contacts.DISPLAY_NAME,
            ContactsContract.Contacts._ID};

    int[] views = new int[]{R.id.contactName, R.id.contactID};
    SimpleCursorAdapter adapter;
```

```
        adapter = new SimpleCursorAdapter(
                this, R.layout.activity_main, c, columns, views,
                CursorAdapter.FLAG_REGISTER_CONTENT_OBSERVER);

        this.setListAdapter(adapter);
    }
}
```

4. Add the following bolded statements to the `AndroidManifest.xml` file. Be sure to change all instances of `com.jfdimarzio` to your package name:

```
<?xml version="1.0" encoding="utf-8"?>
<manifest xmlns:android="http://schemas.android.com/apk/res/android"
    package="com.jfdimarzio.provider">
    <uses-permission android:name="android.permission.READ_CONTACTS"/>
    <application
        android:allowBackup="true"
        android:icon="@mipmap/ic_launcher"
        android:label="@string/app_name"
        android:supportsRtl="true"
        android:theme="@style/AppTheme">
        <activity android:name=".MainActivity">
            <intent-filter>
                <action android:name="android.intent.action.MAIN" />

                <category android:name="android.intent.category.LAUNCHER" />
            </intent-filter>
        </activity>
    </application>

</manifest>
```

5. Launch an AVD and create a few contacts in the Android Emulator. To add a contact, go to the Phone application and click the Contact icon at the top (see Figure 8-1). You see a warning about backing up your contacts. Click the Keep Local button and enter the name, phone number, and email address of a few people.
6. Press Shift+F9 to debug the application on the Android emulator. Note that the first thing that happens is Android displays a request for permission—as shown in Figure 8-2. If you click Allow, you should see a list of your contacts, as shown in Figure 8-3.

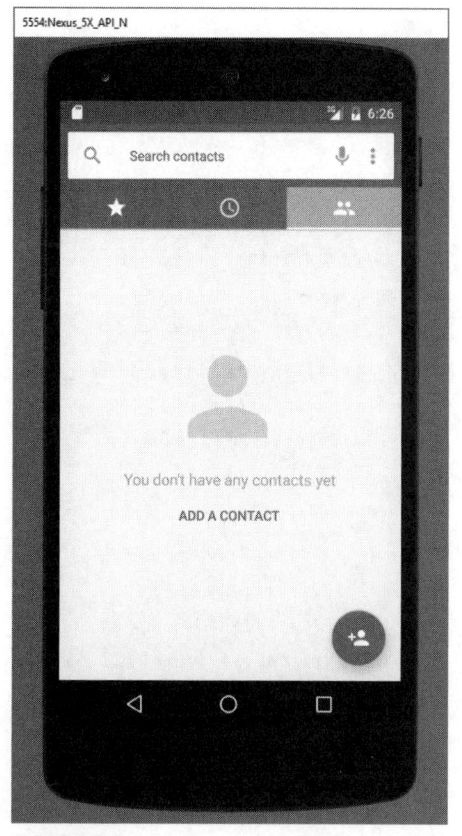

FIGURE 8-1

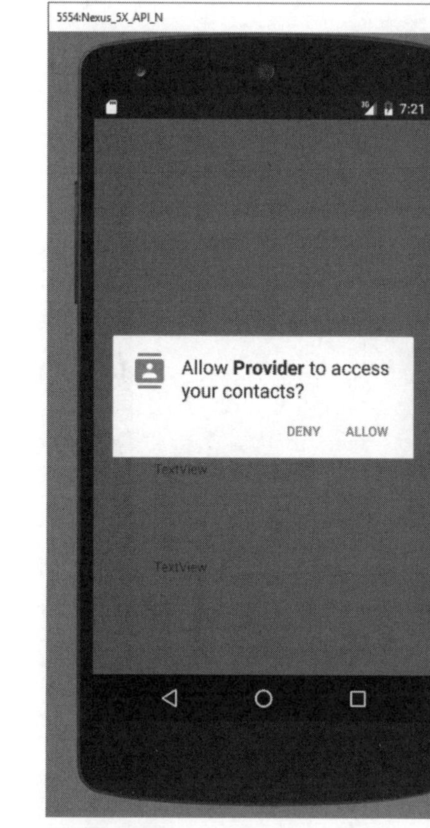

FIGURE 8-2

How It Works

In this example, you retrieved the contacts stored in the Contacts application and displayed them in the `ListView`.

First, you specify the URI for accessing the Contacts application:

```
Uri allContacts = Uri.parse("content://contacts/people");
```

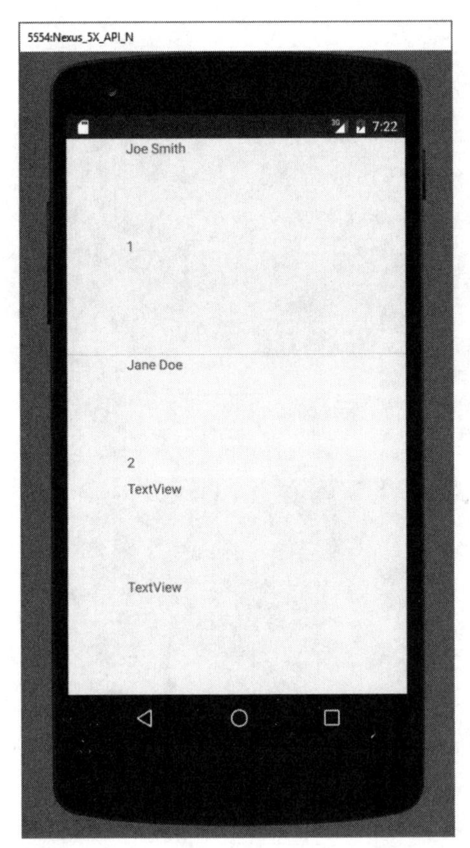

FIGURE 8-3

Next, you must check that your app has permission to access the Contacts:

```
if (ContextCompat.checkSelfPermission(this,
                Manifest.permission.READ_CONTACTS)
                != PackageManager.PERMISSION_GRANTED) {

            ActivityCompat.requestPermissions(this,
                    new String[]{Manifest.permission.READ_CONTACTS},
                    REQUEST_READ_CONTACTS);
        } else{
            ListContacts();
        }
```

If the application does not have permission, a request for permission is issued (causing Android to pop the permission dialog). If the application does have permission, the `ListContacts()` method is called.

The `getContentResolver()` method returns a `ContentResolver` object, which helps to resolve a content URI with the appropriate content provider.

The `CursorLoader` class (only available beginning with Android API level 11 and later) performs the cursor query on a background thread and therefore does not block the application UI.

```
CursorLoader cursorLoader = new CursorLoader(
        this,
        allContacts,
        null,
        null,
        null ,
        null);
c = cursorLoader.loadInBackground();
```

The `SimpleCursorAdapter` object maps a cursor to `TextViews` (or `ImageViews`) defined in your XML file (`activity_main.xml`). It maps the data (as represented by `columns`) to views (as represented by `views`):

```
String[] columns = new String[] {
    ContactsContract.Contacts.DISPLAY_NAME,
    ContactsContract.Contacts._ID};

int[] views = new int[] {R.id.contactName, R.id.contactID};
SimpleCursorAdapter adapter;



this.setListAdapter(adapter);
```

Like the `managedQuery()` method, one of the constructors for the `SimpleCursorAdapter` class has been deprecated. For devices running Honeycomb or later versions, you need to use the new constructor for the `SimpleCursorAdapter` class with one additional argument:

```
//---Honeycomb and later---
adapter = new SimpleCursorAdapter(
        this, R.layout.main, c, columns, views,
        CursorAdapter.FLAG_REGISTER_CONTENT_OBSERVER);
```

The flag registers the adapter to be informed when there is a change in the content provider.

Note that for your application to access the Contacts application, you need to have the `READ_CONTACTS` permission in your `AndroidManifest.xml` file.

Predefined Query String Constants

Besides using the query URI, you can use a list of predefined query string constants in Android to specify the URI for the different data types. For example, besides using the query `content://contacts/people`, you can rewrite this statement:

```
Uri allContacts = Uri.parse("content://contacts/people");
```

using one of the predefined constants in Android, as follows:

```
Uri allContacts = ContactsContract.Contacts.CONTENT_URI;
```

The `PrintContacts()` method prints the following in the logcat window:

```
12-13 08:32:50.471: V/Content Providers(12346): 1, Wei-Meng Lee
12-13 08:32:50.471: V/Content Providers(12346): 2, Linda Chen
12-13 08:32:50.471: V/Content Providers(12346): 3, Joanna Yip
```

It prints the ID and name of each contact stored in the Contacts application. In this case, you access the `ContactsContract.Contacts._ID` field to obtain the ID of a contact, and `ContactsContract.Contacts.DISPLAY_NAME` for the name of a contact. If you want to display the phone number of a contact, you need to query the content provider again, as the information is stored in another table:

```
private void PrintContacts(Cursor c)
{
    if (c.moveToFirst()) {
        do{
            String contactID = c.getString(c.getColumnIndex(
                    ContactsContract.Contacts._ID));
            String contactDisplayName =
                    c.getString(c.getColumnIndex(
                            ContactsContract.Contacts.DISPLAY_NAME));
            Log.v("Content Providers", contactID + ", " +
                    contactDisplayName);
            //---get phone number---

                Cursor phoneCursor =
                    getContentResolver().query(
                        ContactsContract.CommonDataKinds.Phone.CONTENT_URI, null,
                        ContactsContract.CommonDataKinds.Phone.CONTACT_ID + " = " +
                        contactID, null, null);
                while (phoneCursor.moveToNext()) {
                    Log.v("Content Providers",
                        phoneCursor.getString(
                            phoneCursor.getColumnIndex(
                                ContactsContract.CommonDataKinds.Phone.NUMBER)));
                }
                phoneCursor.close();
        } while (c.moveToNext());
    }
}
```

> **NOTE** *To access the phone number of a contact, you need to query against the URI stored in* `ContactsContract.CommonDataKinds.Phone.CONTENT_URI`.

In the preceding code snippet, you first check whether a contact has a phone number using the `ContactsContract.Contacts.HAS_PHONE_NUMBER` field. If the contact has at least a phone number, you then query the content provider again based on the ID of the contact. After the phone numbers are retrieved, you then iterate through them and print out the numbers. You should see something like this:

```
12-13 08:59:31.881: V/Content Providers(13351): 1, Wei-Meng Lee
12-13 08:59:32.311: V/Content Providers(13351): +651234567
12-13 08:59:32.321: V/Content Providers(13351): 2, Linda Chen
12-13 08:59:32.511: V/Content Providers(13351): +1 876-543-21
12-13 08:59:32.545: V/Content Providers(13351): 3, Joanna Yip
12-13 08:59:32.641: V/Content Providers(13351): +239 846 5522
```

Projections

The third parameter for the `CursorLoader` class controls how many columns are returned by the query. This parameter is known as the *projection*. Earlier, you specified `null`:

```
Cursor c;

    CursorLoader cursorLoader = new CursorLoader(
            this,
            allContacts,
            null,
            null,
            null ,
            null);
    c = cursorLoader.loadInBackground();
```

You can specify the exact columns to return by creating an array containing the name of the column to return, like this:

```
String[] projection = new String[]
        {ContactsContract.Contacts._ID,
         ContactsContract.Contacts.DISPLAY_NAME,
         ContactsContract.Contacts.HAS_PHONE_NUMBER};

Cursor c;

    CursorLoader cursorLoader = new CursorLoader(
            this,
            allContacts,
            projection,
            null,
```

```
                null ,
                null);
        c = cursorLoader.loadInBackground();
```

In the preceding example, the `_ID`, `DISPLAY_NAME`, and `HAS_PHONE_NUMBER` fields are retrieved.

Filtering

The fourth and fifth parameters for the `CursorLoader` class enable you to specify a SQL `WHERE` clause to filter the result of the query. For example, the following statement retrieves only the people whose name ends with "Lee":

```
Cursor c;
    CursorLoader cursorLoader = new CursorLoader(
            this,
            allContacts,
            projection,
            ContactsContract.Contacts.DISPLAY_NAME + " LIKE '%Lee'",
            null ,
            null);
    c = cursorLoader.loadInBackground();
```

Here, the fourth parameter for the `CursorLoader` constructor contains a SQL statement containing the name to search for ("Lee"). You can also put the search string into the next argument of the method/constructor, like this:

```
Cursor c;

    //---Honeycomb and later---
    CursorLoader cursorLoader = new CursorLoader(
            this,
            allContacts,
            projection,
            ContactsContract.Contacts.DISPLAY_NAME + " LIKE ?",
             new String[] {"%Lee"},
            null);
    c = cursorLoader.loadInBackground();
```

Sorting

The last parameter of the `CursorLoader` class enables you to specify a SQL `ORDER BY` clause to sort the result of the query. For example, the following statement sorts the contact names in ascending order:

```
Cursor c;
    CursorLoader cursorLoader = new CursorLoader(
            this,
            allContacts,
            projection,
            ContactsContract.Contacts.DISPLAY_NAME + " LIKE ?",
            new String[] {"%Lee"},
            ContactsContract.Contacts.DISPLAY_NAME + " ASC");
    c = cursorLoader.loadInBackground();
```

CREATING YOUR OWN CONTENT PROVIDERS

Creating your own content provider in Android is relatively simple. All you need to do is extend the abstract `ContentProvider` class and override the various methods defined within it.

This section explains how to create a simple content provider that stores a list of books.

TRY IT OUT Creating Your Own Content Provider (ContentProviders.zip)

1. Using Android Studio, create a new Android project and name it ContentProviders.
2. In the `src` folder of the project, add a new Java class file and name it BooksProvider.
3. Populate the `BooksProvider.java` file as follows. Be sure to change all instances of `com.jfdimarzio` to your package name:

```
import android.content.ContentProvider;
import android.content.ContentUris;
import android.content.ContentValues;
import android.content.Context;
import android.content.UriMatcher;
import android.database.Cursor;
import android.database.SQLException;
import android.database.sqlite.SQLiteDatabase;
import android.database.sqlite.SQLiteOpenHelper;
import android.database.sqlite.SQLiteQueryBuilder;
import android.net.Uri;
import android.text.TextUtils;
import android.util.Log;

public class BooksProvider extends ContentProvider {
    static final String PROVIDER_NAME = "com.jfdimarzio.provider.Books";
    static final Uri CONTENT_URI =
    Uri.parse("content://"+ PROVIDER_NAME + "/books");
    static final String _ID = "_id";
    static final String TITLE = "title";
    static final String ISBN = "isbn";
    static final int BOOKS = 1;
    static final int BOOK_ID = 2;
    private static final UriMatcher uriMatcher;
    static{
        uriMatcher = new UriMatcher(UriMatcher.NO_MATCH);
        uriMatcher.addURI(PROVIDER_NAME, "books", BOOKS);
        uriMatcher.addURI(PROVIDER_NAME, "books/#", BOOK_ID);
    }
    //---for database use---
    SQLiteDatabase booksDB;
    static final String DATABASE_NAME = "Books";
    static final String DATABASE_TABLE = "titles";
    static final int DATABASE_VERSION = 1;
    static final String DATABASE_CREATE =
            "create table " + DATABASE_TABLE +
                    " (_id integer primary key autoincrement, "
                    + "title text not null, isbn text not null);";
```

```
private static class DatabaseHelper extends SQLiteOpenHelper
{
    DatabaseHelper(Context context) {
        super(context, DATABASE_NAME, null, DATABASE_VERSION);
    }
    @Override
    public void onCreate(SQLiteDatabase db)
    {
        db.execSQL(DATABASE_CREATE);
    }
    @Override
    public void onUpgrade(SQLiteDatabase db, int oldVersion,
                          int newVersion) {
        Log.w("Provider database",
                "Upgrading database from version " +
                        oldVersion + " to " + newVersion +
                        ", which will destroy all old data");
        db.execSQL("DROP TABLE IF EXISTS titles");
        onCreate(db);
    }
}

@Override
public int delete(Uri arg0, String arg1, String[] arg2) {
    // arg0 = uri
    // arg1 = selection
    // arg2 = selectionArgs
    int count=0;
    switch (uriMatcher.match(arg0)){
        case BOOKS:
            count = booksDB.delete(
                    DATABASE_TABLE,
                    arg1,
                    arg2);
            break;
        case BOOK_ID:
            String id = arg0.getPathSegments().get(1);
            count = booksDB.delete(
                    DATABASE_TABLE,
                    _ID + " = " + id +
                            (!TextUtils.isEmpty(arg1) ? " AND (" +
                                    arg1 + ')' : ""),
            arg2);
            break;
        default: throw new IllegalArgumentException("Unknown URI " + arg0);
    }
    getContext().getContentResolver().notifyChange(arg0, null);
    return count;
}
@Override
public String getType(Uri uri) {
    switch (uriMatcher.match(uri)){
        //---get all books---
        case BOOKS:
            return "vnd.android.cursor.dir/vnd.learn2develop.books ";
```

```
            //---get a particular book---
            case BOOK_ID:
                return "vnd.android.cursor.item/vnd.learn2develop.books ";

            default:
                throw new IllegalArgumentException("Unsupported URI: " + uri);
        }
    }
    @Override
    public Uri insert(Uri uri, ContentValues values) {
        //---add a new book---
        long rowID = booksDB.insert(
                DATABASE_TABLE,
                "",
                values);
        //---if added successfully---
        if (rowID>0)
        {
            Uri _uri = ContentUris.withAppendedId(CONTENT_URI, rowID);
            getContext().getContentResolver().notifyChange(_uri, null);
            return _uri;
        }
        throw new SQLException("Failed to insert row into " + uri);
    }
    @Override
    public boolean onCreate() {
        Context context = getContext();
        DatabaseHelper dbHelper = new DatabaseHelper(context);
        booksDB = dbHelper.getWritableDatabase();
        return (booksDB == null)? false:true;
    }
    @Override
    public Cursor query(Uri uri, String[] projection, String selection,
                        String[] selectionArgs, String sortOrder) {
        SQLiteQueryBuilder sqlBuilder = new SQLiteQueryBuilder();
        sqlBuilder.setTables(DATABASE_TABLE);
        if (uriMatcher.match(uri) == BOOK_ID)
            //---if getting a particular book---
            sqlBuilder.appendWhere(
                    _ID + " = " + uri.getPathSegments().get(1));
        if (sortOrder==null || sortOrder=="")
            sortOrder = TITLE;
        Cursor c = sqlBuilder.query(
                booksDB,
                projection,
                selection,
                selectionArgs,
                null,
                null,
                sortOrder);
        //---register to watch a content URI for changes---
        c.setNotificationUri(getContext().getContentResolver(), uri);
        return c;
    }
```

```
    @Override
    public int update(Uri uri, ContentValues values, String selection,
                      String[] selectionArgs) {
        int count = 0;
        switch (uriMatcher.match(uri)){
            case BOOKS:
                count = booksDB.update(
                        DATABASE_TABLE,
                        values,
                        selection,
                        selectionArgs);
                break;
            case BOOK_ID:
                count = booksDB.update(
                        DATABASE_TABLE,
                        values,
                        _ID + " = " + uri.getPathSegments().get(1) +
                                (!TextUtils.isEmpty(selection) ? " AND (" +
                                        selection + ')' : ""),
                selectionArgs);
                break;
            default: throw new IllegalArgumentException("Unknown URI " + uri);
        }
        getContext().getContentResolver().notifyChange(uri, null);
        return count;
    }
}
```

4. Add the following bolded statements to the `AndroidManifest.xml` file. Be sure to change all instances of `com.jfdimarzio` to your package name:

```
<?xml version="1.0" encoding="utf-8"?>
<manifest xmlns:android="http://schemas.android.com/apk/res/android"
  , package="com.jfdimarzio.contentproviders">

    <application
        android:allowBackup="true"
        android:icon="@mipmap/ic_launcher"
        android:label="@string/app_name"
        android:supportsRtl="true"
        android:theme="@style/AppTheme">
        <activity android:name=".MainActivity">
            <intent-filter>
                <action android:name="android.intent.action.MAIN" />

                <category android:name="android.intent.category.LAUNCHER" />
            </intent-filter>
        </activity>
        <provider android:name="BooksProvider"
         android:authorities="com.jfdimarzio.provider.Books">
    </provider>
```

```
    </application>

    </manifest>
```

How It Works

In this example, you first create a class named `BooksProvider` that extends the `ContentProvider` base class. The various methods to override in this class are as follows:

- `getType()`—Returns the MIME type of the data at the given URI.
- `onCreate()`—Called when the provider is started.
- `query()`—Receives a request from a client. The result is returned as a `Cursor` object.
- `insert()`—Inserts a new record into the content provider.
- `delete()`—Deletes an existing record from the content provider.
- `update()`—Updates an existing record from the content provider.

Within your content provider, you are free to choose how you want to store your data—in a traditional file system, XML, a database, or even through web services. For this example, you use the SQLite database approach discussed in the previous chapter.

You then define the following constants within the `BooksProvider` class:

```
static final String PROVIDER_NAME =
    "com.jfdimarzio.Books";
static final Uri CONTENT_URI =
    Uri.parse("content://"+ PROVIDER_NAME + "/books");
static final String _ID = "_id";
static final String TITLE = "title";
static final String ISBN = "isbn";
static final int BOOKS = 1;
static final int BOOK_ID = 2;
private static final UriMatcher uriMatcher;
static{
    uriMatcher = new UriMatcher(UriMatcher.NO_MATCH);
    uriMatcher.addURI(PROVIDER_NAME, "books", BOOKS);
    uriMatcher.addURI(PROVIDER_NAME, "books/#", BOOK_ID);
}
//---for database use---
SQLiteDatabase booksDB;
static final String DATABASE_NAME = "Books";
static final String DATABASE_TABLE = "titles";
static final int DATABASE_VERSION = 1;
static final String DATABASE_CREATE =
    "create table " + DATABASE_TABLE +
    " (_id integer primary key autoincrement, "
    + "title text not null, isbn text not null);";
```

Observe in the preceding code that you used an `UriMatcher` object to parse the content URI that is passed to the content provider through a `ContentResolver`. For example, the following content URI represents a request for all books in the content provider:

```
content://com.jfdimarzio.provider.Books/books
```

The following represents a request for a particular book with `_id 5`:

```
content://com.jfdimarzio.provider.Books/books/5
```

Your content provider uses a SQLite database to store the books. Note that you use the `SQLiteOpenHelper` helper class to help manage your database:

```
private static class DatabaseHelper extends SQLiteOpenHelper
{
    DatabaseHelper(Context context) {
        super(context, DATABASE_NAME, null, DATABASE_VERSION);
    }
    @Override
    public void onCreate(SQLiteDatabase db)
    {
        db.execSQL(DATABASE_CREATE);
    }
    @Override
    public void onUpgrade(SQLiteDatabase db, int oldVersion,
            int newVersion) {
        Log.w("Provider database",
                "Upgrading database from version " +
                        oldVersion + " to " + newVersion +
                ", which will destroy all old data");
        db.execSQL("DROP TABLE IF EXISTS titles");
        onCreate(db);
    }
}
```

Next, you override the `getType()` method to uniquely describe the data type for your content provider. Using the `UriMatcher` object, `vnd.android.cursor.item/vnd.<package name>.books` is returned for a single book, and `vnd.android.cursor.dir/vnd.<package name>.books` is returned for multiple books:

```
@Override
public String getType(Uri uri) {
    switch (uriMatcher.match(uri)){
    //---get all books---
    case BOOKS:
        return "vnd.android.cursor.dir/vnd.jfdimarzio.books ";

    //---get a particular book---
    case BOOK_ID:
        return "vnd.android.cursor.item/vnd.jfdimarzio.books ";

    default:
        throw new IllegalArgumentException("Unsupported URI: " + uri);
    }
}
```

Next, you override the `onCreate()` method to open a connection to the database when the content provider is started:

```
@Override
public boolean onCreate() {
    Context context = getContext();
    DatabaseHelper dbHelper = new DatabaseHelper(context);
    booksDB = dbHelper.getWritableDatabase();
    return (booksDB == null)? false:true;
}
```

Now, you override the `query()` method to allow clients to query for books:

```
@Override
public Cursor query(Uri uri, String[] projection, String selection,
        String[] selectionArgs, String sortOrder) {
    SQLiteQueryBuilder sqlBuilder = new SQLiteQueryBuilder();
    sqlBuilder.setTables(DATABASE_TABLE);
    if (uriMatcher.match(uri) == BOOK_ID)
        //---if getting a particular book---
        sqlBuilder.appendWhere(
                _ID + " = " + uri.getPathSegments().get(1));
    if (sortOrder==null || sortOrder=="")
        sortOrder = TITLE;
    Cursor c = sqlBuilder.query(
        booksDB,
        projection,
        selection,
        selectionArgs,
        null,
        null,
        sortOrder);
    //---register to watch a content URI for changes---
    c.setNotificationUri(getContext().getContentResolver(), uri);
    return c;
}
```

By default, the result of the query is sorted using the `title` field. The resulting query is returned as a `Cursor` object.

To allow a new book to be inserted into the content provider, you override the `insert()` method:

```
@Override
public Uri insert(Uri uri, ContentValues values) {
    //---add a new book---
    long rowID = booksDB.insert(
            DATABASE_TABLE,
            "",
            values);
    //---if added successfully---
    if (rowID>0)
    {
        Uri _uri = ContentUris.withAppendedId(CONTENT_URI, rowID);
        getContext().getContentResolver().notifyChange(_uri, null);
        return _uri;
```

```
        }
        throw new SQLException("Failed to insert row into " + uri);
    }
```

After the record is inserted successfully, you call the `notifyChange()` method of the `ContentResolver`. This notifies registered observers that a row was updated.

To delete a book, you override the `delete()` method:

```
    @Override
    public int delete(Uri arg0, String arg1, String[] arg2) {
        // arg0 = uri
        // arg1 = selection
        // arg2 = selectionArgs
        int count=0;
        switch (uriMatcher.match(arg0)){
        case BOOKS:
            count = booksDB.delete(
                    DATABASE_TABLE,
                    arg1,
                    arg2);
            break;
        case BOOK_ID:
            String id = arg0.getPathSegments().get(1);
            count = booksDB.delete(
                    DATABASE_TABLE,
                    _ID + " = " + id +
                    (!TextUtils.isEmpty(arg1) ? " AND (" +
                            arg1 + ')' : ""),
                            arg2);
            break;
        default: throw new IllegalArgumentException("Unknown URI " + arg0);
        }
        getContext().getContentResolver().notifyChange(arg0, null);
        return count;
    }
```

Likewise, call the `notifyChange()` method of the `ContentResolver` after the deletion. This notifies registered observers that a row was deleted.

To update a book, you override the `update()` method:

```
    @Override
    public int update(Uri uri, ContentValues values, String selection,
            String[] selectionArgs) {
        int count = 0;
        switch (uriMatcher.match(uri)){
        case BOOKS:
            count = booksDB.update(
                    DATABASE_TABLE,
                    values,
                    selection,
                    selectionArgs);
            break;
        case BOOK_ID:
            count = booksDB.update(
```

```
                    DATABASE_TABLE,
                    values,
                    _ID + " = " + uri.getPathSegments().get(1) +
                    (!TextUtils.isEmpty(selection) ? " AND (" +
                            selection + ')' : ""),
                            selectionArgs);
            break;
        default: throw new IllegalArgumentException("Unknown URI " + uri);
        }
        getContext().getContentResolver().notifyChange(uri, null);
        return count;
    }
```

As with the `insert()` and `delete()` methods, you called the `notifyChange()` method of the `ContentResolver` after the update. This notifies registered observers that a row was updated.

Finally, to register your content provider with Android, modify the `AndroidManifest.xml` file by adding the `<provider>` element.

USING THE CONTENT PROVIDER

Now that you have built your new content provider, you can test it from within your Android application. The following Try It Out demonstrates how to do that.

TRY IT OUT Using the Newly Created Content Provider

1. Using the same project created in the previous section, add the following bolded statements to the `activity_main.xml` file. Be sure to change all instances of `com.jfdimarzio` to your package name:

```
<?xml version="1.0" encoding="utf-8"?>
<android.support.constraint.ConstraintLayout xmlns:android=
    "http://schemas.android.com/apk/res/android"
    xmlns:app="http://schemas.android.com/apk/res-auto"
    xmlns:tools="http://schemas.android.com/tools"
    android:id="@+id/activity_main"
    android:layout_width="match_parent"
    android:layout_height="match_parent"
    tools:context="com.jfdimarzio.contentproviders.MainActivity">

    <TextView
        android:text="ISBN"
        android:layout_width="wrap_content"
        android:layout_height="wrap_content"
        android:id="@+id/textView"
        app:layout_constraintLeft_toLeftOf="@+id/activity_main"
        tools:layout_constraintLeft_creator="1"
        app:layout_constraintTop_toTopOf="@+id/activity_main"
```

```
        android:layout_marginTop="16dp"
        app:layout_constraintRight_toRightOf="@+id/activity_main"
        tools:layout_constraintRight_creator="1" />

    <EditText
        android:layout_width="wrap_content"
        android:layout_height="wrap_content"
        android:inputType="text"
        android:ems="10"
        android:id="@+id/txtISBN"
        app:layout_constraintLeft_toLeftOf="@+id/activity_main"
        tools:layout_constraintLeft_creator="1"
        app:layout_constraintTop_toBottomOf="@+id/textView"
        android:layout_marginTop="8dp"
        app:layout_constraintRight_toRightOf="@+id/activity_main"
        tools:layout_constraintRight_creator="1"
        app:layout_constraintBottom_toTopOf="@+id/textView2"
        android:layout_marginBottom="8dp"
        app:layout_constraintHorizontal_bias="0.46"
        app:layout_constraintVertical_bias="0.100000024" />

    <TextView
        android:text="Title"
        android:layout_width="wrap_content"
        android:layout_height="wrap_content"
        android:id="@+id/textView2"
        app:layout_constraintLeft_toLeftOf="@+id/activity_main"
        tools:layout_constraintLeft_creator="1"
        app:layout_constraintTop_toTopOf="@+id/activity_main"
        android:layout_marginTop="142dp"
        tools:layout_constraintTop_creator="1"
        app:layout_constraintRight_toRightOf="@+id/activity_main"
        tools:layout_constraintRight_creator="1" />

    <EditText
        android:layout_width="wrap_content"
        android:layout_height="wrap_content"
        android:inputType="text"
        android:ems="10"
        android:id="@+id/txtTitle"
        app:layout_constraintLeft_toLeftOf="@+id/activity_main"
        tools:layout_constraintLeft_creator="1"
        app:layout_constraintTop_toBottomOf="@+id/textView2"
        android:layout_marginTop="8dp"
        app:layout_constraintRight_toRightOf="@+id/activity_main"
        tools:layout_constraintRight_creator="1" />

    <Button
        android:text="Add Title"
        android:layout_width="wrap_content"
        android:layout_height="wrap_content"
        android:id="@+id/btnAdd"
        app:layout_constraintLeft_toLeftOf="@+id/activity_main"
        tools:layout_constraintLeft_creator="1"
        app:layout_constraintTop_toBottomOf="@+id/txtTitle"
        android:layout_marginTop="112dp"
        app:layout_constraintRight_toRightOf="@+id/activity_main"
```

```
        tools:layout_constraintRight_creator="1"
        android:onClick="onClickAddTitle" />

    <Button
        android:text="Retrieve Titles"
        android:layout_width="wrap_content"
        android:layout_height="wrap_content"
        android:id="@+id/btnRetrieve"
        app:layout_constraintLeft_toLeftOf="@+id/activity_main"
        tools:layout_constraintLeft_creator="1"
        app:layout_constraintTop_toBottomOf="@+id/btnAdd"
        android:layout_marginTop="32dp"
        app:layout_constraintRight_toRightOf="@+id/activity_main"
        tools:layout_constraintRight_creator="1"
        android:onClick="onClickRetrieveTitles"  />
</android.support.constraint.ConstraintLayout>
```

2. In the `MainActivity.java` file, add the following bolded statements. Be sure to change all instances of `com.jfdimarzio` to your package name:

```
import android.content.ContentValues;
import android.content.CursorLoader;
import android.database.Cursor;
import android.net.Uri;
import android.support.v7.app.AppCompatActivity;
import android.os.Bundle;
import android.view.View;
import android.widget.EditText;
import android.widget.Toast;

public class MainActivity extends AppCompatActivity {

    @Override
    protected void onCreate(Bundle savedInstanceState) {
        super.onCreate(savedInstanceState);
        setContentView(R.layout.activity_main);
    }
    public void onClickAddTitle(View view) {
        //---add a book---
        ContentValues values = new ContentValues();
        values.put(BooksProvider.TITLE, ((EditText)
                findViewById(R.id.txtTitle)).getText().toString());
        values.put(BooksProvider.ISBN, ((EditText)
                findViewById(R.id.txtISBN)).getText().toString());
        Uri uri = getContentResolver().insert(
                BooksProvider.CONTENT_URI, values);
        Toast.makeText(getBaseContext(),uri.toString(),
                Toast.LENGTH_LONG).show();
    }
    public void onClickRetrieveTitles(View view) {
        //---retrieve the titles---
        Uri allTitles = Uri.parse(
                "content://com.jfdimarzio.provider.Books/books");
        Cursor c;
        CursorLoader cursorLoader = new CursorLoader(
                    this,
```

```
                    allTitles, null, null, null,
                    "title desc");
            c = cursorLoader.loadInBackground();
        if (c.moveToFirst()) {
            do{
                Toast.makeText(this,
                        c.getString(c.getColumnIndex(
                                BooksProvider._ID)) + ", " +
                                c.getString(c.getColumnIndex(
                                        BooksProvider.TITLE)) + ", " +
                                c.getString(c.getColumnIndex(
                                        BooksProvider.ISBN)),
                        Toast.LENGTH_SHORT).show();
            } while (c.moveToNext());
        }
    }
}
```

3. Press Shift+F9 to debug the application on the Android emulator.
4. Enter an ISBN and title for a book and click the Add Title button. Figure 8-4 shows the `Toast` class displaying the URI of the book added to the content provider. To retrieve all the titles stored in the content provider, click the Retrieve Titles button and observe the values displayed using the `Toast` class.

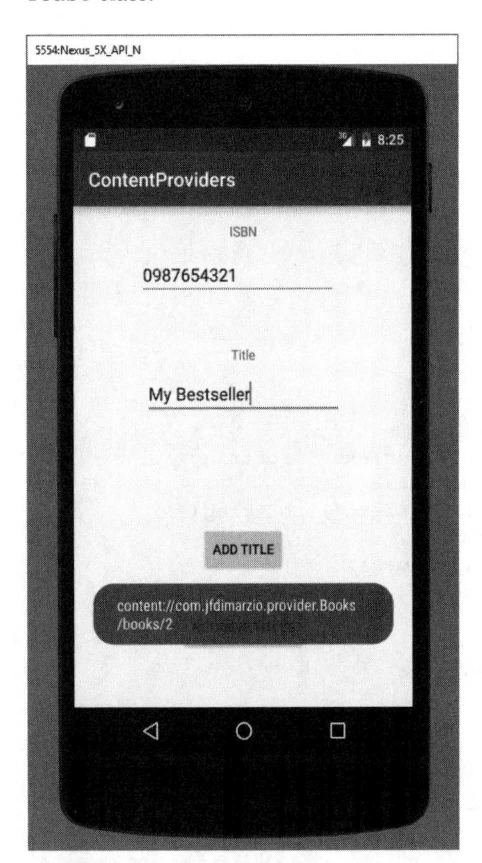

FIGURE 8-4

How It Works

First, you modify the activity so that users can enter a book's ISBN and title to add to the content provider that you have just created.

To add a book to the content provider, you create a new `ContentValues` object and then populate it with the various information about a book:

```
//---add a book---
ContentValues values = new ContentValues();
values.put(BooksProvider.TITLE, ((EditText)
        findViewById(R.id.txtTitle)).getText().toString());
values.put(BooksProvider.ISBN, ((EditText)
        findViewById(R.id.txtISBN)).getText().toString());
Uri uri = getContentResolver().insert(
        BooksProvider.CONTENT_URI, values);
```

Notice that because your content provider is in the same package, you can use the `BooksProvider.TITLE` and the `BooksProvider.ISBN` constants to refer to the `"title"` and `"isbn"` fields, respectively. If you were accessing this content provider from another package, then you would not be able to use these constants. In that case, you need to specify the field name directly, like this:

```
ContentValues values = new ContentValues();
values.put("title", ((EditText)
    findViewById(R.id.txtTitle)).getText().toString());
values.put("isbn", ((EditText)
    findViewById(R.id.txtISBN)).getText().toString());
Uri uri = getContentResolver().insert(
        Uri.parse(
            "content://com.jfdimarzio.provider.Books/books"),
            values);
```

Also note that for external packages, you need to refer to the content URI using the fully qualified content URI:

```
        Uri.parse(
            "content://com.jfdimarzio.provider.Books/books"),
```

To retrieve all the titles in the content provider, you use the following code snippets:

```
//---retrieve the titles---
Uri allTitles = Uri.parse(
        "content://com.jfdimarzio.provider.Books/books");
Cursor c;
if (android.os.Build.VERSION.SDK_INT <11) {
    //---before Honeycomb---
    c = managedQuery(allTitles, null, null, null,
            "title desc");
} else {
    //---Honeycomb and later---
    CursorLoader cursorLoader = new CursorLoader(
            this,
            allTitles, null, null, null,
            "title desc");
    c = cursorLoader.loadInBackground();
}
```

```
if (c.moveToFirst()) {
    do{
        Toast.makeText(this,
            c.getString(c.getColumnIndex(
                BooksProvider._ID)) + ", " +
            c.getString(c.getColumnIndex(
                BooksProvider.TITLE)) + ", " +
            c.getString(c.getColumnIndex(
                BooksProvider.ISBN)),
            Toast.LENGTH_SHORT).show();
    } while (c.moveToNext());
}
```

The preceding query returns the result sorted in descending order based on the `title` field.

If you want to update a book's detail, call the `update()` method with the content URI, indicating the book's ID (the number 2 at the end of the following example):

```
ContentValues editedValues = new ContentValues();
editedValues.put(BooksProvider.TITLE, "Android Tips and Tricks");
getContentResolver().update(
    Uri.parse(
        "content://com.jfdimarzio.provider.Books/books/2"),
        editedValues,
        null,
        null);
```

To delete a book, use the `delete()` method with the content URI, indicating the book's ID:

```
//---delete a title---
getContentResolver().delete(
        Uri.parse("content://com.jfdimarzio.provider.Books/books/2"),
        null, null);
```

To delete all books, simply omit the book's ID in your content URI:

```
//---delete all titles---
getContentResolver().delete(
        Uri.parse("content://com.jfdimarzio.provider.Books/books"),
        null, null);
```

SUMMARY

In this chapter, you learned what content providers are and how to use some of the built-in content providers in Android. In particular, you have seen how to use the Contacts content provider. Google's decision to provide content providers enables applications to share data through a standard set of programming interfaces. In addition to the built-in content providers, you can also create your own custom content provider to share data with other packages.

EXERCISES

1. Write the query to retrieve all contacts from the Contacts application that contain the word "jack."

2. Name the methods that you need to override in your own implementation of a content provider.

3. How do you register a content provider in your `AndroidManifest.xml` file?

You can find answers to the exercises in the appendix.

▶ WHAT YOU LEARNED IN THIS CHAPTER

TOPIC	KEY CONCEPTS
Retrieving a managed cursor	Use the `CursorLoader` class.
Two ways to specify a query for a content provider	Use either a query URI or a predefined query string constant.
Retrieving the value of a column in a content provider	Use the `getColumnIndex()` method.
Querying URI for accessing a contact's name	`ContactsContract.Contacts.CONTENT_URI`
Querying URI for accessing a contact's phone number	`ContactsContract.CommonDataKinds.Phone.CONTENT_URI`
Creating your own content provider	Create a class and extend the `ContentProvider` class.

Messaging

WHAT YOU WILL LEARN IN THIS CHAPTER

- How to send SMS messages programmatically from within your application
- How to send SMS messages using the built-in Messaging application
- How to receive incoming SMS messages
- How to send email messages from your application

> ***CODE DOWNLOAD*** *The wrox.com code downloads for this chapter are found at* `www.wrox.com/go/beginningandroidprog` *on the Download Code tab. The code is in the chapter 09 download and individually named according to the names throughout the chapter.*

After you have your basic Android application up and running, the next interesting thing you can add to it is the capability to communicate with the outside world. You might want your application to send an SMS message to another phone when an event happens (such as when a particular geographical location is reached), or you might want to access a web service that provides certain services (such as currency exchange, weather, and so on).

This chapter demonstrates how to send and receive SMS messages programmatically from within your Android application. You also find out how to invoke the Mail application from within your Android application to send email messages to other users.

SMS MESSAGING

SMS messaging is one of the main functions on a mobile phone today—for some users, it's as necessary as the device itself. Today, any mobile phone you buy will have SMS messaging capabilities, and nearly all users of any age know how to send and receive such messages. Android comes with a built-in SMS application that enables you to send and receive SMS messages. However, in some cases, you might want to integrate SMS capabilities into your Android application. For example, you might want to write an application that automatically sends an SMS message at regular time intervals. For example, this would be useful if you wanted to track the location of your kids—simply give them an Android device that sends out an SMS message containing its geographical location every 30 minutes. Now you know if they really went to the library after school! (Of course, such a capability also means you would have to pay the fees incurred from sending all those SMS messages.)

This section describes how you can programmatically send and receive SMS messages in your Android applications. The good news for Android developers is that you don't need a real device to test SMS messaging: The free Android emulator provides that capability. In fact, when looking at your emulator window, the four-digit number that appears above your emulator is its "phone number." The first emulator session that you open is typically 5554, with each subsequent session being incremented by 1.

Sending SMS Messages Programmatically

The first example explains how to send SMS messages programmatically from within your application. Using this approach, your application can automatically send an SMS message to a recipient without user intervention. The following Try It Out shows you how.

TRY IT OUT Sending SMS Messages (SMS.zip)

1. Using Android Studio, create a new Android project and name it **SMS**.
2. Replace the `TextView` with the following bolded statements in the `activity_main.xml` file. Be sure to replace instances of `com.jfdimarzio` with the package used in your project:

```
<?xml version="1.0" encoding="utf-8"?>
<android.support.constraint.ConstraintLayout xmlns:android=
    "http://schemas.android.com/apk/res/android"
    xmlns:app="http://schemas.android.com/apk/res-auto"
    xmlns:tools="http://schemas.android.com/tools"
    android:id="@+id/activity_main"
    android:layout_width="match_parent"
    android:layout_height="match_parent"
    tools:context="com.jfdimarzio.sms.MainActivity">

    <Button
        android:text="Send SMS"
        android:layout_width="wrap_content"
        android:layout_height="wrap_content"
        android:id="@+id/btnSendSMS"
        app:layout_constraintLeft_toLeftOf="@+id/activity_main"
        app:layout_constraintTop_toTopOf="@+id/activity_main"
```

```
        android:layout_marginTop="16dp"
        app:layout_constraintRight_toRightOf="@+id/activity_main"
        app:layout_constraintBottom_toBottomOf="@+id/activity_main"
        android:layout_marginBottom="16dp"
        android:onClick="onClick" />
</android.support.constraint.ConstraintLayout>
```

3. In the `AndroidManifest.xml` file, add the following bolded statements. Be sure to replace instances of `com.jfdimarzio` with the package used in your project:

```
<?xml version="1.0" encoding="utf-8"?>
<manifest xmlns:android="http://schemas.android.com/apk/res/android"
    package="com.jfdimarzio.sms">
    <uses-permission android:name="android.permission.SEND_SMS"/>
    <application
        android:allowBackup="true"
        android:icon="@mipmap/ic_launcher"
        android:label="@string/app_name"
        android:supportsRtl="true"
        android:theme="@style/AppTheme">

        <activity android:name=".MainActivity">
            <intent-filter>
                <action android:name="android.intent.action.MAIN" />

                <category android:name="android.intent.category.LAUNCHER" />
            </intent-filter>
        </activity>
    </application>

</manifest>
```

4. Add the following statements in bold to the `MainActivity.java` file:

```
import android.Manifest;
import android.content.pm.PackageManager;
import android.support.v4.app.ActivityCompat;
import android.support.v4.content.ContextCompat;
import android.support.v7.app.AppCompatActivity;
import android.os.Bundle;
import android.telephony.SmsManager;
import android.view.View;
import android.widget.Toast;

public class MainActivity extends AppCompatActivity {
    final private int REQUEST_SEND_SMS = 123;
    @Override
    protected void onCreate(Bundle savedInstanceState) {
        super.onCreate(savedInstanceState);
        setContentView(R.layout.activity_main);

        if (ContextCompat.checkSelfPermission(this,
                Manifest.permission.SEND_SMS)
                != PackageManager.PERMISSION_GRANTED) {
```

```
                ActivityCompat.requestPermissions(this,
                        new String[]{Manifest.permission.SEND_SMS},
                        REQUEST_SEND_SMS);
            }
        }
        @Override
        public void onRequestPermissionsResult(int requestCode,
         String[] permissions, int[] grantResults) {
            switch (requestCode) {
                case REQUEST_SEND_SMS:
                    if (grantResults[0] == PackageManager.PERMISSION_GRANTED) {
                        Toast.makeText(MainActivity.this,
         "Permission Granted", Toast.LENGTH_SHORT).show();
                    } else {
                        Toast.makeText(MainActivity.this,
         "Permission Denied", Toast.LENGTH_SHORT).show();
                    }
                    break;
                default:
                    super.onRequestPermissionsResult(requestCode,
          permissions, grantResults);
            }
        }

        public void onClick(View v) {
        //---the "phone number" of your emulator should be 5554---
            sendSMS("5554", "Hello my friends!");

        }

        //---sends an SMS message---
        private void sendSMS(String phoneNumber, String message)
        {
            SmsManager sms = SmsManager.getDefault();
            sms.sendTextMessage(phoneNumber, null, message, null, null);
        }

    }
```

5. Press Shift+F9 to debug the application on the Android emulator. Grant the application permission to SEND_SMS when asked.
6. Click the Send SMS button to send an SMS message. Figure 9-1 shows the SMS message received (view it by opening the messaging app on the emulator).

How It Works

Android uses a permissions-based policy whereby all the permissions needed by an application must be specified in the `AndroidManifest.xml` file. This ensures that when the application is installed, the user knows exactly which access permissions it requires. As shown in the Providers example in Chapter 8, the application asks the user to either grant or deny permissions.

FIGURE 9-1

To send an SMS message programmatically, you use the `SmsManager` class. Unlike other classes, you do not directly instantiate this class. Instead, you call the `getDefault()` static method to obtain an `SmsManager` object. You then send the SMS message using the `sendTextMessage()` method:

```
//---sends an SMS message---
private void sendSMS(String phoneNumber, String message)
{
    SmsManager sms = SmsManager.getDefault();
    sms.sendTextMessage(phoneNumber, null, message, null, null);
}
```

Following are the five arguments to the `sendTextMessage()` method:

- `destinationAddress`—Phone number of the recipient
- `scAddress`—Service center address; use `null` for default SMSC
- `text`—Content of the SMS message

- `sentIntent`—Pending intent to invoke when the message is sent (discussed in more detail in the next section)
- `deliveryIntent`—Pending intent to invoke when the message has been delivered (discussed in more detail in the next section)

> **NOTE** *If you send an SMS message programmatically using the* `SmsManager` *class, the message sent does not appear in the sender's built-in Messaging application.*

Sending SMS Messages Using Intent

Using the `SmsManager` class, you can send SMS messages from within your application without the need to involve the built-in Messaging application. However, sometimes it would be easier if you could simply invoke the built-in Messaging application and let it handle sending the message.

To activate the built-in Messaging application from within your application, you can use an `Intent` object with the MIME type `"vnd.android-dir/mms-sms"`, as shown in the following code snippet:

```
Intent i = new
        Intent(android.content.Intent.ACTION_VIEW);
i.putExtra("address", "5556; 5558; 5560");
i.putExtra("sms_body", "Hello my friends!");
i.setType("vnd.android-dir/mms-sms");
startActivity(i);
```

This code invokes the Messaging application directly. Note that you can send your SMS to multiple recipients by separating each phone number with a semicolon (in the `putExtra()` method). The numbers are separated using commas in the Messaging application.

> **NOTE** *If you use this method to invoke the Messaging application, there is no need to ask for the* `SEND_SMS` *permission in* `AndroidManifest.xml` *because your application is ultimately not the one sending the message.*

Receiving SMS Messages

Besides sending SMS messages from your Android applications, you can also receive incoming SMS messages from within your applications by using a `BroadcastReceiver` object. This is useful when you want your application to perform an action when a certain SMS message is received. For example, you might want to track the location of your phone in case it is lost or stolen. In this case, you can write an application that automatically listens for SMS messages containing some secret code. When that message is received, you can then send an SMS message containing the location's coordinates back to the sender.

The following Try It Out shows how to programmatically listen for incoming SMS messages.

TRY IT OUT Receiving SMS Messages

1. Using the same project created in the previous section, add the following bolded statements to the `AndroidManifest.xml` file. Please be sure to replace all instances of `com.jfdimarzio` with the package used in your project:

```
<?xml version="1.0" encoding="utf-8"?>
<manifest xmlns:android="http://schemas.android.com/apk/res/android"
    package="com.jfdimarzio.sms">
    <uses-permission android:name="android.permission.SEND_SMS"/>
    <uses-permission android:name="android.permission.RECEIVE_SMS"/>
    <application
        android:allowBackup="true"
        android:icon="@mipmap/ic_launcher"
        android:label="@string/app_name"
        android:supportsRtl="true"
        android:theme="@style/AppTheme">

        <activity android:name=".MainActivity">
            <intent-filter>
                <action android:name="android.intent.action.MAIN" />

                <category android:name="android.intent.category.LAUNCHER" />
            </intent-filter>
        </activity>

        <receiver android:name=".SMSReceiver" android:exported="true"
             android:permission="android.permission.BROADCAST_SMS">
             <intent-filter android:priority="9000">
                 <action android:name="android.provider.Telephony.SMS_RECEIVED" />
             </intent-filter>
         </receiver>

    </application>

</manifest>
```

2. In the `src` folder of the project, add a new Class file to the package name and call it **SMSReceiver** (see Figure 9-2).

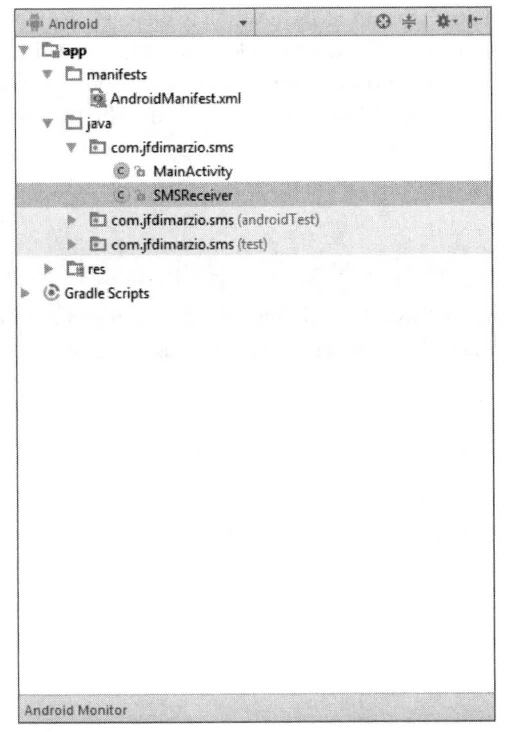

FIGURE 9-2

3. Code the `SMSReceiver.java` file as follows:

```
import android.content.BroadcastReceiver;
import android.content.Context;
import android.content.Intent;
import android.os.Bundle;
import android.telephony.SmsMessage;
import android.util.Log;
import android.widget.Toast;
public class SMSReceiver extends BroadcastReceiver
{
    @Override
    public void onReceive(Context context, Intent intent)
    {
        //---get the SMS message passed in---
        Bundle bundle = intent.getExtras();
        SmsMessage[] msgs = null;
        String str = "SMS from ";
        if (bundle != null)
        {
            //---retrieve the SMS message received---
            msgs = Telephony.Sms.Intents.getMessagesFromIntent(intent);
```

```
                for (int i=0; i<msgs.length; i++){
                    str += msgs[i].getMessageBody().toString();
                }

                    //---get the message body---
                    str += msgs[i].getMessageBody().toString();
                }
                //---display the new SMS message---
                Toast.makeText(context, str, Toast.LENGTH_SHORT).show();
                Log.d("SMSReceiver", str);
            }
        }
    }
```

4. Press Shift+F9 to debug the application on the Android emulator.
5. Using the `More` setting on the emulator, select `Phone` and `Send Message`, send a message to the emulator. Your application should be able to receive the message and display it using the `Toast` class (see Figure 9-3).

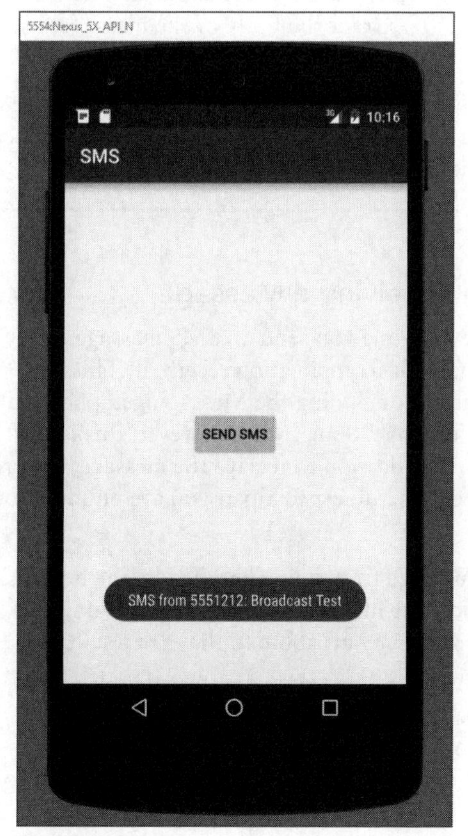

FIGURE 9-3

How It Works

To listen for incoming SMS messages, you create a `BroadcastReceiver` class. The `BroadcastReceiver` class enables your application to receive intents sent by other applications using the `sendBroadcast()` method. Essentially, it enables your application to handle events raised by other applications. When an intent is received, the `onReceive()` method is called, which needs to be overridden.

When an incoming SMS message is received, the `onReceive()` method is fired. The SMS message is contained in the `Intent` object (`intent`, which is the second parameter in the `onReceive()` method) via a `Bundle` object. Note that each SMS message received invokes the `onReceive()` method. If your device receives five SMS messages then the `onReceive()` method is called five times.

Each SMS message is stored in an `Object` array. If the SMS message is fewer than 160 characters then the array has one element. If an SMS message contains more than 160 characters the message is split into multiple smaller messages and is stored as multiple elements in the array.

To extract the content of each message, use the static `getMessagesFromIntent()` method from `Telephony.Sms`. The phone number of the sender is obtained via the `getOriginatingAddress()` method. Therefore, if you need to send an autoreply to the sender, use the `getOriginating-Address()` method to obtain the sender's phone number. To extract the body of the message, use the `getMessageBody()` method.

One interesting characteristic of the `BroadcastReceiver` is that your application continues to listen for incoming SMS messages even if it is not running. As long as the application is installed on the device, any incoming SMS messages are received by the application.

Preventing the Messaging Application from Receiving a Message

In the previous section, you might have noticed that every time you send an SMS message to the emulator (or device), both your application and the built-in application receive it. This is because when an SMS message is received, all applications (including the Messaging application) on the Android device take turns handling the incoming message. Sometimes, however, this is not the behavior you want. For example, you might want your application to receive the message and prevent it from being sent to other applications. This is very useful, especially if you are building some kind of tracking application.

The solution is very simple. To prevent an incoming message from being handled by the built-in Messaging application, your application needs to handle the message before the Messaging app has the chance to do it. To do this, add the `android:priority` attribute to the `<intent-filter>` element, like this:

```
<receiver android:name=".SMSReceiver">
    <intent-filter android:priority="100">
        <action android:name=
            "android.provider.Telephony.SMS_RECEIVED" />
    </intent-filter>
</receiver>
```

Set this attribute to a high number, such as 100. The higher the number, the earlier Android executes your application. When an incoming message is received, your application executes first, and you can decide what to do with the message. To prevent other applications from seeing the message, simply call the `abortBroadcast()` method in your `BroadcastReceiver` class:

```
@Override
public void onReceive(Context context, Intent intent)
{
    //---get the SMS message passed in---
    Bundle bundle = intent.getExtras();
    SmsMessage[] msgs = null;
    String str = "SMS from ";
    if (bundle != null)
    {
        //---retrieve the SMS message received---
        Object[] pdus = (Object[]) bundle.get("pdus");
        msgs = new SmsMessage[pdus.length];
        for (int i=0; i<msgs.length; i++){
            msgs[i] = SmsMessage.createFromPdu((byte[])pdus[i]);
            if (i==0) {
                //---get the sender address/phone number---
                str += msgs[i].getOriginatingAddress();
                str += ": ";
            }
            //---get the message body---
            str += msgs[i].getMessageBody().toString();
        }

        //---display the new SMS message---
        Toast.makeText(context, str, Toast.LENGTH_SHORT).show();
        Log.d("SMSReceiver", str);

        //---stop the SMS message from being broadcasted---
        this.abortBroadcast();
    }
}
```

After you do this, no other applications are able to receive your SMS messages.

> ***NOTE*** *Be aware that after the preceding application is installed on your device, all incoming SMS messages will be intercepted by your application and will not appear in your Messaging application again.*

Updating an Activity from a BroadcastReceiver

The previous section demonstrates how you can use a `BroadcastReceiver` class to listen for incoming SMS messages and then use the `Toast` class to display the received SMS message. Often, you'll want to send the SMS message back to the main activity of your application. For example, you might want to display the message in a `TextView`. The following Try It Out demonstrates how you can do this.

TRY IT OUT Creating a View-Based Application Project

1. Using the same project from the previous section, add the following bolded lines to the `activity_main.xml` file. Be sure to replace all instances of `com.jfdimarzio` with the package used in your project:

```
<?xml version="1.0" encoding="utf-8"?>
<android.support.constraint.ConstraintLayout xmlns:android=
    "http://schemas.android.com/apk/res/android"
    xmlns:app="http://schemas.android.com/apk/res-auto"
    xmlns:tools="http://schemas.android.com/tools"
    android:id="@+id/activity_main"
    android:layout_width="match_parent"
    android:layout_height="match_parent"
    tools:context="com.jfdimarzio.sms.MainActivity">

    <Button
        android:text="Send SMS"
        android:layout_width="wrap_content"
        android:layout_height="wrap_content"
        android:id="@+id/btnSendSMS"
        android:onClick="onClick"
        app:layout_constraintLeft_toLeftOf="@+id/activity_main"
        app:layout_constraintTop_toTopOf="@+id/activity_main"
        android:layout_marginTop="16dp"
        app:layout_constraintRight_toRightOf="@+id/activity_main"
        app:layout_constraintBottom_toBottomOf="@+id/activity_main"
        android:layout_marginBottom="16dp" />

    <TextView
        android:text="TextView"
        android:layout_width="wrap_content"
        android:layout_height="wrap_content"
        android:id="@+id/textView"
        app:layout_constraintLeft_toLeftOf="@+id/btnSendSMS"
        app:layout_constraintTop_toBottomOf="@+id/btnSendSMS"
        android:layout_marginTop="8dp"
        app:layout_constraintRight_toRightOf="@+id/btnSendSMS"
        app:layout_constraintBottom_toBottomOf="@+id/activity_main"
        android:layout_marginBottom="16dp" />
</android.support.constraint.ConstraintLayout>
```

2. Add the following bolded statements to the `SMSReceiver.java` file:

```
import android.content.BroadcastReceiver;
import android.content.Context;
import android.content.Intent;
import android.os.Bundle;
import android.telephony.SmsMessage;
import android.util.Log;
import android.widget.Toast;
public class SMSReceiver extends BroadcastReceiver
{
    @Override
```

```
        public void onReceive(Context context, Intent intent)
        {
            //---get the SMS message passed in---
            Bundle bundle = intent.getExtras();
            SmsMessage[] msgs = null;
            String str = "SMS from ";
            if (bundle != null)
            {
                //---retrieve the SMS message received---
                Object[] pdus = (Object[]) bundle.get("pdus");
                msgs = new SmsMessage[pdus.length];
                for (int i=0; i<msgs.length; i++){
                    msgs[i] = SmsMessage.createFromPdu((byte[])pdus[i]);
                    if (i==0) {
                        //---get the sender address/phone number---
                        str += msgs[i].getOriginatingAddress();
                        str += ": ";
                    }
                    //---get the message body---
                    str += msgs[i].getMessageBody().toString();
                }
                //---display the new SMS message---
                Toast.makeText(context, str, Toast.LENGTH_SHORT).show();
                Log.d("SMSReceiver", str);

                Intent broadcastIntent = new Intent();
                broadcastIntent.setAction("SMS_RECEIVED_ACTION");
                broadcastIntent.putExtra("sms", str);
                context.sendBroadcast(broadcastIntent);

            }
        }
    }
```

3. Add the following bolded statements to the `MainActivity.java` file:

```
import android.Manifest;
import android.content.BroadcastReceiver;
import android.content.Context;
import android.content.Intent;
import android.content.IntentFilter;
import android.content.pm.PackageManager;
import android.support.v4.app.ActivityCompat;
import android.support.v4.content.ContextCompat;
import android.support.v7.app.AppCompatActivity;
import android.os.Bundle;
import android.telephony.SmsManager;
import android.view.View;
import android.widget.TextView;
import android.widget.Toast;

import static android.Manifest.permission_group.SMS;

public class MainActivity extends AppCompatActivity {
    final private int REQUEST_SEND_SMS = 123;
```

```
final private int REQUEST_REC_SMS = 321;
BroadcastReceiver smsSentReceiver;
IntentFilter intentFilter;

private BroadcastReceiver intentReceiver = new BroadcastReceiver() {
    @Override
    public void onReceive(Context context, Intent intent) {
        //---display the SMS received in the TextView---
        TextView SMSes = (TextView) findViewById(R.id.textView);
        SMSes.setText(intent.getExtras().getString("sms"));
    }
};

@Override
protected void onCreate(Bundle savedInstanceState) {
    super.onCreate(savedInstanceState);
    setContentView(R.layout.activity_main);

    if (ContextCompat.checkSelfPermission(this,
            Manifest.permission.SEND_SMS)
            != PackageManager.PERMISSION_GRANTED ) {

            ActivityCompat.requestPermissions(this,
                    new String[]{Manifest.permission.SEND_SMS},
                    REQUEST_SEND_SMS);
    }

    if (ContextCompat.checkSelfPermission(this,
            Manifest.permission.RECEIVE_SMS)
            != PackageManager.PERMISSION_GRANTED ) {

        ActivityCompat.requestPermissions(this,
                new String[]{Manifest.permission.RECEIVE_SMS},
                REQUEST_REC_SMS);
    }

    intentFilter = new IntentFilter();
    intentFilter.addAction("SMS_RECEIVED_ACTION");

}

@Override
public void onResume() {
    super.onResume();
    //---register the receiver---
    registerReceiver(intentReceiver, intentFilter);

}
@Override
public void onPause() {
    super.onPause();
```

```
        //---unregister the receiver---
        unregisterReceiver(intentReceiver);
    }

    @Override
    public void onRequestPermissionsResult(int requestCode,
    String[] permissions, int[] grantResults) {
        switch (requestCode) {
            case REQUEST_SEND_SMS:
                if (grantResults[0] == PackageManager.PERMISSION_GRANTED) {
                    Toast.makeText(MainActivity.this,
    "SEND Permission Granted", Toast.LENGTH_SHORT).show();
                } else {
                    Toast.makeText(MainActivity.this,
    "SEND Permission Denied", Toast.LENGTH_SHORT).show();
                }
                break;
            case REQUEST_REC_SMS:
                if (grantResults[0] == PackageManager.PERMISSION_GRANTED) {
                    Toast.makeText(MainActivity.this,
    "RECEIVE Permission Granted", Toast.LENGTH_SHORT).show();
                } else {
                    Toast.makeText(MainActivity.this,
    "RECEIVE Permission Denied", Toast.LENGTH_SHORT).show();
                }
                break;
            default:
                super.onRequestPermissionsResult(requestCode,
    permissions, grantResults);
        }
    }

    public void onClick(View v) {

        sendSMS("5554", "Hello my friends!");

    }

    //---sends an SMS message to another device---
    private void sendSMS(String phoneNumber, String message)
    {
        SmsManager sms = SmsManager.getDefault();
        sms.sendTextMessage(phoneNumber, null, message, null, null);
    }

}
```

4. Press Shift+F9 to debug the application on the Android emulator. Using the DDMS, send an SMS message to the emulator. Figure 9-4 shows the `Toast` class displaying the message received, and the `TextView` showing the message received.

FIGURE 9-4

How It Works

You first add a `TextView` to your activity so that it can be used to display the received SMS message.

Next, you modify the `SMSReceiver` class so that when it receives an SMS message, it broadcasts another `Intent` object so that any applications listening for this intent can be notified (which is the next thing you implement). The SMS received is also sent out via this intent:

```
//---send a broadcast intent to update the SMS received in the activity
Intent broadcastIntent = new Intent();
broadcastIntent.setAction("SMS_RECEIVED_ACTION");
broadcastIntent.putExtra("sms", str);
context.sendBroadcast(broadcastIntent);
```

In your activity you create a `BroadcastReceiver` object to listen for broadcast intents:

```
private BroadcastReceiver intentReceiver = new BroadcastReceiver() {
    @Override
    public void onReceive(Context context, Intent intent) {
```

```
            //---display the SMS received in the TextView---
            TextView SMSes = (TextView) findViewById(R.id.textView1);
            SMSes.setText(intent.getExtras().getString("sms"));
        }
    };
```

When a broadcast intent is received, you update the SMS message in the `TextView`.

You need to create an `IntentFilter` object so that you can listen for a particular intent. In this case, the intent is `"SMS_RECEIVED_ACTION"`:

```
    @Override
    public void onCreate(Bundle savedInstanceState) {
        super.onCreate(savedInstanceState);
        setContentView(R.layout.main);

        //---intent to filter for SMS messages received---
        intentFilter = new IntentFilter();
        intentFilter.addAction("SMS_RECEIVED_ACTION");
    }
```

Finally, you register the `BroadcastReceiver` in the activity's `onResume()` event and unregister it in the `onPause()` event:

```
    @Override
    public void onResume() {
        super.onResume();
        //---register the receiver---
        registerReceiver(intentReceiver, intentFilter);

    }
    @Override
    public void onPause() {
        super.onPause();

        //---unregister the receiver---
        unregisterReceiver(intentReceiver);
    }
```

This means that the `TextView` displays the SMS message only when the message is received while the activity is visible on the screen. If the SMS message is received when the activity is not in the foreground, the `TextView` is not updated.

Invoking an Activity from a BroadcastReceiver

The previous example shows how you can pass the SMS message received to be displayed in the activity. However, in many situations your activity might be in the background when the SMS message is received. In this case, it would be useful to be able to bring the activity to the foreground when a message is received. The following Try It Out shows you how.

TRY IT OUT Invoking an Activity

1. Using the same project used in the previous section, add the following bolded lines to the `MainActivity.java` file:

```
import android.Manifest;
import android.content.BroadcastReceiver;
import android.content.Context;
import android.content.Intent;
import android.content.IntentFilter;
import android.content.pm.PackageManager;
import android.support.v4.app.ActivityCompat;
import android.support.v4.content.ContextCompat;
import android.support.v7.app.AppCompatActivity;
import android.os.Bundle;
import android.telephony.SmsManager;
import android.view.View;
import android.widget.TextView;
import android.widget.Toast;

import static android.Manifest.permission_group.SMS;

public class MainActivity extends AppCompatActivity {
    final private int REQUEST_SEND_SMS = 123;
    final private int REQUEST_REC_SMS = 321;
    BroadcastReceiver smsSentReceiver;
    IntentFilter intentFilter;

    private BroadcastReceiver intentReceiver = new BroadcastReceiver() {
        @Override
        public void onReceive(Context context, Intent intent) {
            //---display the SMS received in the TextView---
            TextView SMSes = (TextView) findViewById(R.id.textView);
            SMSes.setText(intent.getExtras().getString("sms"));
        }
    };

    @Override
    protected void onCreate(Bundle savedInstanceState) {
        super.onCreate(savedInstanceState);
        setContentView(R.layout.activity_main);

        if (ContextCompat.checkSelfPermission(this,
                Manifest.permission.SEND_SMS)
                != PackageManager.PERMISSION_GRANTED ) {

                ActivityCompat.requestPermissions(this,
                        new String[]{Manifest.permission.SEND_SMS},
                        REQUEST_SEND_SMS);
        }

        if (ContextCompat.checkSelfPermission(this,
                Manifest.permission.RECEIVE_SMS)
                != PackageManager.PERMISSION_GRANTED ) {
```

```
            ActivityCompat.requestPermissions(this,
                    new String[]{Manifest.permission.RECEIVE_SMS},
                    REQUEST_REC_SMS);
        }

        intentFilter = new IntentFilter();
        intentFilter.addAction("SMS_RECEIVED_ACTION");

        registerReceiver(intentReceiver, intentFilter);
    }

    @Override
    public void onResume() {
        super.onResume();
        //---register the receiver---
        //registerReceiver(intentReceiver, intentFilter);

    }
    @Override
    public void onPause() {
        super.onPause();

        //---unregister the receiver---
        unregisterReceiver(intentReceiver);
    }


@Override
    public void onRequestPermissionsResult(int requestCode,
    String[] permissions, int[] grantResults) {
        switch (requestCode) {
            case REQUEST_SEND_SMS:
                if (grantResults[0] == PackageManager.PERMISSION_GRANTED) {
                    Toast.makeText(MainActivity.this,
    "SEND Permission Granted", Toast.LENGTH_SHORT).show();
                } else {
                    Toast.makeText(MainActivity.this,
    "SEND Permission Denied", Toast.LENGTH_SHORT).show();
                }
                break;
            case REQUEST_REC_SMS:
                if (grantResults[0] == PackageManager.PERMISSION_GRANTED) {
                    Toast.makeText(MainActivity.this,
    "RECEIVE Permission Granted", Toast.LENGTH_SHORT).show();
                } else {
                    Toast.makeText(MainActivity.this,
    "RECEIVE Permission Denied", Toast.LENGTH_SHORT).show();
                }
                break;
            default:
                super.onRequestPermissionsResult(requestCode,
    permissions, grantResults);
        }
    }
```

```
        public void onClick(View v) {

            sendSMS("5554", "Hello my friends!");

        }

        //---sends an SMS message to another device---
        private void sendSMS(String phoneNumber, String message)
        {
            SmsManager sms = SmsManager.getDefault();
            sms.sendTextMessage(phoneNumber, null, message, null, null);
        }

    }
```

2. Add the following bolded statements to the `SMSReceiver.java` file:

```
import android.content.BroadcastReceiver;
import android.content.Context;
import android.content.Intent;
import android.os.Bundle;
import android.telephony.SmsMessage;
import android.util.Log;
import android.widget.Toast;
public class SMSReceiver extends BroadcastReceiver
{
    @Override
    public void onReceive(Context context, Intent intent)
    {
        //---get the SMS message passed in---
        Bundle bundle = intent.getExtras();
        SmsMessage[] msgs = null;
        String str = "SMS from ";
        if (bundle != null)
        {
            //---retrieve the SMS message received---
            Object[] pdus = (Object[]) bundle.get("pdus");
            msgs = new SmsMessage[pdus.length];
            for (int i=0; i<msgs.length; i++){
                msgs[i] = SmsMessage.createFromPdu((byte[])pdus[i]);
                if (i==0) {
                    //---get the sender address/phone number---
                    str += msgs[i].getOriginatingAddress();
                    str += ": ";
                }
                //---get the message body---
                str += msgs[i].getMessageBody().toString();
            }
            //---display the new SMS message---
            Toast.makeText(context, str, Toast.LENGTH_SHORT).show();
            Log.d("SMSReceiver", str);

            //---launch the SMSActivity---
```

```
                Intent mainActivityIntent = new Intent(context, MainActivity.class);
                mainActivityIntent.setFlags(Intent.FLAG_ACTIVITY_NEW_TASK);
                context.startActivity(mainActivityIntent);

                Intent broadcastIntent = new Intent();
                broadcastIntent.setAction("SMS_RECEIVED_ACTION");
                broadcastIntent.putExtra("sms", str);
                context.sendBroadcast(broadcastIntent);

            }
        }
    }
```

3. Modify the `AndroidManifest.xml` file as shown in bold:

```
<?xml version="1.0" encoding="utf-8"?>
<manifest xmlns:android="http://schemas.android.com/apk/res/android"
    package="com.jfdimarzio.sms">
    <uses-permission android:name="android.permission.SEND_SMS"/>
    <uses-permission android:name="android.permission.RECEIVE_SMS"/>
    <application
        android:allowBackup="true"
        android:icon="@mipmap/ic_launcher"
        android:label="@string/app_name"
        android:supportsRtl="true"
        android:launchMode="singleTask"
        android:theme="@style/AppTheme">

        <activity android:name=".MainActivity">
            <intent-filter>
                <action android:name="android.intent.action.MAIN" />

                <category android:name="android.intent.category.LAUNCHER" />
            </intent-filter>
        </activity>

        <receiver android:name=".SMSReceiver" android:exported="true"
            android:permission="android.permission.BROADCAST_SMS">
            <intent-filter android:priority="5822">
                <action android:name="android.provider.Telephony.SMS_RECEIVED" />
            </intent-filter>
        </receiver>

    </application>

</manifest>
```

4. Press Shift+F9 to debug the application on the Android emulator. When the `MainActivity` is shown, click the Home button to send the activity to the background.
5. Use the DDMS to send an SMS message to the emulator again. This time, note that the activity is brought to the foreground, displaying the SMS message received.

How It Works

In the MainActivity class, you first registered the BroadcastReceiver in the activity's onCreate() event, instead of the onResume() event. Instead of unregistering it in the onPause() event, you unregister it in the onDestroy() event. This ensures that even if the activity is in the background, it is still able to listen for the broadcast intent.

Next, you modify the onReceive() event in the SMSReceiver class by using an intent to bring the activity to the foreground before broadcasting another intent:

```
//---launch the SMSActivity---
Intent mainActivityIntent = new Intent(context, SMSActivity.class);

mainActivityIntent.setFlags(Intent.FLAG_ACTIVITY_NEW_TASK);
context.startActivity(mainActivityIntent);

//---send a broadcast intent to update the SMS received in the activity---
Intent broadcastIntent = new Intent();

broadcastIntent.setAction("SMS_RECEIVED_ACTION");
broadcastIntent.putExtra("sms", str);
context.sendBroadcast(broadcastIntent);
```

The startActivity() method launches the activity and brings it to the foreground. Note that you need to set the Intent.FLAG_ACTIVITY_NEW_TASK flag because calling startActivity() from outside of an activity context requires the FLAG_ACTIVITY_NEW_TASK flag.

You also need to set the launchMode attribute of the <activity> element in the AndroidManifest.xml file to singleTask:

```
<activity
    android:label="@string/app_name"
    android:name=".SMSActivity"
    android:launchMode="singleTask" >
```

If you don't set this, multiple instances of the activity are launched as your application receives SMS messages.

Note that in this example, when the activity is in the background (such as when you click the Home button to show the home screen), the activity is brought to the foreground and its TextView is updated with the SMS received. However, if the activity was killed (such as when you click the Back button to destroy it), the activity is launched again but the TextView is not updated.

Caveats and Warnings

Although the capability to send and receive SMS messages makes Android a very compelling platform for developing sophisticated applications, this flexibility comes with a price. A seemingly innocent application might send SMS messages behind the scene without the user knowing, as demonstrated by a recent case of an SMS-based Trojan Android application (see http://www.tripwire.com/state-of-security/security-data-protection/android-malware-sms/).

The app claims to be a media player, but when it's installed it sends SMS messages to a premium-rate number, resulting in huge phone bills for the user.

The user needs to explicitly give permissions (such as accessing the Internet, sending and receiving SMS messages, and so on) to your application; however, the request for permissions is shown only at installation time. If the user clicks the Install button, he or she is considered to have granted the application permission to send and receive SMS messages. This is dangerous because after the application is installed it can send and receive SMS messages without ever prompting the user again.

In addition to this, the application also can "sniff" for incoming SMS messages. For example, based on the techniques you learned from the previous section, you can easily write an application that checks for certain keywords in the SMS message. When an SMS message contains the keyword you are looking for, you can then use the Location Manager (discussed in Chapter 8) to obtain your geographical location and then send the coordinates back to the sender of the SMS message. The sender could then easily track your location. All these tasks can be done easily without the user knowing it! That said, users should try to avoid installing Android applications that come from dubious sources, such as from unknown websites or strangers.

SENDING EMAIL

Like SMS messaging, Android also supports email. The Gmail/Email application on Android enables you to configure an email account using POP3 or IMAP. Besides sending and receiving emails using the Gmail/Email application, you can also send email messages programmatically from within your Android application. The following Try It Out shows you how.

For the following example to work properly, you must configure the Email app on your emulator. Simply click the Email app on the emulator and follow the on-screen prompts to set up the application. If you do not, you receive a message stating that no application is configured to handle the Email intent.

TRY IT OUT Sending Email Programmatically (Emails.zip)

1. Using Android Studio, create a new Android project and name it **Emails**.
2. Add the following bolded statements to the `activity_main.xml` file, replacing the `TextView`. Please be sure to replace all instances of `com.jfdimarzio` with the package used in your project:

```
<?xml version="1.0" encoding="utf-8"?>
<android.support.constraint.ConstraintLayout xmlns:android=
    "http://schemas.android.com/apk/res/android"
    xmlns:app="http://schemas.android.com/apk/res-auto"
    xmlns:tools="http://schemas.android.com/tools"
    android:id="@+id/activity_main"
    android:layout_width="match_parent"
    android:layout_height="match_parent"
    tools:context="com.jfdimarzio.emails.MainActivity">


    <Button
        android:text="Send Email"
        android:layout_width="wrap_content"
```

```
        android:layout_height="wrap_content"
        android:id="@+id/btnSendEmail"
        app:layout_constraintLeft_toLeftOf="@+id/activity_main"
        app:layout_constraintTop_toTopOf="@+id/activity_main"
        app:layout_constraintRight_toRightOf="@+id/activity_main"
        app:layout_constraintBottom_toBottomOf="@+id/activity_main" />
</android.support.constraint.ConstraintLayout>
```

3. Add the following bolded statements to the `MainActivity.java` file:

```
import android.content.Intent;
import android.net.Uri;
import android.support.v7.app.AppCompatActivity;
import android.os.Bundle;
import android.view.View;

public class MainActivity extends AppCompatActivity {

    @Override
    protected void onCreate(Bundle savedInstanceState) {
        super.onCreate(savedInstanceState);
        setContentView(R.layout.activity_main);
    }
    public void onClick(View v) {
        //---replace the following email addresses with real ones---
        String[] to =
                {"someguy@example.com",
                        "anotherguy@example.com"};
        String[] cc = {"busybody@example.com"};
        sendEmail(to, cc, "Hello", "Hello my friends!");
    }

    private void sendEmail(String[] emailAddresses, String[] carbonCopies,
                           String subject, String message)
    {
        Intent emailIntent = new Intent(Intent.ACTION_SEND);
        emailIntent.setData(Uri.parse("mailto:"));
        String[] to = emailAddresses;
        String[] cc = carbonCopies;
        emailIntent.putExtra(Intent.EXTRA_EMAIL, to);
        emailIntent.putExtra(Intent.EXTRA_CC, cc);
        emailIntent.putExtra(Intent.EXTRA_SUBJECT, subject);
        emailIntent.putExtra(Intent.EXTRA_TEXT, message);
        emailIntent.setType("message/rfc822");
        startActivity(Intent.createChooser(emailIntent, "Email"));
    }
}
```

4. Press Shift+F9 to test the application on the Android emulator/device (ensure that you have configured your email before trying this example).

5. Click the Send Email button. If you configured the Email service on your emulator, you should see the Email application launched in your emulator/device. Otherwise you see the message shown in Figure 9-5.

FIGURE 9-5

How It Works

In this example, you are launching the built-in Email application to send an email message. You use an `Intent` object and set the various parameters using the `setData()`, `putExtra()`, and `setType()` methods:

```
Intent emailIntent = new Intent(Intent.ACTION_SEND);
emailIntent.setData(Uri.parse("mailto:"));
String[] to = emailAddresses;
String[] cc = carbonCopies;
emailIntent.putExtra(Intent.EXTRA_EMAIL, to);
emailIntent.putExtra(Intent.EXTRA_CC, cc);
emailIntent.putExtra(Intent.EXTRA_SUBJECT, subject);
emailIntent.putExtra(Intent.EXTRA_TEXT, message);
emailIntent.setType("message/rfc822");
startActivity(Intent.createChooser(emailIntent, "Email"));
```

SUMMARY

This chapter described the two key ways for your application to communicate with the outside world. You first learned how to send and receive SMS messages. Using SMS, you can build a variety of applications that rely on the service provided by your mobile operator. Chapter 8 shows you a good example of how to use SMS messaging to build a location tracker application.

You also learned how to send email messages from within your Android application. You do that by invoking the built-in Email application through the use of an `Intent` object.

EXERCISES

1. Name the two ways in which you can send SMS messages in your Android application.

2. Name the permissions you need to declare in your `AndroidManifest.xml` file for sending and receiving SMS messages.

3. How do you notify an activity from a `BroadcastReceiver`?

You can find answers to the exercises in the appendix.

▶ WHAT YOU LEARNED IN THIS CHAPTER

TOPIC	KEY CONCEPTS
Programmatically sending SMS messages	Use the `SmsManager` class.
Sending SMS messages using Intent	Set the intent type to `vnd.android-dir/mms-sms`.
Receiving SMS messages	Implement a `BroadcastReceiver` and set it in the `AndroidManifest.xml` file.
Sending email using Intent	Set the intent type to `message/rfc822`.

10

Location-Based Services

WHAT YOU WILL LEARN IN THIS CHAPTER

- Displaying Google Maps in your Android application
- Displaying zoom controls on the map
- Switching between the different map views
- Retrieving the address location touched on the map
- Performing geocoding and reverse geocoding
- Obtaining geographical data using GPS, Cell-ID, and Wi-Fi triangulation
- Monitoring for a location
- Building a location tracker application

> ***CODE DOWNLOAD*** *The wrox.com code downloads for this chapter are found at* `www.wrox.com/go/beginningandroidprog` *on the Download Code tab. The code is in the chapter 10 download and individually named according to the names throughout the chapter.*

You have seen the explosive growth of mobile apps in recent years. One category of apps that is very popular is Location-Based Services, commonly known as LBS. LBS apps track your location, and might offer additional services such as locating amenities nearby, offering suggestions for route planning, and so on. Of course, one of the key ingredients in an LBS app is maps, which present a visual representation of your location.

This chapter shows you how to make use of Google Maps in your Android application, as well as how to manipulate the map view programmatically. In addition, you find out how to obtain your geographical location using the `LocationManager` class available in the Android SDK. This chapter ends with a project to build a location tracker application that you can install on an Android device and use to track the location of friends and relatives using SMS messaging.

DISPLAYING MAPS

Google Maps is one of the many applications bundled with the Android platform. In addition to simply using the Maps application, you can also embed it into your own applications and make it do some very cool things. This section describes how to use Google Maps in your Android applications and programmatically perform the following:

- Change the views of Google Maps.
- Obtain the latitude and longitude of locations in Google Maps.
- Perform geocoding and reverse geocoding (translating an address to latitude and longitude and vice versa).

Creating the Project

To get started, you need to first create an Android project so that you can display Google Maps in your activity:

1. Using Android Studio, create an Android project and name it LBS.
2. From the Create New Project Wizard, select Google Maps Activity as shown in Figure 10-1.

Obtaining the Maps API Key

Beginning with the Android SDK release v1.0, you need to apply for a free Google Maps API key before you can integrate Google Maps into your Android application. When you apply for the key, you must also agree to Google's terms of use, so be sure to read them carefully.

To get a Google Maps key, open the `google_maps_api.xml` file that was created in your LBS project. Within this file is a link to create a new Google Maps key. Simply copy and paste the link into your browser and follow the instructions. Make note of the key that Google gives you because you need it later in this project.

Displaying the Map

You are now ready to display Google Maps in your Android application.

The following Try It Out shows you how.

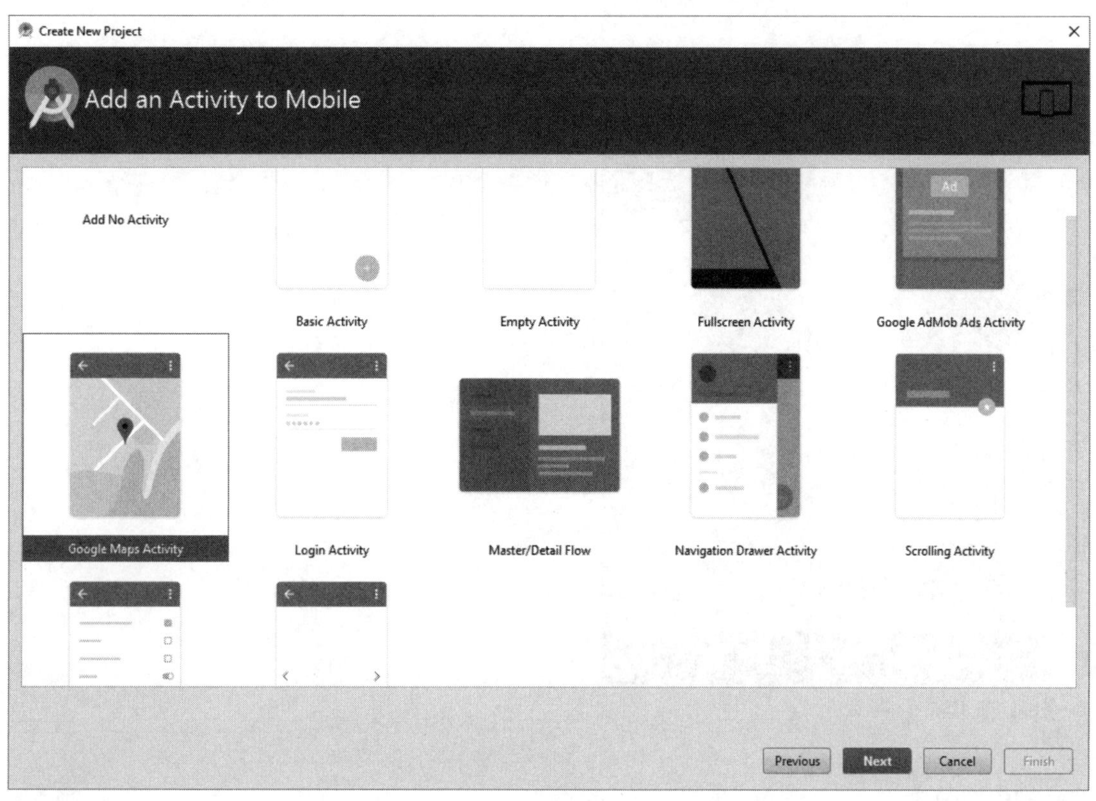

FIGURE 10-1

TRY IT OUT Displaying Google Maps (LBS.zip)

1. Using the project created in the previous section, replace the `YOUR_KEY_HERE` placeholder in the `google_maps_api.xml` with your Google Maps key.

2. Press Shift+F9 to debug the application on the Android emulator. Figure 10-2 shows Google Maps displayed in the application's activity. (Keep in mind, depending on the specs of your computer, this example might take a while to load the first time you run it.)

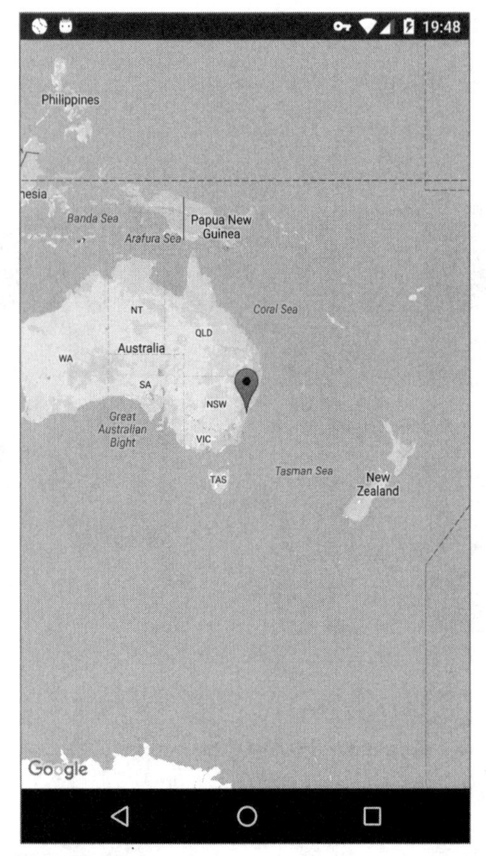

FIGURE 10-2

How It Works

To display Google Maps in your application, you first need the `ACCESS_FINE_LOCATION` permission in your manifest file. This is created for you automatically when you selected to set up a Google Maps Activity. You can see the line if you open the `AndroidManifest.xml`.

```
<uses-permission android:name="android.permission.ACCESS_FINE_LOCATION" />
```

In order to test your application on the Android emulator, be sure to create an Emulator with an SDK version that includes Google Play Services as the selected target.

CAN'T SEE THE MAP?

If instead of seeing Google Maps displayed you see an empty screen with grids, then most likely you are using the wrong API key in the `google_maps_api.xml` file. You might also want to ensure that you have Internet access on your emulator/devices. Finally, make sure that the package name that you supplied when you registered for your key matches the package name in your application.

Displaying the Zoom Control

The previous section showed how you can display Google Maps in your Android application. You can pan the map to any desired location and it updates on-the-fly. However, there is no way to use the emulator to zoom in or out from a particular location (on a real Android device you can pinch the map to zoom it). Thus, in this section, you find out how you can enable users to zoom in or out of the map using the built-in zoom controls.

TRY IT OUT Displaying the Built-In Zoom Controls

1. Using the project created in the previous section, add the following bolded statement to `activity_maps.xml`. Please be sure to replace all instances of `com.jfdimarzio` with a reference to the package used in your application:

```
<fragment xmlns:android="http://schemas.android.com/apk/res/android"
    xmlns:tools="http://schemas.android.com/tools"
    xmlns:map="http://schemas.android.com/apk/res-auto"
    android:layout_width="match_parent"
    android:layout_height="match_parent"
    android:id="@+id/map"
    tools:context="com.jfdimarzio.locationservices.MapsActivity"
    android:name="com.google.android.gms.maps.SupportMapFragment"
    map:uiZoomControls="true"
    />
```

2. Press Shift+F9 to debug the application on the Android emulator. Observe the built-in zoom controls that appear at the bottom of the map when you click and drag the map (see Figure 10-3). You can click the minus (–) icon to zoom out of the map, and the plus (+) icon to zoom into the map.

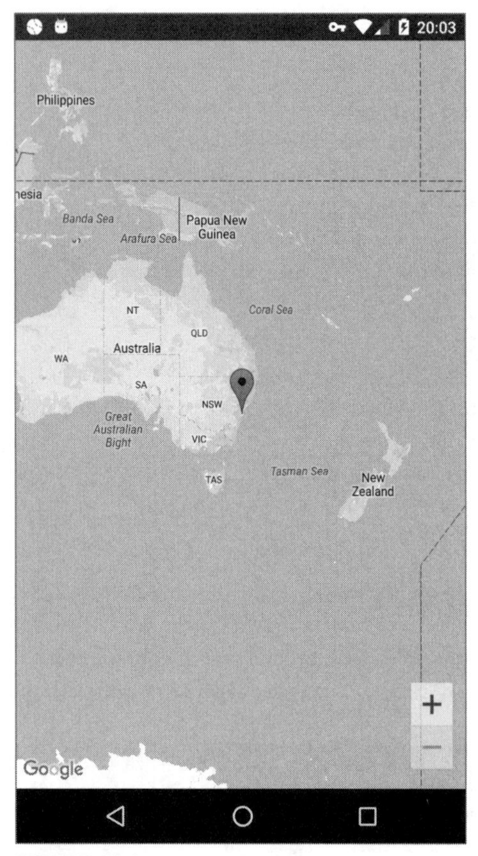

FIGURE 10-3

How It Works

To display the built-in zoom controls, you must add a parameter to `activity_maps.xml` that sets the `uiZoomControls` to `true`:

```
map:uiZoomControls="true"
```

Besides displaying the zoom controls, you can also programmatically zoom in or out of the map using the `animateCamera()` method of the `GoogleMap` class. The following Try It Out shows you how to achieve this.

TRY IT OUT Programmatically Zooming In or Out of the Map

1. Using the project created in the previous section, add the following bolded statements to the `MapsActivity.java` file:

```
import android.support.v4.app.FragmentActivity;
import android.os.Bundle;
import android.view.KeyEvent;

import com.google.android.gms.maps.CameraUpdateFactory;
import com.google.android.gms.maps.GoogleMap;
import com.google.android.gms.maps.OnMapReadyCallback;
import com.google.android.gms.maps.SupportMapFragment;
import com.google.android.gms.maps.model.LatLng;
import com.google.android.gms.maps.model.MarkerOptions;

public class MapsActivity extends FragmentActivity implements OnMapReadyCallback {

    private GoogleMap mMap;

    @Override
    protected void onCreate(Bundle savedInstanceState) {
        super.onCreate(savedInstanceState);
        setContentView(R.layout.activity_maps);
        // Obtain the SupportMapFragment and get notified
        // when the map is ready to be used.
        SupportMapFragment mapFragment =
(SupportMapFragment) getSupportFragmentManager()
                .findFragmentById(R.id.map);
        mapFragment.getMapAsync(this);
    }

    @Override
    public void onMapReady(GoogleMap googleMap) {
        mMap = googleMap;

        // Add a marker in Sydney and move the camera
        LatLng sydney = new LatLng(-34, 151);
        mMap.addMarker(new MarkerOptions().position(sydney).title(
"Marker in Sydney"));
        mMap.moveCamera(CameraUpdateFactory.newLatLng(sydney));

    }
    public boolean onKeyDown(int keyCode, KeyEvent event)
    {
        switch (keyCode)
        {
            case KeyEvent.KEYCODE_3:
```

```
                    mMap.animateCamera(CameraUpdateFactory.zoomIn());
                    break;
                case KeyEvent.KEYCODE_1:
                    mMap.animateCamera(CameraUpdateFactory.zoomOut());
                    break;
            }
            return super.onKeyDown(keyCode, event);
        }

    }
```

2. Press Shift+F9 to debug the application on the Android emulator. You can now zoom into the map by clicking the numeric 3 key on the emulator. To zoom out of the map, click the numeric 1 key.

How It Works

To handle key presses on your activity, you handle the `onKeyDown` event:

```
public boolean onKeyDown(int keyCode, KeyEvent event)
    {
        switch (keyCode)
        {
            case KeyEvent.KEYCODE_3:
                mMap.animateCamera(CameraUpdateFactory.zoomIn());
                break;
            case KeyEvent.KEYCODE_1:
                mMap.animateCamera(CameraUpdateFactory.zoomOut());
                break;
        }
        return super.onKeyDown(keyCode, event);
    }
```

Note that if you deploy the application on a real Android device, you might not be able to test the zooming feature because most Android devices today do not have a physical keyboard.

Changing Views

By default, Google Maps is displayed in *map view*, which is basically drawings of streets and places of interest. You can also set Google Maps to display in *satellite view* using the `setMapType()` method of the `GoogleMap` class:

```
    public void onMapReady(GoogleMap googleMap) {
        mMap = googleMap;

        // Add a marker in Sydney and move the camera
        LatLng sydney = new LatLng(-34, 151);
        mMap.addMarker(new MarkerOptions().position(sydney).title(
"Marker in Sydney"));
```

```
        mMap.moveCamera(CameraUpdateFactory.newLatLng(sydney));
        mMap.setMapType(GoogleMap.MAP_TYPE_SATELLITE);
    }
```

Figure 10-4 shows Google Maps displayed in satellite view.

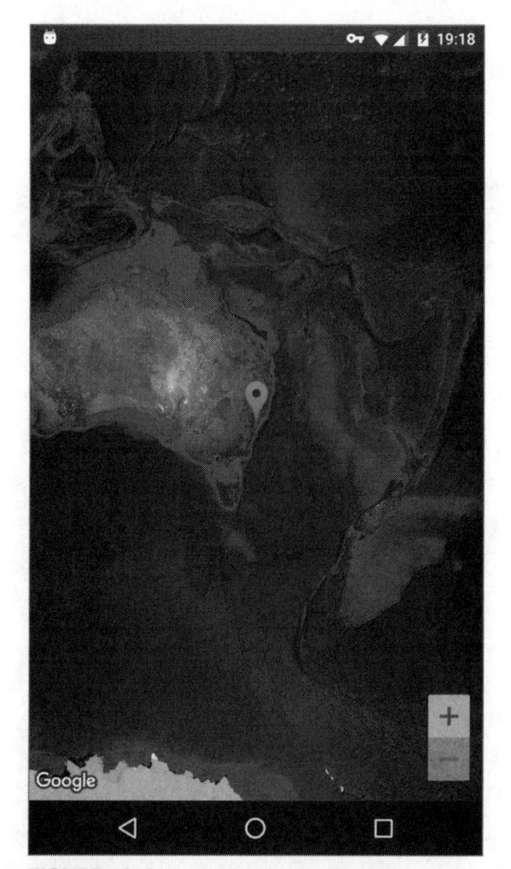

FIGURE 10-4

Navigating to a Specific Location

By default, Google Maps displays the map of Australia when it is first loaded. However, you can set Google Maps to display a particular location. To do so, you can use the `moveCamera()` method of the `GoogleMap` class.

The following Try It Out shows how you can programmatically animate Google Maps to a particular location.

TRY IT OUT Navigating the Map to Display a Specific Location

1. Using the project created in the previous section, change the following bolded statements to the `MapsActivity.java` file:

```
import android.support.v4.app.FragmentActivity;
import android.os.Bundle;

import com.google.android.gms.maps.CameraUpdateFactory;
import com.google.android.gms.maps.GoogleMap;
import com.google.android.gms.maps.OnMapReadyCallback;
import com.google.android.gms.maps.SupportMapFragment;
import com.google.android.gms.maps.model.LatLng;
import com.google.android.gms.maps.model.MarkerOptions;

public class MapsActivity extends FragmentActivity implements OnMapReadyCallback {

    private GoogleMap mMap;

    @Override
    protected void onCreate(Bundle savedInstanceState) {
        super.onCreate(savedInstanceState);
        setContentView(R.layout.activity_maps);
        // Obtain the SupportMapFragment and get notified
        // when the map is ready to be used.
        SupportMapFragment mapFragment =
    (SupportMapFragment) getSupportFragmentManager()
                .findFragmentById(R.id.map);
        mapFragment.getMapAsync(this);
    }

    @Override
    public void onMapReady(GoogleMap googleMap) {
        mMap = googleMap;

        LatLng boston = new LatLng(42.3601, -71.0589);
        mMap.addMarker(new MarkerOptions().position(boston).title(
"Boston, Mass"));
        mMap.moveCamera(CameraUpdateFactory.newLatLng(boston));
    }


}
```

2. Press Shift+F9 to debug the application on the Android emulator. When the map is loaded, observe that it now animates to a particular location in Boston, Massachusetts (see Figure 10-5).

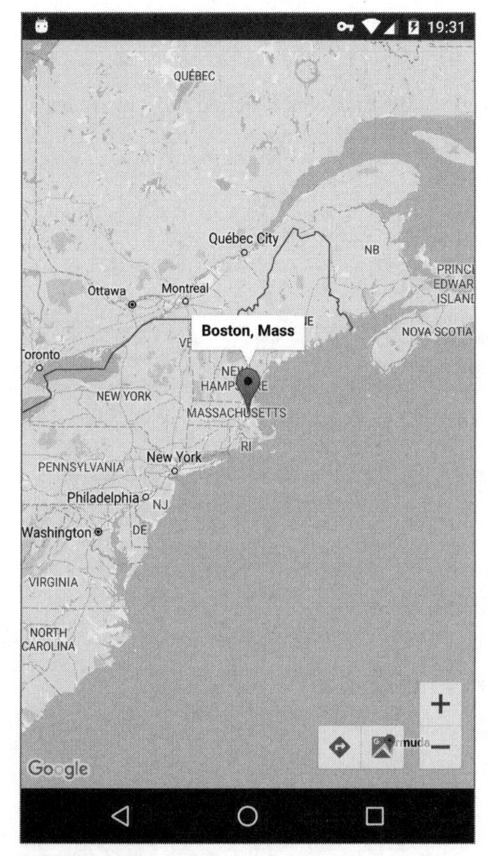

FIGURE 10-5

How It Works

In the preceding code, a `LatLng` object is created and set to the new coordinates of 42.3601 N, 71.0589 W (the coordinates of Boston). Notice that to represent either W (west) or S (south) you use the negative value of the coordinate.

Getting the Location That Was Touched

After using Google Maps for a while, you might want to know the latitude and longitude of a location corresponding to the position on the screen that was just touched. Knowing this information is very useful because you can determine a location's address—a process known as *reverse geocoding* (you find out how this is done in the next section).

To get the latitude and longitude of a point on the Google Map that was touched, you must set a `onMapClickListener`:

```
import android.support.v4.app.FragmentActivity;
import android.os.Bundle;
import android.util.Log;

import com.google.android.gms.maps.CameraUpdateFactory;
import com.google.android.gms.maps.GoogleMap;
import com.google.android.gms.maps.OnMapReadyCallback;
import com.google.android.gms.maps.SupportMapFragment;
import com.google.android.gms.maps.model.LatLng;
import com.google.android.gms.maps.model.MarkerOptions;

public class MapsActivity extends FragmentActivity implements OnMapReadyCallback {

    private GoogleMap mMap;

    @Override
    protected void onCreate(Bundle savedInstanceState) {
        super.onCreate(savedInstanceState);
        setContentView(R.layout.activity_maps);
        // Obtain the SupportMapFragment and get notified
        // when the map is ready to be used.
        SupportMapFragment mapFragment =
(SupportMapFragment) getSupportFragmentManager()
                .findFragmentById(R.id.map);
        mapFragment.getMapAsync(this);
    }

    @Override
    public void onMapReady(GoogleMap googleMap) {
        mMap = googleMap;

        LatLng boston = new LatLng(42.3601, -71.0589);
        mMap.addMarker(new MarkerOptions().position(boston).title("Boston, Mass"));
        mMap.moveCamera(CameraUpdateFactory.newLatLng(boston));

        mMap.setOnMapClickListener(new GoogleMap.OnMapClickListener() {
            @Override
            public void onMapClick(LatLng point) {
```

```
                Log.d("DEBUG","Map clicked [" + point.latitude +
" / " + point.longitude + "]");

            }
        });
    }


}
```

You should see a logcat entry similar to this if you run the preceding code:

```
D/DEBUG: Map clicked [37.15198779979302 / -83.76536171883345]
```

Geocoding and Reverse Geocoding

As mentioned in the preceding section, if you know the latitude and longitude of a location, you can find out its address using a process known as reverse geocoding. Google Maps in Android supports reverse geocoding via the `Geocoder` class. The following code snippet shows how you can retrieve the address of a location just touched using the `getFromLocation()` method:

```
import android.location.Address;
import android.location.Geocoder;
import android.support.v4.app.FragmentActivity;
import android.os.Bundle;
import android.widget.Toast;

import com.google.android.gms.maps.CameraUpdateFactory;
import com.google.android.gms.maps.GoogleMap;
import com.google.android.gms.maps.OnMapReadyCallback;
import com.google.android.gms.maps.SupportMapFragment;
import com.google.android.gms.maps.model.LatLng;
import com.google.android.gms.maps.model.MarkerOptions;

import java.io.IOException;
import java.util.List;
import java.util.Locale;

public class MapsActivity extends FragmentActivity implements OnMapReadyCallback {

    private GoogleMap mMap;

    @Override
    protected void onCreate(Bundle savedInstanceState) {
```

```
        super.onCreate(savedInstanceState);
        setContentView(R.layout.activity_maps);
        // Obtain the SupportMapFragment and get notified
        // when the map is ready to be used.
        SupportMapFragment mapFragment =
(SupportMapFragment) getSupportFragmentManager()
                .findFragmentById(R.id.map);
        mapFragment.getMapAsync(this);
    }

    @Override
    public void onMapReady(GoogleMap googleMap) {
        mMap = googleMap;

        LatLng boston = new LatLng(42.3601, -71.0589);
        mMap.addMarker(new MarkerOptions().position(boston).title("Boston, Mass"));
        mMap.moveCamera(CameraUpdateFactory.newLatLng(boston));

        mMap.setOnMapClickListener(new GoogleMap.OnMapClickListener() {
            @Override
            public void onMapClick(LatLng point) {
                Geocoder geoCoder = new Geocoder(
                        getBaseContext(), Locale.getDefault());
                try {
                    List<Address> addresses = geoCoder.getFromLocation(
point.latitude,point.longitude,1);
                    String add = "";
                    if (addresses.size() > 0)
                    {
                        for (int i=0; i<addresses.get(0).
getMaxAddressLineIndex();
                             i++)
                            add += addresses.get(0).getAddressLine(i) + "\n";
                    }
                    Toast.makeText(getBaseContext()
, add, Toast.LENGTH_SHORT).show();
                }
                catch (IOException e) {
                    e.printStackTrace();
                }

            }
        });
    }


}
```

The `Geocoder` object converts the latitude and longitude into an address using the `getFromLocation()` method. After the address is obtained, you display it using the `Toast` class. Keep in mind that pin will not move. In this example, we are only getting the address of a location that you touch. Figure 10-6 shows the application displaying the address of a location that was touched on the map.

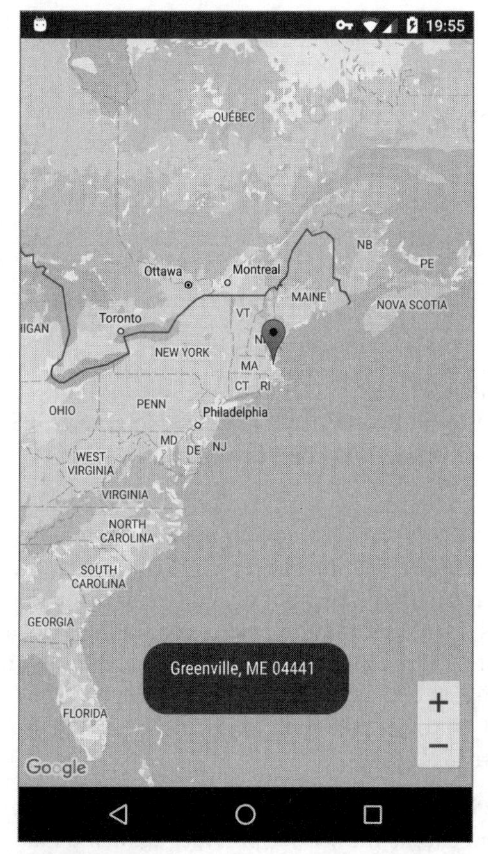

FIGURE 10-6

If you know the address of a location but want to know its latitude and longitude, you can do so via geocoding. Again, you can use the `Geocoder` class for this purpose. The following code shows how you can find the exact location of the Empire State Building by using the `getFromLocationName()` method:

```
Geocoder geoCoder = new Geocoder(
                getBaseContext(), Locale.getDefault());

        try {
```

```
            List<Address> addresses = geoCoder.getFromLocationName(
                    "empire state building", 5);

            if (addresses.size() > 0) {
                LatLng p = new LatLng(
                        (int) (addresses.get(0).getLatitude()),
                        (int) (addresses.get(0).getLongitude()));
                mMap.moveCamera(CameraUpdateFactory.newLatLng(p));
            }
        } catch (IOException e) {
            e.printStackTrace();
        }
```

GETTING LOCATION DATA

Nowadays, mobile devices are commonly equipped with GPS receivers. Because of the many satellites orbiting the earth, you can use a GPS receiver to find your location easily. However, GPS requires a clear sky to work and hence does not always work indoors or where satellites can't penetrate (such as a tunnel through a mountain).

Another effective way to locate your position is through *cell tower triangulation*. When a mobile phone is switched on, it is constantly in contact with base stations surrounding it. By knowing the identity of cell towers, it is possible to translate this information into a physical location through the use of various databases containing the cell towers' identities and their exact geographical locations. The advantage of cell tower triangulation is that it works indoors, without the need to obtain information from satellites. However, it is not as precise as GPS because its accuracy depends on overlapping signal coverage, which varies quite a bit. Cell tower triangulation works best in densely populated areas where the cell towers are closely located.

A third method of locating your position is to rely on Wi-Fi triangulation. Rather than connect to cell towers, the device connects to a Wi-Fi network and checks the service provider against databases to determine the location serviced by the provider. Of the three methods described here, Wi-Fi triangulation is the least accurate.

On the Android platform, the SDK provides the `LocationManager` class to help your device determine the user's physical location. The following Try It Out shows how this is done in code.

TRY IT OUT Navigating the Map to a Specific Location

1. Using the same project created in the previous section, add the following bolded statements to the `MapsActivity.java` file:

```
import android.content.Context;
import android.content.pm.PackageManager;
import android.location.Location;
import android.location.LocationListener;
import android.location.LocationManager;
import android.support.v4.app.ActivityCompat;
import android.support.v4.app.FragmentActivity;
import android.os.Bundle;
import android.widget.Toast;
```

```
import com.google.android.gms.maps.CameraUpdateFactory;
import com.google.android.gms.maps.GoogleMap;
import com.google.android.gms.maps.OnMapReadyCallback;
import com.google.android.gms.maps.SupportMapFragment;
import com.google.android.gms.maps.model.LatLng;

public class MapsActivity extends FragmentActivity implements OnMapReadyCallback {
    final private int REQUEST_COURSE_ACCESS = 123;
    boolean permissionGranted = false;
    private GoogleMap mMap;
    LocationManager lm;
    LocationListener locationListener;

    @Override
    protected void onCreate(Bundle savedInstanceState) {
        super.onCreate(savedInstanceState);
        setContentView(R.layout.activity_maps);
        // Obtain the SupportMapFragment and get notified
        // when the map is ready to be used.
        SupportMapFragment mapFragment =
(SupportMapFragment) getSupportFragmentManager()
                .findFragmentById(R.id.map);
        mapFragment.getMapAsync(this);
    }

    @Override
    public void onPause() {
        super.onPause();

        //---remove the location listener---
        if (ActivityCompat.checkSelfPermission(this,
    android.Manifest.permission.ACCESS_FINE_LOCATION)
!= PackageManager.PERMISSION_GRANTED && ActivityCompat.checkSelfPermission(
this, android.Manifest.permission.ACCESS_COARSE_LOCATION)
!= PackageManager.PERMISSION_GRANTED) {
            ActivityCompat.requestPermissions(this,
                    new String[]{
android.Manifest.permission.ACCESS_COARSE_LOCATION},
                    REQUEST_COURSE_ACCESS);
            return;
        }else{
            permissionGranted = true;
        }
        if(permissionGranted) {
            lm.removeUpdates(locationListener);
        }
    }
    @Override
    public void onMapReady(GoogleMap googleMap) {
        mMap = googleMap;


        lm = (LocationManager)getSystemService(Context.LOCATION_SERVICE);
```

```
        locationListener = new MyLocationListener();

        if (ActivityCompat.checkSelfPermission(this,
    android.Manifest.permission.ACCESS_FINE_LOCATION)
!= PackageManager.PERMISSION_GRANTED && ActivityCompat.checkSelfPermission(
this, android.Manifest.permission.ACCESS_COARSE_LOCATION)
!= PackageManager.PERMISSION_GRANTED) {
            ActivityCompat.requestPermissions(this,
                    new String[]{
android.Manifest.permission.ACCESS_COARSE_LOCATION},
                    REQUEST_COURSE_ACCESS);
            return;
        }else{
            permissionGranted = true;
        }
        if(permissionGranted) {
            lm.requestLocationUpdates(LocationManager.GPS_PROVIDER, 0, 0,
 locationListener);
        }

    }
    @Override
    public void onRequestPermissionsResult(int requestCode,
String[] permissions,
 int[] grantResults) {
        switch (requestCode) {
            case REQUEST_COURSE_ACCESS:
                if (grantResults[0] == PackageManager.PERMISSION_GRANTED) {

                    permissionGranted = true;

                } else {
                    permissionGranted = false;
                }
                break;
            default:
                super.onRequestPermissionsResult(requestCode, permissions,
 grantResults);
        }
    }
    private class MyLocationListener implements LocationListener
    {
        public void onLocationChanged(Location loc) {
            if (loc != null) {
                Toast.makeText(getBaseContext(),
                       "Location changed : Lat: " + loc.getLatitude() +
                " Lng: " + loc.getLongitude(),
                        Toast.LENGTH_SHORT).show();
                LatLng p = new LatLng(
                        (int) (loc.getLatitude()),
                        (int) (loc.getLongitude()));
                mMap.moveCamera(CameraUpdateFactory.newLatLng(p));
                mMap.animateCamera(CameraUpdateFactory.zoomTo(7));
            }
        }
```

```
            public void onProviderDisabled(String provider) {
            }
            public void onProviderEnabled(String provider) {
            }
            public void onStatusChanged(String provider, int status,
                                        Bundle extras) {
            }
        }

}
```

2. Add the following bolded line to the `AndroidManifest.xml` file.0 Please be sure to replace all instances of `com.jfdimarzio` with a reference to the package used in your application:

```
<?xml version="1.0" encoding="utf-8"?>
<manifest xmlns:android="http://schemas.android.com/apk/res/android"
    package="com.jfdimarzio.locationservices" >

    <!--
         The ACCESS_COARSE/FINE_LOCATION permissions are not required to use
         Google Maps Android API v2, but you must specify either coarse or fine
         location permissions for the 'MyLocation' functionality.
    -->
    <uses-permission android:name="android.permission.ACCESS_FINE_LOCATION" />
    <uses-permission android:name="android.permission.ACCESS_COARSE_LOCATION" />

    <application
        android:allowBackup="true"
        android:icon="@mipmap/ic_launcher"
        android:label="@string/app_name"
        android:supportsRtl="true"
        android:theme="@style/AppTheme" >

        <!--
             The API key for Google Maps-based APIs is defined as a string resource
             (See the file "res/values/google_maps_api.xml").
             Note that the API key is linked to the encryption
             key used to sign the APK.
             You need a different API key for each encryption key,
             including the release key that is used to
             sign the APK for publishing.
             You can define the keys for the debug and release targets in
             src/debug/ and src/release/.
        -->
        <meta-data
            android:name="com.google.android.geo.API_KEY"
            android:value="@string/google_maps_key" />

        <activity
            android:name=".MapsActivity"
            android:label="@string/title_activity_maps" >
            <intent-filter>
                <action android:name="android.intent.action.MAIN" />

                <category android:name="android.intent.category.LAUNCHER" />
```

```
            </intent-filter>
        </activity>
    </application>

</manifest>
```

3. Press Shift+F9 to debug the application on the Android emulator.
4. To simulate GPS data received by the Android emulator, you use the Location Controls tool on the right-hand side of the emulator.
5. Observe that the map on the emulator now animates to another location (see Figure 10-7). This proves that the application has received the GPS data.

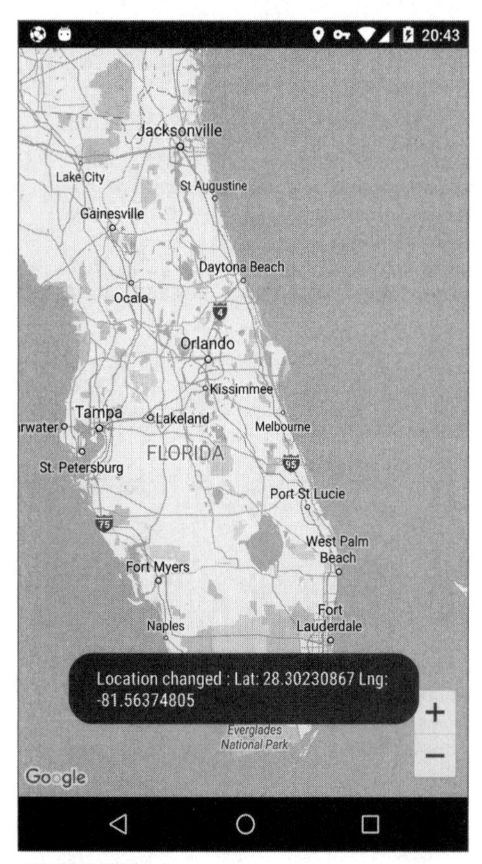

FIGURE 10-7

How It Works

In Android, location-based services are provided by the `LocationManager` class, located in the `android.location` package. Using the `LocationManager` class, your application can obtain periodic updates of the device's geographical locations, as well as fire an intent when it enters the proximity of a certain location.

In the `MapsActivity.java` file, you first check for permission to use the Course Locations. Then you obtain a reference to the `LocationManager` class using the `getSystemService()` method. You do this in the `onCreate()` method of the `LBSActivity`:

```
//---use the LocationManager class to obtain locations data---
lm = (LocationManager)
    getSystemService(Context.LOCATION_SERVICE);
locationListener = new MyLocationListener();
```

Next, you create an instance of the `MyLocationListener` class, which you define later in the class.

The `MyLocationListener` class implements the `LocationListener` abstract class. You need to override four methods in this implementation:

- `onLocationChanged(Location location)`—Called when the location has changed
- `onProviderDisabled(String provider)`—Called when the provider is disabled by the user
- `onProviderEnabled(String provider)`—Called when the provider is enabled by the user
- `onStatusChanged(String provider, int status, Bundle extras)`—Called when the provider status changes

In this example, you're more interested in what happens when a location changes, so you write your code in the `onLocationChanged()` method. Specifically, when a location changes, you display a small dialog on the screen showing the new location information: latitude and longitude. You show this dialog using the `Toast` class:

```
public void onLocationChanged(Location loc) {
    if (loc != null) {
        Toast.makeText(getBaseContext(),
                "Location changed : Lat: " + loc.getLatitude() +
        " Lng: " + loc.getLongitude(),
                Toast.LENGTH_SHORT).show();
        LatLng p = new LatLng(
                (int) (loc.getLatitude()),
                (int) (loc.getLongitude()));
        mMap.moveCamera(CameraUpdateFactory.newLatLng(p));
        mMap.animateCamera(CameraUpdateFactory.zoomTo(7));
    }
}
```

In the preceding method, you also navigate the map to the location that you have received.

To be notified whenever there is a change in location, you needed to register a request for location changes so that your program can be notified periodically. You do this via the `requestLocationUpdates()` method:

```
if(permissionGranted) {
            lm.requestLocationUpdates(LocationManager.GPS_PROVIDER, 0, 0,
 locationListener);
        }
```

The `requestLocationUpdates()` method takes four arguments:

- `provider`—The name of the provider with which you register. In this case, you are using GPS to obtain your geographical location data.
- `minTime`—The minimum time interval for notifications, in milliseconds. 0 indicates that you want to be continually informed of location changes.
- `minDistance`—The minimum distance interval for notifications, in meters. 0 indicates that you want to be continually informed of location changes.
- `listener`—An object whose `onLocationChanged()` method will be called for each location update

Finally, in the `onPause()` method, you remove the listener when the activity is destroyed or goes into the background (so that the application no longer listens for changes in location, thereby saving the battery of the device). You do that using the `removeUpdates()` method:

```
    @Override
    public void onPause() {
        super.onPause();

        //---remove the location listener---
        if (ActivityCompat.checkSelfPermission(this,
    android.Manifest.permission.ACCESS_FINE_LOCATION)
!= PackageManager.PERMISSION_GRANTED && ActivityCompat.checkSelfPermission(
this, android.Manifest.permission.ACCESS_COARSE_LOCATION)
!= PackageManager.PERMISSION_GRANTED) {
            ActivityCompat.requestPermissions(this,
                    new String[]{
android.Manifest.permission.ACCESS_COARSE_LOCATION},
                    REQUEST_COURSE_ACCESS);
            return;
        }else{
            permissionGranted = true;
        }
        if(permissionGranted) {
            lm.removeUpdates(locationListener);
        }
    }
```

> ***NOTE*** *The network provider will not work on the Android emulator. If you test the preceding code on the emulator, it results in an illegal argument exception. You need to test the code on a real device.*

You can combine both the GPS location provider with the network location provider within your application:

```
    @Override
    public void onResume() {
```

```
        super.onResume();

        //---request for location updates---
        lm.requestLocationUpdates(
                LocationManager.GPS_PROVIDER,
                0,
                0,
                locationListener);

        //---request for location updates---
        lm.requestLocationUpdates(
                LocationManager.NETWORK_PROVIDER,
                0,
                0,
                locationListener);
    }
```

However, be aware that doing so will cause your application to receive two different sets of coordinates, as both the GPS provider and the NETWORK provider will try to get your location using their own methods (GPS versus Wi-Fi and cell ID triangulation). Hence, it is important that you monitor the status of the two providers in your device and use the appropriate one. You can check the status of the two providers by implementing the following three methods (shown in bold) of the `MyLocationListener` class:

```
    private class MyLocationListener implements LocationListener
    {
        ...

        //---called when the provider is disabled---
        public void onProviderDisabled(String provider) {
            Toast.makeText(getBaseContext(),
                    provider + " disabled",
                    Toast.LENGTH_SHORT).show();
        }
        //---called when the provider is enabled---
        public void onProviderEnabled(String provider) {
            Toast.makeText(getBaseContext(),
                    provider + " enabled",
                    Toast.LENGTH_SHORT).show();
        }
        //---called when there is a change in the provider status---
        public void onStatusChanged(String provider, int status,
            Bundle extras) {
            String statusString = "";
            switch (status) {
                case android.location.LocationProvider.AVAILABLE:
                    statusString = "available";
                case android.location.LocationProvider.OUT_OF_SERVICE:
                    statusString = "out of service";
                case android.location.LocationProvider.TEMPORARILY_UNAVAILABLE:
                    statusString = "temporarily unavailable";
            }
```

```
                Toast.makeText(getBaseContext(),
                        provider + " " + statusString,
                        Toast.LENGTH_SHORT).show();
            }
        }
```

MONITORING A LOCATION

One very cool feature of the `LocationManager` class is its ability to monitor a specific location. This is achieved using the `addProximityAlert()` method.

The following code snippet shows how to monitor a particular location such that if the user is within a five-meter radius from that location, your application will fire an intent to launch the web browser:

```
import android.app.PendingIntent;
import android.content.Intent;
import android.net.Uri;
        //---use the LocationManager class to obtain locations data---
        lm = (LocationManager)
            getSystemService(Context.LOCATION_SERVICE);
        //---PendingIntent to launch activity if the user is within
        // some locations---
        PendingIntent pendingIntent = PendingIntent.getActivity(
            this, 0, new
            Intent(android.content.Intent.ACTION_VIEW,
              Uri.parse("http://www.amazon.com")), 0);
        lm.addProximityAlert(37.422006, -122.084095, 5, -1, pendingIntent);
```

The `addProximityAlert()` method takes five arguments:

- Latitude
- Longitude
- Radius (in meters)
- Expiration (duration for which the proximity alert is valid, after which it is deleted; –1 for no expiration)
- Pending intent

Note that if the Android device's screen goes to sleep, the proximity is also checked once every four minutes in order to preserve the battery life of the device.

SUMMARY

This chapter took a whirlwind tour of the `GoogleMap` object, which displays Google Maps in your Android application. You have learned the various ways in which the map can be manipulated. You also have also seen how you can obtain geographical location data using the various network providers: GPS, cell ID, or Wi-Fi triangulation.

EXERCISES

1. If you have embedded the Google Maps API into your Android application but it does not show the map when the application is loaded, what could be the likely reasons?
2. What is the difference between geocoding and reverse geocoding?
3. Name the two location providers that you can use to obtain your location data.

You can find answers to the exercises in the appendix.

▶ WHAT YOU LEARNED IN THIS CHAPTER

TOPIC	KEY CONCEPTS
Displaying the GoogleMap	`<string name="google_maps_key" templateMergeStrategy="prese` `rve" translatable="false">YOUR_KEY_HERE</string>`
Displaying the zoom controls	`map:uiZoomControls="true"`
Programmatically zooming in or out of the map	`mMap.animateCamera(CameraUpdateFactory.zoomTo(7));`
Changing views	`mMap.setMapType(GoogleMap.MAP_TYPE_SATELLITE);`

Animating to a particular location	`LatLng boston = new LatLng(42.3601, -71.0589);`
	
	`mMap.addMarker(new MarkerOptions().position(boston).`
	`title("Boston, Mass"));`
	`        mMap.moveCamera(CameraUpdateFactory.`
	`newLatLng(boston));`

Getting the location of the map touched	`                mMap.setOnMapClickListener(new GoogleMap.`
	`OnMapClickListener() {`
	`            @Override`
	`            public void onMapClick(LatLng point) {`
	`                Log.d("DEBUG","Map clicked [" + point.latitude`
	`+ " / " + point.longitude + "]");`
	
	`            }`
	`        });`

Geocoding and reverse geocoding	Use the `Geocoder` class
Setting a Proximity Alert	`lm.addProximityAlert(37.422006, -122.084095, 5, -1,` `    pendingIntent);`

11

Networking

WHAT YOU WILL LEARN IN THIS CHAPTER

- How to connect to the web using HTTP
- How to consume XML web services
- How to consume JSON web services
- How to connect to a Socket server

> ***CODE DOWNLOAD*** *The wrox.com code downloads for this chapter are found at* `www.wrox.com/go/beginningandroidprog` *on the Download Code tab. The code is in the chapter 11 download and individually named according to the names throughout the chapter.*

Chapter 11 explains how your application can talk to the outside world through the use of SMS messaging and emails. Another way to communicate with the outside world is through the wireless network available on your Android device. In this chapter, you find out how to use the HTTP protocol to talk to web servers so that you can download text and binary data. Also, you see how to parse XML files to extract the relevant parts of an XML document—a technique that is useful if you are accessing web services. In addition to XML web services, this chapter also covers JSON (JavaScript Object Notation), which is a lightweight alternative to XML. You make use of the classes available in the Android SDK to manipulate JSON content.

Finally, this chapter also demonstrates how to write an Android application to connect to servers using TCP sockets. Using sockets programming, you can write sophisticated, interesting networked applications.

CONSUMING WEB SERVICES USING HTTP

One common way to communicate with the outside world is through HTTP. HTTP is no stranger to most people; it is the protocol that drives much of the web's success. Using the HTTP protocol, you can perform a variety of tasks, such as downloading web pages from a web server, downloading binary data, and more.

The following Try It Out creates an Android project so you can use the HTTP protocol to connect to the web to download all sorts of content.

TRY IT OUT Creating the Base Project for HTTP Connection (Networking.zip)

1. Using Android Studio, create a new Android project and name it **Networking**.
2. Add the following bolded statement to the `AndroidManifest.xml` file. Please be sure to replace all instances of `com.jfdimarzio` with the package name used in your application:

```
<?xml version="1.0" encoding="utf-8"?>
<manifest xmlns:android="http://schemas.android.com/apk/res/android"
    package="com.jfdimarzio.networking">
    <uses-permission android:name="android.permission.INTERNET"/>
    <application
        android:allowBackup="true"
        android:icon="@mipmap/ic_launcher"
        android:label="@string/app_name"
        android:supportsRtl="true"
        android:theme="@style/AppTheme">

        <activity android:name=".MainActivity">
            <intent-filter>
                <action android:name="android.intent.action.MAIN" />

                <category android:name="android.intent.category.LAUNCHER" />
            </intent-filter>
        </activity>
    </application>

</manifest>
```

3. Import the following packages in bold to the `MainActivity.java` file:

```
import android.support.v7.app.AppCompatActivity;
import android.os.Bundle;
import android.util.Log;

import java.io.IOException;
import java.io.InputStream;
import java.net.HttpURLConnection;
import java.net.URL;
import java.net.URLConnection;
```

4. Define the `OpenHttpConnection()` method in the `MainActivity.java` file:

```
public class MainActivity extends AppCompatActivity {
    private InputStream OpenHttpConnection(String urlString) throws IOException
    {
        InputStream in = null;
        int response = -1;

        URL url = new URL(urlString);
        URLConnection conn = url.openConnection();

        if (!(conn instanceof HttpURLConnection))
            throw new IOException("Not an HTTP connection");
        try{
            HttpURLConnection httpConn = (HttpURLConnection) conn;
            httpConn.setAllowUserInteraction(false);
            httpConn.setInstanceFollowRedirects(true);
            httpConn.setRequestMethod("GET");
            httpConn.connect();
            response = httpConn.getResponseCode();
            if (response == HttpURLConnection.HTTP_OK) {
                in = httpConn.getInputStream();
            }
        }
        catch (Exception ex)
        {
            Log.d("Networking", ex.getLocalizedMessage());
            throw new IOException("Error connecting");
        }
        return in;
    }

    @Override
    protected void onCreate(Bundle savedInstanceState) {
        super.onCreate(savedInstanceState);
        setContentView(R.layout.activity_main);
    }
}
```

How It Works

Before you finish the app, let's discuss what's happened to this point. Because you are using the HTTP protocol to connect to the web, your application needs the `INTERNET` permission. That means the first thing you do is add the permission in the `AndroidManifest.xml` file.

You then define the `OpenHttpConnection()` method, which takes a URL string and returns an `InputStream` object. Using an `InputStream` object, you can download the data by reading bytes from the stream object. In this method, you make use of the `HttpURLConnection` object to open an HTTP connection with a remote URL. You set all the various properties of the connection, such as the request method, and so on:

```
HttpURLConnection httpConn = (HttpURLConnection) conn;
httpConn.setAllowUserInteraction(false);
httpConn.setInstanceFollowRedirects(true);
httpConn.setRequestMethod("GET");
```

After trying to establish a connection with the server, the HTTP response code is returned. If the connection is established (via the response code `HTTP_OK`), then you proceed to get an `InputStream` object from the connection:

```
httpConn.connect();
response = httpConn.getResponseCode();
if (response == HttpURLConnection.HTTP_OK) {
    in = httpConn.getInputStream();
}
```

Using the `InputStream` object, you can then start to download the data from the server.

Downloading Binary Data

A common task you need to perform is downloading binary data from the web. For example, you might want to download an image from a server so that you can display it in your application. The following Try It Out shows how this is done.

TRY IT OUT Downloading Binary Data

1. Using the same project created earlier in this chapter (see "Creating the Base Project for HTTP Connection"), replace the default `TextView` with the following bolded statements to the `main.xml` file:

```
<?xml version="1.0" encoding="utf-8"?>
<android.support.constraint.ConstraintLayout xmlns:android=
    "http://schemas.android.com/apk/res/android"
    xmlns:app="http://schemas.android.com/apk/res-auto"
    xmlns:tools="http://schemas.android.com/tools"
    android:id="@+id/activity_main"
    android:layout_width="match_parent"
    android:layout_height="match_parent"
    tools:context="com.jfdimarzio.networking.MainActivity">


    <ImageView
        android:src="@color/material_grey_300"
        android:layout_width="209dp"
        android:layout_height="272dp"
        android:id="@+id/imageView"
        app:layout_constraintLeft_toLeftOf="@+id/activity_main"
        app:layout_constraintTop_toTopOf="@+id/activity_main"
        app:layout_constraintRight_toRightOf="@+id/activity_main"
        app:layout_constraintBottom_toBottomOf="@+id/activity_main" />
</android.support.constraint.ConstraintLayout>
```

2. Add the following bolded statements to the `MainActivity.java` file:

```
import android.Manifest;
import android.content.pm.PackageManager;
import android.graphics.Bitmap;
```

```
import android.graphics.BitmapFactory;
import android.os.AsyncTask;
import android.support.v4.app.ActivityCompat;
import android.support.v4.content.ContextCompat;
import android.support.v7.app.AppCompatActivity;
import android.os.Bundle;
import android.util.Log;
import android.widget.ImageView;
import android.widget.Toast;

import java.io.IOException;
import java.io.InputStream;
import java.net.HttpURLConnection;
import java.net.URL;
import java.net.URLConnection;

public class MainActivity extends AppCompatActivity {
    ImageView img;
    final private int REQUEST_INTERNET = 123;
    private InputStream OpenHttpConnection(String urlString) throws IOException
    {
        InputStream in = null;
        int response = -1;

        URL url = new URL(urlString);
        URLConnection conn = url.openConnection();

        if (!(conn instanceof HttpURLConnection))
            throw new IOException("Not an HTTP connection");
        try{
            HttpURLConnection httpConn = (HttpURLConnection) conn;
            httpConn.setAllowUserInteraction(false);
            httpConn.setInstanceFollowRedirects(true);
            httpConn.setRequestMethod("GET");
            httpConn.connect();
            response = httpConn.getResponseCode();
            if (response == HttpURLConnection.HTTP_OK) {
                in = httpConn.getInputStream();
            }
        }
        catch (Exception ex)
        {
            Log.d("Networking", ex.getLocalizedMessage());
            throw new IOException("Error connecting");
        }
        return in;
    }
    private Bitmap DownloadImage(String URL)
    {
        Bitmap bitmap = null;
        InputStream in = null;
        try {
            in = OpenHttpConnection(URL);
            bitmap = BitmapFactory.decodeStream(in);
            in.close();
```

```
        } catch (IOException e1) {
            Log.d("NetworkingActivity", e1.getLocalizedMessage());
        }
        return bitmap;
    }

    private class DownloadImageTask extends AsyncTask<String, Void, Bitmap> {
        protected Bitmap doInBackground(String... urls) {
            return DownloadImage(urls[0]);
        }

        protected void onPostExecute(Bitmap result) {
            ImageView img = (ImageView) findViewById(R.id.imageView);
            img.setImageBitmap(result);
        }
    }

    @Override
    protected void onCreate(Bundle savedInstanceState) {
        super.onCreate(savedInstanceState);
        setContentView(R.layout.activity_main);

        if (ContextCompat.checkSelfPermission(this,
                Manifest.permission.INTERNET)
                != PackageManager.PERMISSION_GRANTED) {

                ActivityCompat.requestPermissions(this,
                        new String[]{Manifest.permission.INTERNET},
                        REQUEST_INTERNET);

        } else{
            new DownloadImageTask().execute(
    "http://www.jfdimarzio.com/butterfly.png");
        }

    }
    @Override
    public void onRequestPermissionsResult(int requestCode,
    String[] permissions, int[] grantResults) {
        switch (requestCode) {
            case REQUEST_INTERNET:
                if (grantResults[0] == PackageManager.PERMISSION_GRANTED) {

                    new DownloadImageTask().execute(
    "http://www.jfdimarzio.com/butterfly.png");

                } else {
                    Toast.makeText(MainActivity.this,
    "Permission Denied", Toast.LENGTH_SHORT).show();
                }
                break;
            default:
                super.onRequestPermissionsResult(requestCode,
    permissions, grantResults);
        }
    }
}
```

3. Press Shift+F9 to debug the application on the Android emulator. Figure 11-1 shows the image downloaded from the web and then displayed in the `ImageView`.

FIGURE 11-1

How It Works

The `DownloadImage()` method takes the URL of the image to download and then opens the connection to the server using the `OpenHttpConnection()` method that you have defined earlier in this chapter. Using the `InputStream` object returned by the connection, the `decodeStream()` method from the `BitmapFactory` class is used to download and decode the data into a `Bitmap` object. The `DownloadImage()` method returns a `Bitmap` object.

To download an image and display it on the activity, you call the `DownloadImage()` method. However, starting with Android 3.0, synchronous operations can no longer be run directly from a UI thread. If you try to call the `DownloadImage()` method directly in your `onCreate()` method (as shown in the following code snippet), your application crashes when it is run on a device running Android 3.0 and later:

```
/** Called when the activity is first created. */
@Override
public void onCreate(Bundle savedInstanceState) {
```

```
        super.onCreate(savedInstanceState);
        setContentView(R.layout.main);
        //---download an image---
        //---code will not run in Android 3.0 and beyond---
        Bitmap bitmap =
            DownloadImage("http://www.mayoff.com/5-01cablecarDCP01934.jpg");
        img = (ImageView) findViewById(R.id.img);
        img.setImageBitmap(bitmap);
    }
```

Because the `DownloadImage()` method is synchronous—that is, it will not return control until the image is downloaded—calling it directly freezes the UI of your activity. This is not allowed in Android 3.0 and later. All synchronous code must be wrapped using an `AsyncTask` class. Using `AsyncTask` enables you to perform background tasks in a separate thread and then return the result in a UI thread. That way, you can perform background operations without needing to handle complex threading issues.

To call the `DownloadImage()` method asynchronously, you need to wrap the code in a subclass of the `AsyncTask` class, as shown here:

```
    private class DownloadImageTask extends AsyncTask<String, Void, Bitmap> {
        protected Bitmap doInBackground(String... urls) {
            return DownloadImage(urls[0]);
        }
        protected void onPostExecute(Bitmap result) {
            ImageView img = (ImageView) findViewById(R.id.img);
            img.setImageBitmap(result);
        }
    }
```

Basically, you define a class (`DownloadImageTask`) that extends the `AsyncTask` class. In this case, there are two methods within the `DownloadImageTask` class: `doInBackground()` and `onPostExecute()`.

You put all the code that needs to be run asynchronously in the `doInBackground()` method. When the task is completed, the result is passed back via the `onPostExecute()` method.

In this case, you use the `ImageView` to display the downloaded image.

RUNNING SYNCHRONOUS OPERATIONS IN A UI THREAD

To be specific, if you set the `android:minSdkVersion` attribute in your `AndroidManifest.xml` file to a value of 9 or less (though it's not recommended) and then run your application on an Android 3.0 or later device, your synchronous code still works in a UI thread. However, if the `android:minSdkVersion` attribute value is set to 10 or higher, your synchronous code does not work in a UI thread.

NOTE *Chapter 12 discusses the AsyncTask class in more detail.*

To call the `DownloadImageTask` class, create an instance of it and then call its `execute()` method, which passes the image's URL:

```
    @Override
    public void onCreate(Bundle savedInstanceState) {
        super.onCreate(savedInstanceState);
        setContentView(R.layout.main);
        new DownloadImageTask().execute(
            "http://www.jfdimarzio.com/butterfly.png");
    }
```

If you want to download a series of images asynchronously, you can modify the `DownloadImageTask` class as follows:

```
...
import android.widget.Toast;
...
    private class DownloadImageTask extends AsyncTask
    <String, Bitmap, Long> {
        //---takes in a list of image URLs in String type---
        protected Long doInBackground(String... urls) {
            long imagesCount = 0;
            for (int i = 0; i < urls.length; i++) {
                //---download the image---
                Bitmap imageDownloaded = DownloadImage(urls[i]);
                if (imageDownloaded != null)  {
                    //---increment the image count---
                    imagesCount++;
                    try {
                        //---insert a delay of 3 seconds---
                        Thread.sleep(3000);
                    } catch (InterruptedException e) {
                        e.printStackTrace();
                    }
                    //---return the image downloaded---
                    publishProgress(imageDownloaded);
                }
            }
            //---return the total images downloaded count---
            return imagesCount;
        }
        //---display the image downloaded---
        protected void onProgressUpdate(Bitmap... bitmap) {
            img.setImageBitmap(bitmap[0]);
        }
        //---when all the images have been downloaded---
        protected void onPostExecute(Long imagesDownloaded) {
            Toast.makeText(getBaseContext(),
                  "Total " + imagesDownloaded + " images downloaded" ,
                  Toast.LENGTH_LONG).show();
        }
    }
```

In this example, the `DownloadImageTask` class has one more method: `onProgressUpdate()`. Because the task to be performed inside an `AsyncTask` class can be lengthy, you call the `publishProgress()`

method to update the progress of the operation. This triggers the `onProgressUpdate()` method, which in this case displays the image to be downloaded. The `onProgressUpdate()` method is executed on the UI thread. That means it is thread-safe to update the `ImageView` with the bitmap downloaded from the server.

To download a series of images asynchronously in the background, create an instance of the `BackgroundTask` class and call its `execute()` method, like this:

```
@Override
public void onCreate(Bundle savedInstanceState) {
    super.onCreate(savedInstanceState);
    setContentView(R.layout.main);

    /* new DownloadImageTask().execute(
        "http://www.mayoff.com/5-01cablecarDCP01934.jpg");
   */

    img = (ImageView) findViewById(R.id.img);
    new DownloadImageTask().execute(
            "http://www.mayoff.com/5-01cablecarDCP01934.jpg",
            "http://www.hartiesinfo.net/greybox/Cable_Car_
              Hartbeespoort.jpg",
            "http://mcmanuslab.ucsf.edu/sites/default/files/
              imagepicker/m/mmcmanus/
              CaliforniaSanFranciscoPaintedLadiesHz.jpg",
            "http://www.fantom-xp.com/wallpapers/63/San_Francisco
              _-_Sunset.jpg",
            "http://travel.roro44.com/europe/france/
              Paris_France.jpg",
            "http://wwp.greenwichmeantime.com/time-zone/usa/nevada
               /las-vegas/hotel/the-strip/paris-las-vegas/paris-
               las-vegas-hotel.jpg",
            "http://designheaven.files.wordpress.com/2010/04/
               eiffel_tower_paris_france.jpg");
}
```

When you run the preceding code, the images are downloaded in the background and displayed at an interval of three seconds. When the last image has been downloaded, the `Toast` class displays the total number of images downloaded.

REFERRING TO LOCALHOST FROM YOUR EMULATOR

When working with the Android emulator, you might frequently need to access data hosted on the local web server using `localhost`. For example, your own web services are likely to be hosted on your local computer during development, and you'll want to test them on the same development machine you use to write your Android applications. In such cases, you should use the special IP address of 10.0.2.2 (not 127.0.0.1) to refer to the host computer's loopback interface. From the Android emulator's perspective, `localhost` (127.0.0.1) refers to its own loopback interface.

Downloading Text Content

Besides downloading binary data, you can also download plain-text content. For example, you might want to access a web service that returns a string of random quotes. The following Try It Out shows how you can download a string from a web service in your application.

TRY IT OUT Downloading Plain-Text Content

1. Using the same project created earlier, add the following bolded statements to the `MainActivity.java` file:

```
import android.Manifest;
import android.content.pm.PackageManager;
import android.graphics.Bitmap;
import android.graphics.BitmapFactory;
import android.os.AsyncTask;
import android.support.v4.app.ActivityCompat;
import android.support.v4.content.ContextCompat;
import android.support.v7.app.AppCompatActivity;
import android.os.Bundle;
import android.util.Log;
import android.widget.ImageView;
import android.widget.Toast;

import java.io.IOException;
import java.io.InputStream;
import java.io.InputStreamReader;
import java.net.HttpURLConnection;
import java.net.URL;
import java.net.URLConnection;

public class MainActivity extends AppCompatActivity {
    ImageView img;
    final private int REQUEST_INTERNET = 123;
    private InputStream OpenHttpConnection(String urlString) throws IOException
    {
        InputStream in = null;
        int response = -1;

        URL url = new URL(urlString);
        URLConnection conn = url.openConnection();

        if (!(conn instanceof HttpURLConnection))
            throw new IOException("Not an HTTP connection");
        try{
            HttpURLConnection httpConn = (HttpURLConnection) conn;
            httpConn.setAllowUserInteraction(false);
            httpConn.setInstanceFollowRedirects(true);
            httpConn.setRequestMethod("GET");
            httpConn.connect();
            response = httpConn.getResponseCode();
            if (response == HttpURLConnection.HTTP_OK) {
                in = httpConn.getInputStream();
            }
        }
```

```
        catch (Exception ex)
        {
            Log.d("Networking", ex.getLocalizedMessage());
            throw new IOException("Error connecting");
        }
        return in;
    }
    private String DownloadText(String URL)
    {
        int BUFFER_SIZE = 2000;
        InputStream in = null;
        try {
            in = OpenHttpConnection(URL);
        } catch (IOException e) {
            Log.d("Networking", e.getLocalizedMessage());
            return "";
        }

        InputStreamReader isr = new InputStreamReader(in);
        int charRead;
        String str = "";
        char[] inputBuffer = new char[BUFFER_SIZE];
        try {
            while ((charRead = isr.read(inputBuffer))>0) {
                //---convert the chars to a String---
                String readString =
                        String.copyValueOf(inputBuffer, 0, charRead);
                str += readString;
                inputBuffer = new char[BUFFER_SIZE];
            }
            in.close();
        } catch (IOException e) {
            Log.d("Networking", e.getLocalizedMessage());
            return "";
        }
        return str;
    }
    private class DownloadTextTask extends AsyncTask<String, Void, String> {
        protected String doInBackground(String... urls) {
            return DownloadText(urls[0]);
        }
        @Override
        protected void onPostExecute(String result) {
            Toast.makeText(getBaseContext(), result, Toast.LENGTH_LONG).show();
        }
    }

    @Override
    protected void onCreate(Bundle savedInstanceState) {
        super.onCreate(savedInstanceState);
        setContentView(R.layout.activity_main);
```

```
        if (ContextCompat.checkSelfPermission(this,
                Manifest.permission.INTERNET)
                != PackageManager.PERMISSION_GRANTED) {

            ActivityCompat.requestPermissions(this,
                    new String[]{Manifest.permission.INTERNET},
                    REQUEST_INTERNET);

        } else{

            new DownloadTextTask().execute("http://jfdimarzio.com/test.htm");

        }

    }

}
```

2. Press Shift+F9 to debug the application on the Android emulator. Figure 11-2 shows the random quote downloaded and displayed using the `Toast` class.

FIGURE 11-2

How It Works

The `DownloadText()` method accesses the text file's URL, downloads the text file, and then returns the desired string of text. It basically opens an HTTP connection to the server and then uses an `InputStreamReader` object to read each character from the stream and save it in a `String` object. As shown in the previous section, you had to create a subclass of the `AsyncTask` class to call the `DownloadText()` method asynchronously.

Accessing Web Services Using the GET Method

So far, this chapter has showed you how to download images and text from the web. The previous section demonstrated how to download some plain text from a server. Very often, you need to download XML files and parse the contents (a good example of this is consuming web services). Therefore, in this section you learn how to connect to a web service using the HTTP `GET` method. After the web service returns a result in XML, you extract the relevant parts and display its content using the `Toast` class.

In this example, you use the web method from `http://services.aonaware.com/DictService/DictService.asmx?op=Define`. This web method is from a dictionary web service that returns the definition of a given word.

The web method takes a request in the following format:

```
GET /DictService/DictService.asmx/Define?word=string HTTP/1.1
Host: services.aonaware.com
HTTP/1.1 200 OK
Content-Type: text/xml; charset=utf-8
Content-Length: length
```

It returns a response in the following format:

```
<?xml version="1.0" encoding="utf-8"?>
<WordDefinition xmlns="http://services.aonaware.com/webservices/">
  <Word>string</Word>
  <Definitions>
    <Definition>
      <Word>string</Word>
      <Dictionary>
        <Id>string</Id>
        <Name>string</Name>
      </Dictionary>
      <WordDefinition>string</WordDefinition>
    </Definition>
    <Definition>
      <Word>string</Word>
      <Dictionary>
        <Id>string</Id>
        <Name>string</Name>
      </Dictionary>
      <WordDefinition>string</WordDefinition>
```

```
      </Definition>
    </Definitions>
  </WordDefinition>
```

Hence, to obtain the definition of a word, you need to establish an HTTP connection to the web method and then parse the XML result that is returned. The following Try It Out shows you how.

TRY IT OUT Consuming Web Services

1. Using the same project we have been adding to throughout this chapter, add the following bolded statements to the `MainActivity.java` file:

```
import org.w3c.dom.Document;
import org.w3c.dom.Element;
import org.w3c.dom.Node;
import org.w3c.dom.NodeList;

import javax.xml.parsers.DocumentBuilder;
import javax.xml.parsers.DocumentBuilderFactory;
import javax.xml.parsers.ParserConfigurationException;

public class MainActivity extends AppCompatActivity {
    ImageView img;
    final private int REQUEST_INTERNET = 123;
    private InputStream OpenHttpConnection(String urlString) throws IOException
    {
        InputStream in = null;
        int response = -1;

        URL url = new URL(urlString);
        URLConnection conn = url.openConnection();

        if (!(conn instanceof HttpURLConnection))
            throw new IOException("Not an HTTP connection");
        try{
            HttpURLConnection httpConn = (HttpURLConnection) conn;
            httpConn.setAllowUserInteraction(false);
            httpConn.setInstanceFollowRedirects(true);
            httpConn.setRequestMethod("GET");
            httpConn.connect();
            response = httpConn.getResponseCode();
            if (response == HttpURLConnection.HTTP_OK) {
                in = httpConn.getInputStream();
            }
        }
        catch (Exception ex)
        {
            Log.d("Networking", ex.getLocalizedMessage());
            throw new IOException("Error connecting");
        }
        return in;
    }
    private String WordDefinition(String word) {
        InputStream in = null;
```

```
        String strDefinition = "";
        try {
            in = OpenHttpConnection(
                    "http://services.aonaware.com" +
"/DictService/DictService.asmx/Define?word=" + word);
            Document doc = null;
            DocumentBuilderFactory dbf =
                    DocumentBuilderFactory.newInstance();
            DocumentBuilder db;
            try {
                db = dbf.newDocumentBuilder();
                doc = db.parse(in);
            } catch (ParserConfigurationException e) {
                // TODO Auto-generated catch block
                e.printStackTrace();
            } catch (Exception e) {
                // TODO Auto-generated catch block
                e.printStackTrace();
            }
            doc.getDocumentElement().normalize();

            //---retrieve all the <Definition> elements---
            NodeList definitionElements =
                    doc.getElementsByTagName("Definition");

            //---iterate through each <Definition> elements---
            for (int i = 0; i < definitionElements.getLength(); i++) {
                Node itemNode = definitionElements.item(i);
                if (itemNode.getNodeType() == Node.ELEMENT_NODE)
                {
                    //---convert the Definition node into an Element---
                    Element definitionElement = (Element) itemNode;

                    //---get all the <WordDefinition> elements under
                    // the <Definition> element---
                    NodeList wordDefinitionElements =
                            (definitionElement).getElementsByTagName(
                                    "WordDefinition");

                    strDefinition = "";
                    //---iterate through each <WordDefinition> elements---
                    for (int j = 0; j < wordDefinitionElements.getLength(); j++) {
                        //---convert a <WordDefinition> node into an Element---
                        Element wordDefinitionElement =
                                (Element) wordDefinitionElements.item(j);

                        //---get all the child nodes under the
                        // <WordDefinition> element---
```

```
                        NodeList textNodes =
                                ((Node) wordDefinitionElement).getChildNodes();

                        strDefinition +=
                                ((Node) textNodes.item(0)).getNodeValue() + ". \n";
                    }

                }
            }
        } catch (IOException e1) {
            Log.d("NetworkingActivity", e1.getLocalizedMessage());
        }
        //---return the definitions of the word---
        return strDefinition;
    }
    private class AccessWebServiceTask extends AsyncTask<String, Void, String> {
        protected String doInBackground(String... urls) {
            return WordDefinition(urls[0]);
        }

        protected void onPostExecute(String result) {
            Toast.makeText(getBaseContext(), result, Toast.LENGTH_LONG).show();
        }
    }

    @Override
    protected void onCreate(Bundle savedInstanceState) {
        super.onCreate(savedInstanceState);
        setContentView(R.layout.activity_main);

        if (ContextCompat.checkSelfPermission(this,
                Manifest.permission.INTERNET)
                != PackageManager.PERMISSION_GRANTED) {

            ActivityCompat.requestPermissions(this,
                    new String[]{Manifest.permission.INTERNET},
                    REQUEST_INTERNET);

        } else{
            new AccessWebServiceTask().execute("apple");
        }

    }
}
```

2. Press Shift+F9 to debug the application on the Android emulator. Figure 11-3 shows the result of the web service call being parsed and then displayed using the `Toast` class.

FIGURE 11-3

How It Works

The `WordDefinition()` method first opens an HTTP connection to the web service, passing in the word for which you want the definition:

```
            in = OpenHttpConnection(
"http://services.aonaware.com/DictService/DictService.asmx/Define?word=" + word);
```

It then uses the `DocumentBuilderFactory` and `DocumentBuilder` objects to obtain a `Document` (DOM) object from an XML file (which is the XML result returned by the web service):

```
            Document doc = null;
            DocumentBuilderFactory dbf =
                DocumentBuilderFactory.newInstance();
            DocumentBuilder db;
            try {
                db = dbf.newDocumentBuilder();
                doc = db.parse(in);
            } catch (ParserConfigurationException e) {
                // TODO Auto-generated catch block
                e.printStackTrace();
```

```
    } catch (Exception e) {
        // TODO Auto-generated catch block
        e.printStackTrace();
    }
    doc.getDocumentElement().normalize();
```

When the `Document` object is obtained, you find all the elements with the `<Definition>` tag:

```
    //---retrieve all the <Definition> elements---
    NodeList definitionElements =
        doc.getElementsByTagName("Definition");
```

Because the definition of a word is contained within the `<WordDefinition>` element, you then proceed to extract all the definitions:

```
    //---iterate through each <Definition> elements---
    for (int i = 0; i < definitionElements.getLength(); i++) {
        Node itemNode = definitionElements.item(i);
        if (itemNode.getNodeType() == Node.ELEMENT_NODE)
        {
            //---convert the Definition node into an Element---
            Element definitionElement = (Element) itemNode;

            //---get all the <WordDefinition> elements under
            // the <Definition> element---
            NodeList wordDefinitionElements =
                (definitionElement).getElementsByTagName(
                "WordDefinition");

            strDefinition = "";
            //---iterate through each <WordDefinition> elements---
            for (int j = 0; j < wordDefinitionElements.getLength(); j++) {
                //---convert a <WordDefinition> node into an Element---
                Element wordDefinitionElement =
                    (Element) wordDefinitionElements.item(j);

                //---get all the child nodes under the
                // <WordDefinition> element---
                NodeList textNodes =
                    ((Node) wordDefinitionElement).getChildNodes();

                strDefinition +=
                    ((Node) textNodes.item(0)).getNodeValue() + ". \n";
            }
        }
    }
```

The preceding code loops through all the `<Definition>` elements looking for a child element named `<WordDefinition>`. The text content of the `<WordDefinition>` element contains the definition of a word, and the definitions of a word are then concatenated and returned by the `WordDefinition()` method:

```
    //---return the definitions of the word---
    return strDefinition;
```

As usual, you need to create a subclass of the `AsyncTask` class to call the `WordDefinition()` method asynchronously:

```
private class AccessWebServiceTask extends AsyncTask<String, Void, String> {
    protected String doInBackground(String... urls) {
        return WordDefinition(urls[0]);
    }

    protected void onPostExecute(String result) {
        Toast.makeText(getBaseContext(), result, Toast.LENGTH_LONG).show();
    }
}
```

Finally, you access the web service asynchronously using the `execute()` method:

```
    //---access a Web Service using GET---
    new AccessWebServiceTask().execute("apple");
```

CONSUMING JSON SERVICES

In the previous section, you learned how to consume XML web services by using HTTP to connect to the web server and then obtain the results in XML. You also learned how to use DOM to parse the result of the XML document. However, manipulating XML documents is a computationally expensive operation for mobile devices, for the following reasons:

- XML documents are lengthy. They use tags to embed information, and the size of an XML document can pretty quickly become large. A large XML document means that your device must use more bandwidth to download it, which translates into higher cost.
- XML documents are more difficult to process. As shown earlier, when using the `DocumentBuilderFactory`, you must use DOM to traverse the tree in order to locate the information you want. In addition, DOM itself has to build the entire document in memory as a tree structure before you can traverse it. This is both memory and CPU intensive.

A much more efficient way to represent information exists in the form of JSON (JavaScript Object Notation). JSON is a lightweight data-interchange format that is easy for humans to read and write. It is also easy for machines to parse and generate. The following lines of code show what a JSON message looks like:

```
[
    {
        "appeId":"1",
        "survId":"1",
        "location":"",
        "surveyDate":"2008-03 14",
        "surveyTime":"12:19:47",
        "inputUserId":"1",
        "inputTime":"2008-03-14 12:21:51",
        "modifyTime":"0000-00-00 00:00:00"
```

```
    },
    {
        "appeId":"2",
        "survId":"32",
        "location":"",
        "surveyDate":"2008-03-14",
        "surveyTime":"22:43:09",
        "inputUserId":"32",
        "inputTime":"2008-03-14 22:43:37",
        "modifyTime":"0000-00-00 00:00:00"
    },
    {
        "appeId":"3",
        "survId":"32",
        "location":"",
        "surveyDate":"2008-03-15",
        "surveyTime":"07:59:33",
        "inputUserId":"32",
        "inputTime":"2008-03-15 08:00:44",
        "modifyTime":"0000-00-00 00:00:00"
    },
    {
        "appeId":"4",
        "survId":"1",
        "location":"",
        "surveyDate":"2008-03-15",
        "surveyTime":"10:45:42",
        "inputUserId":"1",
        "inputTime":"2008-03-15 10:46:04",
        "modifyTime":"0000-00-00 00:00:00"
    },
    {
        "appeId":"5",
        "survId":"32",
        "location":"",
        "surveyDate":"2008-03-16",
        "surveyTime":"08:04:49",
        "inputUserId":"32",
        "inputTime":"2008-03-16 08:05:26",
        "modifyTime":"0000-00-00 00:00:00"
    },
    {
        "appeId":"6",
        "survId":"32",
        "location":"",
        "surveyDate":"2008-03-20",
        "surveyTime":"20:19:01",
        "inputUserId":"32",
        "inputTime":"2008-03-20 20:19:32",
        "modifyTime":"0000-00-00 00:00:00"
    }
]
```

The preceding block of lines represents a set of data taken for a survey. Note that the information is represented as a collection of key/value pairs, and that each key/value pair is grouped into an ordered list of objects. Unlike XML, there are no lengthy tag names. Instead, there are only brackets and braces.

The following Try It Out demonstrates how to process JSON messages easily using the `JSONArray` and `JSONObject` classes available in the Android SDK.

TRY IT OUT Consuming JSON Services

1. Using Android Studio, create a new Android project and name it **JSON**.

2. Add the following bolded line to the `AndroidManifest.xml` file. Please be sure to replace any instance of `com.jfdimarzio` with the name of the package used in your application:

```
<?xml version="1.0" encoding="utf-8"?>
<manifest xmlns:android="http://schemas.android.com/apk/res/android"
    package="com.jfdimarzio.json">
    <uses-permission android:name="android.permission.INTERNET"/>
    <application
        android:allowBackup="true"
        android:icon="@mipmap/ic_launcher"
        android:label="@string/app_name"
        android:supportsRtl="true"
        android:theme="@style/AppTheme">
        <activity android:name=".MainActivity">
            <intent-filter>
                <action android:name="android.intent.action.MAIN" />

                <category android:name="android.intent.category.LAUNCHER" />
            </intent-filter>
        </activity>
    </application>

</manifest>
```

3. Add the following lines of code in bold to the `MainActivity.java` file:

```
import android.os.AsyncTask;
import android.support.v7.app.AppCompatActivity;
import android.os.Bundle;
import android.util.Log;
import android.widget.Toast;

import org.json.JSONArray;
import org.json.JSONObject;

import java.io.BufferedInputStream;
import java.io.BufferedReader;
import java.io.IOException;
import java.io.InputStream;
import java.io.InputStreamReader;
import java.net.HttpURLConnection;
import java.net.MalformedURLException;
import java.net.URL;
```

```
public class MainActivity extends AppCompatActivity {
    public String readJSONFeed(String address) {
        URL url = null;
        try {
            url = new URL(address);
        } catch (MalformedURLException e) {
            e.printStackTrace();
        };
        StringBuilder stringBuilder = new StringBuilder();
        HttpURLConnection urlConnection = null;
        try {
            urlConnection = (HttpURLConnection) url.openConnection();
        } catch (IOException e) {
            e.printStackTrace();
        }
        try {
            InputStream content = new BufferedInputStream(
    urlConnection.getInputStream());
            BufferedReader reader = new BufferedReader(
    new InputStreamReader(content));
            String line;
            while ((line = reader.readLine()) != null) {
                stringBuilder.append(line);
            }
        } catch (IOException e) {
            e.printStackTrace();
        } finally {
            urlConnection.disconnect();
        }
        return stringBuilder.toString();
    }
    private class ReadJSONFeedTask extends AsyncTask<String, Void, String> {
        protected String doInBackground(String... urls) {
            return readJSONFeed(urls[0]);
        }

        protected void onPostExecute(String result) {
            try {
                JSONArray jsonArray = new JSONArray(result);
                Log.i("JSON", "Number of surveys in feed: " +
                        jsonArray.length());
                //---print out the content of the json feed---
                for (int i = 0; i < jsonArray.length(); i++) {
                    JSONObject jsonObject = jsonArray.getJSONObject(i);
                    Toast.makeText(getBaseContext(),
    jsonObject.getString("appeId") +
                                    " - " + jsonObject.getString("inputTime"),
                            Toast.LENGTH_SHORT).show();
                }
            } catch (Exception e) {
                e.printStackTrace();
            }
        }
```

```
        }

        @Override
        protected void onCreate(Bundle savedInstanceState) {
            super.onCreate(savedInstanceState);
            setContentView(R.layout.activity_main);

             new ReadJSONFeedTask().execute(
        "http://extjs.org.cn/extjs/examples/grid/survey.html");

        }
    }
```

4. Press Shift+F9 to debug the application on the Android emulator. You see the `Toast` class appear a couple of times, displaying the information (see Figure 11-4).

FIGURE 11-4

How It Works

The first thing you do in this project is define the `readJSONFeed()` method:

```
public String readJSONFeed(String address) {
        URL url = null;
        try {
            url = new URL(address);
        } catch (MalformedURLException e) {
            e.printStackTrace();
        };
        StringBuilder stringBuilder = new StringBuilder();
        HttpURLConnection urlConnection = null;
        try {
            urlConnection = (HttpURLConnection) url.openConnection();
        } catch (IOException e) {
            e.printStackTrace();
        }
        try {
            InputStream content = new BufferedInputStream(
    urlConnection.getInputStream());
            BufferedReader reader = new BufferedReader(
    new InputStreamReader(content));
            String line;
            while ((line = reader.readLine()) != null) {
                 stringBuilder.append(line);
            }
        } catch (IOException e) {
            e.printStackTrace();
        } finally {
            urlConnection.disconnect();
        }
        return stringBuilder.toString();
    }
```

This method simply connects to the specified URL and then reads the response from the web server. It returns a string as the result.

To call the `readJSONFeed()` method asynchronously, you created a subclass of the `AsyncTask` class:

```
    private class ReadJSONFeedTask extends AsyncTask<String, Void, String> {
        protected String doInBackground(String... urls) {
            return readJSONFeed(urls[0]);
        }

        protected void onPostExecute(String result) {
            try {
                JSONArray jsonArray = new JSONArray(result);
                Log.i("JSON", "Number of surveys in feed: " +
                        jsonArray.length());
```

```
                //---print out the content of the json feed---
                for (int i = 0; i < jsonArray.length(); i++) {
                    JSONObject jsonObject = jsonArray.getJSONObject(i);
                    Toast.makeText(getBaseContext(), jsonObject.getString("appeId") +
                            " - " + jsonObject.getString("inputTime"),
                            Toast.LENGTH_SHORT).show();
                }
            } catch (Exception e) {
                e.printStackTrace();
            }
        }
    }
```

You call the `readJSONFeed()` method in the `doInBackground()` method, and the JSON string that you fetch is passed in through the `onPostExecute()` method. The JSON string used in this example (and as illustrated earlier in the introduction to "Consuming JSON Services") is from `http://extjs.org.cn/extjs/examples/grid/survey.html`.

To obtain the list of objects in the JSON string, you use the `JSONArray` class, passing it the JSON feed as the constructor for the class:

```
JSONArray jsonArray = new JSONArray(result);
Log.i("JSON", "Number of surveys in feed: " +
        jsonArray.length());
```

The `length()` method returns the number of objects in the `jsonArray` object. With the list of objects stored in the `jsonArray` object, you iterate through it to obtain each object using the `getJSONObject()` method:

```
//---print out the content of the json feed---
for (int i = 0; i < jsonArray.length(); i++) {
    JSONObject jsonObject = jsonArray.getJSONObject(i);
    Toast.makeText(this, jsonObject.getString("appeId") +
            " - " + jsonObject.getString("inputTime"),
            Toast.LENGTH_SHORT).show();
}
```

The `getJSONObject()` method returns an object of type `JSONObject`. To obtain the value of the key/value pair stored inside the object, you use the `getString()` method (you can also use the `getInt()`, `getLong()`, and `getBoolean()` methods for other data types).

Finally, you access the JSON feed asynchronously using the `execute()` method:

```
new ReadJSONFeedTask().execute(
    "http://extjs.org.cn/extjs/examples/grid/survey.html");
```

The preceding example shows how you can consume a JSON service and quickly parse its result. A much more interesting example is to use a real-life scenario: Twitter. The following changes make the application fetch my latest tweets from Twitter and then display the tweets in the `Toast` class (see Figure 10-6):

```
private class ReadJSONFeedTask extends AsyncTask<String, Void, String> {
    protected String doInBackground(String... urls) {
```

```
            return readJSONFeed(urls[0]);
        }

        protected void onPostExecute(String result) {
            try {
                JSONArray jsonArray = new JSONArray(result);
                Log.i("JSON", "Number of surveys in feed: " +
                        jsonArray.length());
                //---print out the content of the json feed---
                for (int i = 0; i < jsonArray.length(); i++) {
                    JSONObject jsonObject = jsonArray.getJSONObject(i);
                    /*
                    Toast.makeText(getBaseContext(),
jsonObject.getString("appeId") +
                            " - " + jsonObject.getString("inputTime"),
                            Toast.LENGTH_SHORT).show();
                    */

                    Toast.makeText(getBaseContext(),
jsonObject.getString("text") +
                            " - " + jsonObject.getString("created_at"),
                            Toast.LENGTH_SHORT).show();
                }
            } catch (Exception e) {
                e.printStackTrace();
            }
        }
    }
    /** Called when the activity is first created. */
    @Override
    public void onCreate(Bundle savedInstanceState) {
        super.onCreate(savedInstanceState);
        setContentView(R.layout.main);
        /*
        new ReadJSONFeedTask().execute(
            "http://extjs.org.cn/extjs/examples/grid/survey.html");
        */
        new ReadJSONFeedTask().execute(
            "https://twitter.com/statuses/user_timeline/weimenglee.json");
    }
```

SUMMARY

In this chapter, you learned how your application can connect with the outside world through the use of the HTTP protocol. Using the HTTP protocol, you can download various types of data from web servers. One good application of this is to talk to web services, whereby you need to parse XML files. In addition to XML web services, you also saw how to consume JSON services, which are more lightweight than XML web services. Finally, you saw an alternative to HTTP: using sockets for communication. Sockets enable your application to remain connected to a server so that it can receive data as it becomes available. An important lesson in this chapter is that all synchronous operations must be encapsulated using the `AsyncTask` class. Otherwise, your application does not work on devices running Honeycomb or later.

EXERCISES

1. Name the permissions you need to declare in your `AndroidManifest.xml` file for an HTTP connection.

2. Name the classes used for dealing with JSON messages.

3. Name the class for performing background asynchronous tasks.

You can find answers to the exercises in the appendix.

▶ WHAT YOU LEARNED IN THIS CHAPTER

TOPIC	KEY CONCEPTS
Establishing an HTTP connection	Use the `HttpURLConnection` class.
Accessing XML web services	Use the `Document`, `DocumentBuilderFactory`, and `DocumentBuilder` classes to parse the XML result returned by the web service.
Dealing with JSON messages	Use the `JSONArray` and `JSONObject` classes.
Sockets programming	Use the `Socket` class to establish a TCP connection. Use the `InputStream` and `OutputStream` objects for receiving and sending data, respectively.
The three methods in an **`AsyncTask`** class	The three methods are `doInBackground()`, `onProgressUpdate()`, and `onPostExecute()`.

12

Developing Android Services

WHAT YOU WILL LEARN IN THIS CHAPTER

- How to create a service that runs in the background
- How to perform long-running tasks in a separate thread
- How to perform repeated tasks in a service
- How an activity and a service communicate

> ***CODE DOWNLOAD*** *The wrox.com code downloads for this chapter are found at* `www.wrox.com/go/beginningandroidprog` *on the Download Code tab. The code is in the chapter 12 download and individually named according to the names throughout the chapter.*

A *service* is an application in Android that runs in the background without needing to interact with the user. For example, while using an application, you might want to play some background music at the same time. In this case, the code that is playing the background music has no need to interact with the user; therefore, it can be run as a service. Also, services are ideal for situations in which there is no need to present a user interface (UI) to the user. A good example of this scenario is an application that continually logs the geographical coordinates of the device. In this case, you can write a service to do that in the background. In this chapter, you find out how to create your own services and use them to perform background tasks asynchronously.

CREATING YOUR OWN SERVICES

The best way to understand how a service works is by creating one. The following Try It Out shows you the steps to create a simple service. Subsequent sections add more functionality to this service. For now, you see how to start and stop a service.

TRY IT OUT Creating a Simple Service (Services.zip)

1. Using Android Studio, create a new Android project and name it **Services.**
2. Add a new Java Class file to the project and name it **MyService**. Populate the `MyService.java` file with the following code:

```
import android.app.Service;
import android.content.Intent;
import android.os.IBinder;
import android.widget.Toast;

public class MyService extends Service {
    @Override
    public IBinder onBind(Intent arg0) {
        return null;
    }
    @Override
    public int onStartCommand(Intent intent, int flags, int startId) {
        // We want this service to continue running until it is explicitly
        // stopped, so return sticky.
        Toast.makeText(this, "Service Started", Toast.LENGTH_LONG).show();
        return START_STICKY;
    }
    @Override
    public void onDestroy() {
        super.onDestroy();
        Toast.makeText(this, "Service Destroyed", Toast.LENGTH_LONG).show();
    }
}
```

3. In the `AndroidManifest.xml` file, add the following bolded statement. Please be sure to replace all instances of `com.jfdimarzio` with the package used in your application:

```
<?xml version="1.0" encoding="utf-8"?>
<manifest xmlns:android="http://schemas.android.com/apk/res/android"
    package="com.jfdimarzio.services">

    <application
        android:allowBackup="true"
        android:icon="@mipmap/ic_launcher"
        android:label="@string/app_name"
        android:supportsRtl="true"
        android:theme="@style/AppTheme">
        <activity android:name=".MainActivity">
            <intent-filter>
                <action android:name="android.intent.action.MAIN" />
```

```
                <category android:name="android.intent.category.LAUNCHER" />
            </intent-filter>
        </activity>
        <service android:name=".MyService" />
    </application>

</manifest>
```

4. In the `main.xml` file, add the following bolded statements, replacing `TextView`. Please be sure to replace all instances of `com.jfdimarzio` with the package used in your application:

```
<?xml version="1.0" encoding="utf-8"?>
android.support.constraint.ConstraintLayout xmlns:android=
    "http://schemas.android.com/apk/res/android"
    xmlns:app="http://schemas.android.com/apk/res-auto"
    xmlns:tools="http://schemas.android.com/tools"
    android:id="@+id/activity_main"
    android:layout_width="match_parent"
    android:layout_height="match_parent"
    tools:context="com.jfdimarzio.services.MainActivity">


    <Button
        android:text="Start Service"
        android:layout_width="90dp"
        android:layout_height="50dp"
        android:id="@+id/btnStartService"
        app:layout_constraintLeft_toLeftOf="@+id/activity_main"
        app:layout_constraintTop_toTopOf="@+id/activity_main"
        android:layout_marginTop="16dp"
        app:layout_constraintRight_toRightOf="@+id/activity_main"
        app:layout_constraintBottom_toTopOf="@+id/btnStopService"
        android:layout_marginBottom="8dp"
        android:onClick="startService"  />

    <Button
        android:text="Stop Service"
        android:layout_width="88dp"
        android:layout_height="48dp"
        android:id="@+id/btnStopService"
        app:layout_constraintLeft_toLeftOf="@+id/activity_main"
        android:layout_marginStart="16dp"
        app:layout_constraintTop_toTopOf="@+id/activity_main"
        app:layout_constraintRight_toRightOf="@+id/activity_main"
        android:layout_marginEnd="16dp"
        app:layout_constraintBottom_toBottomOf="@+id/activity_main"
        android:onClick="stopService"  />
</android.support.constraint.ConstraintLayout>
```

5. Add the following bolded `startService` and `stopService` statements to the `MainActivity.java` file:

```
package net.learn2develop.Services;
import android.support.v7.app.AppCompatActivity;
import android.content.Intent;
```

```
import android.os.Bundle;
import android.view.View;
public class MainActivity extends AppCompatActivity {
    /** Called when the activity is first created. */
    @Override
    public void onCreate(Bundle savedInstanceState) {
        super.onCreate(savedInstanceState);
        setContentView(R.layout.main);
    }

    public void startService(View view) {
        startService(new Intent(getBaseContext(), MyService.class));
    }

    public void stopService(View view) {
        stopService(new Intent(getBaseContext(), MyService.class));
    }
}
```

6. Press Shift+F9 to debug the application on the Android emulator.
7. Clicking Start Service starts the service (see Figure 12-1). To stop the service, click Stop Service.

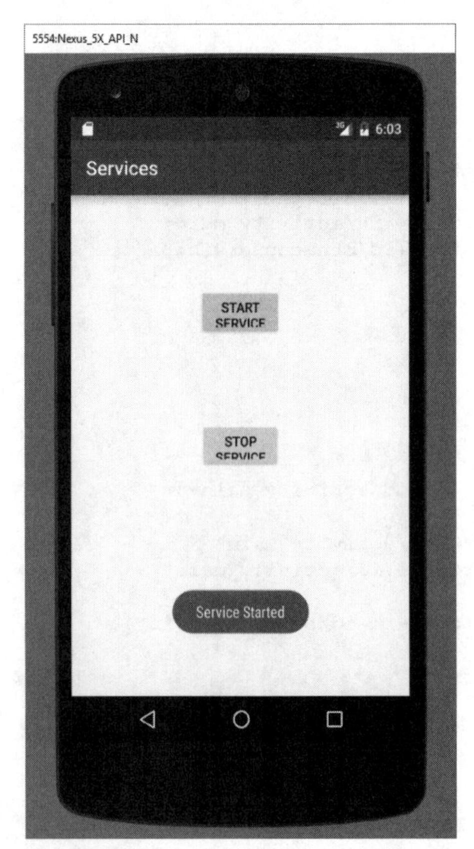

FIGURE 12-1

How It Works

This example demonstrated the simplest service that you can create. The service itself is not doing anything useful, of course, but it serves to illustrate how a service is created.

First, you define a class that extends the `Service` base class. All services extend the `Service` class:

```
public class MyService extends Service {
}
```

Within the `MyService` class, you implement three methods:

```
@Override
public IBinder onBind(Intent arg0) {  ...  }
@Override
public int onStartCommand(Intent intent, int flags, int startId) { ... }
@Override
public void onDestroy() { ... }
```

- The `onBind()` method enables you to bind an activity to a service. This in turn enables an activity to directly access members and methods inside a service. For now, you simply return a `null` for this method. Later in this chapter, you find out more about binding.
- The `onStartCommand()` method is called when you start the service explicitly using the `startService()` method (discussed shortly). This method signifies the start of the service, and you code it to do the things you need to do for your service. In this method, you returned the constant `START_STICKY` so that the service continues to run until it is explicitly stopped.
- The `onDestroy()` method is called when the service is stopped using the `stopService()` method. This is where you clean up the resources used by your service.

All services that you have created must be declared in the `AndroidManifest.xml` file, like this:

```
<service android:name=".MyService" />
```

If you want your service to be available to other applications, you can always add an intent filter with an action name, like this:

```
<service android:name=".MyService">
    <intent-filter>
        <action android:name="net.learn2develop.MyService" />
    </intent-filter>
</service>
```

To start a service, you use the `startService()` method, like this:

```
startService(new Intent(getBaseContext(), MyService.class));
```

If you are calling this service from an external application, then the call to the `startService()` method looks like this:

```
startService(new Intent("net.learn2develop.MyService"));
```

To stop a service, use the `stopService()` method:

```
stopService(new Intent(getBaseContext(), MyService.class));
```

Performing Long-Running Tasks in a Service

Because the service you created in the previous section does not do anything useful, in this section you modify it so that it performs a task. In the following Try It Out, you simulate the service of downloading a file from the Internet.

TRY IT OUT Making Your Service Useful

1. Using the Services project created in the first example, add the following bolded statements to the `MyService.java` file:

```
import android.app.Service;
import android.content.Intent;
import android.os.IBinder;
import android.widget.Toast;

import java.net.MalformedURLException;
import java.net.URL;

public class MyService extends Service {
    @Override
    public IBinder onBind(Intent arg0) {
        return null;
    }
    @Override
    public int onStartCommand(Intent intent, int flags, int startId) {
        // We want this service to continue running until it is explicitly
        // stopped, so return sticky.
        //Toast.makeText(this, "Service Started", Toast.LENGTH_LONG).show();

        try {
            int result =
DownloadFile(new URL("http://www.amazon.com/somefile.pdf"));
            Toast.makeText(getBaseContext(),
                    "Downloaded " + result + " bytes",
            Toast.LENGTH_LONG).show();
        } catch (MalformedURLException e) {
            // TODO Auto-generated catch block
            e.printStackTrace();
        }
        return START_STICKY;
    }

    private int DownloadFile(URL url) {
        try {
            //---simulate taking some time to download a file---
            Thread.sleep(5000);
        } catch (InterruptedException e) {
            e.printStackTrace();
        }
        //---return an arbitrary number representing
        // the size of the file downloaded---
        return 100;
```

```
        }
        @Override
        public void onDestroy() {
            super.onDestroy();
            Toast.makeText(this, "Service Destroyed", Toast.LENGTH_LONG).show();
        }
    }
```

2. Press Shift+F9 to debug the application on the Android emulator.
3. Click the Start Service button to start the service to download the file. Note that the activity is frozen for a few seconds before the `Toast` class displays the "Downloaded 100 bytes" message (see Figure 12-2).

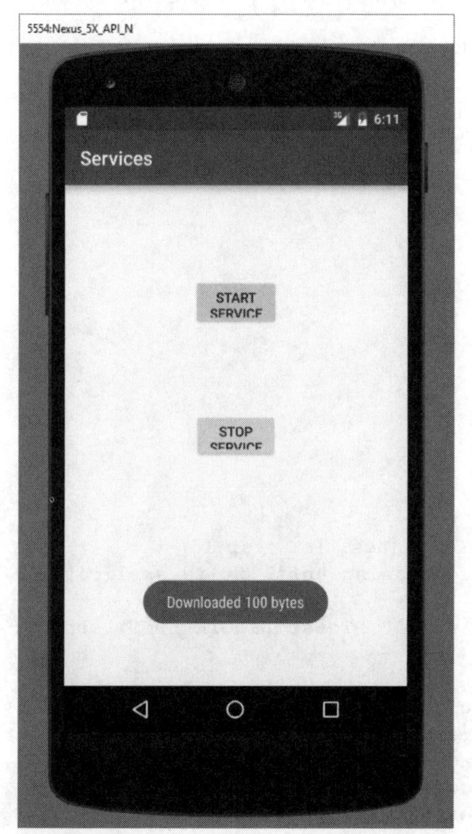

FIGURE 12-2

How It Works

In this example, your service calls the `DownloadFile()` method to simulate downloading a file from a given URL. This method returns the total number of bytes downloaded (which is hardcoded as 100). To simulate the delays experienced by the service when downloading the file, you use the `Thread.Sleep()` method to pause the service for five seconds (5,000 milliseconds).

As you start the service, note that the activity is suspended for about five seconds. This is the time taken for the file to be downloaded from the Internet. During this time, the entire activity is not responsive, demonstrating a very important point: The service runs on the same thread as your activity. In this case, because the service is suspended for five seconds, so is the activity.

That means for a long-running service, it is important that you put all long-running code into a separate thread so that it does not tie up the application that calls it. The following Try It Out shows you how.

TRY IT OUT Performing Tasks in a Service Asynchronously (Services.zip)

1. Using the Services project created in the first example, add the following bolded statements to the `MyService.java` file:

```
import android.app.Service;
import android.content.Intent;
import android.os.AsyncTask;
import android.os.IBinder;
import android.util.Log;
import android.widget.Toast;

import java.net.MalformedURLException;
import java.net.URL;

public class MyService extends Service {
    @Override
    public IBinder onBind(Intent arg0) {
        return null;
    }
    @Override
    public int onStartCommand(Intent intent, int flags, int startId) {
        // We want this service to continue running until it is explicitly
        // stopped, so return sticky.
        //Toast.makeText(this, "Service Started", Toast.LENGTH_LONG).show();

        try {
            new DoBackgroundTask().execute(
                    new URL("http://www.amazon.com/somefiles.pdf"),
                    new URL("http://www.wrox.com/somefiles.pdf"),
                    new URL("http://www.google.com/somefiles.pdf"),
                    new URL("http://www.learn2develop.net/somefiles.pdf"));
        } catch (MalformedURLException e) {
            // TODO Auto-generated catch block
            e.printStackTrace();
        }
        return START_STICKY;
    }

    private int DownloadFile(URL url) {
        try {
```

```
            //---simulate taking some time to download a file---
            Thread.sleep(5000);
        } catch (InterruptedException e) {
            e.printStackTrace();
        }
        //---return an arbitrary number representing
        // the size of the file downloaded---
        return 100;
    }
    private class DoBackgroundTask extends AsyncTask<URL, Integer, Long> {
        protected Long doInBackground(URL... urls) {
            int count = urls.length;
            long totalBytesDownloaded = 0;
            for (int i = 0; i < count; i++) {
                totalBytesDownloaded += DownloadFile(urls[i]);
                //---calculate percentage downloaded and
                // report its progress---
                publishProgress((int) (((i+1) / (float) count) * 100));
            }
            return totalBytesDownloaded;
        }
        protected void onProgressUpdate(Integer... progress) {
            Log.d("Downloading files",
                    String.valueOf(progress[0]) + "% downloaded");
            Toast.makeText(getBaseContext(),
                    String.valueOf(progress[0]) + "% downloaded",
                    Toast.LENGTH_LONG).show();
        }
        protected void onPostExecute(Long result) {
            Toast.makeText(getBaseContext(),
                    "Downloaded " + result + " bytes",
                    Toast.LENGTH_LONG).show();
            stopSelf();
        }
    }
    @Override
    public void onDestroy() {
        super.onDestroy();
        Toast.makeText(this, "Service Destroyed", Toast.LENGTH_LONG).show();
    }
}
```

2. Press Shift+F9 to debug the application on the Android emulator.
3. Click the Start Service button. The `Toast` class displays a message indicating what percentage of the download is completed. You should see four of them: 25 percent, 50 percent, 75 percent, and 100 percent.
4. You can see output similar to the following in the LogCat window:

```
12-06 01:58:24.967: D/Downloading files(6020): 25% downloaded
12-06 01:58:30.019: D/Downloading files(6020): 50% downloaded
12-06 01:58:35.078: D/Downloading files(6020): 75% downloaded
12-06 01:58:40.096: D/Downloading files(6020): 100% downloaded
```

How It Works

This example illustrates one way in which you can execute a task asynchronously within your service. You do so by creating an inner class that extends the `AsyncTask` class. The `AsyncTask` class enables you to perform background execution without needing to manually handle threads and handlers.

The `DoBackgroundTask` class extends the `AsyncTask` class by specifying three generic types:

```
private class DoBackgroundTask extends AsyncTask<URL, Integer, Long> {
```

In this case, the three types specified are `URL`, `Integer`, and `Long`. These three types specify the data type used by the following three methods that you implement in an `AsyncTask` class:

- `doInBackground()`—This method accepts an array of the first generic type specified earlier. In this case, the type is `URL`. This method is executed in the background thread and is where you put your long-running code. To report the progress of your task, you call the `publishProgress()` method, which invokes the next method, `onProgressUpdate()`. This is implemented in an `AsyncTask` class. The return type of this method takes the third generic type specified earlier, which is `Long` in this case.
- `onProgressUpdate()`—This method is invoked in the UI thread and is called when you call the `publishProgress()` method. It accepts an array of the second generic type specified earlier. In this case, the type is `Integer`. Use this method to report the progress of the background task to the user.
- `onPostExecute()`—This method is invoked in the UI thread and is called when the `doInBackground()` method has finished execution. This method accepts an argument of the third generic type specified earlier, which in this case is a `Long`.

To download multiple files in the background, you create an instance of the `DoBackgroundTask` class and then call its `execute()` method by passing in an array of `URLs`:

```
try {
    new DoBackgroundTask().execute(
            new URL("http://www.amazon.com/somefiles.pdf"),
            new URL("http://www.wrox.com/somefiles.pdf"),
            new URL("http://www.google.com/somefiles.pdf"),
            new URL("http://www.learn2develop.net/somefiles.pdf"));
} catch (MalformedURLException e) {
    // TODO Auto-generated catch block
    e.printStackTrace();
}
```

The preceding causes the service to download the files in the background, and reports the progress as a percentage of files downloaded. More important, the activity remains responsive while the files are downloaded in the background, on a separate thread.

Note that when the background thread has finished execution, you can manually call the `stopSelf()` method to stop the service:

```
protected void onPostExecute(Long result) {
    Toast.makeText(getBaseContext(),
```

```
                "Downloaded " + result + " bytes",
                Toast.LENGTH_LONG).show();
        stopSelf();
    }
```

The `stopSelf()` method is the equivalent of calling the `stopService()` method to stop the service.

Performing Repeated Tasks in a Service

In addition to performing long-running tasks in a service, you might also perform some repeated tasks in a service. For example, you could write an alarm clock service that runs persistently in the background. In this case, your service might need to periodically execute some code to check whether a prescheduled time has been reached so that an alarm can be sounded. To execute a block of code to be executed at a regular time interval, you can use the `Timer` class within your service. The following Try It Out shows you how.

TRY IT OUT Running Repeated Tasks Using the Timer Class (Services.zip)

1. Using the Services project again, add the following bolded statements to the `MyService.java` file:

```
import android.app.Service;
        import android.content.Intent;
        import android.os.AsyncTask;
        import android.os.IBinder;
        import android.util.Log;
        import android.widget.Toast;

        import java.net.MalformedURLException;
        import java.net.URL;
        import java.util.Timer;
        import java.util.TimerTask;

public class MyService extends Service {
    int counter = 0;
    static final int UPDATE_INTERVAL = 1000;
    private Timer timer = new Timer();

    @Override
    public IBinder onBind(Intent arg0) {
        return null;
    }
    @Override
    public int onStartCommand(Intent intent, int flags, int startId) {
        // We want this service to continue running until it is explicitly
         // stopped, so return sticky.
         //Toast.makeText(this, "Service Started", Toast.LENGTH_LONG).show();

        doSomethingRepeatedly();
```

```
        try {
            new DoBackgroundTask().execute(
                    new URL("http://www.amazon.com/somefiles.pdf"),
                    new URL("http://www.wrox.com/somefiles.pdf"),
                    new URL("http://www.google.com/somefiles.pdf"),
                    new URL("http://www.learn2develop.net/somefiles.pdf"));
        } catch (MalformedURLException e) {
            // TODO Auto-generated catch block
            e.printStackTrace();
        }
        return START_STICKY;
    }

    private void doSomethingRepeatedly() {
        timer.scheduleAtFixedRate(new TimerTask() {
            public void run() {
                Log.d("MyService", String.valueOf(++counter));
            }
        }, 0, UPDATE_INTERVAL);
    }

    private int DownloadFile(URL url) {
        try {
            //---simulate taking some time to download a file---
            Thread.sleep(5000);
        } catch (InterruptedException e) {
            e.printStackTrace();
        }
        //---return an arbitrary number representing
        // the size of the file downloaded---
        return 100;
    }
    private class DoBackgroundTask extends AsyncTask<URL, Integer, Long> {
        protected Long doInBackground(URL... urls) {
            int count = urls.length;
            long totalBytesDownloaded = 0;
            for (int i = 0; i < count; i++) {
                totalBytesDownloaded += DownloadFile(urls[i]);
                //---calculate percentage downloaded and
                // report its progress---
                publishProgress((int) (((i+1) / (float) count) * 100));
            }
            return totalBytesDownloaded;
        }
        protected void onProgressUpdate(Integer... progress) {
            Log.d("Downloading files",
                    String.valueOf(progress[0]) + "% downloaded");
            Toast.makeText(getBaseContext(),
                    String.valueOf(progress[0]) + "% downloaded",
                    Toast.LENGTH_LONG).show();
        }
        protected void onPostExecute(Long result) {
            Toast.makeText(getBaseContext(),
                    "Downloaded " + result + " bytes",
                    Toast.LENGTH_LONG).show();
```

```
                stopSelf();
            }
        }

        @Override
        public void onDestroy() {
            super.onDestroy();

            if (timer != null){
                timer.cancel();
            }

            Toast.makeText(this, "Service Destroyed", Toast.LENGTH_LONG).show();
        }

    }
```

2. Press Shift+F9 to debug the application on the Android emulator.
3. Click the Start Service button.
4. Observe the output displayed in the LogCat window. It will be similar to the following:

```
12-06 02:37:54.118: D/MyService(7752): 1
12-06 02:37:55.109: D/MyService(7752): 2
12-06 02:37:56.120: D/MyService(7752): 3
12-06 02:37:57.111: D/MyService(7752): 4
12-06 02:37:58.125: D/MyService(7752): 5
12-06 02:37:59.137: D/MyService(7752): 6
```

How It Works

In this example, you create a `Timer` object and call its `scheduleAtFixedRate()` method inside the `doSomethingRepeatedly()` method that you have defined:

```
    private void doSomethingRepeatedly() {
        timer.scheduleAtFixedRate( new TimerTask() {
            public void run() {
                Log.d("MyService", String.valueOf(++counter));
            }
        }, 0, UPDATE_INTERVAL);
    }
```

You pass an instance of the `TimerTask` class to the `scheduleAtFixedRate()` method so that you can repeatedly execute the block of code within the `run()` method. The second parameter to the `scheduleAtFixedRate()` method specifies the amount of time, in milliseconds, before first execution. The third parameter specifies the amount of time, in milliseconds, between subsequent executions.

In the preceding example, you essentially print the value of the counter every second (1,000 milliseconds). The service repeatedly prints the value of `counter` until the service is terminated:

```
    @Override
    public void onDestroy() {
        super.onDestroy();

        if (timer != null){
```

```
            timer.cancel();
        }

        Toast.makeText(this, "Service Destroyed", Toast.LENGTH_LONG).show();
    }
```

For the `scheduleAtFixedRate()` method, your code is executed at fixed time intervals, regardless of how long each task takes. For example, if the code within your `run()` method takes two seconds to complete, then your second task starts immediately after the first task has ended. Similarly, if your delay is set to three seconds and the task takes two seconds to complete, then the second task waits for one second before starting.

Also, notice that you call the `doSomethingRepeatedly()` method directly in the `onStartCommand()` method, without needing to wrap it in a subclass of the `AsyncTask` class. This is because the `TimerTask` class itself implements the `Runnable` interface, which allows it to run on a separate thread.

Executing Asynchronous Tasks on Separate Threads Using IntentService

Earlier in this chapter, you learned how to start a service using the `startService()` method and stop a service using the `stopService()` method. You have also seen how you should execute long-running tasks on a separate thread—not the same thread as the calling activities. It is important to note that once your service has finished executing a task, it should be stopped as soon as possible so that it does not unnecessarily hold up valuable resources. That's why you use the `stopSelf()` method to stop the service when a task has been completed. Unfortunately, a lot of developers often forget to terminate a service when it is done performing its task. To easily create a service that runs a task asynchronously and terminates itself when it is done, you can use the `IntentService` class.

The `IntentService` class is a base class for `Service` that handles asynchronous requests on demand. It is started just like a normal service; and it executes its task within a worker thread and terminates itself when the task is completed. The following Try It Out demonstrates how to use the `IntentService` class.

TRY IT OUT Using the IntentService Class to Auto-Stop a Service (Services.zip)

1. Using the Services project created in the first example, add a new Class file named **MyIntentService .java**.

2. Populate the `MyIntentService.java` file as follows:

```
import android.app.IntentService;
import android.content.Intent;
import android.util.Log;

import java.net.MalformedURLException;
import java.net.URL;

public class MyIntentService extends IntentService {
private Thread thread = new Thread();
```

```
    public MyIntentService() {
        super("MyIntentServiceName");
    }
    @Override
    protected void onHandleIntent(Intent intent) {
        thread.start();
        try {
            int result =
                    DownloadFile(new URL("http://www.amazon.com/somefile.pdf"));
            Log.d("IntentService", "Downloaded " + result + " bytes");
        } catch (MalformedURLException e) {
            e.printStackTrace();
        }
    }
    private int DownloadFile(URL url) {
        try {
            //---simulate taking some time to download a file---
            thread.sleep(5000);
        } catch (InterruptedException e) {
            e.printStackTrace();
        }
        return 100;
    }

}
```

3. Add the following bolded statement to the `AndroidManifest.xml` file. Please note, replace all instances of `com.jfdimarzio` to the package used in your application:

```
<?xml version="1.0" encoding="utf-8"?>
<manifest xmlns:android="http://schemas.android.com/apk/res/android"
package="com.jfdimarzio.services">

<application
    android:allowBackup="true"
    android:icon="@mipmap/ic_launcher"
    android:label="@string/app_name"
    android:supportsRtl="true"
    android:theme="@style/AppTheme">
    <activity android:name=".MainActivity">
        <intent-filter>
            <action android:name="android.intent.action.MAIN" />

            <category android:name="android.intent.category.LAUNCHER" />
        </intent-filter>
    </activity>
    <service android:name=".MyService">
    <intent-filter>
        <action android:name="net.learn2develop.MyService" />
    </intent-filter>
</service>
    <service android:name=".MyIntentService" />

</application>

</manifest>
```

4. Add the following bolded statement to the `MainActivity.java` file:

```
public void startService(View view) {
    //startService(new Intent(getBaseContext(), MyService.class));
    //OR
    //startService(new Intent("net.learn2develop.MyService"));
    startService(new Intent(getBaseContext(), MyIntentService.class));
}
public void stopService(View view) {

    stopService(new Intent(MainActivity.this, MyIntentService.class));
}
```

5. Press Shift+F9 to debug the application on the Android emulator.

6. Click the Start Service button. After about five seconds, you should see something similar to the following statement in the LogCat window. Try it again; however, this time click the Start Service button and then the Stop Service button:

```
12-06 13:35:32.181: D/IntentService(861): Downloaded 100 bytes
```

How It Works

First, you define the `MyIntentService` class, which extends the `IntentService` class instead of the `Service` class:

```
public class MyIntentService extends IntentService {
}
```

You need to implement a constructor for the class and call its superclass with the name of the intent service (setting it with a string):

```
public MyIntentService() {
    super("MyIntentServiceName");
}
```

You then implement the `onHandleIntent()` method, which is executed on a worker thread:

```
@Override
protected void onHandleIntent(Intent intent) {
    try {
        int result =
            DownloadFile(new URL("http://www.amazon.com/somefile.pdf"));
        Log.d("IntentService", "Downloaded " + result + " bytes");
    } catch (MalformedURLException e) {
        e.printStackTrace();
    }
}
```

The `onHandleIntent()` method is where you place the code that needs to be executed on a separate thread, such as downloading a file from a server. When the code has finished executing, the thread is terminated and the service is stopped automatically.

ESTABLISHING COMMUNICATION BETWEEN A SERVICE AND AN ACTIVITY

Often a service simply executes in its own thread, independently of the activity that calls it. This doesn't pose a problem if you simply want the service to perform some tasks periodically and the activity does not need to be notified about the service's status. For example, you might have a service that periodically logs the geographical location of the device to a database. In this case, there is no need for your service to interact with any activities, because its main purpose is to save the coordinates into a database. However, suppose you want to monitor for a particular location. When the service logs an address that is near the location you are monitoring, it might need to communicate that information to the activity. If so, you need to devise a way for the service to interact with the activity.

The following Try It Out demonstrates how a service can communicate with an activity using a `BroadcastReceiver`.

TRY IT OUT Invoking an Activity from a Service (Services.zip)

1. Using the Services project created earlier, add the following statements in bold to the `MyIntentService.java` file:

```
import android.app.IntentService;
import android.content.Intent;
import android.util.Log;

import java.net.MalformedURLException;
import java.net.URL;

public class MyIntentService extends IntentService {
    public MyIntentService() {
        super("MyIntentServiceName");
    }
    @Override
    protected void onHandleIntent(Intent intent) {
        try {
            int result =
                    DownloadFile(new URL("http://www.amazon.com/somefile.pdf"));
            Log.d("IntentService", "Downloaded " + result + " bytes");

            //---send a broadcast to inform the activity
            // that the file has been downloaded---
            Intent broadcastIntent = new Intent();
            broadcastIntent.setAction("FILE_DOWNLOADED_ACTION");
            getBaseContext().sendBroadcast(broadcastIntent);
        } catch (MalformedURLException e) {
            e.printStackTrace();
        }
    }
    private int DownloadFile(URL url) {
        try {
```

```
                //---simulate taking some time to download a file---
                Thread.sleep(5000);
            } catch (InterruptedException e) {
                // TODO Auto-generated catch block
                e.printStackTrace();
            }
            return 100;
        }

}
```

2. Add the following bolded statements to the `MainActivity.java` file:

```
import android.content.BroadcastReceiver;
import android.content.Context;
import android.content.Intent;
import android.content.IntentFilter;
import android.support.v7.app.AppCompatActivity;
import android.os.Bundle;
import android.view.View;
import android.widget.Toast;

public class MainActivity extends AppCompatActivity {
    IntentFilter intentFilter;

    /** Called when the activity is first created. */
    @Override
    public void onCreate(Bundle savedInstanceState) {
        super.onCreate(savedInstanceState);
        setContentView(R.layout.activity_main);
    }

    @Override
    public void onResume() {
        super.onResume();
        //---intent to filter for file downloaded intent---
        intentFilter = new IntentFilter();
        intentFilter.addAction("FILE_DOWNLOADED_ACTION");
        //---register the receiver---
        registerReceiver(intentReceiver, intentFilter);
    }

    @Override
    public void onPause() {
        super.onPause();

        //---unregister the receiver---
        unregisterReceiver(intentReceiver);
    }

    public void startService(View view) {
        //startService(new Intent(getBaseContext(), MyService.class));
        //OR
```

```
        //startService(new Intent("net.learn2develop.MyService"));
        startService(new Intent(getBaseContext(), MyIntentService.class));
    }

    public void stopService(View view) {
        stopService(new Intent(getBaseContext(), MyService.class));
    }
    private BroadcastReceiver intentReceiver = new BroadcastReceiver() {
        @Override
        public void onReceive(Context context, Intent intent) {
            Toast.makeText(getBaseContext(), "File downloaded!",
            Toast.LENGTH_LONG).show();
        }
    };
}
```

3. Press Shift+F9 to debug the application on the Android emulator.
4. Click the Start Service button. After about five seconds, the `Toast` class displays a message indicating that the file has been downloaded (see Figure 12-3).

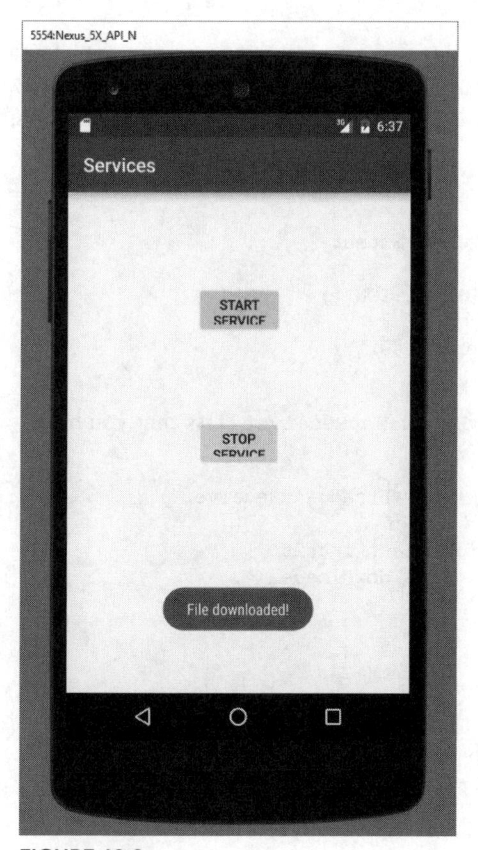

FIGURE 12-3

How It Works

To notify an activity when a service has finished its execution, you broadcast an intent using the `sendBroadcast()` method:

```
@Override
protected void onHandleIntent(Intent intent) {
    try {
        int result =
            DownloadFile(new URL("http://www.amazon.com/somefile.pdf"));
        Log.d("IntentService", "Downloaded " + result + " bytes");

        //---send a broadcast to inform the activity
        // that the file has been downloaded---
        Intent broadcastIntent = new Intent();
        broadcastIntent.setAction("FILE_DOWNLOADED_ACTION");
        getBaseContext().sendBroadcast(broadcastIntent);
    } catch (MalformedURLException e) {
        e.printStackTrace();
    }
}
```

The action of this intent that you are broadcasting is set to `"FILE_DOWNLOADED_ACTION"`, which means any activity that is listening for this intent will be invoked. That means in your `MainActivity.java` file, you listen for this intent using the `registerReceiver()` method from the `IntentFilter` class:

```
@Override
public void onResume() {
    super.onResume();
    //---intent to filter for file downloaded intent---
    intentFilter = new IntentFilter();
    intentFilter.addAction("FILE_DOWNLOADED_ACTION");
    //---register the receiver---
    registerReceiver(intentReceiver, intentFilter);
}
```

When the intent is received, it invokes an instance of the `BroadcastReceiver` class that you have defined:

```
private BroadcastReceiver intentReceiver = new BroadcastReceiver() {
    @Override
    public void onReceive(Context context, Intent intent) {
        Toast.makeText(getBaseContext(), "File downloaded!",
                Toast.LENGTH_LONG).show();
    }
};
```

> **NOTE** *Chapter 9 discusses the* `BroadcastReceiver` *class in more detail.*

In this Try It Out, the message "File downloaded!" is displayed. Of course, if you need to pass some data from the service to the activity, you can make use of the `Intent` object. The next section discusses this.

BINDING ACTIVITIES TO SERVICES

So far, you have seen how services are created, how they are called, and how they are terminated when they are done with their task. All the services that you have seen are simple—either they start with a counter and increment at regular intervals or they download a fixed set of files from the Internet. However, real-world services are usually much more sophisticated, requiring the passing of data so that they can do the job correctly for you.

Using the service demonstrated earlier that downloads a set of files, suppose you now want to let the calling activity determine what files to download, instead of hardcoding them in the service. Here is what you need to do.

1. First, in the calling activity, you create an `Intent` object, specifying the service name:

```
public void startService(View view) {
    Intent intent = new Intent(getBaseContext(), MyService.class);
}
```

2. You then create an array of `URL` objects and assign it to the `Intent` object through its `putExtra()` method.
3. You start the service using the `Intent` object:

```
public void startService(View view) {
    Intent intent = new Intent(getBaseContext(), MyService.class);
    try {
        URL[] urls = new URL[] {
                new URL("http://www.amazon.com/somefiles.pdf"),
                new URL("http://www.wrox.com/somefiles.pdf"),
                new URL("http://www.google.com/somefiles.pdf"),
                new URL("http://www.learn2develop.net/somefiles.pdf")};
        intent.putExtra("URLs", urls);
    } catch (MalformedURLException e) {
        e.printStackTrace();
    }
    startService(intent);
}
```

4. Note that the `URL` array is assigned to the `Intent` object as an `Object` array.
5. On the service's end, you need to extract the data passed in through the `Intent` object in the `onStartCommand()` method:

```
@Override
public int onStartCommand(Intent intent, int flags, int startId) {
    // We want this service to continue running until it is explicitly
    // stopped, so return sticky.
    Toast.makeText(this, "Service Started", Toast.LENGTH_LONG).show();
    Object[] objUrls = (Object[]) intent.getExtras().get("URLs");
    URL[] urls = new URL[objUrls.length];
    for (int i=0; i<objUrls.length-1; i++) {
        urls[i] = (URL) objUrls[i];
    }
    new DoBackgroundTask().execute(urls);
    return START_STICKY;
}
```

6. The preceding first extracts the data using the `getExtras()` method to return a `Bundle` object.
7. It then uses the `get()` method to extract the `URL` array as an `Object` array.
8. Because in Java you cannot directly cast an array from one type to another, you must create a loop and cast each member of the array individually.
9. Finally, you execute the background task by passing the URL array into the `execute()` method.

This is one way in which your activity can pass values to the service. As you can see, if you have relatively complex data to pass to the service, you must do some additional work to ensure that the data is passed correctly. A better way to pass data is to bind the activity directly to the service so that the activity can call any public members and methods on the service directly. The following Try It Out shows you how to bind an activity to a service.

TRY IT OUT Accessing Members of a Property Directly Through Binding (Services.zip)

1. Using the Services project created earlier, add the following bolded statements to the `MyService.java` file (note that you are modifying the existing `onStartCommand()`):

```
        import android.app.Service;
        import android.content.Intent;
        import android.os.AsyncTask;
        import android.os.Binder;
        import android.os.IBinder;
        import android.util.Log;
        import android.widget.Toast;

        import java.net.MalformedURLException;
        import java.net.URL;
        import java.util.Timer;
        import java.util.TimerTask;

public class MyService extends Service {
    int counter = 0;
    URL[] urls;
    static final int UPDATE_INTERVAL = 1000;
    private Timer timer = new Timer();
    private final IBinder binder = new MyBinder();
    public class MyBinder extends Binder {
        MyService getService() {
            return MyService.this;
        }
    }
    @Override
    public IBinder onBind(Intent arg0) {
        return binder;
    }
    @Override
    public int onStartCommand(Intent intent, int flags, int startId) {
```

```
        // We want this service to continue running until it is explicitly
        // stopped, so return sticky.
        Toast.makeText(this, "Service Started", Toast.LENGTH_LONG).show();
        new DoBackgroundTask().execute(urls);
        return START_STICKY;
    }

    private void doSomethingRepeatedly() {...}

    private int DownloadFile(URL url) {...}
    private class DoBackgroundTask extends AsyncTask<URL, Integer, Long> {...}
        protected void onProgressUpdate(Integer... progress) {...}

    @Override
    public void onDestroy() {...}

}
```

2. In the `MainActivity.java` file, add the following bolded statements (note the change to the existing `startService()` method):

```
import android.content.BroadcastReceiver;
import android.content.ComponentName;
import android.content.Context;
import android.content.Intent;
import android.content.IntentFilter;
import android.content.ServiceConnection;
import android.os.IBinder;
import android.support.v7.app.AppCompatActivity;
import android.os.Bundle;
import android.view.View;
import android.widget.Toast;

import java.net.MalformedURLException;
import java.net.URL;

public class MainActivity extends AppCompatActivity {
    IntentFilter intentFilter;

    MyService serviceBinder;
    Intent i;
    private ServiceConnection connection = new ServiceConnection() {
        public void onServiceConnected(
                ComponentName className, IBinder service) {
            //—-called when the connection is made—-
            serviceBinder = ((MyService.MyBinder)service).getService();
            try {
                URL[] urls = new URL[] {
                        new URL("http://www.amazon.com/somefiles.pdf"),
                        new URL("http://www.wrox.com/somefiles.pdf"),
                        new URL("http://www.google.com/somefiles.pdf"),
                        new URL("http://www.learn2develop.net/somefiles.pdf")};
                //---assign the URLs to the service through the
                // serviceBinder object---
                serviceBinder.urls = urls;
```

```
            } catch (MalformedURLException e) {
                e.printStackTrace();
            }
            startService(i);
        }
        public void onServiceDisconnected(ComponentName className) {
            //---called when the service disconnects---
            serviceBinder = null;
        }
    };
    /** Called when the activity is first created. */
    @Override
    public void onCreate(Bundle savedInstanceState) {...}

    @Override
    public void onResume() {...}

    @Override
    public void onPause() {...}

    public void startService(View view) {
        i = new Intent(MainActivity.this, MyService.class);
        bindService(i, connection, Context.BIND_AUTO_CREATE);

    }

    public void stopService(View view) {...}
    private BroadcastReceiver intentReceiver = new BroadcastReceiver() {...};
}
```

3. Press Shift+F9 to debug the application. Clicking the Start Service button starts the service as normal.

How It Works

To bind activities to a service, you must first declare an inner class in your service that extends the `Binder` class:

```
public class MyBinder extends Binder {
    MyService getService() {
        return MyService.this;
    }
}
```

Within this class you implement the `getService()` method, which returns an instance of the service.

You then create an instance of the `MyBinder` class:

```
private final IBinder binder = new MyBinder();
```

You also modify the `onBind()` method to return the `MyBinder` instance:

```
@Override
public IBinder onBind(Intent arg0) {
    return binder;
}
```

In the onStartCommand() method, you then call the execute() method using the urls array, which you declare as a public member in your service:

```
public class MyService extends Service {
    int counter = 0;
    URL[] urls;
...
...
    @Override
    public int onStartCommand(Intent intent, int flags, int startId) {
        // We want this service to continue running until it is explicitly
        // stopped, so return sticky.
        Toast.makeText(this, "Service Started", Toast.LENGTH_LONG).show();
        new DoBackgroundTask().execute(urls);
        return START_STICKY;
    }
}
```

Next, this URL array must be set directly from your activity.

In the MainActivity.java file, you first declare an instance of your service and an Intent object:

```
MyService serviceBinder;
Intent i;
```

The serviceBinder object will be used as a reference to the service, which you access directly.

You then create an instance of the ServiceConnection class so that you can monitor the state of the service:

```
private ServiceConnection connection = new ServiceConnection() {
    public void onServiceConnected(
        ComponentName className, IBinder service) {
        //---called when the connection is made---
        serviceBinder = ((MyService.MyBinder)service).getService();
        try {
            URL[] urls = new URL[] {
                new URL("http://www.amazon.com/somefiles.pdf"),
                new URL("http://www.wrox.com/somefiles.pdf"),
                new URL("http://www.google.com/somefiles.pdf"),
                new URL("http://www.learn2develop.net/somefiles.pdf")};
                //---assign the URLs to the service through the
                // serviceBinder object---
                serviceBinder.urls = urls;
        } catch (MalformedURLException e) {
                e.printStackTrace();
        }
        startService(i);
    }
    public void onServiceDisconnected(ComponentName className) {
        //---called when the service disconnects---
        serviceBinder = null;
    }
};
```

You need to implement two methods: onServiceConnected() and onServiceDisconnected().

- The `onServiceConnected()` method is called when the activity is connected to the service.
- The `onServiceDisconnected()` method is called when the service is disconnected from the activity.

When the activity is connected to the service, you obtain an instance of the service from the `onServiceConnected()` method by using the `getService()` method of the `service` argument. You then assign it to the `serviceBinder` object. The `serviceBinder` object is a reference to the service, and all the members and methods in the service can be accessed through this object. Here, you create a URL array and then directly assign it to the public member in the service:

```
URL[] urls = new URL[] {
    new URL("http://www.amazon.com/somefiles.pdf"),
    new URL("http://www.wrox.com/somefiles.pdf"),
    new URL("http://www.google.com/somefiles.pdf"),
    new URL("http://www.learn2develop.net/somefiles.pdf")};
    //---assign the URLs to the service through the
    // serviceBinder object---
    serviceBinder.urls = urls;
```

You then start the service using an `Intent` object:

```
startService(i);
```

Before you can start the service, you must bind the activity to the service. This is done in the `startService()` method of the Start Service button:

```
public void startService(View view) {
    i = new Intent(MainActivity.this, MyService.class);
    bindService(i, connection, Context.BIND_AUTO_CREATE);
}
```

The `bindService()` method enables your activity to be connected to the service. It takes three arguments:

- An `Intent` object
- A `ServiceConnection` object
- A flag to indicate how the service should be bound

UNDERSTANDING THREADING

So far, you have seen how services are created and why it is important to ensure that your long-running tasks are properly handled, especially when updating the UI thread. Earlier in this chapter (as well as in Chapter 9), you also saw how to use the `AsyncTask` class for executing long-running code in the background. This section briefly summarizes the various ways to handle long-running tasks correctly using a variety of methods available.

For this discussion, assume that you have an Android project named Threading. The `main.xml` file contains a `Button` and `TextView`:

```
<?xml version="1.0" encoding="utf-8"?>
<LinearLayout xmlns:android="http://schemas.android.com/apk/res/android"
    android:layout_width="fill_parent"
    android:layout_height="fill_parent"
    android:orientation="vertical" >
    <TextView
        android:layout_width="fill_parent"
        android:layout_height="wrap_content"
        android:text="@string/hello" />
    <Button
        android:id="@+id/btnStartCounter"
        android:layout_width="match_parent"
        android:layout_height="wrap_content"
        android:text="Start"
        android:onClick="startCounter" />
    <TextView
        android:id="@+id/textView1"
        android:layout_width="match_parent"
        android:layout_height="wrap_content"
        android:text="TextView" />
    </LinearLayout>
```

Suppose you want to display a counter on the activity, from 0 to 1,000. In your `ThreadingActivity` class, you have the following code:

```
package net.learn2develop.Threading;
import android.app.Activity;
import android.os.Bundle;
import android.util.Log;
import android.view.View;
import android.widget.TextView;
public class ThreadingActivity extends Activity {
    TextView txtView1;

    /** Called when the activity is first created. */
    @Override
    public void onCreate(Bundle savedInstanceState) {
        super.onCreate(savedInstanceState);
        setContentView(R.layout.main);

        txtView1 = (TextView) findViewById(R.id.textView1);
    }

    public void startCounter(View view) {
        for (int i=0; i<=1000; i++) {
            txtView1.setText(String.valueOf(i));
            try {
                Thread.sleep(1000);
            } catch (InterruptedException e) {
                Log.d("Threading", e.getLocalizedMessage());
            }
        }
    }
}
```

When you run the application and click the Start button, the application is briefly frozen.

The UI freezes because the application is continuously trying to display the value of the counter at the same time it is pausing for one second after it has been displayed. This ties up the UI, which is waiting for the display of the numbers to be completed. The result is a nonresponsive application that will frustrate your users.

To solve this problem, one option is to wrap the part of the code that contains the loop using a `Thread` and `Runnable` class, like this:

```
public void startCounter(View view) {
    new Thread(new Runnable() {
        public void run() {
            for (int i=0; i<=1000; i++) {
                txtView1.setText(String.valueOf(i));
                try {
                    Thread.sleep(1000);
                } catch (InterruptedException e) {
                    Log.d("Threading", e.getLocalizedMessage());
                }
            }
        }
    }).start();
}
```

In the preceding code, you first create a class that implements the `Runnable` interface. Within this class, you put your long-running code within the `run()` method. The `Runnable` block is then started using the `Thread` class.

> **NOTE** *A `Runnable` is a block of code that can be executed by a thread.*

However, the preceding application will not work, and it will crash if you try to run it. This code that is placed inside the `Runnable` block is on a separate thread, and in the preceding example you are trying to update the UI from another thread, which is not a safe thing to do because Android UIs are not thread-safe. To resolve this, you need to use the `post()` method of a `View` to create another `Runnable` block to be added to the message queue. In short, the new `Runnable` block created will be executed in the UI thread, so it would now be safe to execute your application:

```
public void startCounter(View view) {
    new Thread(new Runnable() {
        @Override
        public void run() {
            for (int i=0; i<=1000; i++) {
                final int valueOfi = i;

                //---update UI---
                txtView1.post(new Runnable() {
                    public void run() {
                        //---UI thread for updating---
```

```
                        txtView1.setText(String.valueOf(valueOfi));
                    }
                });

                //---insert a delay
                try {
                    Thread.sleep(1000);
                } catch (InterruptedException e) {
                    Log.d("Threading", e.getLocalizedMessage());
                }
            }
        }
    }).start();
}
```

This application will now work correctly, but it is complicated and makes your code difficult to maintain.

A second option to update the UI from another thread is to use the `Handler` class. A `Handler` enables you to send and process messages, similar to using the `post()` method of a `View`. The following code snippet shows a `Handler` class called `UIupdater` that updates the UI using the message that it receives:

> **NOTE** *For the following code to work, you must import the* `android.os.Handler` *package as well as add the* `static` *modifier to* `txtView1`.

```
//---used for updating the UI on the main activity---
static Handler UIupdater = new Handler() {
    @Override
    public void handleMessage(Message msg) {
        byte[] buffer = (byte[]) msg.obj;

        //---convert the entire byte array to string---
        String strReceived = new String(buffer);
        //---display the text received on the TextView---
        txtView1.setText(strReceived);
        Log.d("Threading", "running");
    }
};

public void startCounter(View view) {
    new Thread(new Runnable() {
        @Override
        public void run() {
            for (int i=0; i<=1000; i++) {
                //---update the main activity UI---
                ThreadingActivity.UIupdater.obtainMessage(
                    0, String.valueOf(i).getBytes() ).sendToTarget();
                //---insert a delay
                try {
                    Thread.sleep(1000);
```

```
                    } catch (InterruptedException e) {
                        Log.d("Threading", e.getLocalizedMessage());
                    }
                }
            }
        }).start();
    }

}
```

A detailed discussion of the `Handler` class is beyond the scope of this book. For more details, check out the documentation at `https://developer.android.com/reference/android/os/Handler.html`.

So far, the two methods just described enable you to update the UI from a separate thread. In Android, you could use the simpler `AsyncTask` class to do this. Using the `AsyncTask`, you could rewrite the preceding code as follows:

```
private class DoCountingTask extends AsyncTask<Void, Integer, Void> {
    protected Void doInBackground(Void... params) {
        for (int i = 0; i < 1000; i++) {
            //---report its progress---
            publishProgress(i);
            try {
                Thread.sleep(1000);
            } catch (InterruptedException e) {
                Log.d("Threading", e.getLocalizedMessage());
            }
        }
        return null;
    }
    protected void onProgressUpdate(Integer... progress) {
        txtView1.setText(progress[0].toString());
        Log.d("Threading", "updating...");
    }
}
public void startCounter(View view) {
    new DoCountingTask().execute();
}
```

The preceding code will update the UI safely from another thread. What about stopping the task? If you run the preceding application and then click the Start button, the counter will start to display from zero. However, if you press the back button on the emulator/device, the task will continue to run even though the activity has been destroyed. You can verify this through the LogCat window. If you want to stop the task, use the following code snippets:

```
public class ThreadingActivity extends Activity {
    static TextView txtView1;
    DoCountingTask task;

    /** Called when the activity is first created. */
    @Override
    public void onCreate(Bundle savedInstanceState) {
        super.onCreate(savedInstanceState);
```

```
        setContentView(R.layout.main);

        txtView1 = (TextView) findViewById(R.id.textView1);
    }

    public void startCounter(View view) {
        task = (DoCountingTask) new DoCountingTask().execute();
    }

    public void stopCounter(View view) {
        task.cancel(true);
    }

    private class DoCountingTask extends AsyncTask<Void, Integer, Void> {
        protected Void doInBackground(Void... params) {
            for (int i = 0; i < 1000; i++) {
                //---report its progress---
                publishProgress(i);
                try {
                    Thread.sleep(1000);
                } catch (InterruptedException e) {
                    Log.d("Threading", e.getLocalizedMessage());
                }
                if (isCancelled()) break;
            }
            return null;
        }
        protected void onProgressUpdate(Integer... progress) {
            txtView1.setText(progress[0].toString());
            Log.d("Threading", "updating...");
        }
    }
    @Override
    protected void onPause() {
        super.onPause();
        stopCounter(txtView1);
    }
}
```

To stop the `AsyncTask` subclass, you need to get an instance of it first. To stop the task, call its `cancel()` method. Within the task, you call the `isCancelled()` method to check whether the task should be terminated.

SUMMARY

In this chapter, you learned how to create a service in your Android project to execute long-running tasks. You have seen the many approaches you can use to ensure that the background task is executed in an asynchronous fashion, without tying up the main calling activity. You have also learned how an activity can pass data into a service, and how you can alternatively bind to an activity so that it can access a service more directly.

EXERCISES

1. Why is it important to put long-running code in a service on a separate thread?

2. What is the purpose of the `IntentService` class?

3. Name the three methods you need to implement in an `AsyncTask` class.

4. How can a service notify an activity of an event happening?

5. For threading, what is the recommended method to ensure that your code runs without tying up the UI of your application?

You can find answers to the exercises in the appendix.

▸ WHAT YOU LEARNED IN THIS CHAPTER

TOPIC	KEY CONCEPTS
Creating a service	Create a class and extend the `Service` class.
Implementing the methods in a service	Implement the following methods: `onBind()`, `onStartCommand()`, and `onDestroy()`.
Starting a service	Use the `startService()` method.
Stopping a service	Use the `stopService()` method.
Performing long-running tasks	Use the `AsyncTask` class and implement three methods: `doInBackground()`, `onProgressUpdate()`, and `onPostExecute()`.
Performing repeated tasks	Use the `Timer` class and call its `scheduleAtFixedRate()` method.
Executing tasks on a separate thread and auto-stopping a service	Use the `IntentService` class.
Enabling communication between an activity and a service	Use the `Intent` object to pass data into the service. For a service, broadcast an `Intent` to notify an activity.
Binding an activity to a service	Use the `Binder` class in your service and implement the `ServiceConnection` class in your calling activity.
Updating the UI from a `Runnable` block	Use the `post()` method of a view to update the UI. Alternatively, you can also use a `Handler` class. The recommended way is to use the `AsyncTask` class.

Appendix

Answers to Exercises

This appendix includes the answers to the end-of-chapter exercises.

CHAPTER 1 ANSWERS

1. An AVD is an Android Virtual Device. It represents an Android emulator, which emulates a particular configuration of an actual Android device.
2. Because Jelly Bean had the largest install base at the time.
3. Software Development Kit.

CHAPTER 2 ANSWERS

1. The company domain is used to name the Java package to which your code will belong.
2. This screen adds commonly used features to your project at the time the project is created.
3. Code completion is an invaluable tool that shows you contextual options for completing the piece of code that you are trying to write.
4. Breakpoints are mechanisms that enable Android Studio to temporarily pause execution of your code to let you examine the condition of your application.

CHAPTER 3 ANSWERS

1. Activity
2. `android:theme`
3. `onCreateDialog()`

4. Intents
5. `startActivityForResult()`

CHAPTER 4 ANSWERS

1. The `dp` unit is density independent and `1dp` is equivalent to one pixel on a 160-dpi screen. The `px` unit corresponds to an actual pixel on screen. You should always use the `dp` unit because it enables your activity to scale properly when run on devices of varying screen size.
2. With the advent of devices with different screen sizes, using `AbsoluteLayout` makes it difficult for your application to have a consistent look and feel across devices.
3. The `onPause()` event is fired whenever an activity is killed or sent to the background. The `onSaveInstanceState()` event is similar to the `onPause()` event, except that it is not always called, such as when the user presses the Back button to kill the activity.
4. The three events are `onPause()`, `onSaveInstanceState()`, and `onRetainNonConfigurationInstance()`.
   - You generally use the `onPause()` method to preserve the activity's state because the method is always called when the activity is about to be destroyed.
   - For screen orientation changes, however, it is easier to use the `onSaveInstanceState()` method to save the state of the activity (such as the data entered by the user) using a Bundle object.
   - The `onRetainNonConfigurationInstance()` method is useful for momentarily saving data (such as images or files downloaded from a web service) that might be too large to fit into a Bundle object.
5. Adding action items to the Action Bar is similar to creating menu items for an options menu — simply handle the `onCreateOptionsMenu()` and `onOptionsItemSelected()` events.

CHAPTER 5 ANSWERS

1. You should inspect the `isChecked()` method of each `RadioButton` to determine whether it has been selected.
2. You can use the `getResources()` method.
3. The code snippet to obtain the current date is as follows:

```
//--get the current date--
Calendar today = Calendar.getInstance();
yr = today.get(Calendar.YEAR);
month = today.get(Calendar.MONTH);
day = today.get(Calendar.DAY_OF_MONTH);
showDialog(DATE_DIALOG_ID);
```

4. The three specialized fragments are `ListFragment`, `DialogFragment`, and `PreferenceFragment`.

   - The `ListFragment` is useful for displaying a list of items, such as an RSS listing of news items.
   - The `DialogFragment` allows you to display a dialog window modally and is useful when you want a response from the user before allowing him to continue with your application.
   - The `PreferenceFragment` displays a window containing your application's preferences and allows the user to edit them directly in your application.

CHAPTER 6 ANSWERS

1. The `ImageSwitcher` enables images to be displayed with animation. You can animate the image when it is being displayed, as well as when it is being replaced by another image.
2. The two methods are `onCreateOptionsMenu()` and `onOptionsItemSelected()`.
3. The two methods are `onCreateContextMenu()` and `onContextItemSelected()`.
4. To prevent launching the device's web browser, you need to implement the `WebViewClient` class and override the `shouldOverrideUrlLoading()` method.

CHAPTER 7 ANSWERS

1. You can use the `PreferenceActivity` class.
2. The method name is `getExternalStorageDirectory()`.
3. The permission is `WRITE_EXTERNAL_STORAGE`.

CHAPTER 8 ANSWERS

1. The code is as follows:

```
Cursor c;
if (android.os.Build.VERSION.SDK_INT <11) {
    //---before Honeycomb---
    c = managedQuery(allContacts, projection,
            ContactsContract.Contacts.DISPLAY_NAME + " LIKE ?",
            new String[] {"%jack"},
            ContactsContract.Contacts.DISPLAY_NAME + " ASC");
} else {
    //---Honeycomb and later---
    CursorLoader cursorLoader = new CursorLoader(
```

```
                this,
                allContacts,
                projection,
                ContactsContract.Contacts.DISPLAY_NAME + " LIKE ?",
                new String[] {"%jack"},
                ContactsContract.Contacts.DISPLAY_NAME + " ASC");
        c = cursorLoader.loadInBackground();
    }
```

2. The methods are `getType()`, `onCreate()`, `query()`, `insert()`, `delete()`, and `update()`.
3. The code is as follows:

```
<provider android:name="BooksProvider"
        android:authorities="net.learn2develop.provider.Books" />
```

CHAPTER 9 ANSWERS

1. You can either programmatically send an SMS message from within your Android application or invoke the built-in Messaging application to send it on your application's behalf.
2. The two permissions are `SEND_SMS` and `RECEIVE_SMS`.
3. `onUpgrade()`

CHAPTER 10 ANSWERS

1. The likely reasons are as follows:
   - No Internet connection
   - Incorrect placement of the `<uses-library>` element in the `AndroidManifest.xml` file
   - Missing `INTERNET` permission in the `AndroidManifest.xml` file
2. Geocoding is the act of converting an address into its coordinates (latitude and longitude). Reverse geocoding converts a pair of location coordinates into an address.
3. The two providers are as follows:
   - `LocationManager.GPS_PROVIDER`
   - `LocationManager.NETWORK_PROVIDER`
4. The method is `addProximityAlert()`.

CHAPTER 11 ANSWERS

1. The permission is `INTERNET`.
2. The classes are `JSONArray` and `JSONObject`.
3. The class is `AsyncTask`.

CHAPTER 12 ANSWERS

1. A separate thread should be used because a service runs on the same process as the calling activity. If a service is long-running, you need to run it on a separate thread so that it does not block the activity.
2. The `IntentService` class is similar to the `Service` class except that it runs the tasks in a separate thread and automatically stops the service when the task has finished execution.
3. The three methods are `doInBackground()`, `onProgressUpdate()`, and `onPostExecute()`.
4. The service can broadcast an intent, and the activity can register an intent using an `IntentFilter` class.
5. The recommended method is to create a class that uses `AsyncTask`. This ensures that the UI is updated in a thread-safe manner.

INDEX

A

E

F

G

M

N

O

P

Q

T

U

V

W

X

Y

Z